Drug smuggler nation

Manchester University Press

Drug smuggler nation

Narcotics and the Netherlands, 1920–1995

STEPHEN SNELDERS

Manchester University Press

Copyright © Stephen Snelders 2021

The right of Stephen Snelders to be identified as the author of this work has been asserted by him in accordance with the Copyright, Designs and Patents Act 1988.

Published by Manchester University Press
Oxford Road, Manchester M13 9PL
www.manchesteruniversitypress.co.uk

British Library Cataloguing-in-Publication Data
A catalogue record for this book is available from the British Library

ISBN   978 1 5261 5139 1   hardback
ISBN   978 1 5261 6722 4   paperback

First published 2021
Paperback published 2023

The publisher has no responsibility for the persistence or accuracy of URLs for any external or third-party internet websites referred to in this book, and does not guarantee that any content on such websites is, or will remain, accurate or appropriate.

Typeset
by New Best-set Typesetters Ltd

Contents

List of figures		*page* vi
Acknowledgements		vii
1	Introduction: The drug regulatory regime vs. criminal anarchy	1
2	The interwar period	23
3	Global perils I: Chinese and Greek drug smugglers	41
4	Cannabis, counterculture, and criminals: The rise of cannabis smuggling	74
5	Global perils II: Chinese triads, Turkish families, and heroin	110
6	The expansion of the cannabis trade after 1976	153
7	Global perils III: Colombian syndicates and cocaine	188
8	The floodgates of criminal anarchy: Synthetic drugs and subverting the state	215
9	Conclusion	266
	Appendix: Graphs of arrests and seizures	272
	Bibliography	275
	Index	293

Figures

1 Offences against the Opium Act, 1963–1972. K. H. Meijring, *Recht en verdovende middelen* (The Hague: VUGA-Uitgeverij), pp. 115, 118   page 272
2 Offences against the Opium Act in relation to cannabis, 1967–1972. K. H. Meijring, *Recht en verdovende middelen* (The Hague: VUGA-Uitgeverij), p. 120   273
3 Arrests of importers of illegal drugs in the Netherlands, 1967–1972. K. H. Meijring, *Recht en verdovende middelen* (The Hague: VUGA-Uitgeverij), p. 120   273
4 Seizures of marihuana and hashish in the Netherlands, in kilograms, 1967–1972. K. H. Meijring, *Recht en verdovende middelen* (The Hague: VUGA-Uitgeverij), p. 22   274
5 Seizures of cocaine in the Netherlands, in kilograms, 1980–1998. G. Farrell, K. Mansur, and M. Tulis, 'Cocaine and heroin in Europe 1983–93', *British Journal of Criminology* 36 (1996) 255–81, p. 258; D. Zaitch, *Trafficking Cocaine: Colombian Drug Entrepeneurs in the Netherlands* (The Hague: Kluwers), p. 305   274

Acknowledgements

When I first started as a historian of drugs my focus was almost exclusively on the demand side of the drug market. The hows and whys of illegal drug supply fell mostly outside my research interests. I assumed that, given a demand for illegal drugs, supply would 'somehow' come into existence and provide users with the desired substances. In retrospect, like many of my contemporaries I had a naive belief in the workings of the market, even an illegal one. It took a 'global turn' in my research focus to awaken my interest in how this 'somehow' in creating drug supply had actually worked in history. This global turn was part of the ongoing discussions within the drug history projects at Utrecht University (embedded in the Descartes Centre for the History and Philosophy of the Sciences, and in the Freudenthal Institute of the Faculty of Science) in the Netherlands: especially with Toine Pieters. Many thanks go to Toine for our collaborations in the adventures of historical research.

In 2015 Toine suggested that I should take a closer look at the global trade routes that seem a constant in the production and distribution of intoxicants and medicines since Columbus's 'discovery' of America. The project received support from the Descartes Centre and its director Wijnand Mijnhart, as well as his successor Bert Theunissen. The Centre financed a three-month sabbatical to develop my research ideas. The resulting project was incorporated in *The Imperative of Regulation*, a collaborative research programme with James Kennedy (University College Utrecht) and Gemma Blok (then University of Amsterdam, since moved to the Open University Heerlen) that aimed to produce a fresh historical perspective on the history of drugs in the Netherlands. James Kennedy and Toine Pieters successfully applied for financing of this research programme to the Dutch Research Council (NWO). Many thanks go to NWO for supporting the programme (project no. 360–52–180) and to the project team – consisting of Gemma, James, Toine, and the researchers Berrie van der Molen,

Arjan Nuijten, and Rafalea de Quadros Rigoni – for the subsequent support and discussions of my ventures into the often shadowy and murky historical data on illegal drug supply.

Ideas in this book have been discussed at conferences and seminars, especially those organized by the Social History of Alcohol and Drugs group that I have happily attended since 2004. Naming all of the colleagues involved in these discussions is impossible, naming only a select few risks being unjust to those not named. Nevertheless, special thanks go to David Courtwright, Jim Mills, Patricia Barton, and Charles D. Kaplan for more than a decade of discussing the history of drugs and how to think outside the box of present-day misunderstandings and facile opinions. I also wish to thank those law enforcement officials, traders, and users who over the years shared their views on the illegal trade with me.

Research findings and perspectives in this book were presented and discussed in a number of paper presentations. Parts of Chapter 2 were presented at the workshop 'Intoxication, Discourses and Social Practices in Cultural and Historical Perspective', Sheffield University, 30 September–1 October 2016, organized by Phil Withington and Rysosuke Yokoe. My perspective on Chinese drug trafficking and the triads (parts of Chapters 3 and 5) was presented at the biannual Alcohol and Drugs History Society conference that we hosted at Utrecht University, 22–25 June 2017. The rise of the Netherlands as a nexus in the international illegal cannabis trade (part of Chapter 4) was discussed at the symposium 'Cannabis: Global Histories', organized by Jim Mills and Lucas Ritchert at the University of Strathclyde, Glasgow, 19–20 April 2018. Dutch cannabis smuggling after 1976 (part of Chapter 6) was revisited at the panel 'From Kabul to California: Building a global illicit drug market in the 20th century', organized with James Bradford and Haggai Ram at the Alcohol and Drugs History Society conference at the David F. Musto Center for Drug Policy Studies, Shanghai University, China, 12–15 June 2019. Big thank yous to all the organizers and participants for their hospitality and involvement.

Finally, thanks are due to Joost Gijselhart, Kostis Gkotsinas, Nicole Maalsté, Haggai Ram, Toine Spapens, Bengt Svensson, Dolf Tops, and Damiàn Zaitch for generously assisting in making available and sharing sources and information; and to Patricia Piolon for her assistance in understanding Swedish texts.

1

Introduction: The drug regulatory regime vs. criminal anarchy

Despite more than a century of increasing state regulation on a global scale, drug trafficking today is the most profitable illegal trade in the world. A conservative estimate valued the illicit drug retail market in Europe (including the UK) alone in 2013 at 24 billion euros. According to the United Nations Office on Drugs and Crime (UNODC), illegal drugs account for 17 to 25 per cent of all proceeds of global crime, and for between 0.1 and 0.6 per cent of the gross domestic product (GDP) in member states of the European Union (including the UK).[1]

In the Netherlands the contribution of illegal activities to the GDP has been estimated at 0.4 per cent or 2.6 billion euros. Half of this comes from the trade in illegal drugs. The export value of indoor cultivated *nederwiet* ('Netherweed' or Dutch marihuana) alone was estimated at 1 billion euros in 2010.[2] Today the country is one of the most important sources of synthetic drugs such as MDMA (XTC) and amphetamines and functions as a major transit hub for other drugs, for example of cocaine to the UK.[3] A 2018 report on the Dutch production and export of synthetic drugs came to a staggering (but in the view of the report's authors still conservative) estimate of a global retail value of 18.9 billion euros.[4]

These estimates give some kind of indication of the economic value of the illegal drug trade, even when based on limited data provided by police detective units and only giving approximate indications of the total volume of the illegal drug trade. The estimates do not give an idea of other major impacts of the drug trade on society, such as cross-overs with and financing of other criminal activities, entanglements with the legitimate economy, corruption and threatening of civil servants, and effects on public and individual health. States and civil society are struggling with the unintended consequences of drug regulatory policies and the successes of the drug trade, such as problems of addiction, overdoses, and gang wars. Of crucial importance in coming to terms with these consequences is an understanding of the patterns and nature of the illegal drug trade.

The rise and implementation of an international drug regulatory regime in the twentieth century restricted and transformed the traditional Dutch production and trade in drugs. At the same time it created new opportunities for Dutch entrepreneurs. The increasing state regulations and interventions necessary to control the illegal drug trade and consumption, combined with the increasing public demand for these illegal drugs, led to the proliferation of a 'hydra' of small, anarchic groups and networks ideally suited to circumventing the enforcement of regulation. When one head of this hydra was chopped off, another one grew in its place. In the course of the twentieth century these groups and networks included sailor smugglers, idealists from countercultural drug scenes, and criminal opportunists. They included native Dutch people as well as criminal entrepreneurs from other ethnic backgrounds in the Netherlands (Chinese, Turkish, and Kurdish, Moroccan etc.). They were often working together in temporary alliances, and in tandem with a legitimate 'upperworld', especially within the chemical and maritime industries. Smugglers in the Netherlands used the excellent logistics and infrastructure of the country and its superb connections by ship, train, or plane to places of supply and demand, and stimulated the development of illegal drug production, from Afghanistan to Morocco. Smugglers transformed the Netherlands into a transit hub for the international drug trade, supplying other European countries and the UK. They developed direct and indirect connections between supply countries and demand in the Americas. They also created a thriving underground industry of illegal synthetic drug laboratories and indoor cannabis cultivation in the Netherlands itself.

The drug regulatory regime and the illegal drug market stimulated an enormous expansion of 'organized crime' that took the Netherlands by surprise. In 1974 the Rotterdam police commissioner Jan Blaauw warned of the existence of 'organized crime groups' that had partly developed out of smuggler networks. He estimated the total number of people involved at less than a hundred.[5] Little more than fifteen years later the Centrale Recherche Informatiedienst (CRI – Criminal Intelligence Unit) of the Dutch police produced a list of more than 260 'drug gangs', most of them also involved in other criminal activities such as armed robberies, car thefts, and possession of illegal firearms.[6] By the year 2000 the American Drug Enforcement Administration (DEA) estimated that around one hundred criminal groups were active in the illegal drug trade in Amsterdam alone. Besides Dutch people these included Turkish, Colombian, Kurdish, Chinese, Nigerian, Israeli, Moroccan, British, and Irish groups.[7] Blaauw's one hundred organized criminals had multiplied and were creating havoc in Dutch society. Concerns over these developments led to the widely publicized parliamentary inquiry of 1994–1996 that concluded that the illegal drug trade and organized crime had become firmly embedded in society.[8]

In order to understand the patterns in the rise of the illegal drug trade and its relation to organized crime, from the enactment of the first Dutch drug law in 1920 to the parliamentary and societal debates around 1995, this book synthesizes the results of case studies of and reports on twentieth-century illegal drug smuggling and production – works by historians, criminologists, and investigative journalists together with archival research. The (often bewildering) multiplications of the supply side of the market are investigated from the perspective of their emergence and development as the necessary antithesis to the creation and implementation of a drug regulatory regime by the state.

The global drug regulatory regime

The Dutch drug regulatory regime developed within the context of an international drug regulatory regime that was inaugurated by the International Opium Convention of 1912 and expanded in subsequent treaties. I use the term 'regime' here in the definition of historians Timothy Brook and Bob Tadashi Wakabayashi, 'to signify a system in which an authority declares its right to control certain practices, and develops policies and mechanisms to exercise that right within its presumed domain'.[9] Although this book is not primarily concerned with the grounds and dynamics of this regime, a short overview of its development is in order.

The global drug regulatory regime worked from the international level (multilateral treaties between states and from 1919 onwards supervision by supra-national organizations, the League of Nations, and the United Nations) to the local level (legislation and policies of states) in order to control non-medical and recreational use of prohibited drugs. In doing so the regime created a reaction that went the other way: non-state actors such as criminal entrepreneurs and their networks started activities at the local level (e.g., cultures of smuggling in cities and provinces) and expanded internationally. This led to more global regulation and prohibition that led again to more opportunities for local entrepreneurs to expand their activities.

The twentieth century is the key period for understanding our present-day policies and problems of drug control. There is, however, a 'pre-history' of the regulation of drugs such as opium that goes back into the seventeenth century. For instance, the Dutch East India Company (VOC) tried to establish a monopoly on the opium trade on Java in the Dutch East Indies (now Indonesia) as early as the 1670s. In 1678 the company prohibited the sale of crude opium not distributed from its own warehouses. A few years earlier, in 1674, the VOC had prohibited opium use among the agricultural workers on the Moluccas out of fears of a decrease in their productivity.[10] Opium trade and consumption would become hotly contested in Asia in the eighteenth and nineteenth centuries, leading, for instance, to the infamous Opium Wars of 1839–1842 and 1856–1860 in which Britain and France forced China to open its borders for the opium trade. By the early twentieth century most colonial powers, including the Netherlands, had established monopolies on the distribution of opium in their colonies (for more detail on the Dutch opium monopoly, see Chapter 3).

Attempts at global drug regulation started in the early 1900s. The United States and China especially promoted the enactment of drug regulation in international law and international treaties. The meetings of the International Opium Commission in Shanghai in 1909 and the International Opium Conference in The Hague in the Netherlands in 1912 led to the first international opium convention. This convention was aimed at controlling the non-medical and 'illegitimate' use of opium and opiates derived from opium such as morphine and heroin, as well as of cocaine. (The latter three drugs were all relatively new substances that had been developed by the pharmaceutical industry in the nineteenth century.) The United States particularly became the driving force behind prohibitionist global drug regulation. As political scientist David Bewley-Taylor has written:

> Since the beginning of the twentieth century, the United States has been consistent in its intention to confront the issue of drug use from the prohibitionist perspective and locate the sources of domestic [drug] problems beyond the boundaries of American society [...] the emergence of a universal norm dictating national responses to illicit drug use could emerge only given the influence possessed by a superpower [the United States].[11]

Not all countries were at first enthusiastic about global drug regulation, since it ran counter to economic interests. These interests concerned, for instance, the colonial opium monopolies, the German and Dutch pharmaceutical industry, and the position of the Japanese as distributors of cocaine and morphine in Asia. The rise of the United States as a global superpower driving the expansion of a global regulatory regime was therefore crucial. The Allied victory in the First World War led to a decisive step. The Hague Convention of 1912 and its ratification became part of the Treaty of Versailles of 1919. Moreover, a 'permanent international control machinery was created: the League of Nations was entrusted with general supervision over the execution of agreements with regard to traffic in [...] opium and other dangerous drugs'.[12] By 1919 membership of the international regime of drug control had become almost a prerequisite for states to participate fully in the international community.[13]

Although the United States did not become a member of the League of Nations, in the interwar period it worked closely with the League of Nations Opium Advisory Committee, the supervisory international body on drug regulation. After the Second World War and the creation of the United Nations (UN) the role of the League of Nations Advisory Committee was taken over by the Commission on Narcotic Drugs of the UN Economic and Social Council. The prohibitive framework that consisted of the scheduling of drugs, obligations to effectuate global drug control, and international cooperation against illicit trade was further embodied in new treaties. These were the 1961 Single Convention of Narcotic Drugs, the 1971 Convention on Psychotropic Substances, and the 1988 Vienna Convention against Illicit Traffic in Narcotic Drugs and Psychotropic Substances. In principle this UN regime was and is 'promotional': it has to be executed by the national states, not by the UN itself. However, any state not adhering to the regime has been in danger of being classified as 'deviant' and becoming the butt of international criticism.[14]

Since the 1909 Shanghai Commission meeting, international drug regulation has been driven by the imperative of further regulation. This because, as will be seen throughout this book, interventions by international bodies and national states encountered practices of smuggling and supply by non-state actors. This had already started in the interwar period. These actors responded on a national and an international level to a continuing, and from 1965 onwards even massively increasing, demand for illicit drugs. In other words, the very lack of success in actually controlling drug use necessitated a continual expansion of the prohibitive framework.

The regime became more rigorously executed and embodied in European national legislation such as the Dutch *Opiumwet* (Opium Act) and the UK Dangerous Drugs Act (which both came into effect in 1920). The first Dutch Opium Act was enacted only in 1919 in reaction to the Treaty of Versailles, even though the Hague Convention had already been ratified by the Netherlands as early as 1914. The Opium Act prohibited the production and sale of opium and its derivatives (such as heroin and morphine) and of cocaine for other than medical purposes. This Dutch regulatory regime was continually expanded over the century. The second Opium Act of 1928 criminalized non-medical possession and use of the drugs as well, and prohibited the import and transit of cannabis. In 1953 the use and possession of cannabis were also criminalized. In 1966 the use and possession of hallucinogens followed. The revision of the Act in 1976 decriminalized use, but not possession. It introduced a differentiation between a List 1 of 'hard drugs', which now also included amphetamines, and a List 2 of 'soft drugs' (hashish and marihuana). As a consequence, possession of small amounts of cannabis was decriminalized as well. MDMA was included in List 1 in 1988, followed by similar compounds (generally known as XTC).

In the course of the century penalties for violation of the Opium Act were increased. In 1919 the maximum sentence was three months in prison or a fine of 1,000 Dutch guilders for a first offence; six months in prison or a 3,000-guilder fine for reoffending. In 1928 the maximum sentence was increased to one year, and two years for reoffending. These sentences were relatively light compared with those elsewhere. To keep the Netherlands more in line with other nations (e.g., the UK Dangerous Drugs Act had the provision of a maximum sentence of ten years' imprisonment), in 1953 the maximum sentence was increased to four years in prison. After the explosion of the problem of illegal drug use in the 1960s and 1970s the revision of the Opium Act of 1976 increased the maximum sentence for the domestic trade in hard drugs to eight years in prison, and for import and export of these drugs to twelve years. The maximum sentence for the import or export of soft drugs remained four years in prison, but for domestic trade the maximum sentence was decreased to two years.[15]

At the same time the Netherlands became globally (in)famous because of its tolerance of the demand side of the illegal drug market from the later 1970s. Opponents of liberal policies claimed that these made the Netherlands a Mecca of the trade and use of drugs.[16] The revised Opium Act of 1976 had unintended consequences, such as the tolerated concentration of the retail of cannabis in the so-called 'coffee shops' and their expansive growth in the 1980s, and the cultural transformation of cannabis use from an act of resistance into an act of everyday consumption. The Dutch furthermore started to pioneer policies of 'harm reduction' towards heroin use such as the introduction of user rooms where heroin could be safely consumed, and in the 1980s of needle exchange programmes to prevent the spread of HIV through the shared use of needles. However, tolerant Dutch drug policies did not extend to wholesale smuggling and distribution. After 1976, far from taking a liberal attitude towards the drug trade, Dutch law enforcement intensified its fight against smuggling and wholesale trading and its cooperation with other national and international police organizations. For instance, in the 1980s the fight against drugs contributed to a shortage of prison cells, and of 2,000 new cells that were built by 1990, 1,200 had been reserved for offenders under the Opium Act.[17]

The political economy of illegal drugs

While the drug regulatory regime expanded, the illegal drug market in the Netherlands did not move in the direction predicted by some observers: of monopolization and higher prices. A 1983 study of the American heroin market by Robert McBride argued that the structure of the heroin distribution industry was much the same as that for the distribution of legal intoxicants such as coffee, tea, and tobacco. McBride concluded that criminalization of the market led to reduced competition and monopolization. The market would have powerful importers and wholesalers, dominating the producers (such as opium farmers) and retailers. The price of heroin was in his view inelastic, since addicted users would purchase the same amounts despite price fluctuations. Combined with a lack of free competition, this would lead to artificially high prices. Repression and law enforcement would stimulate the tendency to higher prices and higher profits, and to economies of scale, leading to the rise of organized crime syndicates. McBride's conclusions were taken over by the Dutch sociologist Jan-Willem Gerritsen and extrapolated to all regulated drug markets.[18]

Predictions of increasing monopolization of the market, higher prices, and control by vertically organized 'enterprises' have, however, not been validated; rather the contrary.[19] The theory that regulation and law enforcement increase the prices of drugs is discredited. For instance, studies into the price elasticity of heroin have suggested that demand is not inflexible, but that users respond moderately to changes in prices.[20] Between 1983 and 1993 wholesale and retail prices of cocaine in the Netherlands went down in a period of increasing demand. In the same period retail and wholesale prices of heroin went down, despite a stable demand.[21] This while the Dutch police left retail mostly alone and concentrated their activities against wholesale distribution, which should have led to an increase in wholesale prices. According to the calculations of the Dutch Central Bureau for Statistics (CBS), a government agency, average prices of illegal drugs in the Netherlands have actually decreased since 1999.[22] The response of the drug market in the Netherlands to illegalization has been one of increased competition and increased availability, finding its own dark niche in the economic system. Rather than moving to monopolization, the illegal drug market was characterized by a pattern of 'criminal anarchy'.

The pattern of criminal anarchy

The drug regulatory regime evoked in the Netherlands, as it did in other countries, its own antithesis: the development of illegal drug trade and production. As the following chapters will show, drug smuggling and production showed a recurrent pattern. While the design and implementation of the drug regulatory regime was institutionalized and directed from above, the patterns of the ways of operation of smugglers and producers show all the elements of a spontaneous order that I will call 'criminal anarchy'. These ways of operation were not decreed from above but the result of initiatives by individuals and small groups organized in connecting networks that were often temporary and constituted very fluidly. Sometimes they allied with each other, at other times they fought each other; mostly they ignored each other. Together these individuals, groups, and networks constituted a hydra opposed to the regulatory regime. Heads of this hydra could and were cut off. However, new heads always grew somewhere else on the hydra.

By defining the patterns of the hydra as 'criminal anarchy' I do not mean that they were purely chaotic and random. As this book will show, horizontal organizations and connections could go perfectly together with efficient smuggling and other trafficking operations. Moreover, an essential prerequisite for their successful functioning was their embeddedness in the society they operated in, or the ability to forge alliances within this society. 'Anarchy' here refers to a dominantly horizontal organizational model characterized by spontaneous order. Its patterns were 'criminal' in a twofold sense. First, the creation by the regulatory regime of an illegal market meant the criminalization of suppliers on this market. Not all of these suppliers were criminals before they started operating in this market. Second, however, professional criminals and criminal entrepreneurs operating in other illegal markets were drawn to the drug market and by the end of the twentieth century had come to dominate supply and production. To understand the historical vicissitudes in the seemingly chaotic and unpredictable world of drug trafficking it is essential to observe the patterns of criminal anarchy.

The myth of *Cigars of the Pharaoh*

From an early age most of us have become acquainted with the image of the sinister drug lord controlling a vast empire and an organization of minions who obey his every order on pain of violent retribution if they fail to do so. This drug lord figures prominently in an influential manifestation in the guise of the Greek villain Rastapopoulos. He is the opponent of Tintin in the seminal comic books *Cigars of the Pharaoh* (1934) and *The Blue Lotus* (1936) by the Belgian artist Hergé, comic books that remained popular in the Low Countries and elsewhere throughout the twentieth century. In 1999 the French readers of *Le Monde* elected *The Blue Lotus* the eighteenth best book of the twentieth century.

The figure of Rastapopoulos and other elements of the illegal drug trade in these comics did not spring solely from Hergé's fantasy. They follow quite closely contemporary media reports about the 'real' world. One can read Hergé in conjunction with these reports and see the associations and images that inspired popular perceptions of drug users and traffickers. For instance, Hergé would have read in his daily newspaper about major drug seizures in the port of Antwerp, one of the largest harbours in Europe and a major transit hub for the international illegal drug trade. In May 1931 four chests containing 1,200 kilograms of opium were found in the harbour by the Belgian police. A firm in Istanbul had sent the chests to the Netherlands labelled as 'dried fruit'. From the Netherlands the drugs had been sent to Antwerp with the United States as the intended final destination.

Hergé's drug cartel that smuggles opium in cigars is an international octopus, with its tentacles across the world. It is organized as a secret society ruthlessly controlled by its master. The identity of this master is only revealed at the end of *The Blue Lotus* to be Greek film director and millionaire Rastapopoulos. Here again Hergé shows that he has read his newspapers. Greeks performed important roles in the international drug traffic and were regularly caught, as we will see in the next chapter. Rastapopoulos mostly resembles, and not only in his name, the Greek drug trafficker Elie Eliopoulos. Described by historians Kathryn Meyer and Terry Parssinen as 'having a Mephistophelean appearance', and characterized by Harry Anslinger of the US Federal Bureau of Narcotics (FBN) as 'head of a dangerous narcotics gang', Eliopoulos was a key player in the illicit drug trade in the early 1930s. Did Hergé read that in May 1932 the Berlin police arrested the Greek on a German express train, and that it was claimed that an international organization of drug traffickers with branches in all parts of the world had been busted? However, Eliopoulos was less a sinister Dr No or Dr Evil leading a large hierarchical organization than a businessman who operated in illegal markets, a facilitator who connected supply and demand on an international scale.[23] His activities were possible within a framework of criminal anarchy in which loosely connected networks were able to access illegal markets.

Disenchantment with the pyramid model

The organization of Rastapopoulos is a typical example of a pyramid model. The pyramid has a small top, becoming broader at the bottom. The pyramid is hierarchical and based on existing power relations. The leader stands at the top, surrounded by their closest associates and dealing in large amounts. Going down the pyramid the criminals are more subservient, less powerful, dealing in smaller and smaller amounts.[24]

However, by 1990 disenchantment with this model was widespread in criminological research. The very constraints of the illegal market make it hardly possible for large hierarchically organized enterprises to operate. To reduce the risk of detection by law enforcement agencies the number of people involved should be as low as possible, including customers. Operations should take place locally and not directed from afar. Large-scale marketing and advertising would only increase visibility and hence increase chances of detection.[25] Dutch criminologists found that organizational structures in the illegal drug market were diverse, not strictly hierarchic or vertical, and in some cases even 'democratic'.[26] A study by the Scientific Research and Documentation Centre (WODC) of the Ministry of Justice, based on police files and published in 1990, pioneered an analysis of organized crime groups as 'crime enterprises'. The criminal entrepreneur was a kind of market vendor who could be removed from the market at any time, since he had no licence. Even the largest of the criminal enterprises had to adjust its ways of operation and tactics to the strategies of the state. These ways of operation should therefore leave as few traces as possible – that is, leave no evidence. Because of the haphazard nature of organizing transport and distribution, crime enterprises remained loose temporary groups that needed above all to be flexible.[27] The study was fundamental to the approach that has since been taken in the reports of the WODC on organized crime in the Netherlands.[28]

The practice of everyday smuggling

When production, distribution, and consumption of drugs are illegal, but this illegality is contested, the contestants need to devise their own methods to make the market function.[29] Since the normal method of regulating a market and reducing the risks of operators and consumers (i.e. regulation by the state) disappears, self-regulation takes its place. The illegal drug trade is from this perspective a response, a series of countermeasures of social groups and individuals (with their own cultures and traditions) against the politics of the state. In the Netherlands these groups and individuals have been highly diverse and differentiated in all kinds of aspects including ethnicity, kin, commercial interests, and motivation. The illegal traders have ranged from marginalized Chinese labour migrants in the interwar period to prominent members of south Netherlands communities at the end of the twentieth century.

Michel de Certeau in his *The Practice of Everyday Life* (*L'Invention du quotidien*) has made the distinction between what he called the strategies from 'above' (the state) and the counteractions or tactics from 'below'. The major difference between these two – and herein lies the usefulness of this distinction for an investigation of the illegal drug trade in the Netherlands – is that the state controls a certain territory, and the traffickers do not. In the words of de Certeau a strategy is 'the calculation or manipulation of power relationships that becomes possible as soon as a subject with land power can be isolated. It postulates a *place* that can be delimited as its *own* and serve as the base from which relations with an *exteriority* composed of targets or threats can be managed.' For our purposes the subject is here the Dutch state implementing the drug regulatory regime. In response to the manipulation of power relationships by the state (in order to control the drug market), tactics are used by smugglers and others. In de Certeau's definition a tactic is:

> a calculated action determined by the absence of a proper locus. No delimitation of an exteriority, then, provides it with the condition necessary for autonomy. The space of a tactic is the space of the other. Thus it must play on and with a terrain imposed on it and organized by the law of a foreign power […] It operates in isolated actions, blow by blow. It takes advantage of 'opportunities' […] What it wins it cannot keep.[30]

To operate in the terrain of the other (the state) one needs to produce and develop practices, or what de Certeau calls 'ways of operating'. Invisibility, trickery, ruses, and wit are important elements of these practices. After all, when the state is visible and controls the territory, the smugglers are weaker and have to resort to deception.

Smuggling is a case par excellence in which these kinds of tactics have been developed over decades and even centuries.[31]

As this book will show, two elements have been essential for the successful development of these ways of operating by smugglers. One is the organizational structure of the operations. Invisibility and flexibility are paramount: the models here are the bands of the Scarlet Pimpernel or the Swamp Fox, small groups that evade the sight of the authorities, rather than Scarface with his highly visible gangster image. The second is the historical social and cultural embeddedness of the smugglers in society.

Anarchy as organization

The theory of anarchy as organization rather than as chaos, as developed by political theorists such as Peter Kropotkin and other anarchists, is useful in understanding the ways of operation of smugglers. Pivotal in this theory is the idea of anarchy as spontaneous order: 'the theory that, given a common need, a collection of people will, by trial and error, by improvisation and experiment, evolve order out of the situation'.[32] Applying this theory to the illegal drug markets of the twentieth century, the common need is the demand for psychoactive drugs made illegal by the drug regulatory regime. In response autonomous individuals and small groups, loosely confederated in networks, took direct action and developed the ways of operation of supplying the market. In contrast to political anarchy, criminal anarchy was of course not always motivated by political aims, but more often by the prospect of financial gain. I say 'not always' because politically and idealistically motivated smugglers did perform important roles in illegal drug supply, especially from the 1960s onwards, particularly in the supply of cannabis, LSD, and XTC. Moreover, many smugglers who were also users were at some point minimally commercially motivated in organizing supply for themselves and their social networks: for instance, Chinese sailor smugglers or again 1960s cannabis users.[33]

Applying a theory of anarchy as spontaneous order to the illegal drug market has close affinities with criminological perspectives on crime as essentially disorganized or the application to 'organized crime' of a 'garbage can model' of functioning in a state of 'disorganized anarchy'.[34] However, the term 'disorganized' is misleading. Smugglers can be very well organized, and anarchy is itself a form of organization.

Applying the theory of anarchy as spontaneous order emphasizes, moreover, the emergence of this order in a dialectical relationship with the drug regulatory regime.

While anarchically organized and embedded in society, smugglers and their rings show variety in other respects – in fact, this is another key element in the theory of anarchy as organization. An important differentiation in groups taking up the illegal drug trade is that between 'power syndicates' and 'enterprise syndicates', a distinction made by historian of crime Alan Block. The lines between these two ideal types are in practice fluid but in general 'power syndicates' offer protection and attempt to control certain illegal markets – for instance, gambling and prostitution. 'Enterprise syndicates' merely offer services, such as access to illegal drugs.[35] As we will see, in the Netherlands the illegal drug trade was taken up by 'specialized' smugglers and traders as well as by criminal entrepreneurs pursuing various sideline activities. The networks in which they were organized also took different forms, ranging from temporary connections of 'lone wolves' to more permanent mutual aid societies with shared cultural capital such as the Chinese triads.[36]

There is one problem in applying the theory of anarchy as organization to the illegal drug trade. Anarchism stresses the dissolution of leadership. While I reject the idea of shadowy masterminds behind the world of drug smuggling and recognize that the smuggling rings are essentially fragmented and localized phenomena, to me this does not mean that these groups do not know *any* kind of leadership. Key figures play prominent roles, even if they are not indispensable to the functioning of the illegal market as a whole. Some people in smuggling groups have dominated others with a mixture of success, charisma, and if necessary threatening or executing violence. The model here, however, is once again not a Dr No or a Dr Evil ruling a hierarchical organization, but bandit chiefs or pirate captains needing the consensus of their men to operate.[37]

Embeddedness

To operate successfully and to develop their spontaneous order the smugglers need connections to society. This is a general characteristic of successful criminal activity. For example, sociologist Louis Corsino has emphasized that the success of the Chicago outfit of Al Capone in Prohibition Chicago was based on its social capital: on the one hand it had closure, i.e., it was a tight and closed group that defended its own niche, but it was also capable of brokerage between different social networks, thus making it possible to operate in a wider social environment.[38] Ethnicity and a shared social and cultural background are of crucial importance since they are the basis of closure and solidity in networks.

To use the important criminological concept of embeddedness: smuggling needs to be embedded in society socially, culturally, and historically.[39] Drug smuggling has been socially embedded in personal relationships including suppliers, clients, and collaborators. It has been embedded in places such as bars, ships, underground laboratories etc. Smugglers have had a cultural embeddedness in shared meanings, values, and attitudes that characterized them and connected them to other persons, groups, and institutions in society. This embeddedness has had a historical character: it developed and changed in a long-term dynamic of decades and even centuries. A major question that this book will therefore address is where to find this embeddedness in a long-term historical perspective.

Methods

Criminal anarchy is a pattern that can be perceived again and again in the historical sources on twentieth-century drug trafficking. However, the very nature of these sources creates problems for the historian. Crime does not advertise its exact doings and it attempts to hide from the attention of law enforcement and public media. In the research for this book I have tried to work around these problems by correlating data from different kinds of sources. These include statistics on the illegal drug trade collated by law enforcement agencies, often in the context of reports to international organizations; published and unpublished police reports; newspaper articles and other publications by crime journalists; publications and reports by academic criminologists; and ego documents and memoirs of traffickers and law enforcement officers, often told to and refashioned by journalists. The availability of these sources is not evenly distributed across the period of research. For instance, police reports form the interwar period that are still present in the National Archive in The Hague are far more detailed and name those involved to an extent not available in the post-war period. On the other hand Dutch criminologists 'discovered' the problem of the illegal drug trade at the end of the 1980s and have produced a very rich literature on developments in the last decade of our research. In their publications and in police reports of the 1980s and 1990s there is, with some exceptions, a general tendency to focus on aggregative conclusions and common denominators. Publications by crime journalists go the opposite way and tend to focus on the unique and on the activities and agency of individuals. None of these sources can be taken at its face value, whether it concerns the seemingly 'hard' but disputable statistical data, the self-presentations of criminal entrepreneurs, or the insights from police officers and criminologists. Taken individually, each source only adds to a bewildering variety of practices and operations on the illegal drug market.

There are clearly limits to a research approach attempting to discover the exact facts behind the presented data. I therefore accepted what one crime historian has called the 'irreducible dimension of opacity and not-knowing about the past' and focused on the patterns that could be noticed in this variety of sources.[40] Patterns emerged that connected Chinese seamen smuggling opium in the 1920s with 1960s hippies and 1980s criminal 'villains'. In looking for these patterns I attempted to contextualize the data on criminal activities within the existing historical, sociological and anthropological literature on the societies in which they took place. In doing so, behind the opacity of the data one bleak pattern emerged and seemed to recur again and again: the bewildering variety of data turned out to *be* the pattern of criminal anarchy.

Contents

Chapters 2 to 8 present the empirical data in a more or less chronological history. Although the markets in different illegal drugs were not necessarily separated, for the sake of clarity the chapters follow the trajectories of different (categories of) illegal drugs. Chapter 2 investigates how after the introduction of the Opium Act forms of supply adapted. Legal production spilled over in illegal markets, and networks of smugglers and distributors came into existence, manifesting the pattern of criminal anarchy. While Chapter 2 focuses on the involvement and tactics of native Dutch smugglers, Chapter 3 examines how smuggling in the interwar period was taken up by other nationalities. 'Chinatowns' had come into existence in the major ports of Amsterdam and Rotterdam on the eve of the First World War, socially and culturally embedding Chinese drug trafficking in the heart of Dutch society and economy. Another group of foreign drug traffickers presenting a global danger in the interwar period came from the Mediterranean. Greek networks originating from the trade networks of the former Ottoman Empire succeeded in establishing alliances with wholesale and retail traders in the Netherlands embedded in Dutch society, both Chinese and native Dutch.

Chapter 4 turns to the post-war period and the rise of cannabis smuggling. In the later 1960s and the early 1970s Dutch smugglers started to build international networks to supply European cannabis markets on a larger scale. These smugglers were socially and culturally embedded in the new hippie counterculture and in longer-existing maritime and criminal cultures. The counterculture of the 1960s produced smugglers who perceived cannabis use and trade in the context of a rebellion against 'straight' society. These smugglers were minimally commercially driven. However, by 1971 the illegal cannabis market became an increasingly interesting and profitable business for more commercially minded smugglers and criminal entrepreneurs moved in. The operations of these smugglers were further stimulated by favourable conditions such as the geographical position of the Netherlands, the connections of criminal entrepreneurs with Dutch maritime trading culture, and the socio-economic and political situation in supply countries such as Lebanon and Morocco.

Chapter 5 returns to the Chinese opiates trade and investigates how on the basis of the social and cultural embeddedness of the Chinese in Dutch society, and linking to a new demand for powerful opiates among the Dutch population, the global opium networks of the interwar period developed into the heroin trade networks of the 1970s that fuelled the heroin epidemics in Western cities. The demand for heroin also attracted new competitors to the market. The chapter discusses the Turkish and Kurdish drug smugglers that made use of their own ethnic networks and 'embeddedness' in migrant communities in the Netherlands and elsewhere, and of the smuggling routes by land that built on the traditional Silk Road trade routes from Europe through the Middle East and into Afghanistan.

After 1976 the demand for cannabis continued to grow in a political climate of liberal attitudes on cannabis consumption. More and more traders and smugglers of various nationalities and ethnic backgrounds observed this and took their chance to enter the cannabis market. Chapter 6 discusses the expansion of the cannabis trade after 1976 and how the market came to be dominated by entrepreneurs with a criminal background. Idealism did not, though, completely disappear from the market. For instance, the influence of the 1960s counterculture was paramount in the development of extensive indoor cultivation of marihuana in the Netherlands. However, criminal entrepreneurs quickly entered this cultivation as well. By 1995 the Netherlands was central in the distribution of cannabis in Europe.

Chapter 7 turns to another global peril. In the 1980s cocaine increased in popularity. The supply of this drug was perceived as a global danger, this time not coming from the East (as was the case with heroin) but from the West: South America. While Chinese and Turkish smugglers were firmly embedded in migrant communities, the Colombian export syndicates essential to the rise of illegal cocaine supply in the later 1980s and the 1990s more resembled the interwar period Greek smugglers in making successful alliances with importers and distributors from native Dutch and other backgrounds, all of whom made use of Dutch infrastructure and maritime culture.

Finally, Chapter 8 discusses the development of the production and smuggling of illegal synthetic drugs in the Netherlands. This underground industry was based on a powerful combination of chemical expertise and criminal entrepreneurship. From the 1960s onwards idealists were involved in setting up global chains of production and distribution of 'mind-liberating' drugs such as LSD and, by 1990, XTC. At the same time bank robbers and other criminal entrepreneurs from the south of the Netherlands had become involved in amphetamine smuggling and moved into amphetamine and later XTC production. Borderlines between idealists and criminals became blurred, creating a highly successful illegal export industry.

The drug regulatory regime in the Netherlands had created its antithesis in the operations of drug smugglers and producers. After seventy-five years the state seemed unable to halt the expansion of either the demand for or the supply of illegal drugs. The conclusions in Chapter 9 summarize the results of our historical analysis of this failure of policies, and discuss the significance of understanding the ways in which criminal anarchy reconstructed the political economy of the drug market in the Netherlands in the twentieth century.

Notes

1. European Monitoring Centre for Drugs and Drug Addiction and Europol, 'EU drug markets report: In-depth analysis' (EMCDDA–Europol joint publication, Luxembourg: Publications Office of the European Union, 2016); B. Edens and M. Bruil, 'Inclusion of non-observed economy in Dutch national accounts after the 2010 ESA revision' (The Hague: Centraal Bureau voor de Statistiek, 2014), p. 13; M. Rensman, 'Illegale activiteiten in de nationale rekeningen', in *De Nederlandse economie in 2013* (The Hague: Centraal Bureau voor de Statistiek, 2014), pp. 178–93.
2. Rensman, 'Illegale activiteiten', p. 187.
3. European Monitoring Centre for Drugs and Drug Addiction, 'United Kingdom country drug report' (EMCDDA–Europol joint publication, Luxembourg: Publications Office of the European Union, 2018).
4. P. Tops, J. van Valkenhoef et al., *Waar een klein land groot in kan zijn. Nederland en synthetische drugs in de afgelopen 50 jaar* (The Hague: Boom, 2018).
5. J. A. Blaauw, 'De bestrijding van de georganiseerde misdaad in Nederland', *Algemeen Politieblad* 123 (1974) 227–36.
6. Centrale Recherche Informatiedienst (CRI), annual report 1991, p. 20.
7. Gruppo Abele, 'Synthetic drugs trafficking in three European cities: Major trends and the involvement of organised crime' (Turin: Gruppo Abele, 2003), p. 28.
8. Parlementaire Enquêtecommissie Opsporingsmethoden, Tweede Kamer der Staten-Generaal, 1995–1996, 24 072 (hereafter PEO).
9. T. Brook and B. Tadashi Wakabayashi, 'Introduction: Opium's history in China', in: T. Book and B. Tadashi Wakabayashi (eds), *Opium Regimes: China, Britain and Japan, 1839–1952* (Berkeley: University of California Press, 2000), p. 4.
10. On the early history of opium regulation by the VOC, see W. K. Baron van Dedem, *Eene bijdrage tot de studie der opiumquaestie op Java. De officiëele literatuur* (Amsterdam: J. H. de Bussy, 1881); K. H. Meijring, *Recht en verdovende middelen* (The Hague: VUGA-Boekerij, 1974), pp. 75–6; E. Vanvugt, *Wettig opium. 350 jaar Nederlandse opiumhandel in de Indische archipel* (Haarlem: In de Knipscheer, 1985).
11. D. R. Bewley-Taylor, *The United States and International Drug Control 1909–1997* (London: Continuum, 2001), p. 6.
12. R. Lines, *Drug Control and Human Rights in International Law* (Cambridge: Cambridge University Press, 2017), p. 3.

13 See S. Rimner, *Opium's Long Shadow: From Asian Revolt to Global Drug Control* (Cambridge: Harvard University Press, 2018).
14 Bewley-Taylor, *United States and International Drug Control*.
15 On the development of the Opium Act regulatory regime in the Netherlands: Meijring, *Recht en verdovende middelen*; M. de Kort, *Tussen patiënt en delinquent. Geschiedenis van het Nederlandse drugsbeleid* (Hilversum: Verloren, 1995); T. Boekhout van Solinge, *Drugs and Decision-Making in the European Union* (Amsterdam: Mets & Schilt, 2002); T. Blom, *Opiumwetgeving en drugsbeleid* (Deventer: Wolters Kluwer, 2015). On its implementation see also T. Spapens, T. Müller, and H. van de Bunt, 'The Dutch drug policy from a regulatory perspective', *European Journal of Crime Policy Research* 21 (2015) 191–205.
16 R. de Quadros Rigoni, '"Drugs paradise": Dutch stereotypes and substance regulation in European collaborations on drug policies in the 1970s', *Contemporary Drug Problems* 46:3 (2019) 219–40.
17 V. Ruggiero and N. South, *Eurodrugs: Drug Use, Markets and Trafficking in Europe* (London: UCL Press, 1995), p. 91. For a nuanced discussion of the differences in tolerance between the Netherlands and the UK see D. M. Downes, *Contrasts in Tolerance: Post-War Penal Policy in the Netherlands and England and Wales* (Oxford: Clarendon Press, 1988).
18 R. B. McBride, 'Business as usual: Heroin distribution in the United States', *Journal of Drug Issues* 13:1 (1983) 147–66; J.-W. Gerritsen, *The Control of Fuddle and Flash: A Sociological History of the Regulation of Alcohol and Opiates* (Leiden: Brill, 2000).
19 On predicted and actual effects of prohibition and legalization: R. J. MacCoun and P. Reuter, *Drug War Heresies: Learning from Other Vices, Times, and Places* (Cambridge: Cambridge University Press, 2001).
20 L. Paoli, V. A. Greenfield, and P. Reuter, *The World Heroin Market: Can Supply Be Cut?* (Oxford: Oxford University Press, 2009), pp. 60–3.
21 G. Farrell, K. Mansur, and M. Tulis, 'Cocaine and heroin in Europe 1983–93', *British Journal of Criminology* 36 (1996) 255–81.
22 B. Kazemier, A. Bruil et al., 'The contribution of illegal activities to national income in the Netherlands', *Public Finance Review* 41:5 (2013) 544–77; Edens and Bruil, 'Inclusion of non-observed economy'; Rensman, 'Illegale activiteiten', p. 187.
23 S. Snelders, 'The adventures of Tintin in the opium empire', Points blog, 9 July 2019, https://pointsadhsblog.wordpress.com/2012/07/09/the-adventures-of-tintin-in-the-opium-empire (accessed 7 August 2020). On Eliopoulos see also A. A. Block, 'European drug traffic and traffickers between the wars: The policy of suppression and its consequences', *Journal of Social History* 23 (1989) 315–37; K. Meyer and T. Parssinen, *Webs of Smoke: Smugglers, Warlords, Spies, and the History of the International*

Drug Trade (Lanham: Rowman & Littlefield, 1998), pp. 117–32; D. Valentine, *The Strength of the Wolf: The Secret History of America's War on Drugs* (London: Verso, 2006); R. Gingeras, *Heroin, Organized Crime, and the Making of Modern Turkey* (Oxford: Oxford University Press, 2014).

24 An influential example of the pyramid model is the analysis of the Cosa Nostra in the United States in D. R. Cressey, *Theft of the Nation: The Structure and Operations of Organized Crime in America* (New York: Harper & Row, 1969).

25 Paoli et al., *World Heroin Market*, pp. 204–5.

26 D. J. Korf and M. de Kort, 'Drugshandel en drugsbestrijding' (University of Amsterdam, Bonger Institute of Criminology, 1990), pp. 35–6, 106; D. Korf and H. Verbraeck, 'Dealers en dienders. Dynamiek tussen drugsbestrijding en de midden- en hogere niveaus van de cannabis-, cocaine-, amfetamine- en ecstasyhandel in Amsterdam' (University of Amsterdam, Bonger Institute of Criminology, 1993), pp. 24–5.

27 P. C. van Duyne, R. F. Kouwenberg and G. Romeijn, *Misdaadondernemingen. Ondernemende misdadigers in Nederland* (Gouda: Quint, 1990), p. 23. On the illegal drug market as a kind of market or bazaar see V. Ruggiero and N. South, 'The late-modern city as a bazaar: Drug markets, illegal enterprise and the "barricades"', *British Journal of Sociology* 48 (1997) 54–70.

28 The first of these reports, the 'WODC-Monitor', was published in 1998: E. R. Kleemans, E. I. A. M. van den Berg, and H. G. van de Bunt, 'Georganiseerde criminaliteit in Nederland. Rapportage op basis van de WODC-monitor' (The Hague: WODC, 1998). Since then four other reports have been published. See also P. P. H. M. Klerks, *Groot in de hasj. Theorie en praktijk van de georganiseerde criminaliteit* (Antwerp: Samsom, 2000); T. Spapens, 'Dutch Crime Networks', in G. Bruinsma and D. Weisbund (eds.), *Encyclopedia of Criminology and Criminal Justice* (New York: Springer, 2014), pp. 1211–19.

29 On the concept of the architecture of illegal markets: J. Becker and M. Dewey (eds.), *The Architecture of Illegal Markets: Towards an Economic Sociology of Illegality in the Economy* (Oxford: Oxford University Press, 2017).

30 M. de Certeau, *The Practice of Everyday Life* (Berkeley: University of California Press, 1984), pp. 35–7 (emphasis in the original).

31 A satisfactory general history of smuggling does not yet exist, despite attempts in A. Karras, *Smuggling: Contraband and Corruption in World History* (Lanham: Rowman & Littlefield, 2009); S. Harvey, *Smuggling: Seven Centuries of Contraband* (London: Reaktion Books, 2016).

32 C. Ward, *Anarchy in Action* (London: Freedom Press, 1982), p. 28.

33 A concept of 'minimally commercial smuggling' is used here that is similar to conceptualizations of a 'social supply' or a 'minimally commercial supply' in retail dealing as developed in R. Coomber and L. Moyle, 'Beyond drug dealing: Developing and extending the concept of "social supply" of illicit drugs to "minimally commercial supply"', *Drugs Education, Policy and Prevention* 21:2 (2013) 157–64. Compare also the typology in N. Dorn, K. Murji, and N. South, *Traffickers: Drug Markets and Law Enforcement* (London: Routledge, 1992), which describes among other types 'trading charities' that operate primarily from ideological motivation and 'mutual societies' of networks of user/dealers based on friendship ties. The tension between and often the fusion of idealistic and commercial motivations for cannabis trafficking can be observed in many Western countries in the 1960s and 1970s. See for instance the history of the Brotherhood of Eternal Love: S. Tendler and D. May, *The Brotherhood of Eternal Love: From Flower Power to Hippie Mafia* (London: Cyan Books, 2007); N. Schou, *Orange Sunshine: The Brotherhood of Eternal Love and Its Quest to Spread Peace, Love, and Acid to the World* (New York: Thomas Dunne Books, 2010).

34 The classic in the field is P. Reuter, *Disorganized Crime: The Economics of the Visible Hand* (Cambridge: MIT Press, 1984). For applying the garbage-can model to the Netherlands: Tops et al., *Waar een klein land groot in kan zijn*).

35 A. Block, *East Side – West Side: Organizing Crime in New York 1930–1950* (Cardiff: University College Cardiff Press, 1980).

36 For mutual aid societies compare L. Paoli, *Mafia Brotherhoods: Organized Crime, Italian Style* (New York: Oxford University Press, 2003).

37 Cf. S. Snelders, *The Devil's Anarchy: The Sea Robberies of the Most Famous Pirate Claes G. Compaen, and Very Remarkable Travels of Jan Erasmus Reyning*, 2nd edn (Brooklyn: Autonomedia 2014).

38 L. Corsino, *The Neighborhood Outfit: Organized Crime in Chicago Heights* (Urbana: University of Illinois Press, 2014).

39 For the concept of the social embeddedness of crime see H. van de Bunt, D. Siegel, and D. Zaitch, 'The social embeddedness of organized crime', in L. Paoli (ed.), *The Oxford Handbook of Organized Crime* (New York: Oxford University Press, 2014), pp. 321–39. This includes relational networks (on the level of persons) as well as structural embeddedness in institutions, places, and environments etc.

40 M. Houlbrook, *Prince of Tricksters: The Incredible True Story of Netley Lucas, Gentleman Crook* (Chicago: University of Chicago Press, 2016), pp. 16–17.

2

The interwar period

In 1919 the Dutch parliament approved the first Opium Act. This acceptance signalled the adherence of the Netherlands to the new international drug regulatory regime gaining force after the Allied victory in the First World War. However, while the approval of the Opium Act inaugurated a century of increasing state intervention in drug markets, at the time it was not a reaction to problems of drug abuse in the Netherlands. The Opium Act was a response to international pressure to become part of the international regime. Among Dutch government authorities there was ambivalence about enforcing the Opium Act and hesitation to take measures detrimental to Dutch economic interests. It therefore took another decade to develop and implement government polices to enforce the regime. Legal production by pharmaceutical companies spilled over in illegal markets and some producers showed a degree of non-compliance with the new regime. Police officers and pharmaceutical inspectors had to strike a balance between law enforcement and the country's economic interests.

After the introduction of the Opium Act, forms of drug supply adapted. This chapter investigates how users, distributors, and producers developed new tactics. While the total volume of the illegal drug market pales into insignificance compared to the volume of the 1970s and after, the interwar period is significant in showing the first manifestations of criminal anarchy in response to the new regulatory regime.

The Opium Act

On 4 October 1919 the government of the Netherlands published the text of the first Opium Act in its official publication the *Staatsblad*, thus pronouncing it law. The act had been accepted unanimously and without debate by the chambers of the Dutch Estates-General or parliament, came into effect in 1920, and prohibited the *production* and *distribution* for other than medical purposes of opium, of opiates derived from opium, such as morphine and heroin, and of cocaine. The revised second Opium Act of 1928 further prohibited the *use* of these drugs without medical prescription, as well as the import and transit trade of *Indische hennep* (cannabis).

The introduction of the Opium Act was not so much a reaction to a landscape of drug abuse as an important factor in its creation. Domestic concerns and ambivalence about the use of psychoactive substances in the Netherlands before 1920 had focused primarily on alcohol.[1] Earlier regulation of other psychoactive substances was directed at the medical retail side. The 1865 *Wet op de Artsenijbereidkunst* (Pharmacy Act) and the 1874 *Wet op de Veeartsenijkunst* (Veterinary Medicine Act) limited the amount of drugs that could be sold in the retail trade by certified pharmacists. Significantly these laws did nothing to regulate wholesale supply and were not meant to harm the economic interests of the pharmaceutical industry.[2] Major concerns about the abuse of what were called *verdoovende middelen* (narcotics) only rose after 1920 and were significantly focused on migrants from abroad: in particular the Chinese who came to be imagined as a global peril undermining Western society and supremacy (see Chapter 3). From the start, the Opium Act regime was connected to the perceived problems of drug abuse among migrants and among other 'races' living in the colonies and potentially upsetting colonial society.[3]

The colonial dimension

Significantly, The Hague Convention of 1912, which became the basis of the post-war international drug regulatory regime (see Chapter 1), had been ratified by the Netherlands as early as 20 June 1914. It took more than five years and the pressure of the Allied victory in the First World War to have the Dutch state actually codify the convention in law. This demonstrates the lack of urgency of the project; after all, a drug problem did not exist in the Netherlands. The eventual introduction of the Opium Act was partly necessitated by the new balance of international relations after the war. Moreover, the Netherlands had to show compliance with the drug regulatory regime in order to salvage its colonial monopoly on non-medical production and distribution in the Dutch East Indies. In 1919 the government informed parliament that it considered a speedy introduction of the Opium Act especially advisable because of the colonial situation: after all, the colonial state itself supplied opium to its subjects in the colonies.[4] Economic and financial interests here were huge. For instance, in 1905–1906 opium sales in the Dutch East Indies provided 16 per cent of tax revenues in the colony. In the interwar period the volume of sales would go down, from 127 to 59 tonnes in 1929, but in that year there were still 1,065 opium dens and 101,000 registered users in the East Indies.[5]

Colonial drug regulation developed out of economic motives: the defence of the opium monopoly of the VOC and since the 1800s of the colonial state against interlopers and smugglers. The dialectics of a regulatory regime were already in place here, confronting Dutch colonial strategies with smugglers' tactics. Around 1800 the prevalence of smuggling became paradoxically an argument against a total ban of opium use in the Indonesian archipelago, since it was thought that such a ban would lead to an increase in the illegal economy. By that time Dutch politicians had reconceptualized opium use. Originally primarily a medical practice among the people of the archipelago, it was now seen as a 'slow-working poison' endangering millions of people. Opium had once been associated with Sumatran warriors going on a rampage, but became more and more related to orientalized images of passivity, its use leading to dependence, diminishing sexual appetites, and reduced work performances by agricultural labourers. Opium use thus conceived was on the one hand a threat to the colonial economy, but on the other hand a source of colonial profits. The answer to this ambiguity was to keep the state's trade monopoly intact and even stimulate the trade's growth, while at the same time taking public health measures against abuse. This view continued to be the basis of Dutch colonial opium policies until the Japanese occupation of Indonesia in 1942. It led to the introduction of the so-called *Opiumregie* (Opium regime) that by 1914 was in force throughout the East Indies. Besides entailing a state monopoly on the import of crude opium it also made the production of *rookopium* (smokable opium) a state monopoly.

Crude opium, derived from the drained and dried juice of poppy heads and the base for the preparation of smokable opium, was imported from British India. The distribution of the prepared product was arranged through a system of concessions, with differentiations in the availability of the drug in certain regions and for particular population groups. In this way the Dutch government hoped to increase profits and at the same time exclude the Chinese intermediate traders, who until then had bought the rights for the distribution of the drug from the state. The new system also facilitated the fight against opium smugglers, since the new standard product of the colonial state factory was easily discernible from illegal products. Not all users were, however, pleased with state opium and many preferred opium of other taste and quality. A police taskforce was set up to fight the illegal opium trade, but had little success. Illegal opium and later opium-based drugs such as heroin and morphine were smuggled in from Malaysia and China. Arguments for the Opiumregie were not limited to economic or public security issues. The Dutch government claimed that increased control of the whole chain of opium import, production, and distribution would lead to a reduction in opium abuse and dependence among the subject populations, who would have less reason and opportunity to turn to non-regulated substances and whose use level could be rigidly controlled. At the same time the majority of Chinese users were vilified: they undermined the lofty purposes of the colonial state's opium trade and/or brought the problems of addiction on themselves.[6]

The contrast between prohibiting opium in the Netherlands and selling it in the East Indies did not escape the notice of critics. In 1931 the lawyer of a Dutch cocaine smuggler asked a Dutch court how it was possible that the Dutch state prohibited in the Netherlands what it did itself in the Dutch East Indies.[7]

On the other side of the globe, in the Dutch West Indies, by 1900 drug policies aimed to regulate consumption of opium and cannabis by immigrant indentured labourers from China, British India, and the Dutch East Indies. These people had brought their drug habits to the colony of Suriname (Dutch Guyana), and from 1872 onwards excise had to be paid on the import of these drugs. The result was a thriving smuggling trade, especially with neighbouring British Guyana, where the use and sale of these drugs had already been regulated in 1861, stimulating illegal production and distribution.[8] In the 1890s Dutch employers in Suriname started to complain about reduced work performance because of drug use among immigrant labourers, while the colonial mental hospital received an increasing number of patients with reported cannabis-induced insanity.[9] In 1896 a new regulation stipulated that opium and cannabis could only be sold on medical prescription.[10] Smuggling increased, and to control the trade in 1908 a new regulation prohibited the import and sale of cannabis and opium except for licensed wholesalers, apothecaries and retail dealers; possession of more than small amounts of opium for personal use was criminalized.[11] In 1910 all opium dens were closed, and in 1918 the complete prohibition of the sale and use of cannabis (except by apothecaries and on medical prescription) and opium was enacted in the colony, anticipating the Opium Act of the next year.[12] The second Opium Act of 1928 was enacted for Suriname as well. However, illegal use of cannabis and opium continued to exist.[13] After the Second World War and especially after the independence of Suriname in 1975, the trade and use of illegal drugs by Surinamese migrants in the Netherlands was prominent in images and realities of the illegal drug market, while the independent state of Suriname would become a major drug trafficker itself (see Chapter 7).

Pharmaceutical companies and new networks of supply

After 1920 pharmaceutical companies in the Netherlands in possession of government permits could still produce morphine, heroin, and cocaine for medical purposes. Cocaine, and in the 1930s morphine, codeine, and other opiates, were produced by the Nederlandsche Cocaïne Fabriek (Dutch Cocaine Factory) in Amsterdam; morphine and other opiates by Pharmaceutical-Chemical Products formerly Bonnema (later to become Zwitsal) in the city of Apeldoorn.[14] It is impossible to establish how much of this production spilled over into the illegal market, for instance by theft from the factories or from pharmacists. Cocaine from the Nederlandsche Cocaïne Fabriek was found, for example, in Italy in 1929; the Dutch Ministry of Foreign Affairs denied all involvement of the firm in this affair.[15] Police reports show that the Netherlands did function as an important transit hub for the illegal trade in products from German, French, and other factories.[16]

Dutch government authorities were reluctant to operate against the interests of the nation's pharmaceutical industry and trade, even when the international regulatory regime led by the League of Nations intensified. The Treaty of Geneva of 1925 established a committee charged with the collection of data on production, distribution, and export of narcotics. From then on, national states had to issue import and export certificates for trade; moreover, these could only be issued for medical and scientific purposes. The introduction of this system by the League of Nations posed new problems for companies to continue their narcotics trade. The Netherlands, as an important producer of narcotics, was far from enthusiastic about the new system, which was a concession to the concerns of the USA (although this country was itself not party to the League of Nations and the treaty). Dutch politicians claimed that not the supply but the demand side should be targeted in order to limit the evils of narcotics use, in an interesting parallel to their statements about drug control in the Dutch East Indies.[17] Not until 1928 did the Netherlands introduce the certificate system for its own imports and exports.[18] This Dutch delay created business opportunities for *corporate non-compliance*: an active refusal to comply with the spirit, if not the letter, of international and national regulatory regimes. In the interwar period the Dutch state occasionally supported this with a kind of *state non-compliance* that obstructed the League of Nations regime, and also went against the spirit of the state's own regulatory regime.

This came to public attention in March 1928 when two police detectives seized 60 kilograms of heroin belonging to the Chemical Factory Naarden (CFN) aboard a ship in the Rotterdam harbour with Shanghai as its destination. The police searched the Naarden factory. Investigations into its administration revealed an extensive drug trade in which the CFN took care of the transit of drugs produced in other countries to destinations such as China, which had by then the biggest illegal narcotics market in the world. However, it turned out that no legal action could be taken against the CFN because it only kept the drugs in transit, with a licence from the Dutch government, and did not formally 'import' them. In transit the drugs were repackaged and relabelled for export. The CFN also did not hesitate to deliver drugs to individual smugglers, for instance to the Dutch drugs and weapons trader Salomon Hoornstra, considered by the Dutch police a major international smuggler who supplied Japanese traffickers.[19]

The CFN was a facilitator connecting European production with distribution, especially in China. Here a huge market in morphine and heroin had come into existence, despite the international regulatory regime and despite anti-opium campaigns in the country. In the 1920s this market was supplied from Europe and Japan. One League of Nations report estimated heroin imports in China through Shanghai and other ports at 5 tonnes each month by the time of the CFN affair.[20] Most of this supply ended up in pills and powders for the illegal market.[21]

Although CFN's actions were, at least according to the Dutch representative in the League of Nations Opium Advisory Committee, in disregard of all moral obligations, the company had not formally transgressed the law. The police felt frustrated, but a leading right-wing Dutch daily newspaper defended the company and the economic freedom of Dutch enterprises. The only action taken was the revoking of the CFN's licence to function as a transit depot, 'at the company's own request'. This face-saver was not such a big loss for the company since the introduction of the certificate system closed the loophole that it had used anyway.[22]

The *Dienst Volksgezondheid* (State Department of Public Health) and its Pharmaceutical Inspectorate had few problems with the transit and export of narcotics. The managing clerk of the CFN, F. M. Nieuwenhuis, now started to work for himself and continued to connect the legal production of pharmaceutical companies to the shady world of international drug traffickers.[23] After leaving the CFN he even received an opium permit in December 1928, allowing him to trade in regulated drugs. He had already started to buy Turkish heroin, morphine, and cocaine from a middleman in Paris before receiving the permit. The Ministry of Justice and its police protested against Nieuwenhuis having the permit, but without result. This despite that both police and customs considered Nieuwenhuis to be the real 'fixer' in the CFN affair, and despite a refusal by the British government the following year to issue an export permit for the delivery of morphine to Nieuwenhuis. It even seems that Nieuwenhuis was to some extent 'protected' by the chief inspector for public health, J. B. M. Coebergh.

Not only did Coebergh intercede on behalf of Nieuwenhuis with Sir Malcolm Delevingne, the British representative in the Opium Advisory Committee, but when Delevingne continued to refuse the permit, Coebergh in his turn refused a permit to a Dutch pharmaceutical company to export morphine to Britain. Under pressure from both the Ministry of Justice and the Ministry of Foreign Affairs, Coebergh had to give in and in January 1930 Nieuwenhuis's opium permit was cancelled.[24]

This did not end Nieuwenhuis's operations, however. In December 1930 the Dutch police, at the request of the French, raided his Amsterdam house. The detectives found extensive and encoded international correspondence with contacts in Japan and the United States, and including Dutch 'colleagues' such as Hoornstra (whose own opium permit had already been revoked in 1925), suppliers in Turkey, and middlemen in France. Through Nieuwenhuis's network Turkish drugs were spread all over the world.[25]

A Dutch police report from 1933 details how this network operated. Nieuwenhuis, when still working for the CFN, had had dealings with a Swiss smuggler named Zimmerli who transported drugs through the Netherlands into Switzerland. After having spent a few years outside of Switzerland to avoid prison Zimmerli had returned to his home base in Basel. In 1933, five years after the CFN affair, he sent a telegram to Nieuwenhuis and asked him to telephone him. In the call Zimmerli asked Nieuwenhuis to set up a conference at the Victoria Hotel in Amsterdam, opposite the city's central railway station. Zimmerli took the train to Amsterdam together with two associates: another international smuggler specialized in operations to the United States, and a pharmaceutical engineer. As a result of the meeting, Nieuwenhuis arranged for the delivery of 2,000 kilograms of codeine or ethylmorphine, obtained through his contacts in the pharmaceutical industry, to a chemical laboratory run by the smugglers in France, where they would work on splitting the substance into morphine and possibly the morphine into heroin. The delivery of codeine in itself was not illegal, but the objective of this delivery (the manufacture of illegal drugs) was. Here was a fine example of non-compliance in which the suppliers did not wish to know what went on in the rest of the chain of distribution.[26]

In 1931 a new problem for the international drug traffickers arose as the League of Nations and the USA agreed on the introduction of a limit on production in each country to that country's estimated medical and scientific needs. This forced pharmaceutical companies to limit their production. The treaty of 1931 created a supply crisis and led to the establishment of production outside Western Europe, first in Eastern Europe, and later in Asia.[27] However, this did not end the corporate non-compliance of European pharmaceutical companies. One of Nieuwenhuis's business associates after leaving the CFN was C. H. Jansen, the director of Pharmaceutical-Chemical Products. In 1934 the chief of the Dutch narcotics squad (established in 1932, as will be seen below) asked for the revocation of Jansen's permit to produce narcotics, since Jansen tried to sell them through Nieuwenhuis. The government refused. The advisor for opium affairs of the Ministry of Foreign Affairs wrote confidentially to the Ministry of Labour that there was nothing to blame Jansen for, since the pharmacist was only trying to make his business profitable.[28] While the Dutch police (functioning under the Ministry of Justice) wished actively to fight the international drug trade, the pharmaceutical inspectors (functioning under the Ministry of Labour) were primarily interested in protecting the viability of the Dutch pharmaceutical industry.

Within this context there was space to manoeuvre for facilitators such as Nieuwenhuis and Hoornstra to connect demand, transport, and supply internationally. Like their foreign colleagues such as Elie Eliopoulos, these facilitators made use of the latest technological innovations of the era, communicating by telegraphic code and using the international banking system.[29] They were not leaders or members of sinister and hierarchical international crime syndicates, but key figures in a relational network that can best be understood as a temporary partner model. Essentially they were hustlers and dealers responding to a demand for illegal goods.[30] Nieuwenhuis was not a member of a criminal underclass, but made use of his personal network, built up in a legitimate business, to test and cross the boundaries between legality and illegality.

Legal production and illegal distribution

It was not long before members of a criminal underclass moved in on the new drug market. Although in theory the production of legal pharmaceuticals and their delivery by the licensed wholesale trade to pharmacists and doctors, and by them to patients, was traceable, the minutes of meetings of the pharmaceutical inspectors show that this was an illusion.[31] Narcotics leaked away in all parts of the production and trade chain. The chain of production, distribution and consumption of cocaine connected all kinds of social circles. In the 1930s morphine and cocaine were smuggled from German factories into the Netherlands, partly destined for transit to Belgium and France. Narcotics smuggling appears to have been a sideline activity of smugglers in the German–Dutch border regions, rather than their main activity. It is impossible to quantify this illegal narcotics trade. There is no archival evidence that shows to what extent drugs produced by pharmaceutical companies in Germany, the Netherlands, or elsewhere ended up in an illegal circuit. What is clear is that incentives to enter the drug market were there, since profitability could be high. A study from 1936 claimed that smugglers were easily prepared to pay 1,800 Dutch guilders for a kilogram of cocaine with an official retail price on the legal medical market of 400 guilders (in today's purchasing power around 4,000 euros).[32] Ten years earlier a pimp from Rotterdam bought five or six grams of cocaine under the counter from an employee of a pharmacy every day for a price of 14 to 16 guilders. The employee thus was selling a kilogram at a price of 2,300 to 3,200 guilders. The pimp repackaged the cocaine in 0.25-gram packets, which he sold for 1 guilder a piece, or 2.5 guilders for three powders, to prostitutes and foreign sailors around the Schiedamschedijk in Rotterdam – a quarter well known for its bars, cabarets, and prostitution. His retail price was thus at least 3,300 guilders per kilogram.[33]

The Schiedamschedijk was a source of concern for A. H. Sirks, the chief police commissioner of Rotterdam, who reported in 1930 that heroin and morphine were also increasingly used there and that the situation was especially bad in wintertime. Under Sirks more police attention was directed to the illegal drug trade, leading to more seizures and hence to increased concerns about the total volume. In 1932 Sirks became the head of a new police unit called the *Nederlandsche Centrale tot bestrijding van de smokkelhandel in verdoovende middelen* (Dutch Centre for the Fight Against Narcotics Trafficking, or the Centrale), based in the police headquarters in Rotterdam and with several sub-units in other cities. The establishment of the Centrale was a result of the new League of Nations treaty of 1931. After Sirks retired in 1933 his successor Einthoven, who was less concerned about the drug problem, would quickly report that narcotics smuggling had significantly reduced.[34]

In 1930 Sirks noted that employees of German pharmaceutical companies such as Merck and Boehringer sold narcotics to smugglers and that it was impossible to control the thousands of barges that moved over the great rivers between Germany, the Netherlands, and Belgium and transported these narcotics.[35] Neither was it considered feasible, at least according to customs, to control all the ships in Rotterdam harbour.[36] The amount of theft of cocaine from the Merck factory in Darmstadt was 'colossal' according to the German police, and Merck was regarded as the main source of the smuggling trade in and through the Netherlands. At the same time this put limits on the availability of cocaine since, unlike when Colombian cocaine hit the European markets in the 1980s, there was no illegal production. In the interwar period cocaine was skimmed off from legitimate production for the medical market by employees in the factories. These employees supplied German smugglers, who in their turn delivered the drugs to Dutch smugglers.

In the late 1920s and early 1930s the Dutch and German police forces kept a close eye on one of the networks that distributed cocaine in northwestern Europe. This international network of hustlers and dealers connected the cities in the border regions of the south of the Netherlands (Heerlen, Kerkrade, and Maastricht, all in the province of Limburg) with Germany (Aachen, Cologne), and was socially embedded in meeting places such as bars and dance halls. These hustlers and dealers were often unreliable, since rip-off deals also occurred.[37] A police report from 1931 gives us more details on the personal relationships in the network. A man named Van der Tuyn lived in Heerlen. At his house were regular meetings between his brother Frederik, who was a pimp from The Hague, a prostitute named Hubertine Tummers who lived with Frederik, and a German named Wilhelm von den Hoff who owned a bar in Kerkrade and was known as a 'notorious cocaine dealer'. An associate of Von den Hoff was the smuggler Peiffer from Vaals in Limburg, who specialized in sugar and was well known to the police. Frederik and Hubertine made regular trips in their red two-seater Buick (which must have been quite noticeable) to the border to pick up consignments of drugs smuggled by the likes of Peiffer. The pimp and the prostitute also drove over the border to Aachen and Cologne. The involvement of Hubertine shows that smuggling was not a purely masculine affair.[38] In Aachen a bar called *Bunte Bühne* was a meeting place for smugglers and suppliers – so was a dance hall called *Libelle*, which was a meeting place for all the 'scum of the town' according to the police. Employees of Merck delivered cocaine from the factory to a German trafficker and his associates, a bar owner and a theatre director in Cologne. They then sold the cocaine to smugglers, who in their turn sold to retail dealers in cities such as Kerkrade. Another form of operation was to send cocaine by post, for instance to a bicycle dealer in Maastricht.[39] Cocaine was also smuggled hidden in furniture.[40]

The distribution chain of stolen drugs was thus dependent on the corruptibility of employees of Merck and on the existence of a network of personal relations involving German, Dutch, and Belgian smugglers (since some of the drugs went to Belgium), as well as retail dealers and their customers. It also relied on the social embeddedness of the smugglers in bars and dance halls, and on the availability of means of transport such as a red Buick two-seater. Knowledge of the safest routes to smuggle drugs over the border was also essential. For instance, the border crossing at Locht, connecting the roads from Kerkrade and Heerlen to Aachen, was rarely controlled at night.[41]

There were limits to the illegal drug trade since the supply of stolen narcotics from Merck could not be endless. Occasionally drugs from other factories appeared on the illegal market, such as the cocaine from the Nederlandsche Cocaïne Fabriek in Amsterdam that in 1929 became lost via an Italian importer (see above). Other cocaine that appeared on the illegal market was bought under the counter in pharmacies or stolen from pharmacies of from a hospital – for instance by Dutch railway employees from a hospital in Berlin.[42] Von den Hoff, the cocaine trader of Kerkrade, was said to have different sources for his cocaine.[43] In this context the name of Nieuwenhuis also reappears: he is said to have delivered cocaine to a dealer in Geldrop in 1932.[44]

Once drugs arrived in the Netherlands all kinds of dealers were involved in their retail: people working in the entertainment industry such as pimps, bar owners, and dance teachers, but also garage keepers, cab drivers and so on.[45] Police files show variety among the people involved in the illegal narcotics trade that closely connected a shady underworld of illegal entrepreneurs to a legal upperworld. For instance, in December 1934 two well-known smugglers from Oud-Beijerland, a small town to the south of Rotterdam, were arrested by officers of the *marechaussee* (the military police in charge of border control) at the border crossing near Roosendaal in possession of 3 kilograms of opium. The smugglers had tried to bring the opium in tins on their motorbike to Belgium. The opium was seized and brought to the headquarters of the Centrale in Rotterdam, where it was found that the tins had been seized before and that the civil servant charged with destroying them had instead sold the contraband to smugglers. The civil servant himself had been cheated, since he was paid in forged banknotes.[46] In 1932 the mayor of the German town of Wehr was said to be involved, so was a retired Dutch police commissioner. A German physician in Gangelt supposedly dealt in opium and cocaine through an invalid mineworker in Heerlen. Across the border with Belgium a chemist and 'adventurer' and his partner smuggled cocaine in their Bugatti car. They boasted of using the drug when participating in the Liège–Rome–Liège automobile race.[47]

Medical and illegal distribution

Besides this illegal traffic in narcotics users could still legally buy products that contained opiates, but in insufficient concentration to be considered narcotics under the regulations of the Opium Act. These were products such as codeine (often used in cough syrups to help asthma) and opium powder (Dover powder).[48] To what extent these led to problematic use is uncertain. The Pharmaceutical Inspectorate began to investigate the numbers of addicts shortly after the introduction of the Opium Act, with inconclusive results. In 1921 the count came to around 360 addicts, but in 1930 it had dropped to only 35 (mainly morphine users). The value of these results was slight: the 1930 investigation was based on a questionnaire sent to 4,360 general practitioners, of whom only 750 cared to respond.[49] Numbers must have been higher. Doctors performed a pivotal role in this corner of the drug market. In 1947 a pharmaceutical inspector concluded that the supply of morphine to doctors and hospitals was twice as much as prescriptions could account for.[50]

The state inspectors encountered cases of doctors who had ordered excessive amounts of morphine for only one patient, and the case of a doctor's wife who used her husband's prescription book to buy morphine for her own use at many different pharmacies.[51] In 1940 mention was made of a suspiciously large amount of heroin used in Rotterdam: it turned out that heroin was regularly prescribed for asthma by insurance doctors.[52] In 1939 a police detective claimed that he knew of one patient who had received morphine prescriptions from no fewer than thirty doctors.[53] Where the police wished to prosecute doctors who couldn't keep their hands out of their own medicine cabinet, or patients who falsified prescriptions to receive more of the intoxicants often prescribed by doctors, the Inspectorate was less keen on reporting them to the police. This was to the latter's frustration, as was shown in a plea in a public lecture in 1939 by one police officer in Rotterdam for prosecution of doctors that prescribed narcotics to patients without proper diagnosis.[54] But all in all it would have taken up too many resources for the regulatory state agencies to really control the drug market.

Conclusion

The introduction of the drug regulatory regime in the Netherlands was necessitated by the need to participate fully in the international community of nations dominated by the Allied victors of the First World War, and to protect the colonial opium monopoly in the Dutch East Indies. However, the introduction had unintended consequences and led to the need for more and more regulation in order to control the now illegal drug markets. From the outset the strategies of the state were confronted with the various tactics of smugglers and traffickers. The main sources of supply of morphine, heroin, and cocaine were legal production and spillovers from the medical market, obtained by theft and corruption. Supply remained limited, even when stricter regulation led production to move from the German industry into Eastern Europe and Turkey. Pharmaceutical companies, pharmacists, doctors, patients, and others all tested the boundaries and possibilities of the new regulatory regime in various practices of non-compliance with the new regime. New connections were forged between this upperworld and an underworld of suppliers and smugglers. Illegal drug supply did not become the province of large criminal organizations reminiscent of Tintin stories, but rather of flexible and temporary networks of individual partners. On the one hand brokers originating from the pharmaceutical industry such as Nieuwenhuis connected new forms of supply and demand. On the other hand criminal entrepreneurs and smugglers began sidelines in the profitable illegal drug market. Distribution chains became socially embedded in bars, dance halls, and brothels. The availability of transport such as fast cars, trains, and river barges, and knowledge of transport routes (border crossings, rivers) that could not be fully controlled by the police made smuggling possible.

In the interwar landscape problems of drug trafficking and abuse were relatively small compared to the landscape that would evolve at the end of the 1960s. Nevertheless in the interwar period the first manifestations of a native Dutch criminal anarchy on the drug markets can already be discovered, embedding drug smuggling in border cities and port towns, and linking to a more respectable upperworld of manufacturers and facilitators.

Notes

1 J. C. van der Stel, *Drinken, drank en dronkenschap. Vijf eeuwen drankbestrijding en alcoholhulpverlening in Nederland* (Hilversum: Verloren, 1995).
2 M. de Kort, *Tussen patiënt en delinquent. Geschiedenis van het Nederlandse drugsbeleid* (Hilversum: Verloren, 1995), p. 27.
3 On the history of Dutch drug legislation see de Kort, *Tussen patiënt en delinquent*; T. Blom, *Opiumwetgeving en drugsbeleid*, 2nd edn (Deventer: Wolters Kluwer, 2015).
4 'Nota van wijziging', 4 September 1919, *Bijlagen Handelingen Tweede Kamer der Staten-Generaal*, 60:5.
5 A. W. McCoy, *The Politics of Heroin: CIA Complicity in the Global Drug Trade*, rev. edn (Chicago: Lawrence Hill Books, 2003), pp. 92–3. See also A. L. Foster, 'The Philippines, the United States, and the origins of global narcotics prohibition', *Social History of Alcohol and Drugs* 33 (2019) 13–36, on p. 16.
6 The major studies on opium in the Dutch East Indies are: W. K. Baron van Dedem, *Eene bijdrage tot de studie der opiumquaestie op Java. De officiëele literatuur* (Amsterdam: J. H. de Bussy, 1881); K. H. Meijring, *Recht en verdovende middelen* (The Hague: VUGA-Boekerij, 1974), pp. 73–101; J. R. Rush, 'Opium farms in nineteenth century Java: Institutional continuity and change in a colonial society' (PhD-thesis, Yale University, 1977); E. Vanvugt, *Wettig opium. 350 jaar Nederlandse opiumhandel in de Indische archipel* (Haarlem: In de Knipscheer, 1985); J. C. van Ours, 'The price elasticity of hard drugs', *Journal of Political Economy* 103 (1995) 261–79; S. Chandra, 'The role of government policy in increasing drug

use: Java, 1875–1914', *Journal of Economic History* 62 (2002), 1116–21; E. V. V. van Luijk and J. C. van Ours, 'The effect of government policy on drug use: Java, 1875–1904', *Journal of Economic History* 61 (2007) 1–18.

7 Delpher digitized newspaper archive (ww.delpher.nl/nl/kranten, hereafter D): 'De Maastrichtse cocaine-zaak', *Limburger Koerier* 15 September 1931. See also J. A. Blaauw, *Narcoticabrigade. De eindeloze strijd tegen drugshandelaren* (Baarn: De Fontein, 1997), pp. 101–4.

8 D: *Nieuwe Surinaamsche Courant* 4 October 1894; *Nieuwe Surinaamsche Courant* 25 April 1901; B. L. Moore, *Cultural Power, Resistance and Pluralism: Colonial Guyana 1838–1900* (Montreal: McGill-Queen's University Press, 1995), pp. 164–7.

9 D: *De West-Indiër* 15 July 1894; J. Scholtens, 'Mededeelingen over het gebruik van Gânjâh (Cannabis Indica) in Suriname en over de krankzinnigheid, die er het gevolg van is (cannabinismus)', *Psychiatrische en Neurologische Bladen* 9 (1905) 244–53; R. Hoefte, *In Place of Slavery: A Social History of British Indian and Javanese Laborers in Suriname* (Gainesville: University Press of Florida, 1998), p. 49.

10 *Gouvernementsblad voor de Kolonie Suriname* (hereafter GB), 1896, edicts 26, 36, 48.

11 GB: 1908, edict 13.

12 GB: 1910, edict 12; 1915, edicts 60, 61.

13 B. Pronk, *Verkenningen op het gebied van de criminaliteit in Suriname* (The Hague: Martinus Nijhoff, 1962).

14 H. H. Bosman, 'The history of the Nederlandsche Cocaïne Fabriek and its successors as manufacturers of narcotic drugs, analysed from an international perspective', 2 vols (PhD thesis, Maastricht University, 2012).

15 Letters from League of Nations and Dutch Consul to Ministry of Foreign Affairs, 18 November and 5 December 1929, in archive of Ministry of Foreign Affairs, A-files, National Archive, The Hague, inv. no. 2.05.03 (hereafter NA/FA), 1535.

16 On international drug trafficking in the interwar period: A. A. Block, 'European drug traffic and traffickers between the wars: The policy of suppression and its consequences', *Journal of Social History* 23 (1989) 315–37; K. Meyer and T. Parssinen, *Webs of Smoke: Smugglers, Warlords, Spies, and the History of the International Drug Trade* (Lanham: Rowman & Littlefield, 1998).

17 Blom, *Opiumwetgeving en drugsbeleid*, pp. 11–13.

18 de Kort, *Tussen patiënt en delinquent*, p. 103.

19 Chief Commissioner Sirks to Minister of Justice, 4 September 1930, NA/FA, 1590; de Kort, *Tussen patiënt en delinquent*, p. 101; Blaauw, *Narcoticabrigade*, pp. 54, 124.

20 F. Dikötter, L. Laamann, and Z. Xun, *Narcotic Culture: A History of Drugs in China*, rev. edn (London: Hurst & Company, 2016), p. 135.
21 When the international regulatory regime succeeded in the 1930s in pushing production out of Europe it stimulated its further development in clandestine laboratories and factories in China and Japanese-occupied Manchuria; Dikötter et al., *Narcotic Culture*, pp. 123–43.
22 de Kort, *Tussen patiënt en delinquent*, pp. 98–105.
23 Police report on Nieuwenhuis 26 June 1933, NA/FA, 1537; Blaauw, *Narcoticabrigade*, pp. 111–23; de Kort, *Tussen patiënt en delinquent*, p. 105.
24 Blaauw, *Narcoticabrigade*, pp. 112–23.
25 Blaauw, *Narcoticabrigade*, pp. 121–3.
26 Report J.C. de Jong and G.W. Valken, 26 June 1933, NA/FA, 1537.
27 Meyer and Parssinen, *Webs of Smoke*, pp. 31–2; de Kort, *Tussen patiënt en delinquent*, p. 109.
28 Letters of the chief of the drug squad, 27 July 1934; of the opium advisor, 6 February 1935, NA/FA, 1537.
29 Meyer and Parssinen, *Webs of Smoke*, pp. 117–39.
30 Compare M. H. Haller, *Illegal Enterprise* (Lanham: University Press of America, 2013).
31 In the archive of Pharmaceutical Inspectorate 1921–1961, National Archive, The Hague, inv. no. 2.15.39 (hereafter NA/PI).
32 C. Offerhaus and C. G. Baert, *Anaesthetica. Speciaal cocaine en novocaine, mede in verband met den smokkelhandel* (Amsterdam: D. B. Centen, 1936), p. 7. Purchasing power of the guilder from International Institute for Social History, www.iisg.nl/hpw/calculate2-nl.php (accessed 7 August 2020).
33 de Kort, *Tussen patiënt en delinquent*, pp. 126–7.
34 Nederlandsche Centrale tot bestrijding van den smokkelhandel in verdoovende middelen (hereafter Nederlandsche Centrale), annual report 1933, NA/FA, 1537.
35 Report by Sirks to Foreign Affairs, 25 April 1930, NA/FA, 1535.
36 Government advisor to Foreign Affairs, 24 March 1930, NA/FA, 1590; Labour Trade and Industry to Foreign Affairs, 11 April 1930, NA/FA, 1535.
37 Most of the cases investigated by the police in 1932 concerned fake drugs: Nederlandsche Centrale, annual report 1932, NA/FA, 1537.
38 On gender aspects of drug trafficking see the special issue of *Gender and Critical Drug Studies* of *The Social History of Alcohol and Drugs*, 31 (2017): 7–143.
39 Chief Inspector of Police A. van den Dolder, 'Rapport betreffende den sluikhandel in verdoovingsmiddelen in het zuiden van de provincie Limburg', 30 July 1931, NA/FA, 1536. For Von den Hoff see 'Verslag

van de internationale politie-vergadering gehouden te Maastricht op 3 november 1932', NA/FA, 1537.
40 Inspector of Public Health A. H. van de Velde to Foreign Affairs, 20 October 1930, NA/FA, 1535.
41 'Verslag van de internationale politie-vergadering gehouden te Heerlen op 26 maart 1931 in Hôtel: "Neerlandia"', NA/FA, 1536.
42 Inspector of Public Health A. H. van de Velde to Foreign Affairs, 3 October 1930, NA/FA, 1535. Pharmacies: e.g., report by Rotterdam police to Ministry of Foreign Affairs, 13 March 1933, NA/FA, 1537.
43 'Verslag van de internationale politie-vergadering gehouden te Heerlen op 26 maart 1931 in Hôtel: "Neerlandia"', NA/FA, 1536.
44 'Verslag van de internationale politie-vergadering gehouden te Maastricht op 3 november 1932', NA/FA, 1537.
45 Van den Dolder, 'Rapport', NA/FA, 1536.
46 D: 'Opium-smokkelaars', *Provinciale Noordbrabantsche en 's Hertogenbossche Courant* 8 April 1935; 'Een zonderlinge ontdekking', *Nieuwe Tilburgsche Courant* 9 April 1935.
47 'Verslag van de internationale politie-vergadering gehouden te Maastricht op 3 november 1932', NA/FA, 1537.
48 *Pharmaceutisch Weekblad*, at pw.nl/archief/historisch-archief (hereafter PW), 1940, p. 30.
49 Letter from Minister of Labour, Trade and Industry to Foreign Affairs, 12 January 1931, NA/FA, 1590.
50 G. D. Hemmes, 'Over het gebruik van morphine', *Nederlandsch Tijdschrift voor Geneeskunde* 91 (1947) 550–2.
51 Nederlandsche Centrale, annual report 1932, NA/FA 1537.
52 NA/PI, annual report 1940.
53 D: *De Telegraaf* 23 February 1939.
54 D: *De Telegraaf* 23 February 1939.

3

Global perils I: Chinese and Greek drug smugglers

The introduction and implementation of the drug regulatory regime in the Netherlands provided new opportunities for criminal entrepreneurs. In the previous chapter we investigated how native Dutch individuals and smugglers took these opportunities. Already in the interwar period the illegal drug market in the Netherlands took on multi-ethnic dimensions as well. In particular Chinese and Greek smugglers became involved in supplying opium and opiates, with the Netherlands as end destination or as transit hub for the illegal trade. The role of the Netherlands in international maritime trade and its extensive shipping industry facilitated narcotics smuggling and was one of the grounds for making effective implementation of the drug regulatory regime almost impossible. Policymakers and law enforcement officials were confronted with a problem similar to the one they had regarding the pharmaceutical industry: how to implement the new drug regime without damaging important economic sectors. 'Chinatowns' had come into existence in the major ports of Amsterdam and Rotterdam on the eve of the First World War. Here on the one hand Chinese drug trafficking was socially and culturally embedded; on the other hand, the Chinese labour force was indispensable to Dutch shipping. These factors assisted networks of Chinese and Greek smugglers to make use of Dutch maritime links to connect supply and demand in the drug markets.

In the Dutch East Indies the strategies of the colonial state to control territories and the opium trade had been countered by the tactics of Chinese societies and smugglers. In the nineteenth century these conflicts gave rise to images and the perception of secret Chinese organizations operating internationally to constitute a 'Yellow Peril' to white dominance. The sociologist Manuel Castells has used the remarkable success in the global drug trade of these so-called 'triads' as an example of the consequences of globalization. According to him, the increased possibilities to migrate in a globalized society made it easier for organized crime to migrate too.[1] This explanation is rather too facile. Criminologist Frederico Varese has suggested that for 'organized crime' in one country to migrate successfully to another, three conditions should be met. The first is a market shift, 'a sudden boom in a local market that is not governed by the state'. Second, in the country to which crime moves, a network of individuals with the ability and predisposition to criminal actions has to be present, as well as a social and political context in which recruitment of these individuals can take place (for instance, the presence of a homogeneous ethnic community). Third, state institutions in the country where crime moves to have to be weak or compromised, or alternatively, disposed to use the criminal organizations for their own goals.[2] Varese's study primarily deals with organized racket crime that is mainly involved in 'protection', but his insights are useful for a study of the illegal drug trade as well. All the factors mentioned were to some degree present in the Netherlands in the interwar period. The illegalization of the opium market created a demand for illegal supply. A Chinese ethnic community was present. Dutch law enforcement did not wish to obstruct the supply of labour for the shipping companies by Chinese shipping masters, even when these were suspected of involvement in illegal trade.

The success of Chinese opiate trafficking was not a consequence of post-Second World War globalization but the result of a much longer-lived globalization of commodity flows and migration of criminal activities that extends to well before the First World War. However, as Varese writes, 'the flow of illicit commodities may be transnational, but their control is essentially local'.[3] This chapter and Chapter 5 investigate the illegal opiates trade from the perspective of criminal anarchy.

Demand for opium

Critical to our understanding of Chinese drug trafficking are the global connections between the Chinese, the Dutch, and opium that go back well into the seventeenth century. While in the twentieth century the Chinese brought opiates to Europe, ironically opium smoking was a habit the Chinese had developed out of their contact with European sailors and merchants. In the seventeenth century the Chinese acquired the habit of smoking a substance from the Portuguese and the Dutch. They 'naturalized' or 'normalized' the smoking of tobacco using pipes. In this way tobacco developed from a luxury good into an everyday consumer good among all classes of society.[4] In Southeast Asia Chinese merchants, labourers, travellers, and migrants also experienced the use of opium, which in China itself was by then still mainly a luxury aphrodisiac and medicine but which became a more accessible consumer good when it came to be smoked in pipes, like tobacco.

Chinese opium habits led to the first reported violent encounter over access to the drug between the Dutch and Chinese. The daily register of the VOC trading post in Jakarta (in present-day Indonesia) mentions that on 22 August 1617 a Dutch boatswain named Willem Jansen was fined three months' wages because he had drunkenly tried to force access to a Chinese house to obtain opium. When refused entry Jansen pulled out a knife and stabbed one of the Chinese doormen in the arm.[5]

Opium had been brought by the Portuguese to the Moluccas, and from there its use had spread to other islands in the Indonesian archipelago. Chinese labourers and sailors in Java became great consumers of opium and they took the habit back to China. The Dutch started to trade opium from Bengal in India to their East Indian possessions and to Europe. Opium as a trade item and as a means of payment followed the Dutch throughout Asia and was supplied by the VOC in Java to Chinese traders as early as 1613.[6] By the 1720s opium smoking was widespread in Taiwan, an island then recently occupied by the Chinese. The Chinese emperor issued edicts to prohibit the trade in opium. A Chinese military official claimed, 'the opium smoke is from Batavia [the Dutch name for Jakarta], Luzon [a Spanish-controlled island in the Philippines] and other ocean countries. It is a prohibited article by sea. Taiwan has many rascals; they mix it with tobacco and smoke it.'[7] The development of an 'opium epidemic' in China was fully underway by 1750, long before the Opium Wars of 1839–1842 and 1856–1860 in which Britain and France forced China to open its border to the opium trade.[8] By 1750 the opium habit had spread further into southern China, to the provinces of Guangdong (the city of Canton and its river delta leading to the ocean and to the islands of Hong Kong and Macao situated just off the coast) and Fujian (an important maritime centre to the east of Guangdong). These provinces would be pivotal in reversing the global flow of opium in the early twentieth century from Asia into the Netherlands.

In the eighteenth century the supply of opium came from outside China: for instance, from the 1780s onwards British traders smuggled the drug into that country.[9] But by the late nineteenth century opium was cultivated in China itself. By then it had completely lost the status of a luxury good and even the poorest coolies could afford the habit, smoking or eating the drug as an energizer and anaesthetic to help them to do their work and to get them through the day. Opium consumption was a necessary, but possibly addictive, additive to the diet.[10] Chinese migrant labourers and seamen took the habit with them overseas to the Western hemisphere.[11]

Opium smoking was not a vicious habit pushed by Western colonizers on the colonized people in Asia and the Far East.[12] Neither was it an Asian vice pushed by the Chinese on the Western world. Opium smoking and its global transmigrations were the result of an 'interadoption' of commodities, technologies, and ideas between China and the West, an exchange that also included diverse social and cultural practices such as tobacco smoking, military tactics and technologies, and Delft blue porcelain.[13] In these processes of interadoption the specific social and cultural causes and effects of the habit changed. Seamen, merchants, and smugglers performed pivotal roles in these processes, transporting not only the drug but also cultural habits of drug use to different social groups and responsive cultures across the world in pre-modern globalization processes.

Opium and the Chinese in the Dutch East Indies

Dutch political authorities were first confronted with Chinese opium use in the possessions in the East Indies. Here they also had their first confrontations with the mysterious secret organizations known as triads. The Dutch responses to opium use and Chinese 'organized crime' in the East Indies show parallels with their policies towards these issues in the Netherlands itself after the introduction of the

Opium Act. Racial 'Othering' was of key importance to these Dutch drug policies and attitudes in the colonies, creating a legacy that would influence policies and attitudes in the home country.

In the system of opium regulation introduced by the Dutch colonial state in 1833, distribution was placed in the hands of so-called 'opium farmers'. The opium farmers were obliged to purchase from the state an established minimum amount of opium and use it for retail.[14] Pivotal to this system was the role of the Chinese in the Dutch East Indies, since significant numbers of both consumers and opium farmers were Chinese. Here as in other fields the relationship between the Dutch and the Chinese was fraught with ambivalence. A Danish traveller in the Dutch East Indies observed in 1878: 'The Chinamen are the principal source of profit to the Dutch Government, as they are the opium farmers.'[15] This source of profit was at the same time a source of anxiety and a potential threat to Dutch colonial authority. The average Dutch colonial official had little knowledge of opium. He considered a moderate consumption by Javanese and Chinese labourers as beneficial to their health, with the added advantage that opium consumption kept the population quiet. In his view it was not consumption, but illegal trafficking that was the major evil. The first drug squads or *opiumjagers* (opium hunters) that were appointed in 1876 had, however, low status in the colonial hierarchy and their activities were very much dependent on information and assistance from the Chinese opium farmers. Part of the latter's supply, however, went into the illegal market. The system functioned because of widespread corruption. According to the calculations of historian Benjamin Rush, 60 per cent of the opium trade in central Java was illegal. Sale to consumers took place in thousands of more or less illegal opium stores, as well as by door-to-door pedlars.[16]

As mentioned in the previous chapter, the Dutch therefore developed a new system to improve their control over the opium trade and its consumption. The Opiumregie was gradually introduced between 1894 and 1914 and entailed state monopolies on the production and trade of smokable opium, while retail sales were limited to licensed opium dens. However, the 3,000-kilometre border of and the sea routes to the colony were impossible to close off to the smuggling of other opium. The Indonesian archipelago, with its thousands of islands, is ideally suited for trafficking outside the control of the state. In 1907 a survey of the opium trade estimated that five-sixths of it was illegal.

To enforce the monopoly a central opium investigation agency was founded in 1927 (five years before the establishment of a similar organization in the Netherlands, the Centrale). The agency achieved little: cheaper opium and later opium-based drugs such as heroin and morphine were smuggled in from Malaysia and China.[17]

Controlling the opium market was made more difficult because of the many social functions the use of opium performed among the Chinese and others in the East Indies. Of 200 opium addicts admitted for treatment to a hospital in Batavia more than half had started to use opium or morphine as a painkiller for self-medication. Around sixty had started smoking or eating opium, or taking morphine, to fight extreme fatigue because of long working hours and hard physical labour. Only around thirty of the addicts, approximately 15 per cent, had become addicts because of recreational use and peer pressure in their social group.[18]

To supply the users, underworld cooperated with upperworld across the frontier.[19] People from beyond the Dutch East Indies (*vreemde Oosterlingen*) were seen by the colonial authorities as the primary threat to border control, although others were involved in smuggling as well: Arabs, Armenians, the local indigenous people, and corrupt officials. Smugglers, in the words of historian Eric Tagliacozzo, 'moved into the interstitial scams between the "sinews" of state power, seeking out places and moments where such attacks had a chance of success'.[20] For this Chinese traffickers had an important asset: cross-border network structures reaching from China to Chinese migrants in Southeast Asia and elsewhere. In the colonial imagination this created the spectre of a new and dangerous enemy: the Chinese secret society. In the 1970s this image would haunt police and press in the Netherlands, but its origins go back to the nineteenth-century Dutch East Indies.

The secret societies

A closer understanding of the secret societies is, however, extremely problematic. As they were secret, we know hardly anything about them, to the extent that their very existence has been doubted. Writers who do accept the existence of the triads have held widely divergent ideas about their organizational structure and their influence. To make some sense of a field in which consensus seems to be lacking to a significant degree, a survey of the historical research is essential and clarifying.

From the 1850s onwards, colonial authorities and European writers sounded alarm bells about the existence of the Chinese societies. In his history and analysis of the opium trade in the Dutch East Indies published in 1853 former Governor-General Jean Chrétien Baud wrote that 'the expansion of the Chinese confederations ensured more and more the impunity of the smugglers'.[21] In 1851 the then Governor-General of the Dutch East Indies, Duymaer van Twist, proclaimed in an edict that any activity of the Chinese societies that undermined 'lawful authority' in the colonies would be opposed and their members unconditionally evicted from the colony.[22] At that time the Dutch colonial army was waging a war against the societies in the western part of Borneo. Chinese labourers had migrated in the second half of the eighteenth century to western Borneo to work the gold mines. By 1774 a few thousand Chinese lived there, before the Dutch had established a presence. The Chinese created small autonomous republics, the so-called *kongsi* (joint undertakings). The kongsi elected their own leaders and administered their own affairs, in a conscious imitation of the political structures of their villages of origin on the Chinese mainland. On Borneo there were twenty-four of these kongsi, each with their own jurisdiction, fighting for control of the gold mines with the native Dayak, with the Malay sultans, with each other, and ultimately with the Dutch who were invited in by a Malay sultan in 1818. Between 1819 and 1823 the Dutch colonial army waged several campaigns against the kongsi. However, when in 1824 a war broke out on Java, all Dutch troops were withdrawn and the kongsi resumed and extended their power. By 1850, when the Dutch returned, there were five kongsi left; in some oligarchic rule had replaced the original democratic structure. The kongsi facilitated extensive opium smuggling in the archipelago. It was not until 1856 that the Dutch colonial army finally defeated the kongsi and brought western Borneo under Dutch control.[23]

The military defeat of the kongsi was not the end of Chinese resistance. According to the eyewitness account of Dutch captain Van Rees, the Chinese resorted to the weapon of the weak: terror. In 1854 the Dutch conquered Montrado, the most important town in western Borneo. Some Chinese leaders and their followers accepted the authority of the Dutch but others remained unruly. Around the time of the

Chinese New Year in February 1855 rumours spread in the town that Chinese outlaws had formed a secret society. Their followers carried a paper with a red stamp issued by the society signifying their adherence to another, shadow authority. The society's name, it was said, was only spoken in whispers; holding up three fingers was the gesture of recognition, since the name of the society was *Sam Tiam Foei* (or *Hui*), the Three Fingers (or, alternatively, Three Dots or strokes of a pen) Society. This society had echoes of an older group, as we will see in the next section. The Dutch believed that the society originated in China and Singapore, where its aim was the overthrow of British colonial rule. It had followers in all classes of society and was gaining support, especially among the miners. It recruited its new members by threats of violence, having them take an oath of absolute obedience endorsed by the drinking of a disgusting mixture of fresh cock's blood and arak, a strong alcoholic liquor. Members of the society used threats, murder, and arson to intimidate Chinese people who collaborated with the Dutch. The nucleus of the band was formed by 'twenty to thirty former kongsi chiefs and a few brawlers [bravos] and murderers'.[24] After a few months of fear and terror a prisoner betrayed to the Dutch the jungle location of the society's nightly rendezvous. A patrol of Dutchmen and Dayak allies attacked, killing some chiefs and taking the society's weapons supply. The heads of the dead chiefs were put on stakes to impress the Chinese population. This heralded the end of the threat of the society.[25]

In the attack on the headquarters of the Three Fingers Society outside Montrado a stamp had been found bearing the inscription 'Ngishin-Lanfong-kongsi'. To Van Rees this made clear that the Three Fingers Society, operating in the territory of the Lanfong-kongsi, was part of the much more widespread 'Ngishin-kongsi': 'The Kongsi of Resurrection of Righteousness and Justice' (alternative Latin spellings are Ngee-Hin, Ngihin, and Ngee Heng). This, Van Rees wrote, 'was one of the most powerful democratic [i.e., revolutionary] societies of China, that had shaken the foundations of world empires'.[26] Others in the Dutch East Indies, such as Governor-General Duymaer van Twist and the German sinologist Johann Joseph Hoffmann, agreed.[27] The British and the Dutch colonizers in Asia represented the Chinese kongsi as extensions of secret societies aiming at world power long before the 'Yellow Peril' became a popular trope in popular Western literature such as in the Fu Manchu novels of the British writer Sax Rohmer.

What were the societies?

Historical research has shed more light on the Chinese societies or *hui*. Although often translated as secret society, the word 'hui' literally means 'gathering'.[28] Like the kongsi, these societies had been an integral part of Chinese social life since at least the Han dynasty (206 BCE–220 CE). Not all of them were criminal, but a significant part consisted of outlaws and bandits, 'banded together by a ritual of initiation and an oath of loyalty and secrecy, and who acknowledged no authority but that of their leaders'.[29] Apart from rejecting established authority, these societies were embedded in local social and economic structures, 'offering' protection and involved in activities such as smuggling and piracy. In south China at the end of the eighteenth century the dominant secret society was called the *Tiandihui* or Heaven and Earth Society, also called the Three Dots Society or the Three United Society (hence the name triad; another variation using the number three is the Three Fingers Society). The origin myths of the Tiandihui went back to the beginnings of the Manchu dynasty (founded in 1644). The first triad was supposed to be founded in 1674 as a resistance organization against the foreign Manchu with the aim of restoring the Chinese Ming dynasty. However, more recent historical research suggests that the hui were not essentially patriotic resistance fighters, neither were they idealistic social bandits. Rather, the hui should be understood as mutual aid fraternities, 'associations created by young men who found themselves at the margins of settled society'.[30] Sinologist Wilfred Blythe wrote: 'Rituals and precepts contained elements from ancestor worship, astral worship, popular Taoism, Buddhism, and Confucianism, with the typical oath of secrecy and brotherhood sealed by the drinking of a mixture of blood and wine.'[31]

The element of mutual aid is crucial. The essence of membership is encountering assistance and mutual aid among fellow members in strange countries.[32] One could describe the hui as a lower-class version of Enlightenment Freemasonry. The secret societies have the role of kinship or family networks, while their organizational structure resembles the more horizontal structure of pirate and robber bands rather than godfather-led vertical pyramids. 'This made them particularly suitable as a social organization for Chinese immigrants, the poorer of whom, in particular, were unable to organize themselves on the basis of kinship.'[33] Informers in Borneo told a Dutch scholar that they joined secret societies because a brother of the society would give them what kin and relatives would normally give: mutual support.[34] Already in 1885 the Dutch sinologist J. J. M. de Groot, who spent three years as a government interpreter among the Chinese in Borneo, made it clear in a radical critique of earlier work on the secret societies that there was no reason at all to assume that the societies in the Indies originated in China, just because they had the same name. Two societies having a similar name did not necessarily imply a connection. To De Groot, who pioneered a sociological perspective on the hui, the structural similarities were explained by the characteristics of Chinese village life, which were used as the basis for the democratic mutual aid associations. When they were legal, the societies were out in the open and called kongsi. However, when they were made illegal, as after the Borneo war, they went underground and became secret societies.[35]

It is difficult to make clear distinctions between criminal groups and secret societies. 'Both bandit gangs and secret societies provided "meeting places for the destitute" and both formed a kind of substitute family for those whose natural relatives were dead, or scattered, or far away.'[36] What migrated among the Chinese in Southeast Asia was not a direct organizational structure, or cells of a centrally led revolutionary or criminal brotherhood. Hui sharing the same name in Singapore or Borneo did not have to be directly connected, rather they shared 'symbols, tracts, and lore'.[37] Historian Mary Somers Heidhues wrote that hui 'were ephemeral, displaying little continuity of action, activity, or even membership. The colonial authorities quickly deported or imprisoned supposed ringleaders, yet when problems arose, the *hui* reappeared. It was not the organization that persisted, however, but its forms.'[38] This furthermore explains why the secret societies kept popping up, even after having been eliminated by the Dutch. Hui were involved in insurrections against the Dutch in Borneo after 1855: in 1874, in 1884, in 1899, and in 1914 when not only Chinese but also Dayak and Malaysians were involved.[39] Secret societies were omnipresent among the Chinese in the East Indies, with goals that were mostly local. Some of these goals were illegal, such as running smuggling operations, but the goals could also be of a more general and non-criminal nature, such as giving assistance in organizing parties, burials, etc. Moreover, not all of these societies were totally secret, although their rituals could be. The major common denominator between them was that members were forced to give financial contributions to the society.[40] Participation in and knowledge of the rituals of a hui were forms of social and cultural capital needed for survival overseas by poorer Chinese migrants who could not fall back on kinship networks. From this perspective forming a secret brotherhood was a normal or natural reaction for the Chinese, a manifestation of a 'spontaneous order' that fits perfectly in the pattern of criminal anarchy.

Ritual specialists travelling from China to Southeast Asia had a role in transmitting the forms of the hui, as did oral traditions and literary sources such as *Romance of the Three Kingdoms* and *Water Margin* with their tales of heroic bandits.[41] The leader of the Three Fingers in the Borneo rising of 1855 had been a member of the Tiandihui in China and had brought his knowledge of organization and rituals to the East Indies.[42] The codes, mantras, and gestures police officials made so much of enabled the members of the hui to recognize each other. The structure of the hui also made them excellent vehicles for the sale of protection and for violent operations. The hui, then, could be at the same time both mutual aid associations and criminal networks. Their flexible structure made them ideal forms for spreading criminal or rebellious activities.

The hui, however, were not necessarily in conflict with society. For example, after the British took possession of Singapore in 1819 great numbers of Chinese labourers migrated to the colony. The Tiandihui (known by the British as the 'Grand Triad Hoey') had an important presence among these labourers. In Singapore they created an autonomous social and economic system that existed alongside to the colonial system. The hui also had an important function for the colonial authorities. While the colonial state in Singapore officially pursued a laissez-faire labour policy, unofficially it took on the hui as partner to manage the Chinese labour force. The hui controlled the pepper and gambier production, gradually shed its democratic structure and became dominated by wealthy merchants. Mutual aid as a leading principle made way for a complex debt structure in which the poorer labourers were indebted to the merchants, and in this way the hui transformed in a coercive agency in the service of the richest Chinese bosses. This further led to a gradual fragmentation of the hui. Other hui contested the power of the Tiandihui and started enforcing and smuggling operations. In spite of this, according to historian Carl Trocki the British development of Singapore could never have taken place without the assistance of the triads.[43] Here we have an exemplary form of 'co-management', as criminologists have called the unofficial cooperation of law enforcement agencies and criminal organizations in managing crime in order to maintain a stable social and economic order.

Historical research thus discredits the notion of centralized triad societies with a global command structure. This is confirmed by criminological studies. In his study of the Hong Kong triads, Yiu Kong Chu concluded that by the end of the twentieth century there were fifty societies with around 160,000 members. However, only about 10 per cent of these members were involved in any criminal activities. Some of the Hong Kong triads had a central committee, but not all. An important example of the latter is the 14K, the society that was seen as responsible for the introduction of heroin in the Netherlands in the early 1970s (see Chapter 5). According to Chu, the 14K is a loose network of independent gangs, each of them operating in its own territory. Every gang has its' own leader and a nucleus of fifteen to twenty members. Below them are a few youth gangs, the members of which will later graduate to full triad membership. A triad is more or less a loose cartel of gangs: instead of one big hierarchical pyramid, there are many smaller ones who exhibit a high degree of competition with each other. Personal connections are much more important than institutional ones.[44]

This reconstruction by Chu is at odds with the most influential traditional account of the Hong Kong triads, published by W. P. Morgan in 1960. Morgan, a Hong Kong police officer, put great emphasis on the rituals and the hierarchical structure of the triads, and this idea was taken on by sensational popular accounts in the last quarter of the century.[45] Other Hong Kong police officials were more sceptical about the global influence of the triads. One of them doubted whether the gangs in Hong Kong could control other gangs overseas, since all of them were primarily driven by local dynamics.[46]

That the triads were and are essentially fragmented and localized phenomena does not mean that they do not know *any* authority. 'Both bandit gangs and secret societies, though sharing a tendency to stress egalitarian sibling ties over traditional hierarchical organization, at the same time allowed a leader to reign as supremely as any Confucian patriarch. Discipline was strict.'[47] Some people in the group could dominate others with a mixture of success, charisma, and violence, not unlike the pirate chiefs of the legendary golden age of piracy.[48] It is this combination of elements (shared cultural capital, localized variations, global networks, and gang discipline) that we need to keep in mind when investigating Chinese opiate trafficking in the Netherlands.

Chinese seamen in the Netherlands

Poor Chinese migrants arriving in the Netherlands had to associate themselves with kongsi- and hui-like organizations in order to survive, to gain employment, and – when users – to have access to opium supplies. In doing so they became involved in the global trafficking networks connected by local members of the hui. In this context the tactics developed needed to operate in the changed architecture of the Dutch market after the introduction of the Opium Act.

From the moment of their first arrival in the Netherlands shortly before the First World War, Chinese migrants were surrounded by negative images in public opinion and the media.[49] This was partly related to the fact that the first generation were brought over in 1911 by Dutch shipping companies to work as sailors, mostly as stokers or firemen and as coal trimmers handling the fires in the engine rooms on the large steamships that worked the transoceanic routes of Europe to Asia and the Americas. To keep the fires that fuelled the engines going was extremely hard work performed in murderous heat. Most stokers and trimmers were burnt out by the time they were 35 years of age. This 'black choir' had a reputation for labour unrest.[50] In hiring Chinese workers the companies were trying to break the power of the trade unions. This of course did not make the Chinese popular among the Dutch working classes, but the Chinese were much cheaper than their Dutch colleagues: between 1920 and 1925 the salary costs of a Dutch boilerman were on average 140 Dutch guilders per month, those of a Chinese worker performing the same work were only 90.[51] Moreover, the companies argued that the hard work in the hot engine rooms was not suited for white people, and should be left to their 'racial inferiors' of the 'yellow race'. By 1927 around 3,200 Chinese workers were employed on the Dutch transport and mercantile fleet, of which 2,500 worked in the engine rooms, especially on the ships of the Stoomvaart Maatschappij Nederland (Steamship Company of The Netherlands) and Rotterdamsche Lloyd (Rotterdam Lloyd).[52] Their number decreased during the economic crisis of the 1930s, but in 1936 there were still around 1,000 Chinese workers living in the Netherlands who were signed up with the merchant fleet.[53]

In the port towns of Amsterdam and Rotterdam small 'Chinatowns' came into existence. These were not segregated areas but neighbourhoods where the Chinese lived among the native Dutch. In Amsterdam the first Chinese seamen who arrived to work for the Stoomvaart Maatschappij were lodged in a storehouse on the Javakade, on an island in the east of the harbour where the steamships moored and the companies had their warehouses. Chinese recruitment agents subsequently set up boarding houses in the inner city, close to the waterfront and overlapping with the town's red-light district, where seamen and in their wake Chinese people working as pedlars found lodgings. Here restaurants, illegal gambling houses, and opium dens formed the city's Chinatown. In Rotterdam a similar development took place. The Lloyd company owned a storehouse in the harbour where Chinese personnel were housed, and recruitment agents opened boarding houses on Katendrecht, an island in the harbour and the location of the city's red-light district.[54] From the 1920s onwards the Dutch police and other authorities produced images associating these Chinatowns with drug use, gangs, and criminal behaviour. Moreover, the steamships on which the Chinese worked were seen as an important means of transport for smuggling rings. For the historian it is hard to establish the exact scale of this smuggling but there is evidence of the smuggling of opium and of guns and ammunition as well as humans, foreign currency, and cigarette papers.[55]

An analysis of Dutch newspapers found that whereas before the introduction of the Opium Act opium was primarily associated with medicinal use, after 1920 the associations changed from 'medicines', 'poisons', 'science', 'pharmacies', 'sleep' or 'narcosis', to 'police', 'contraband trade', 'arrested', 'confiscated'.[56] By the eve of the Second World War opium, deviance, and the Chinese were definitively associated in media publications. On his very first appearance in 1940 detective Dick Bos (the hero of eponymous and extremely popular comics) is on the trail of a gang smuggling cocaine on a Chinese ship. When the gang captures him he is sent to China and put to work as slave on a plantation. Of course he escapes and ultimately helps to capture the gang. In *Dick Bos* opium and cocaine were clearly and visually associated with a dark underworld, low-life taverns, unreliable Chinese people, and harbours.[57]

The large majority of the Chinese seamen in the Netherlands came from the maritime provinces in south China where opium smoking had become popular in the eighteenth century: Guangdong and Fujian, provinces with their own languages and traditions. According to the Amsterdam harbour authority (the *waterschout*), of the 720 *zeemansboekjes* or official papers he had issued to Chinese seamen between 1937 and 1940, 510 (71 per cent) were to people from Guangdong. In 1936 the Rotterdam police counted 350 Guangdonese among a total of 399 Chinese workers (almost all seamen) in the city (88 per cent); in 1939 the count was 164 Guangdonese out of a total of 306 Chinese persons of whom the papers were checked (54 per cent). The majority of the Guangdonese came from two districts in the Pearl River estuary that connected the islands of Hong Kong and Macao with Guangdong: Ba' On and Dongguan.[58] 'Bo On', the name which the Dutch used for Ba' On, was also the name of one of the 'secret societies' fighting for control of the opium trade in Amsterdam and Rotterdam.

Police reports give more details of seizures of opium and arrests of smugglers arriving in Dutch ports. The smugglers were arrested either on board their ships, after docking in the grounds of the shipping company, or in a Chinese boarding house. For the period of 1929 to 1937 there are 68 reports of arrests. Most of these were related to ships of Rotterdamsche Lloyd (19) and the Vereenigde Nederlandsche Scheepvaartmaatschappijen (VNS – the United Dutch Shipping Companies), a consortium of shipping companies in which Lloyd participated (17). Third on the list of numbers of arrests is the Amsterdam-based Stoomvaart Maatschappij Nederland (9). A few ships are mentioned more than once, suggesting that these were vessels on board which smuggling was socially embedded. If we investigate the reports of arrests connected to Rotterdamsche Lloyd in more detail it is striking that almost all of the arrests concern Chinese stokers and firemen, and that almost all of them came from Canton (Guangzhou), the capital of Guangdong province, except for two who gave Hong Kong as their place of origin.[59]

Historian Robert J. Antony has described the maritime cultures of Guangdong and Fujian, cultures in which the borderlines between legal and illegal were flexible and the state was ignored or seen as a a nuisance or an enemy.[60] These provinces are isolated from the mainland of China by a mountain range. On the coastline there are, apart from a few larger ports such as Canton, many inlets, canals, islands, and natural harbours. The people living here had, for a large part, different ethnic backgrounds from the ruling Han Chinese: they were Hokkien (Hoklo) and Dan (Tanka). Around 1800 more than a third of the population consisted of fishermen and seamen, doing a bit of smuggling or piracy when conditions were profitable. Opium use and gambling were normal ingredients of everyday life. The smuggling and pirate gangs were flexible and temporary, organized by networks in which membership of secret societies was important. For instance, in 1804 a pirate founded a Tiandihui that quickly gained hundreds of members. Corrupt officials and merchants selling illegal goods were all related to an underground economy that offered social and economic prospects in a region characterized by poverty and increasing population pressure.[61]

Guangdong was an area full of social and cultural deviance. The Chinese seamen of the Dutch shipping companies took this deviance with them to Amsterdam and Rotterdam. Chinese smugglers brought before Dutch judicial courts or arrested by the Dutch police clearly had little reverence for white officials. Amsterdam police officer Hendrik Voordewind remembered being confronted in 1922 with arrested members of Chinese secret societies involved in opium traffic, and 'although the yellow chappies of course understood sufficient Dutch and English [...] some of them looked at me deadpan; others grinned and looked quite satisfied with the adventure'.[62] Respect was clearly lacking on both sides in this encounter. A court reporter described the behaviour of Chinese smugglers brought before the criminal court as almost serene, showing no remorse and keeping silent.[63] They belonged to a different cultural world than their judges.

Opium smuggling

This was the social and cultural background of the Chinese opium smugglers. The opium itself was taken on board ships in different ports on the route from the Dutch East Indies to the Netherlands.

Rotterdam police detectives seized mainly opium from Turkey, and occasionally opium from China or Japanese-controlled Manchuria.[64] The steamships of Rotterdamsche Lloyd mentioned in the police reports all had touched Marseilles, another key transit hub in the international opium trade. Sometimes the opium was brought on board here.[65]

We do not know about the extent of the trade. Sirks claimed that in the Rotterdam Chinatown alone at least 25 kilogram of opium was consumed each week. If this was the case for Amsterdam as well it would have meant a demand for the import of at least 2,600 kilograms each year, or at least one 'run' of 50 kilograms per week.[66]

Smuggling was profitable. In the 1930s one could buy a kilogram of opium for 27 guilders from smugglers in the port of Rotterdam. The opium was then cooked (losing about 20 per cent of its weight) and, once cooled down, packaged in parchment. In the retail trade smokable opium was sold in packages of 2 grams, sufficient for two pipes and enough to get a moderate user through the day, at a price of 50 cents, making for a retail kilogram price of 250 guilders.[67] One smuggler who ended up in the Amsterdam police court had bought 94 kilograms in the port of Hamburg (with the aim of smuggling it through Amsterdam into the USA) for the price of 7,000 guilders, paying a relatively high kilogram price of 75 guilders. The judge estimated the net profits in the opium trade to be 100 to 200 per cent of the purchase price.[68]

In the Netherlands the buyers of the retail packages were almost all Chinese, although there are reports on a few 'decadent' white people who had picked up the opium habit in the Dutch East Indies.[69] In the 1920s neighbours complained of the sharp odours coming from the boarding houses where the opium was cooked or smoked. Police detectives estimated that 75 per cent of the Chinese living in Amsterdam and Rotterdam smoked opium, but that a decrease in use began in the 1930s.[70] In 1925 the police asked the shipping companies about the numbers of Chinese employees using opium. The shipping companies in their turn asked the shipping masters, who supplied them with their Chinese crews. Ng Yat Min, the shipping master for the Stoomvaart Maatschappij, said one in five; the police did not believe him. The shipping master of Lloyd said 65 to 70 per cent of those from Hong Kong and Canton; and Wang Tsi Nang of the British Ocean Steam Company said one in three.[71] One Chinese man remembered that as a young child in Amsterdam he would be fetched by his mother to get his father out of the gambling house, and that there 'on those mattresses some people were using opium: [it was] dark and [there was] that air, but I did not think it strange'.[72] One was not supposed to talk about opium use, however, another Chinese man recalled: 'One could not say "there is opium smoking in the cellar", and one was not allowed to enter that space.'[73]

The Netherlands were not always the end destination but functioned as a transit hub to other destinations as well. Opium was repackaged in small oval tins and smuggled to Curaçao, the Dutch island in the Caribbean, and from there to Venezuela to supply the needs of Chinese workers for the oil companies – the opposite of the 1980s and 1990s flow of cocaine.[74]

Smuggling was profitable and risks were small. Arrests and seizures were few and occurred primarily in Rotterdam and a few other port towns. Most seizures were only of small amounts. Sentences were no more than two months' imprisonment; for instance, that sentence was given to Kwan-Kai who had smuggled the relatively high amount of 94 kilograms.[75] The arrested smugglers were not always even prosecuted. Rarely did the police arrest big-time traffickers.[76]

The ways that the arrested Chinese men operated were embedded within larger social groups. The shipping companies hired Chinese seamen not as individuals, but in groups led by a 'number one'. The intermediaries were the shipping masters – Chinese recruitment agents, who also controlled the boarding houses in the Chinatowns where the labourers lived when they were not at sea. These boarding houses operated furthermore as stores, gambling houses, and opium dens.[77] It is hard to see how any trafficking could have taken place without the knowledge of the number ones and the shipping masters. In fact, the police were convinced that the opium actually belonged to the number ones, or, when it was successfully smuggled into a Chinese boarding house, to its owner. But this could never be proven, since on seizure someone else always declared himself guilty of the crime, in accordance with the Chinese criminal code.[78]

Shipping masters and societies

Supplying the steamship companies with their crews was a profitable enterprise in itself. The shipping master negotiated the wages of the crew with the shipping companies and sold the position of 'number one'. Around 1930 the master could make a profit of 2,200 to 3,000 guilders when he supplied a crew of thirty-five stokers for a voyage of four months. He also made money by providing boarding for the seamen, hiring apartments for 50 guilders per month and renting them out for 35 to 40 guilders per week. In these lodgings ten to fifteen Chinese had to live in 40 square metres. According to one estimate 90 per cent of the income of a stoker went to his number one and to his landlord. Smuggling was an additional sideline and source of income for the shipping masters.[79] Their income was estimated at around 20,000 guilders per year, around 160,000 to 200,000 euros in today's purchasing power. It is not much compared to the money made by contemporary drug traffickers, but nevertheless at the time it was a considerable income. To increase their prestige among other Chinese workers they flaunted their wealth.[80] A British police report described them as 'Chinese in dark suits and gold-rimmed eyeglasses [who] continued to enjoy harems of wives and fat bank accounts'.[81]

Most of these shipping masters came from the same Chinese districts as the seamen, Bo On and Dongguan.[82] They were connected to 'secret' or not-so-secret societies named the Bo On and the Three Fingers. These did not only function as mutual aid associations for migrant Chinese labourers, they also mediated and passed judgement in disputes, since the Chinese were unwilling to turn to the Dutch authorities, which they could not understand anyway (and vice versa).[83] The Bo On organized migrants from the Ba' On district and opened up the first boarding house in Rotterdam on Katendrecht, in 1914.[84] The Amsterdam Bo On Association held formal meetings in a boarding house in the Binnen Bantammerstraat in Amsterdam's Chinatown. A prominent place in the Bo On network was taken by the Ng family, which originated from villages in Ba' On. The Ngs had offices for recruitment and migration in Kowloon (in Hong Kong), Singapore, Marseilles, London, Amsterdam, Rotterdam, and Willemstad on Curaçao. One family member named Ng Fook ran the office in Rotterdam; his brother Ng Young the office in Amsterdam. Ng Young acted as shipping master for the Stoomvaart Maatschappij. The Ng family also owned a boarding house in the Rotterdam Delistraat managed by a man named Choy Loy and his nephew Cheong Seung Yin. Both were suspected of drugs and weapons smuggling by international police organizations. Cheong was arrested in 1924 in Hong Kong in connection to the seizure of weapons on a German freighter.[85] The reputed Amsterdam 'godfather' of early 1970s heroin trafficking, Chung Mon, was born in Ba' On, according to one DEA-account.[86]

The great rivals of the Bo On were the Three Fingers triad, or the Chung Kong Tong. Its Rotterdam chief Ah Kui Tchai, or Tsoi Sau, a former pirate in the Dutch East Indies, was investigated in 1927 for the smuggling of people to Australia. He was also thought by the police to own a boarding house in Marseilles, in the ancient harbour district that was considered a bulwark of the Three Fingers.[87] In the 1920s the 'first Chinese war' in the Netherlands broke out between the Bo On and the Three Fingers (the second and third Chinese wars would be fought in the 1970s and 1980s, see Chapter 5). The two societies fought each other with guns for control of the Chinese communities, and more especially for the profitable role of recruitment for the shipping companies.[88]

As early as 1918 a Chinese recruitment agent named Liang Yi Van was shot dead in the Amsterdam Chinatown, in the Buiten Bantammerstraat. The murderer gave himself up to the police. Liang's half-brother took revenge by shooting three people in the Chinese storehouse on the Javakade, one of whom died, and killing another one in the Buiten Bantammerstraat. The brother was arrested as well. When interrogated, he and the murderer of Liang Yi Van denounced each other as members of (rival) secret societies, but the authorities did not believe them.[89]

Between 1920 and 1935 the struggle led to at least twenty-six murder attempts known to the police: fifteen in Rotterdam, eleven in Amsterdam. The Amsterdam police were bewildered when in June 1922 a report came in that a Chinese stoker had been shot and seriously wounded in the Chinese storehouse on the Javakade. The 250 Chinese lodging there had seen and heard nothing, so they said. Later that day a fight broke out in the harbour among Chinese wielding guns and knives; one of them was killed. The police rounded up thirty-eight suspects but could make nothing of the event.[90] Two weeks later the foreman of the Three Fingers was beaten up in the Chinese storehouse, and another stoker shot. The police raided the headquarters of the Three Fingers and the boarding houses. The officers seem to have been in some kind of alliance with Ng Young, the foreman of the Bo On, since those boarding houses which were controlled by the Bo On turned out to be almost empty at the time of the raids and Ng Young was asked to select from the arrested Chinese the dangerous and criminal elements who should be extradited. According to one inspector the Three Fingers had put a price on the head of Ng Young of 6,000 or 7,000 guilders and in September Young was shot dead by a member of the Three Fingers on a boat travelling to the docks of the Stoomvaart Maatschappij. The killer, a man named Jie Tjai, was caught and sentenced to five years' imprisonment. The man who was rumoured to have instigated the murder, the former stoker and one of the leaders of the Three Fingers in Amsterdam, Sie Lie Sou, had to flee to Rotterdam. The Bo On took control of Amsterdam. The Three Fingers retreated to and controlled Rotterdam. There they managed the recruitment for Rotterdamsche Lloyd. After his release from prison Jie Tjai managed a boarding house in Rotterdam which seems to have been in the control of the Three Fingers, but he was killed in 1931 when visiting Amsterdam, which remained in the control of the Bo On.[91] Ng Young had been succeeded as shipping master by Ng Sung Kam (who would die in 1942).[92]

After 1925 the shipping masters no longer ventured out without their bodyguards.[93] The police were well aware of the involvement of the shipping masters in the opium trade. The migrant department of the police reported in 1930 that most of them were involved in illegal trafficking.[94] Sirks had an intense dislike of the Chinese, a sentiment that was shared by at least one judge in the Amsterdam police court and shows clear parallels with the Dutch attitude to the Chinese in their colonies.[95] The Rotterdam police commissioner held the opinion that all Chinese should leave the country; however, he was also aware that he could not work against the interests of the shipping companies, who needed cheap labour.[96] In 1930 Lloyd started an 'experiment' using Dutch stokers and trimmers in their engine rooms, but the results of this experiment seem to be unrecorded.[97]

The shipping masters were seen as a necessary evil by Dutch authorities. In the first years of the Opium Act regime a shipping master was arrested in Amsterdam. In a boarding house in the Warmoesstraat Wang Tsi Nan, shipping master of the Ocean Steam Company, was arrested in 1921 for possession of ten packages and ninety-six tins containing opium. He was sentenced to ten days' imprisonment or a 200 guilder fine, but he was not extradited because he quickly married his pregnant Dutch girlfriend.[98] After this, though, the shipping masters seem to have been left alone by the police. As seen above in Amsterdam the police worked together with Ng Young of the Bo On. Sirks thought that in Rotterdam Sie Lie Sou was a key figure in the illegal opium trade, but even when opium and eight revolvers were found in his boarding house in Rotterdam he was not extradited because of technical errors in the procedure.[99]

The line between co-management of crime and outright corruption could be blurred. Ultimately law enforcement agencies were not very interested in the opium traffic or opium consumption, as long as it kept to the Chinese. Cheong Seung Yin, the Bo On trafficker in Rotterdam, was intimate with K. Roetman, one of the 'China experts' of the Rotterdam police. An investigation turned up photographs of Roetman, his wife, and Cheong's wife with two other police officers enjoying a day off at the beach. Roetman claimed that Cheong was his informant in the Bo On. The investigation was halted.[100]

The Greek connection

Tackling the Chinese opium trade was problematic since it was so deeply embedded among the Chinese workers that the authorities preferred some sort of co-management, containing rather than eradicating illegal activities. More promising was attacking the involvement of others in the drug trade. The new regulatory regime of the Opium Act had led to the development of an extensive international opium traffic to supply the needs of the Chinese workers in the Netherlands. The transport connections with Turkey were vital in supplying this opium, which opened up possibilities for Greek smuggling networks with their wide-ranging connections in Turkey and throughout the Middle East.

Why were the Greeks of such importance in the illegal drug trade? There are imperial Ottoman roots here. Smuggling was rife on the borders of the Ottoman Empire at the end of the nineteenth century.[101] Opium was grown in Turkey and other parts of the empire: in the 1860s the Ottoman regime introduced poppy cultivation in Macedonia, and after the Balkan wars of 1912–1913 and the First World War this cultivation was located in the states of Greece, Bulgaria, and Yugoslavia (especially Serbia). Greece also briefly occupied Smyrna, a traditional centre of the opium trade. By 1922 Greece was the sixth producer of opium in the world. In the later 1920s Greek opium production began to dwindle, partly because of stricter regulation, partly because tobacco cultivation was more profitable. However, cultivation in Serbia expanded and opium was exported through the Greek port of Thessalonica.[102]

'[Opium cultivation] provided an important source of livelihood for tens of thousands of peasant families, which tended to make government officials less than draconian in their enforcement efforts. The central governments exercised only minimal control over their borders and their miserably paid officials were chronically susceptible to bribery', write historians Meyer and Parssinen.[103] Greek opiate- and cannabis-smuggling networks (Greece was a major source of cannabis for consumers in Egypt) proliferated in the interwar period. The Greeks made use of their geographical and logistical locations and of the 'routine activities' of their extensive maritime transport industry.[104] Moreover, around 1930 the increased state regulation of the Western European pharmaceutical industry led to a profusion of hundreds of small factories in Turkey, Bulgaria, Albania, and Yugoslavia that turned local opium into heroin for the European and American markets. In the organization of this local production Western European financial resources and technological know-how was of crucial importance. For instance, in October 1929 the French company the Societé Industrièlle de Chimie Organique de Paris built a factory for the production of morphine, heroin, and cocaine close to Istanbul. Its production target for heroin was no less than 400 kilograms per month. By December 150 kilograms could be exported to Marseilles.[105] Increased prosecution of Greek drug smugglers in Egypt led to the extradition of some and their return to Greece, where they carried on their operations. For example, two of them, brothers, operated a heroin laboratory in Athens between 1934 and 1936.[106]

An example of the trafficking networks that used this kind of production can be found in the reports of the US FBN. In 1934 and 1935 the FBN ran an informer inside the operation of Greek pharmacist and trafficker Georges Bakladjagou. Bakladjagou disregarded the new borders between countries within the former Ottoman Empire. Greek by birth, he carried a Turkish passport and had lived for years in Turkey. In 1933 he started a pharmacy in Athens, which was a cover for extensive trafficking deals. Bakladjagou bought heroin from Bulgarian and Turkish factories, without having, or so he claimed, the slightest problems with the Turkish authorities, who turned a blind eye to an economic sector from which Turkey could only profit. He also started his own factory in Tirana in Albania, where codeine was turned into heroin. He bribed Albanian government officials as well as customs agents throughout Europe and America. His products were smuggled by stewards on Italian steamships who picked up 1-kilogram packages of heroin in the harbours of Istanbul, Brindisi, or Naples, and delivered them in New York. Bakladjagou was merely continuing the traditions of Greek trade networks in the former Ottoman Empire, now under the new but no less profitable conditions imposed by the international drug regulatory regime. While the reports of the FBN focus on his trade relations with the USA, other Greek smugglers supplied Europe, including the Netherlands.[107]

Shipping companies and shipping lines were essential for transport. Contacts and facilities in the harbour districts of European cities provided key transit hubs. Marseilles was such a key point on the transit routes. For instance, in June 1930 French customs seized 1,000 kilograms of heroin on the steamship *Italia* coming from Istanbul and arrested the Istanbul-born merchant Salomon Eskanazi.[108] The Dutch police noticed increased smuggling activities in that year, after a rather 'quiet' 1929. The transfer of heroin production to Turkey and the Balkans was responsible for these growing activities. Another cargo of 100 kilograms of heroin was seized by Dutch detectives on the steamship *Cavalla* in the Rotterdam port on its way from Turkey to Hamburg. The crates in which the heroin was hidden had been brought on board in Istanbul (the captain claimed not to know by whom) and were meant to be repackaged in Hamburg and send to China.[109] The police also received more and more detailed information about the smuggling of Turkish and Iranian opium from Marseilles to the Netherlands, decades before the infamous 'French Connection' transporting heroin from Asia to the United States.[110]

Other key transit hubs on the opium routes were the ports of Amsterdam and Rotterdam. In 1927 the British representative in the League of Nations Opium Advisory Committee identified these ports as central in the transport of opium from the Black Sea to cities with Chinese populations.[111] The German police called Amsterdam the 'main location' (*Hauptsitz*) of the illegal drug trade in 1934.[112]

The Greek networks worked closely together with Chinese traffickers. A Greek smuggler named Constantin (also known as Dimitri, or

George) Scordillis even had a child with the wife of suspected Chinese trafficker Chai Fan who lived with his family in the Netherlands.[113] While in their operations in, for instance, Greece and the USA the Greeks could work with local Greek communities, in the Netherlands they demonstrated that they were capable of inter-ethnic cooperation as well – a sign of the pragmatism of the trafficking networks. In 1930 the police noticed regular journeys from Rotterdam to the ports of Marseilles and Le Havre, made by native Dutch men and women whom the police had registered as being in close contact with the Chinese communities.[114] Dutch smugglers went to a hotel in Marseilles and paid money to the Greek hotel owner, Nicholas, who operated as a facilitator in the smuggling network. Nicholas then picked up the opium that had been smuggled in from Turkey and handed it over to the Dutch traffickers. They took the drugs by train to Paris and from there to Le Havre, where sailors on freight ships going to Rotterdam took over the drugs and took them to the Netherlands.[115] Chinese traders made regular payments to their compatriots in Marseilles, presumably to pay for opium and morphine that was smuggled to the Netherlands. Four Greeks undertook train journeys from Marseilles to Rotterdam and Amsterdam with opium hidden below the false bottom of their trunks. In June three Greeks, Scordillis, Anastase Peroulis, and Iphicrates Zoudanos, were arrested with opium destined for Chinese traders in Amsterdam. All three Greeks were born in Corfu and lived in Marseilles. The island of Corfu, close to the Albanian coast, had never been occupied by the Turks but was ideally geographically situated for connecting the Balkans to Italy and the rest of Europe. The opium of the Greek smugglers had been brought to Marseilles on a steamship of the Rotterdamsche Lloyd line. Here a Chinese–Greek connection was unravelled that transported opium from Asia to the Chinatowns of the Netherlands.[116]

In 1934 Peroulis was again arrested, in Amsterdam. Not only were 24 kilograms of opium seized in his possession, but a few days before he had delivered 11 kilograms to a Chinese trader in Rotterdam, and he was expecting a shipment of 58 kilograms. Peroulis was convicted and sentenced to the maximum sentence: one year. Three years later the police believed his smuggling ring was again active.[117] The Dutch police did not succeed in bringing an end to the activities of the Greek networks and the Marseilles connection.

Conclusion

The interwar period already shows one major characteristic of criminal anarchy: the involvement of a series of groups with different ethnic backgrounds in drug smuggling. Chinese and Greek smugglers entered the illegal drug market alongside the native Dutch and built up successful tactics against state strategies to enforce the new drug regulatory regime. They solved a number of puzzles caused by the changed architecture of the market. They found sources of supply and customers and confederates in other countries. They developed means of communication and delivery arrangements with and to these other countries, and methods of transferring payment. Chinese opium smuggling connected supply sources in the Middle East (Iran, Turkey) with the port towns of Europe, and sometimes collaborated with the Greek smuggling networks originating in the former Ottoman Empire. Both networks could operate successfully because of their relatively closed homogeneous ethnic and social composition; their ability to use global maritime connections, routes, and smuggling hubs through their networks in communities overseas; and because of the limitation on competing sources of supply in legal production. Other contributing factors for the Chinese were their role in the co-management of crime and labour together with Dutch law enforcement agencies and shipping companies, and their ability to connect to the demand side of Chinese migrants who lived in a culture of opium smoking as source of relaxation after work and as stimulant during work.

The Chinese networks, spanning from Guangdong and Fujian to Chinese migrant communities in the West, were based on the social needs and cultural capital of Chinese labour migrants. Their activities should be viewed in a long-term historical perspective. The interadoption of habits, goods, and technologies between China and the West had led to the integration of opium smoking in the everyday life of Chinese labourers. Smuggling of opium became embedded in the historical tradition of creating mutual aid societies when migrating to other countries.

In contrast, Greek networks – while standing in longer traditions of smuggling as well – were chain networks with a few mutually related individuals at the core. The Greeks were not so much embedded in Dutch society as capable of establishing international connections with other ethnic groups such as the Chinese and the native Dutch.

The interwar period already shows the pragmatic cooperation between trafficking networks of different ethnic backgrounds that is a characteristic of criminal anarchy. The smuggling networks of the interwar period were willing and able to work with each other. Their decentralization and fragmentation facilitated rather than hindered operations and made access to the market relatively easy.

Notes

1. M. Castells, *End of Millennium*, rev. edn (Oxford: Blackwell, 2000), p. 208.
2. F. Varese, *Mafias on the Move: How Organized Crime Conquers New Territories* (Princeton: Princeton University Press, 2011).
3. M. Shaw, 'Organised crime in late apartheid and the transition to a new criminal order: The rise and fall of the Johannesburg "bouncer mafia"', *Journal of Southern African Studies* 42 (2016) 577–94, on p. 594.
4. F. Dikötter, L. Laamann, and Z. Xhun, *Narcotic Culture: A History of Drugs in China* (Chicago: Chicago University Press, 2004), pp. 22–5.
5. The text actually mentions the drinking of tobacco, but this is unlikely; it probably refers to opium. L. C. D. van Dijk, 'Bijvoegsels tot de proeve eener geschiedenis van den handel en het verbruik van opium in Ned. Indië', *Bijdragen tot de taal-, land- en volkenkunde* 2 (1854) 189–211, on p. 211.
6. J. C. Baud, 'Proeve van eene geschiedenis van den handel en het verbruik van opium in Nederlandsch Indië', *Bijdragen tot de taal-, land- en volkenkunde* 1 (1853) 79–220, on p. 90. On the VOC and the Bengal opium trade the major study is O. Prakash, *The Dutch East India Company and the Economy of Bengal, 1630–1720* (Princeton: Princeton University Press, 1985). See also H. Derks, *History of the Opium Problem: The Assault on the East, ca. 1600–1950* (Leiden: Brill, 2012).
7. Cited in Z. Yangwen, *The Social Life of Opium in China* (Cambridge: Cambridge University Press, 2005), p. 45.
8. On China, opium, and the Dutch East Indies: Baud, 'Proeve'; J. Spence, 'Das Opiumrauchen im China der Ch'ing-Zeit (1644–1911)', *Saeculum* 23 (1972) 397–425; J. Spence, 'Opium smoking in Ch'in China', in F. Wakeman, Jr. and C. Grant (eds), *Conflict and Control in Late Imperial China* (Berkeley: University of California Press, 1975), pp. 143–73; Prakash, *Dutch East India Company*; Dikötter et al., *Narcotic Culture*; Yangwen, *Social Life*, pp. 25–45; T. Brook, *Vermeer's Hat: The Seventeenth Century and the Dawn of the Modern World* (New York: Bloomsbury Press, 2008), pp. 117–51.

9   C. A. Trocki, *Opium, Empire and the Global Political Economy: A Study of the Asian Opium Trade, 1750–1950* (London: Routledge, 1999).
10 J. F. Warren, *Rickshaw Coolie: A People's History of Singapore (1880–1940)* (Singapore: Oxford University Press, 1986); Yangwen, *Social Life*, p. 47.
11 D. Courtwright, *Dark Paradise: Opium Addiction in America before 1940* (Cambridge: Harvard University Press, 1982), pp. 67–70; V. Berridge, *Opium and the People: Opiate Use and Drug Control Policy in Nineteenth and Early Twentieth Century England*, rev. edn (London: Free Association Books, 1999); T. A. Hickman, 'Drugs and race in American culture: Orientalism in the turn-of-the-century discourse of narcotic addiction', *American Studies* 41 (2000) 71–92.
12 As is the claim in Derks, *History of the Opium Problem*.
13 See Brook, *Vermeer's Hat*; T. Andrade, *Lost Colony: The Untold Story of China's First Great Victory over the West* (Princeton: Princeton University Press, 2011).
14 Baud, 'Proeve'; E. Vanvugt, *Wettig opium. 350 jaar Nederlandse opiumhandel in de Indische archipel* (Haarlem: In de Knipscheer, 1985).
15 C. Bock, *The Headhunters of Borneo* (Singapore: Marshall Cavendish, 2009 [1881]), p. 13.
16 J. R. Rush, 'Opium farms in nineteenth century Java: Institutional continuity and change in a colonial society' (PhD-thesis, Yale University, 1977); Vanvugt, *Wettig opium*.
17 K. H. Meijring, *Recht en verdovende middelen* (The Hague: VUGA-Boekerij, 1974), pp. 73–101; Rush, 'Opium farms'; Vanvugt, *Wettig opium*.
18 K. T. Sioe and T. K. Hong, 'The mass treatment of drug addiction by the Medinos' phlycten method', in D. G. Baedyagun and L. S. Subhakich (eds), *Transactions of the Eighth Congress of the Far Eastern Association of Tropical Medicine held in Siam December 1930* (Bangkok: Times Press, 1931), pp. 52–64.
19 See E. Tagliacozzo, *Secret Traders, Porous Borders: Smuggling and States along a Southeast Asian Frontier, 1865–1915* (New Haven: Yale University Press, 2005), p. 194.
20 E. Tagliacozzo, 'Kettle on a slow boil: Batavia's threat perceptions in the Indies' Outer Islands, 1870–1910', *Journal of Southeast Asian Studies* 31 (2000) 70–100.
21 Baud, 'Proeve', 183. All translations from Dutch are by the author.
22 A. J. Duymaer van Twist, 'Het Hemel-Aarde-Verbond, Tien-Ti-Hoei, een geheim genootschap in China en onder de Chinezen in Indië', *Bijdragen tot de taal-, land- en volkenkunde* 1 (1853) 260–90, on pp. 289–90.

23 W. A. van Rees, *Montrado. Geschied- en krijgskundige bijdrage betreffende de onderwerping der Chinezen op Borneo* ('s-Hertogenbosch: Gebr. Muller, 1858); E. B. Kielstra, 'Bijdragen tot de geschiedenis van Borneo's Westerafdeling, X–XIII', *Indische Gids* 12 (1890) 450–77, 682–91, 857–78, 1085–9; S. H. Schaank, 'De kongsi's van Montrado. Bijdrage tot de geschiedenis en de kennis van het wezen der Chineesche vereenigingen op de westkust van Borneo', *Tijdschrift voor Indische Taal-, Land- en Volkenkunde* 35 (1893) 498–612; M. S. Heidhues, 'Chinese organizations in West Borneo and Bangkai: Kongsi and *hui*', in D. Ownby and M. S. Heidhues (eds), *'Secret Societies' Reconsidered: Perspectives on the Social History of Modern South China and Southeast Asia* (Armonk: M. E. Sharpe, 1993), pp. 68–88.
24 van Rees, *Montrado*, p. 251.
25 van Rees, *Montrado*, pp. 218–61; Kielstra, 'Bijdragen'; Heidhues, 'Chinese organizations'.
26 van Rees, *Montrado*, p. 260.
27 J. J. M. de Groot, *Het kongsiwezen van Borneo. Eene voorbereiding over den grondslag en den aard der Chineesche politieke vereenigingen in de koloniën, met eene Chineesche geschiedenis van de kongsi Lanfong* (The Hague: Martinus Nijhoff, 1885).
28 B. J. ter Haar 'Messianism and the Heaven and Earth Society: Approaches to Heaven and Earth texts', in Ownby and Heidhues (eds), *'Secret Societies' Reconsidered*, pp. 153–76, on p. 153.
29 W. Blythe, *The Impact of Chinese Secret Societies in Malaya: A Historical Study* (London: Oxford University Press, 1969), p. 17.
30 D. Ownby, 'Chinese *hui* and the early modern social order: Evidence from eighteenth-century Southeast China', in Ownby and Heidues (eds), *'Secret Societies' Reconsidered*, pp. 34–67, on p. 34. See also Blythe, *Impact*.
31 Blythe, *Impact*, p. 21.
32 Fundamental for the perspective of the police is W. P. Morgan, *Triad Societies in Hong Kong* (London: Routledge, 2002 [1960]). See also J. van Straten, 'For export: Chinese triad societies', *International Crime Police Review* (February 1977): 49–53; M. J. Winterton, 'The collation of crime intelligence with regard to Chinese triads in Holland', *Police Journal* 54 (1981) 34–57; R. Weijenburg, *Drugs en drugsbestrijding in Nederland. Een beschrijving van de aanpak van het gebruik en misbruik van en de (illegal) handel in verdovende middelen* (The Hague: VUGA, 1996), pp. 46–55.
33 L. Nagtegaal, *Riding the Dutch Tiger: The Dutch East Indies Company and the Northeast Coast of Java 1680–1743* (Leiden: KITLV Press, 1996), p. 101.

34 Schaank, 'Kongsi's van Montrado', pp. 583–84.
35 de Groot, 'Kongsiwezen', pp. 171–7; see also C. A. Trocki, 'The rise and fall of the Ngee Hong Kongsi in Singapore', in Ownby and Heidhues (eds), *Secret Societies' Reconisdered*, pp. 89–119, on p. 94.
36 P. Billingsley, *Bandits in Republican China* (Stanford: Stanford University Press, 1988), p. 8.
37 Heidhues, 'Chinese organizations', p. 79.
38 Heidhues, 'Chinese organizations', p. 84.
39 Heidhues, 'Chinese organizations', pp. 79–80.
40 Schaank, 'Kongsi's van Montrado', pp. 588–91.
41 Heidhues, 'Chinese organizations', pp. 84–5.
42 Kielstra, 'Bijdragen', p. 463.
43 Trocki, *Opium and Empire*; Trocki, 'Rise and fall'; see also Blythe, *Impact*.
44 Y. K. Chu, *International Triad Movements: The Threat of Chinese Organised Crime* (London: Research Institute for the Study of Conflict and Terrorism, 1996); Y.K. Chu, *The Triads as Business* (London: Routledge, 2000).
45 Morgan, *Triad Societies*.
46 Chu, *International Triad Movements*, p. 5.
47 Billingsley, *Bandits*, p. 8.
48 S. Snelders, *The Devil's Anarchy: The Sea Robberies of the Most Famous Pirate Claes G. Compaen, and Very Remarkable Travels of Jan Erasmus Reyning*, 2nd edn (Brooklyn: Autonomedia 2014).
49 On the Chinese in the interwar period Netherlands: F. van Heek, *Chineesche immigranten in Nederland* (Amsterdam: J. Emmering, 1936); H. J. J. Wubben, *'Chineezen en ander Aziatisch ongedierte'. Lotgevallen van Chinese immigranten in Nederland, 1911–1940* (Zutphen: De Walburg Pers, 1986; B. Zeven, 'Balancerend op de rand van Nederland. De Chinese minderheid in de jaren 1910–1940', in G. Benton and H. Vermeulen (eds), *De Chinezen* (Muiderberg: Dick Coutinho, 1987), pp. 40–64; M. van Rossum, *Hand aan Hand (Blank en Bruin). Solidariteit en de werking van globalisering, etniciteit en klasse onder zeelieden op de Nederlandse koopvaardij, 1900–1945* (Amsterdam: Aksant, 2009).
50 Wubben, *'Chineezen'*, pp. 54–5.
51 Zeven, 'Balancerend', p. 41.
52 van Heek, *Chineesche immigranten*, p. 18.
53 van Heek, *Chineesche immigranten*, p. 106.
54 van Heek, *Chineesche immigranten*, p. 19; Wubben, *'Chineezen'*, pp. 35–59.
55 van Heek, *Chineesche immigranten*, pp. 81–2; Wubben, *'Chineezen'*.
56 S. Snelders, P. Huijnen et al., 'A digital humanities approach to the history of culture and science', in J. Odijk and A. van Hessen (eds), *CLARIN in the Low Countries* (London: Ubiquity Press, 2017) 325–5.

57   A. Mazure, *Dick Bos. Alle avonturen*, vol. 1 (The Hague: Panda, 2005).
58   Wubben, 'Chineezen', pp. 57–8.
59   Archive of Ministry of Foreign Affairs, A-files, National Archive, The Hague, inv. no. 2.05.03 (hereafter NA/FA) 1533–7, 1589–92.
60   See also Dikötter et al., *Narcotic Culture*, pp. 28–9.
61   R. J. Antony, *Like Froth Floating on the Sea: The World of Pirates and Seafarers in Late Imperial South China* (Berkeley: Institute of East Asian Studies, University of California, 2003).
62   H. Voordewind, *De commissaris vertelt verder* (The Hague: D. A. Daamen, 1950), p. 131.
63   J. Luger, *De kleine misdaad voor den politierechter* (Amsterdam: Blitz, c. 1935), pp. 202–10.
64   van Heek, *Chineesche immigranten*, p. 78.
65   Reports on arrests and seizures, NA/FA, 1533–7, 1589–92.
66   J. A. Blaauw, *Narcoticabrigade. De eindeloze strijd tegen drugshandelaren* (Baarn: De Fontein, 1997), p. 51.
67   van Heek, *Chineesche immigranten*, pp. 57, 78–9; Luger, *Kleine misdaad*, p. 207.
68   Luger, *Kleine misdaad*, p. 209.
69   van Heek, *Chineesche immigranten*, p. 79.
70   van Heek, *Chineesche immigranten*, pp. 56–7; Wubben, 'Chineezen', p. 103.
71   Wubben, 'Chineezen', pp. 104–5.
72   Y. Chong, *De Chinezen van de Binnen Bantammerstraat* (Amsterdam: Het Spinhuis, 2005), p. 156 (author's translation).
73   Chong, *Chinezen*, p. 71 (author's translation).
74   van Heek, *Chineesche immigranten*, p. 79; Wubben, 'Chineezen', pp. 108–9.
75   Luger, *Kleine misdaad*, p. 209.
76   NA/FA, 1533–7, 1589–92.
77   Wubben, 'Chineezen', pp. 48–54.
78   van Heek, *Chineesche immigranten*, pp. 80–1.
79   Wubben, 'Chineezen', pp. 48–54; Zeven, 'Balancerend', p. 49.
80   van Heek, *Chineesche immigranten*, p. 40.
81   P. Knepper, *International Crime in the 20th Century: The League of Nations Era, 1919–1939* (Houndmills: Palgrave Macmillan, 2011), p. 135.
82   Wubben, 'Chineezen', pp. 57–8.
83   van Heek, *Chineesche immigranten*, pp. 34–5.
84   Wubben, 'Chineezen', p. 59.
85   Wubben, 'Chineezen', pp. 58–62, 107–18; Chong, *Chinezen*, pp. 7, 23–4.
86   F. Bresler, *The Trail of the Triads: An Investigation into International Crime* (London: Weidenfeld & Nicolson, 1980), p. 137.
87   Wubben, 'Chineezen', pp. 120–2.
88   For the first Chinese war see especially Wubben, 'Chineezen', pp. 66–74.

89 Wubben, *'Chineezen'*, pp. 37–9.
90 Voordewind, *De commissaris vertelt verder*, pp. 130–6.
91 Wubben, *'Chineezen'*, pp. 66–74, 106–7.
92 Chong, *Chinezen*, p. 24.
93 van Heek, *Chineesche immigranten*, pp. 83–4.
94 Wubben, *'Chineezen'*, p. 93.
95 Luger, *Kleine misdaad*, p. 209.
96 Wubben, *'Chineezen'*, pp. 80–3, 93.
97 Ministry of Labour, Trade and Industry to Foreign Affairs, 13 November 1930, NA/FA, 1535.
98 Wubben, *'Chineezen'*, p. 104.
99 Wubben, *'Chineezen'*, pp. 106–7.
100 Wubben, *'Chineezen'*, p. 111–18.
101 R. Gingeras, *Heroin, Organized Crime, and the Making of Modern Turkey* (Oxford: Oxford University Press, 2014), pp. 43–5.
102 K. Gkotsinas, '"Genuine and natural": Opiates and nation-building in Greece, 1923–1940' (unpublished paper, Association for the Study of Nationalities Conference, 2018).
103 K. Meyer and T. Parssinen, *Webs of Smoke: Smugglers, Warlords, Spies, and the History of the International Drug Trade* (Lanham: Rowman & Littlefield, 1998), p. 132.
104 A. A. Block. 'European drug traffic and traffickers between the wars: The policy of suppression and its consequences', *Journal of Social History* 23 (1989), 315–37, on p. 325; K. Gkotsinas, 'Attitudes towards heroin addicts and addiction in inter-war Greece', *Central Europe* 12 (2014) 174–94; Gkotsinas, '"Genuine and natural"'.
105 *Blacklist of Traffickers and Persons Implicated in the Illicit Traffic in Heroin, Cocaine, Morphine and Allied drugs* (Central Narcotics Intelligence Bureau, Egyptian Government), in League of Nations Archive, United Nations Office, Geneva. Courtesy of Haggai Ram.
106 Gotsinas, 'Attitudes', p. 178.
107 On Bakladjagou, see Meyer and Parssinen, *Webs of Smoke*, pp. 132–6.
108 *Blacklist of Traffickers*.
109 On the Cavalla-affair: Blaauw, *Narcoticabrigade*, pp. 60–9.
110 Report by Sirks to the Minister of Justice, 4 September 1930, NA/FA, 1590; report to League of Nations for the year 1930, NA/FA, 1590.
111 M. de Kort, *Tussen patiënt en delinquent. Geschiedenis van het Nederlandse drugsbeleid* (Hilversum: Verloren, 1995), p. 94.
112 Dr Freitag, 'Rauschgifte und ihre Opfer', *Kriminalistische Monatshefte* 8 (1934) 199–202.
113 Letter from Nederlandsche Centrale ter bestrijding van den Smokkelhandel in verdoovende middelen (hereafter Nederlandsche Centrale) to Ministry of Foreign Affairs, 22 April 1936, NA/FA, 1533.

114 Letter from Sirks to Minister of Foreign Affairs, 27 June 1930, NA/FA, 1533.
115 On the Nicolas affair: Blaauw, *Narcoticabrigade*, pp. 78–89.
116 Letter from Sirks to the Minister of Foreign Affairs, 27 June 1930, NA/FA, 1535; letter from Sirks to the Minister of Labour, 4 July 1930, NA/FA, 1535; report by Rotterdam police to Minister of Justice, 16 July 1930, NA/FA, 1535; Blaauw, *Narcoticabrigade*, pp. 89–92.
117 Report by Nederlandsche Centrale, 10 November 1934, NA/FA, 1470; Nederlandsche Centrale, annual report 1937, NA/FA, 1593; Blaauw, *Narcoticabrigade*, pp. 91–2.

4

Cannabis, counterculture, and criminals: The rise of cannabis smuggling

The introduction of the drug regulatory regime in the Netherlands had unintended consequences and created its own problem: the development of an illegal market. Nevertheless, significant expansion of this market did not occur until the late 1960s. The Second World War led to a temporary disturbance of transit routes. After the defeat of the German army, much of its drug supplies entered the illegal market, but this was only a short-lived source of supply. In the early 1960s, from the perspective of the United Nations and the Dutch state, the drug regulatory regime seemed to be working adequately.

This changed dramatically after 1965 as a consequence of an unprecedented increase in the demand for illegal drugs, especially for cannabis. Cannabis use had been prohibited in 1953 and since then the police had attempted to suppress trade and consumption. Until the mid-1960s cannabis use in the Netherlands remained limited and there was no large-scale supply of the drug. The Sixties youth revolt and the rise of counterculture changed this decisively, creating a huge demand for cannabis. In less than a decade a successful illegal drug supply came into existence, connecting production in countries such as Lebanon, Morocco, and Afghanistan with the Netherlands and other countries. This chapter investigates the early and fundamental developments in cannabis smuggling up to the mid-1970s, the smugglers' embeddedness in broader Dutch society and more specifically in the new hippie counterculture and longer-existing maritime and criminal cultures, and how and why smugglers succeeded in linking demand with supply from countries such as Lebanon and Morocco.

The post-war drug trade

Cannabis use was initially limited to American soldiers, migrants from Suriname, and hipster artists and youngsters.[1] The variety consumed was not the indigenous one, even though use of this plant had a tradition of medical use going back at least to the early eighteenth century.[2] The cannabis that came into fashion after the war was illegally imported from abroad. Illegally, since import had been prohibited in the revised second Opium Act of 1928. It was not until 1953 that a further revision of the act also prohibited use and possession of the drug.[3] Nevertheless, only after 1953 did cannabis become an integral part of the landscape of drug use in the Netherlands, alongside other drugs.

The German capitulation in 1945 had made these other drugs such as morphine and cocaine available from stockpiles of both the German and the Allied armies. For instance, Polish prisoners of war released from the camp at Murnau discovered a huge supply of cocaine left by the German medical services near Garmisch in Bavaria and started to smuggle the drug into France and Italy and sell it on the black market. They used permits from the US Army to move around and also dealt in furs, jewellery, artworks, textiles, wine, and other consumer goods. When supplies ran out, traffickers turned to pilfering drugs from pharmaceutical factories such as that of Merck in Darmstadt. More than one ring involved in this traffic was linked to the upperworld of the military occupation forces and to the underworlds of Germany, Italy, and France.[4] Drugs reached the Netherlands through the British military zone in West Germany. Cocaine was found by the authorities in the spare tyres of jeeps and on small boats crossing the Rhine. In 1947 Dutch police arrested a gang of sixteen people and seized 2 kilograms of cocaine in the town of Enschede in the east of the country. In the same year 1,400 ampules of morphine with the German legend *Sanitätslager* ('hospital') were seized in Amsterdam.[5] The Centrale, which had stopped functioning during the war but had been put back in operation in 1947 as a subdivision of the Ministry of Justice, reported the seizure of six bottles of cocaine in the capital and the arrest of a Polish officer.[6] In 1948 a pharmaceutical inspector claimed that because of the Allied victory so many drugs came into the country that an addict did not need to go to a pharmacy for his supplies any more but could turn to the black market.⁷ After 1948 these military supplies became more and more exhausted, but as late as 1955 a German smuggler was arrested in Amsterdam with his car carrying a large supply of morphine, opium, and other drugs that he had obtained while working for the British occupation force in Germany.⁸

After the war Amsterdam was once again considered a centre for the illegal narcotics trade, and the Amsterdam police established a narcotics squad in 1947; until 1966 this consisted of only two detectives.⁹ This did not mean, however, that that there was no prosecution of drug users in the capital.¹⁰ The two detectives were far from idle and kept a close watch on pharmacists, Chinese opium dens and lodgings, ships docking in the harbour, bars frequented by suspected dealers from Suriname, and the bohemian beatnik scene of Amsterdam.¹¹ After parliament had made possession and use of cannabis illegal in 1953, police raids and sentences of up to eight months' imprisonment for possession of minimal amounts (for instance, one marihuana cigarette or 'joint') were not unusual. Trade was still limited; in November 1965 the police caught a 'well-known drugs trafficker' and found 1 kilogram of marihuana and 1.5 kilograms of hashish in his possession. This was considered a big haul at the time.¹²

In the early 1960s it seemed to policymakers and law enforcement officers in Europe that the drug problem was under control. The drug regulatory regime implemented after the First World War was held to be a success, and the illegal drug trade contained. The UN Committee on Narcotic Drugs stated in 1962: 'In Europe there is not a drug problem.'¹³ In that year the Dutch police reported only a few drug seizures: of opium smuggled by Chinese seamen, and of cannabis smuggled in from Tangier in Morocco, for instance.¹⁴ The next year only five arrests were made: four seamen were caught with small amounts of opium or cannabis, and in Amsterdam two Algerians were taken into custody for possession of hashish. If we may believe the Ministry of Justice there was only a small amount of drug smuggling and abuse in the country, centring on Chinese people smoking opium and a few beatniks and American soldiers stationed in West Germany buying cannabis in the larger cities.¹⁵ A much bigger problem to the Dutch authorities was the hundreds of iatrogenic addicts trying to get morphine on false prescriptions.¹⁶ However, by the mid-1960s the trend started to change and the drug problem became uncontainable for the authorities.

Explosion in demand

From 1964 onwards the number of offences (possession and trade) against the Opium Act increased (see Figure 1 in the Appendix). The definitive turning point was 1967. Over the next five years the number of offences multiplied almost by a factor of ten, most of them related to cannabis: 76 per cent in 1967, 86 per cent in 1972 (see Figure 2 in the Appendix). Until the early 1970s both the number of arrested importers and the seized amounts of cannabis were a relatively small part of the total number of offences, but from 1971 onwards they increase dramatically (see Figures 3 and 4 in the Appendix).

Dutch law enforcement assumed (and assumes) that in general it catches 10 per cent of all smuggled goods.[17] This figure is of course completely arbitrary; its origins can be traced to the interwar period when the military police responsible for border control already assumed this percentage.[18] If we base our calculations on the one-in-ten concept, in 1968 approximately 1,000 kilograms of cannabis (ten times the amount of the seizures) were smuggled into the Netherlands. In 1971 this had doubled to 2,000 kilograms, and in 1972 the number had, compared to 1968, multiplied by twenty into 20,000 kilograms. An increase in users had started to translate into a significant increase in smuggled cannabis. The first seizure of over 100 kilograms took place in 1971 when 110 kilograms of hashish from Morocco, imported by plane by a consortium of Rotterdam criminal entrepreneurs, was seized.[19] In 1972 225 kilograms of hashish were discovered in the false sides of crates containing vases, ashtrays, and press-papers imported from Karachi in Pakistan.[20] In 1973 total seizures had risen to almost 6,000 kilograms.[21]

How did this increase of supply relate to changes in the demand side of the market? It is quite certain that the number of cannabis users increased significantly in the five years from 1967 to 1972. However, estimations at the time varied widely. A field study conducted in 1967–1968 estimated a (rather unreliable) total of between 13,500 and 24,000 illegal drug users, mainly consumers of cannabis.[22] Other studies more or less repeated this number: for instance one calculated an estimated 20,000 users in 1970; another 15,000 users in Amsterdam and 7,000 in Rotterdam.[23] These estimates concerned regular users. In 1971 two surveys estimated a total of 2 to 2.6 per cent of the total population had used drugs at some time.[24] This would mean between 260,000 and 300,000 people had at least smoked a joint at some point. In the same year another report estimated 30,000 regular users and a total of 100,000 to 200,000 people who had smoked cannabis at least once.[25] The estimated percentages of users in secondary education were higher, varying between 4 and 20 per cent of all pupils in 1971–1973, 90 per cent of whom had used cannabis.[26] There were huge regional differences. The percentage of illegal drug users among the Amsterdam youth was estimated in 1972 at almost one-third.[27]

At this time cannabis use was still primarily a habit of rebellious countercultural youth, or of those who pretended to be rebelling. Drug use was learned from peers at schools, and by 1970 long hair and vague or more specific alternative ideas were quite normal among the older pupils. Smoking a joint was part of the youth culture.[28] Rotterdam undercover police detectives thought that around 70 to 80 per cent of the more than 60,000 visitors to the June 1970 Pop Festival in Kralingen smoked hashish and marihuana. This festival had been organized as the Dutch answer to Woodstock, with famous American psychedelic rock bands Jefferson Airplane and The Byrds as chief attractions. 'Especially at night one had the impression of having been caught in a nomad camp, where at the campfire the recognizable hashish pipe with precious stuff circulated', one of the undercover detectives reported.[29]

Cannabis use was not yet 'normalized' in the early 1970s, however. It took another decade before Amsterdam psychologist and drug user Herman Cohen would mourn the demise of the hashish culture and the transformation of cannabis into a normal consumer product.[30] This normalization was dependent on the organization of a sufficient and structural illegal supply, which in its turn was triggered by the expansion of cannabis use in the youth culture. Normalization grew out of deviance. This deviance in its turn was dependent on finding sources of supply of contraband.

Source of supply: Lebanon

It turned out to be relatively easy for smugglers to build up a relational embeddedness in exporting countries. The structural conditions were favourable in the three most important countries of supply: Lebanon, Morocco, and Afghanistan.

When after the First World War Greece embraced the new international drug regulatory regime it brought an end to cannabis cultivation there which had been mainly targeted at supplying the Egyptian market. Lebanon, until 1943 under French control, stepped in – despite an official ban enacted first in 1926, and again after independence in 1946. The hot and dry climate of the 120-kilometre-long Bekaa Valley is especially suited for cannabis cultivation, but the plant was also cultivated in the coastal Jebel Liban mountain range in the west of the country, and the Jebel esh Sharqu mountains in the east at the border with Syria. Accounts differ about the exact chronology, but in the interwar period cannabis cultivation and hashish production were developing in response to the demand from Egypt especially and as a consequence of the new international drug regulatory regime.[31] While the population of the Bekaa Valley is predominantly Muslim, that of the mountain ranges is predominantly Christian. Christian and Muslim, Maronite and Shiite leaders alike offered 'protection' in return for a share in the profits.

One estimate claimed that under French rule more than half of the economy depended on production and smuggling of hashish, 90 per cent of which went to Egypt, while corrupt French officials and police officers took their slice of the cake. The actual smuggling was taken care of by small-time criminal entrepreneurs connected to large landowners and merchants.[32] After the end of the Second World War and the withdrawal of French and British troops in 1946, cultivation only increased. In 1954 the US FBN claimed that Lebanon was the most important supplier of cannabis to the United States, and that the government of the country was deeply involved in the hashish trade. Lebanon was also a transit hub for other drugs such as heroin and cocaine. One historian has described Lebanon as being one of the world's first and foremost 'narco-states', even before the civil war that broke out in 1975 and stimulated illegal drug production and trade.[33] In 1950 the largest cannabis farmer in Lebanon, one Sabri Hamadeh, was also the largest landowner in the Bekaa Valley; moreover, he was also the chairman of the Lebanon's Chamber of Deputies and in effect the ruler of his district. His hashish was smuggled to Egypt or directly to the USA through the ports of Tyre and Sidon. President and prime minister took a share of the profits of the export business. Whenever for the sake of appearances and world opinion officials wished to move in on cultivation they were fiercely and violently fought by local militia supported by the leaders of their communities. For thousands of poor families the hashish trade offered sustenance and livelihood.[34]

Lebanese hashish become more cheaply and easily available to Western European smugglers because of the Six-Day War between Israel and the Arab countries in 1967. As a consequence of the war the smuggling routes between Lebanon and Egypt were cut off, notwithstanding reported attempts by the Israeli secret service Mossad to supply Egyptian soldiers with hashish in order to decrease their fighting abilities. Suppliers were looking for new consumer markets, leading to a significant drop in the price of Lebanese hashish, even though it was considered to be of high quality.[35] Consumption in Lebanon itself was limited: according to one account in 1976 only 1 per cent of the population smoked, using water pipes, and cannabis use was not generally accepted.[36]

In 1972 a UN report found 15,000 persons who earned income from hashish production or trade in the north of Bekaa. This is an area of 2,500 square kilometres comprising the district of Hermel and the northern part of the district of Baalbek, with no industry, few schools or health facilities, and a high level of illiteracy. The government had little power here: the region was controlled by tribal clans and described as a refuge for outlaws and local people suspicious of the government. Most of the profits did not go to the poor farmers, only one-third of whom owned their own land, but to landowners and urban financiers and merchants.[37]

While on smaller farms, further up into the mountains, cultivation was mostly by hand, on the larger farms huge fields were ploughed with tractors, and more chemical fertilizers were used. When the harvest was brought in in September or October, plants were dried for two weeks, then threshed with hay forks between plastic sheets or pieces of cloth, and then the broken flowers were sieved. The resin powder produced was pressed into cakes or bricks of the various qualities of Lebanese hashish. Traditionally wrapped in cotton or linen sacks stamped with designs of planes, stars, lions, camels, crescent moons and stars, or sea freighters, the hashish was ready to be bought by Western smugglers and transported to the demand markets of Europe and elsewhere.[38]

Source of supply: Morocco

Production closer to the Netherlands took place in Morocco. Here as in Lebanon cannabis cultivation and hashish production started to boom in response to growing demand from foreign markets. In Morocco the essential economic innovation took place later than in Lebanon: in the 1960s, with the introduction of the production of hashish in the Rif mountain area in the north of the country.

Cannabis cultivation itself had started on a small scale in the Middle Ages, after the Arab conquest, in private gardens and orchards. From the end of the eighteenth century onwards the main producing region became what is now considered the traditional cultivation region in the north, the Rif: 40 square kilometres around the towns of Ketama in Al Hoceima province and Bab Berred to the west in the province of Chefchaouen, where three Berber tribes (the Beni Bou Nsar, the Beni Seddate, and the Ketama) cultivated the plant on plateaux or terraces on the mountain slopes in the valleys. In 1890 the sultan of Morocco limited the trade, giving five villages of each tribe the right to cultivate. Men smoked the chopped cannabis, a gold-green to brown coloured *kif*, in clay bowls or water pipes, sometimes mixed with tobacco; women made cakes for cosmetic or medicinal purposes.

Hashish was not yet produced; the hashish that was available in the 1930s came from Lebanon. After Morocco's independence in 1956 cultivation was forbidden, but it continued to be tolerated in the Rif since eradication was considered unfeasible. Cultivation even started to expand and by 1960 twelve tribes were involved. For the local population, with scant resources and little work, cannabis cultivation was an important source of income. In the 1950s kif became the romanticized drug of the beat writers and poets visiting Tangier. Its (limited) sale and consumption among the native population (especially the lower classes) was more or less tolerated. In the mid-1960s decisive innovations took place. According to legend, hippies took the knowledge of how to make hashish from kif from Afghanistan to Morocco, a decisive step in the globalization of the illegal drug trade.

As in Lebanon, claims differ of who became the first hashish producer but it seems that travellers on the hippie trail began experimenting with sieving cannabis to produce hashish. The earliest candidate is a traveller named English Richard, who is supposed to have started as early as 1962, but Billy Badman (1965), Mohammed Rifi (1966), and others are also candidates. Their products were not yet of sufficient quality to serve the market, but in 1965 an Algerian hashish maker named Mustafa came to Ketama and taught local farmers how to make hashish from kif. Aslama Chai-Chai is reputed to have been one of the first who started to make his own hashish in 1967. Production increased, creating a surplus available for export to Europe, where demand started to soar. Despite an official anti-cannabis policy and some attempts in 1961/1962 and 1967 to eradicate cannabis cultivation in the Rif mountains, the Moroccan government turned a blind eye, since cannabis export was a great boon for the economy and since resistance to eradication was severe in the Rif. Tacitly the cultivation has since been allowed in the high Rif mountains (an area unsuitable for the cultivation of most other crops) but not elsewhere in Morocco.

From the 1960s only part of the production was meant for consumption in Morocco itself, or was sold by aggressive hustlers to tourists or smuggled into the Spanish enclaves of Melilla and Ceuta. Most of the production went by boat out of the country from harbours such as Al Hoceima and Beni Enzar/Mador. Cannabis cultivation increased from an estimated maximum of 3,000 hectares in the late 1960s to 5,000 to 25,000 hectares in the 1980s, stimulated by the economic crisis and poor harvests of other crops of that decade, and would further increase to 75,000 hectares in 1995 according to a Dutch government report. The wars in Afghanistan and Lebanon further spurred rising Western demand for Moroccan cannabis exports. Cultivation spread to lower elevations and to parts of the Atlas mountains in the south. In 1986–1987 and 1992–1995 the Moroccan government conducted eradication programmes at the lower elevations in response to US political pressure but made little effort in the higher ranges. By 1990 an estimated 20,000 households or 200,000 people were involved in growing cannabis and producing hashish, and the number of middlemen or merchants who sold cannabis abroad directly or through one of the export syndicates was estimated at approximately 2,000.[39]

In 1971 a writer for *Rolling Stone* magazine visited Ketama, the centre of the hashish trade, and the nearby village of Azila where hashish was produced. He had no problem in getting offers for any amount of hashish to take home. In the hashish factory of 'Omar' cannabis seeds were grounded into a powder. The powder was then pressed for long periods under heat in a small compressing machine (looking like a machine-shop vice) and compressed in blocks of hash. The hash was subsequently packaged in cellophane. Omar bought the plants from his neighbours' harvests, and the pressing machine in one of the larger cities like Rabat or Tangier. His product was ordered from one of the large cities by telephone and picked up by (European) buyers in their Landrovers. Omar's biggest customer, a group of three men (two Germans and one American) and an English girl, even picked up the hashish by helicopter and took it to their yacht in the Mediterranean. The police did not give Omar any problems, although they worried the smaller drug tourists.[40] Another visitor in the 1970s observed:

> Leaving Ketama is as easy as entering. The police checkpoints along the highways are sporadic, but thorough. The only way that large quantities of hashish leave the Ketama region is according to well-prepared plans, which are approved by the necessary authorities when they are politely paid. Payment is not considered a bribe, but rather a natural part of the business.[41]

Most cultivators were small-time farmers working small plots irrigated by rain. According to research by Kenza Afsahi undertaken in the first decade of the twenty-first century, by then only one in five cultivated on irrigated land in the large valleys, close to a river or dam. New cultivation areas in the provinces of Chefchaouen, Al Hoceima, and now also Taounate, Larache, and Tétouan had supplemented the traditional areas. Today the villages around Ketama remain the 'training' grounds where seasonal male migrants learn the techniques, to disseminate the knowledge among their women and other kin. Families are the organization units of this cultivation, whether irrigated or on rain-fed plots: members of the family share the ploughing, hoeing, threshing, and the guarding and harvesting of the crops. Use of outside labour is less prevalent in the traditional cultivation areas than in the new ones. In 2003 and 2004 almost 100,000 families, or 800,000 rural inhabitants, were involved. Afsahi found that 100 kilograms of cannabis could be used to produce 2.82 kilograms of hashish using the 'beating method' by which dried cannabis is made into a powder (*chira*). For this only basic tools are needed: bunches of kif are placed on a dark cloth that is stretched over a bowl to act as a sieve. The kif bunches are hit with batons for a couple of hours until they sieve through into the bowl as a powder. The powder is then compressed in flat, rectangular forms using a single compression machine. The farmers bring the hashish into the villages and strike deals with the traffickers buying the goods. Often the latter use threats and rumours of arrests in attempts to lower the prices, sometimes to less than the production costs.[42]

In the process of expansion, the quality of Moroccan cannabis severely deteriorated: it became a mass consumption good rather than a product for connoisseurs. Traditional kif varieties and large well-branched plants disappeared in favour of small, moderately branched plants.[43]

Exporting hashish would not have been possible without the existence of a thriving smuggling culture that dated from long before the 1960s. Smuggling was an age-old Rif tradition. In the nineteenth century arms, ammunition, food, tobacco, and other goods were smuggled through the area. After the Second World War smuggling was essential in the eastern Rif both for subsistence and as a source of cash income. In French territories imports were forbidden, creating attractive economic possibilities: kif grown in the western hills of Spanish Morocco was one of the goods smuggled into French Algeria.[44] By the 1990s the smuggling of humans to Europe had become an important activity as well.

In the 1980s Moroccan hashish smuggled into Europe fetched three to five times the value in Morocco. Smuggling chains had come into existence that connected the producers, wholesale buyers, the specialists in storage and packaging, the preparers of the vehicles and boats, the carriers, and the financiers with the European market. Black money entered the legal economy through construction sites on the beaches of Morocco and the Costa del Sol, and was laundered through offshore banking, especially in Gibraltar, or through currency trade or smuggling with the assistance of labour migrants to Europe visiting their homeland again.[45]

Smuggling was not only an essential ingredient for the economy of Rif because other sources of income were scarce, it was also valued highly in Rif culture. To the Berber population of the area the authority of the king and the state was and is questionable. Smuggling 'is not only an important way of gaining a living but also a strategy to beat the state [and] buttressed by notions of manliness, courage, cunning, a strong emphasis on autonomy, independence, and success. To take risks is part of the ethos of masculinity.'[46] The culture of corruption in state and police both reinforced the distrust of the state and assisted smuggling. This did not mean that there were no objections to certain forms of smuggling in Rif society, such as of drugs. To many Rifians this is sinful; on the other hand, however, financers of the cannabis trade are also known to have donated large amounts of money to their communities or to finance the building of mosques.[47]

Source of supply: Afghanistan

As in Lebanon and Morocco, cannabis cultivation in Afghanistan expanded because of Western demand.[48] Hashish produced in Afghanistan had a particular reputation for quality. Cannabis was cultivated especially in the provinces of Kandahar in the south and of Balkh around Mazar-e-Shari in the north, suitable areas for cultivation because of the dry climate with long, hot summers. British observers wrote in the nineteenth century about the drug's use by 'the debauched', and how it was especially popular among the lower classes. The resin (hashish, or *chars*) was smoked, either pure or mixed with local tobacco, in water and clay pipes. The leaves and seeds (marihuana, or *bang*) were also smoked, mostly dry and without tobacco. Chars was especially attractive to Western users and smugglers.[49]

There is little evidence of systematic trade into other countries before the twentieth century. When the first Western cannabis users arrived in Afghanistan on the hippie trail in the later 1960s they found a culture in which hashish was officially illegal, but could be consumed freely (when the users were discreet) in chai khana (teahouses) and smoking rooms. It was mainly popular among the lower classes, labourers, and farmers, but frowned upon by a Westernized elite, while doctors warned of the dangers of cannabis-induced psychosis. Though it was generally used, most Afghans considered it a bad habit and it was not socially acceptable to smoke in public. Most users did so after work at home or in a teahouse. Afghan hashish was potent and had a high THC content (tetrahydrocannabinol is considered an important psychoactive ingredient), as well as a variety (twenty-five variations were listed) hardly encountered elsewhere.[50]

Hippie travellers quickly saw the commercial prospects of Afghan hashish. Locals bought little round discs of hash for 10 to 20 afghanis

(10 to 25 US cents). Smugglers bought in bulk for about 15 to 20 US dollars per kilogram; in 1973 it was 30 dollars per kilogram.⁵¹ Even when one was cheated to some extent and had to pay expenses and pay off government officials, this meant sizeable profits since these were only one-hundredth of the prices in California. The American Brotherhood of Eternal Love, a group of minimally commercially driven dealers in LSD and other hallucinogens and followers of the teachings of psychedelic guru Timothy Leary, started from 1967 onwards to smuggle hashish and later hash oil from Afghanistan in larger amounts, hidden in buses and vans and driven to India or Europe, from where it was shipped and sometimes flown to the USA or Canada.⁵² The International Narcotics Control Board wrote in their 1971 report: 'the copious streams now flowing from Afghanistan [and Nepal] constitute a serious challenge to the effectiveness of international control'.⁵³

Despite the fact that cannabis was officially illegal in Afghanistan, the economic possibilities of illegal exports were recognized by the Afghan government. This was nothing new in itself. In the 1920s, in accordance with the international drug regulatory regime, Afghanistan had prohibited cannabis use and made it punishable with twenty-five to thirty-nine lashes – but at the same time it encouraged export, legal or illegal, to British India. The enactment of cannabis prohibition was more symbolic than effectuated, as witnessed by the ubiquity of cannabis when the hippie travellers started to arrive in the 1960s.⁵⁴ There were also active Afghan smugglers who transported the drug to southern Iran, from which it went on to Europe or the United States.⁵⁵

It was therefore in line with traditional policies that in 1969 and 1970 the government encouraged farmers to use artificial fertilizers to increase production. 'As a result, cannabis plantations flourished around Heart, Kandahar, and Mazar-e-Sharif, and cannabis plants lined many of the roads between Kabul and neighboring cities.'⁵⁶ Cannabis cultivation had been labour intensive, but now the farmers began to mechanize. Canals were dug to irrigate the spring meltwater from the mountains. Farmers gained access to new technologies, such as tractors.⁵⁷ Cultivating cannabis was more profitable than the cultivation of other crops and became an important source of extra income for farmers.⁵⁸ Large-scale production led to the introduction of a new broad-leaf variety of cannabis. Cloths and metal meshes were introduced to produce sieved hashish. As in Morocco and elsewhere, increasing Western demand led both to modernizing production and to producing more hashish of lower quality and less potency. Connoisseurs complained, 'Modern Afghani smoke does not taste as thick, clean, full, dense, or sweet as traditional Afghani smoke. The decline in quality from traditional to modern Afghani is the result of greedy smugglers increasing their profits by selling larger amounts of very low quality at unjustifiable prices.'[59]

The globalization of cannabis consumption was fuelled by this structural change of cultivation in a developing country. By the early 1970s more and more arrests of Western smugglers took place in Afghanistan itself, while Afghan newspapers reported negatively on the culturally insensitive behaviours of Western travellers: according to one report, there were 5,000 to 6,000 hippies in Kabul in 1973. More and more problems of addiction and social problems because of cannabis use were now reported in Afghanistan itself.[60] Afghan attitudes were not unlike those in the Netherlands after the rise of coffee shops catering to drug tourists. On the one hand cannabis use was not generally socially accepted and frowned upon; on the other hand, money could be made.

Around 1970 much of the drug traffic went by air to Europe. British drug smuggler Howard Marks writes in his memoirs of a chain network centred around the Afghan Mohammed Durrani. Marks claims that Durrani was a member of the royal house of Afghanistan now living in Pakistan and in London. His partner in Karachi oversaw the sending of consignments of black Pakistani and Afghan hashish, partly through Dubai where Durrani had another partner working for a Lebanese airline, into the West. They delivered to the Brotherhood of Eternal Love but also to European middlemen who picked up the consignments at airports such as Frankfurt and drove them to the rest of Europe and the UK. Durrani certainly seemed to be highly connected as, according to Marks, he often used the Pakistani diplomatic mail to deliver his supplies of hashish.[61]

The activities and presence of the Brotherhood of Eternal Love in Afghanistan prompted the US Bureau of Narcotics and Dangerous Drugs, the successor agency of the FBN, to post an agent in Kabul in 1972. He was instrumental in the arrest of Leary, who tried to find asylum in the country, fleeing from American justice.[62] Furthermore, the US paid 47 million dollars to the Afghan royal government to eradicate cannabis (and opium) cultivation. After a coup deposing the king in the summer of 1973 the Afghan army roamed the countryside, burning fields and homes, arresting and killing farmers – ignoring, however, farms owned by government officials. The teahouses were closed. Cannabis farmers relocated, Western smugglers left.[63] At the same time the country was hit by severe droughts, bringing starvation to many. While the economy in the dry climate was heavily dependent on tree crops, fruit and nuts, cannabis (and opium) provided a more rewarding alternative. In 1972 a farmer could make on average 175 US dollars per hectare from fruit, but 300 to 360 US dollars per hectare from opium. The only substitute crop for opium was cannabis.[64] After two years, smuggling increased again; hashish was now transported to Pakistan, which became a major distribution country for Afghan as well as Pakistani cannabis (which is, however, considered inferior to Afghan hashish).[65]

When the Soviet Union occupied Afghanistan in 1980 the flow of Afghan hashish to the West was blocked.[66] However, the northwestern frontier areas on the other side of the border with Pakistan became quarters and training grounds for the mujahideen, the Afghan resistance fighters. This area was also highly suited for cannabis cultivation. Afghan refugees brought Afghan techniques of hashish production to Pakistan, while the mujahideen controlling the area took their share of the profits from the hashish trade. The region is sparsely populated, remote, and inaccessible – ideal smuggling terrain. Smuggling was furthermore made easier because people of the same (Pathan) tribes lived on either side of the border between Afghanistan and Pakistan. This continued after the Soviet withdrawal in 1992. According to a 2014 report Afghan cannabis was processed both in Afghanistan itself and in the Pathan tribal areas of Pakistan.[67]

The carriers who smuggled the drugs into Pakistan were paid only a negligible amount. As had been the case with all kinds of goods through the ages, cannabis was taken over the mountains surrounding the Khyber Pass from Afghanistan to Pakistan, mostly on donkeys, horses, and other pack animals, since there were few tracks and the terrain is rocky. Once in Baluchistan, on the other side of the border, the drugs were carried further through mountain passes on livestock or on foot. There was and is also traffic at the border crossing at Torkham, where the Grand Trunk (GT) Road connects Afghanistan with Pakistan. The GT Road is a part of the Silk Road that had connected South and Central Asia from before the birth of the Buddha, and is now a highway connecting Mazar-e-Sharif, Kabul, and Kandahar in Afghanistan with Peshawar, Lahore, and the port town of Karachi in Pakistan. Once in Pakistan the drugs were stored in private homes, often in remote villages, and waited to be picked up by other traffickers and smuggled hidden in trucks to the market or to destinations overseas. Officials and checkpoint guards were bribed on the way. Other agents then took the drugs on board planes, oil tankers, or fishing boats.[68]

From the latter half of 1982, according to one report, traffickers began to route shipments through the Gulf States.[69] Many vessels set off from the Makran coast. The Makran, the 780-kilometre-long Pakistan coastline of Baluchistan, is especially suited for smuggling operations. Makran is sparsely inhabited, with much of the population living in small port towns (like Gwadar, Pasni, and Somniani) and many smaller fishing villages. Here the drugs were loaded onto small vessels that were hard to intercept for the coastguard, before reaching the high seas where the consignments were transferred to larger vessels. In 2015 it was estimated that between 8,000 and 10,000 fishing boats operated off the coast. Most of them were small, typically no longer than 5 metres. The prawn and fish they caught were sold for fairly high prices on the international market, but the fishermen themselves sold them for incredibly low prices and had barely enough resources to meet basic needs, and none to give their children an education.[70] It was an ideal area to recruit transport vessels for illegal purposes. Although the remuneration at the lowest end of the smuggling chain – the carriers and the households who stored the goods in Pakistan – was not very high (in 2011 it was estimated by the UNODC to be around 90 US dollars per month), for those involved it is a substantial sum: the average monthly income of a household in Baluchistan was in that year only 100 dollars. These activities provided a regular income in areas with few employment possibilities. At the highest end of the chain – among the 'drug lords' or middlemen who provided the drugs for transport overseas – millions of dollars were made, part of it going into offshore accounts but some filtering back into the Pakistani economy.[71] The term 'drug lords' as used in a report is somewhat misleading. At least until the US invasion of Afghanistan these smuggling networks were only loosely organized, consisting of small outfits or local groups.[72]

The hippie trail

In 1995 Morocco produced 35 per cent of the world's cannabis, Pakistan 30 per cent, Lebanon 20 per cent, and Afghanistan 5 per cent, as did India and Nepal together.[73] Western demand and Western smugglers had been instrumental in the growth of cannabis cultivation and hashish production in these countries and in connecting Western consumers to a neo-colonial structure of production and distribution. But how did cannabis reach the Netherlands and other European countries?

The rise of the illegal distribution of drugs since the 1960s shows certain commonalities between different Western countries. The criminologists Nicholas Dorn, Karim Murji, and Nigel South distinguished in a broad chronological perspective three initial phases in the 1960s and 1970s in the import and retail of illegal drugs. In a first phase, described by them as the 'good old days', the illegal supply of drugs was less driven by a profit motive than by the motivation to keep oneself and one's friends supplied, often out of a belief in the consciousness-expanding effects of drug use. In a second phase more commercially inclined traffickers moved in, in operations that were sidelines to other, legitimate as well as illegitimate, business interests. In the 1970s professional criminals took over the drug markets – a professionalization accompanied by the use of intimidation and violence.[74] These phases can be distinguished in general in the rise of Dutch cannabis smuggling as well, but need to be detailed and modified to some extent.

As we have seen, the great expansion of the Dutch cannabis market started in 1967. Herman Cohen closely observed at the time the vicissitudes of the market. In 1967 he did not notice any shortage of supply in Amsterdam, apart from one period of two weeks in which increased police activity made the retail dealers cautious for a short time. Supply at the time was still on a small scale and almost incidental, dependent on individual adventurers who could handle at the most a few kilograms at a time.[75] As we will detail below, these were either people out on the 'hippie trail' or sailors following the time-honoured maritime tradition of smuggling. In 1966 the biggest catch for the police was a Dutch engineer who tried to bring 7 kilograms of cannabis from Tangier into the country.[76] The small and incidental scale of the smuggling accounts for Cohen's observations that supply became scarce, first on the few occasions that the police temporarily cracked down on the retail; second, in wintertime, as in January and December 1968, when the weather was too cold to set out on or come back from the hippie trail; and third, when demand suddenly surged, as when in the summer of 1969 a stream of young tourists eager to explore the Magic Centre of Amsterdam filled the city.[77]

Retail trade was still mainly in the hands of small-time dealers with small profit margins, for whom dealing was part of their lifestyle and partly meant to finance their own consumption. Exceptions were a few opportunists who tried to cheat their customers with an inferior product. Cohen only found three middlemen who at the time imported in larger bulk and supplied the retailers. All three, however, had already stopped their activities.[78] One of Cohen's middlemen might have been a musician from New York who was arrested by the Amsterdam police in January 1968 with 25 kilograms of hashish.[79] As a consequence of the small scale of the smuggling the quality of the smuggled product was far from standardized. One batch of cannabis, even when produced in the same area, could contain five times as much THC as the next one.[80] Interestingly this lack of a reliable product did not seem to have any effect on the demand for the drug. Smoking had become an integral part of a deviant subcultural lifestyle and inferior cannabis was better than no cannabis at all.

Smugglers on the hippie trail were socially embedded in the alternative culture of smokers, both on a relational level (their buyers were friends and acquaintances, and *their* friends and acquaintances) and on an institutional level (they met their relations in certain public spaces frequented by the youth culture such as bars, youth centres, concert halls, and parks). These smugglers could often be described as minimally commercially driven. The quantities of cannabis that could be supplied by them were relatively small. Nevertheless this type of smuggler kept operating in the 1970s and beyond – although not always successful. A 25-year-old student from the University of Amsterdam was caught in Beirut attempting to smuggle 900 grams of hashish out of the country.[81] A painter from the city of Delft regularly drove in his car to Morocco, returning with cargoes of hashish. The police caught him when he was coming back to his hometown with 10 kilograms hidden in the chassis of the car.[82] A 27-year-old television technician from Rotterdam drove with 22 kilograms of Lebanese hashish from Lebanon to the Netherlands and was caught on the way at the Greek border.[83] A 21-year-old was caught at Schiphol airport arriving from Karachi with 8 kilograms of hashish under the false bottom of his suitcase.[84] Afghanistan became another source of supply: in June 1972 an Englishman was arrested at Schiphol airport with 10 kilograms of Afghan hashish under the false bottoms of his cases.[85]

Essential in the evolution of the Dutch drug trade was the capability of smugglers to establish contacts and relationships in countries of supply. To Europeans these have been 'strange' or 'other' countries over the past centuries, part of Islamic territories and empires that have been at war with Christianity. Nevertheless Dutch smugglers working these countries succeeded, in a longer tradition of other outlaws such as Dutch pirates in the seventeenth century, in overcoming these cultural barriers and developing social and economic relationships.[86] For them borders were not insurmountable barriers controlled by the states, but spheres of contact and interaction, 'shifting spaces in which people with different identities and cultural influences meet and deal with each other in various ways'.[87]

The memoirs of English drug smuggler Nigel 'Leaf' Fielding are an example of the ease with which an intrepid entrepreneur could buy kilograms of cannabis in supply countries. His experiences are representative of those of other European smugglers. In 1969 or 1970 Fielding, a university dropout hiking through Europe, met in Florence a compatriot who kept a stash of 8 kilograms of Lebanese hashish under his bed. The compatriot, named 'John', had visited Beirut nine months before and in his hotel had met an American who had been offered the 8 kilograms but was too scared of the police to execute the deal. John went in his place to the hills of Baalbek. There he bought 16 kilograms from a farmer. Back in Beirut he gave eight of them to the American, and the other eight he smuggled to Florence. With similar ease one could buy cannabis in other producing countries, if one was prepared to run a few risks. Fielding's hippie trail brought him to Thailand, where the presence of American soldiers had stimulated the growth of an underground drug economy. He went to a village, bought a few kilograms of cannabis, and smuggled them without problem in his backpack on a plane from Malaysia to Heathrow.

Buying cannabis in Morocco was also unproblematic. In 1973 Fielding took a boat from Spain to Tangier, where he was met by a local hustler who took him to Ketama. Here Fielding was laughed at because he only wanted to buy 0.5 kilogram; he could easily have bought such a small amount in Tangier.[88]

Hippie smugglers such as Fielding were important in establishing the connections between the demand market among the countercultural youth in Europe and the supply markets overseas. Being members of the counterculture themselves, they could easily distribute their products in their home countries, once they had smuggled them in their cars or backpacks into Europe. They were embedded in a relational network that spanned the hippie and youth cultures in the Netherlands, Britain, and other Western European countries to the cannabis farmers of Morocco, Lebanon, and other parts of the world.

Maritime smuggling

The hippie cannabis smuggler was often minimally commercially driven. The profit motive was a bigger motive for another type of cannabis smuggler that actually preceded the hippie type and was deeply rooted and culturally embedded in Dutch maritime history and society. This type of smuggler had existed since the introduction of the first Opium Act in 1920 and even before, since the very first beginnings of the Netherlands as an independent state and a global maritime player. In the seventeenth and eighteenth centuries trading companies tried to maintain their legal monopoly on overseas trade, including that in psychotropic drugs such as opium. However, 'to the great irritation of the authorities [...] by far the greatest competition to the [Dutch East India] Company in the opium trade was probably provided by its own servants engaged in a clandestine trade in the drug. Being a high-value, low-bulk item, opium was clearly suited for the trade', and a nice earner on the side for poorly paid sailors.[89] In the West Indies too sailors pursued small smuggling and trading ventures and were considered the weakest link in the monopoly chain of the Dutch West India Company.[90] After the introduction of the Opium Act the smuggling of opium flourished under the Chinese seamen in the service of the Dutch shipping companies, bringing the drug from the East to the Chinatowns of Amsterdam and Rotterdam.

This tradition of sailors smuggling prohibited goods, expressive of a culture of defiance of legal and disciplinary restrictions, was until the end of the 1960s an important source of cannabis supply. On the routes across the ocean sailors had plenty of opportunity to buy contraband in port towns and bring it to the Netherlands. One of these sailors was known as *Rode Kees* (Red Kees), a red-haired Dutchman who worked on the shipping lines with Indonesia and was a reliable source of supply for users in the Amsterdam beatnik scene. He was relationally and institutionally embedded through his contacts in the pubs and bars of the port towns where one might meet dealers as well as customers.[91] Red Kees does not pop up in police records, since he was never arrested. Other examples of the type were – for instance the Indonesian sailor who was caught in August 1966 in Amsterdam with 4 kilograms of hashish.[92]

In the early 1970s small-time sailor smugglers continued to operate. For example, in February 1972 four Pakistani crewmembers of a West German cargo ship were arrested in the harbour of Rotterdam carrying 20 kilograms of hashish.[93] These sailors continued to make use of the 'old-fashioned' maritime networks, in this case connecting cultivators and traders in Pakistan with the Dutch cannabis market. However, although 20 kilograms was a sizeable quantity in the 1960s, by 1972 this kind of smuggling was becoming relatively small scale.

The activities of sailor smugglers were of increasing interests to entrepreneurs when demand for cannabis started to grow. For example, the woman known as *Blonde Greet* (Fair-headed Greet) who ran the café *De Zeemeeuw* (The Seagull) on the Zeedijk in the Amsterdam's notorious red-light district close to the harbour. According to her daughter (who later became infamous herself as the business partner of drug 'kingpin' Klaas Bruinsma – see Chapter 6), Blonde Greet bought cannabis from sailors on the shipping routes to Indonesia in both the Amsterdam and Rotterdam harbours, and sold the drug on to retailers for twice the price: buying at 500 guilders per kilogram and selling at 1,000 guilders per kilogram.[94] The role of Blonde Greet in these and other transactions (we will meet her again below) shows that smuggling was not purely a masculine activity.

The harbour districts of the port towns with their long tradition of illegal trade, distrust of authority, and shadowy business deals offered the ideal social and cultural environment for the distribution of cannabis.[95] They were also the places where a new type would enter the world of cannabis smuggling: the criminal opportunist.

Foreign smugglers

From the seizures we can deduct that individual hippie and sailor smugglers could bring in quantities of up to 20 kilograms of cannabis hidden on ships, in cars, or in plane luggage. Taken together this must have accounted for a sizeable import. However, as Cohen had observed, these smugglers could not guarantee a regular supply of standardized quality. The expanding market therefore needed new types of supply. A third commercially driven type of cannabis smuggler spotted their chance for export to and transit in the Netherlands, making use of the excellent transport infrastructure of the country. The type itself was again not new: we have already seen its predecessor in the interwar Greek trafficking networks.

In 1972 the Amsterdam police rolled up the 'biggest organization' of hashish smugglers the country had known: ten Pakistani men and one Englishwoman were arrested. The degree of professionalism was previously unheard of. Retail dealers had been arrested with unusually large supplies of dozens of kilogram of hashish in their possession. The police followed the trail from the dealers to their supplier, a 42-year-old Pakistani mechanic who had been living in Amsterdam for a few months. In his bike shed the police discovered not only 42 kilograms of hashish, but also documentation for the import of fruit through Schiphol airport. A Pakistani company turned out to be importing orange crates from its home country to the Netherlands. The papers were in order, there was only one thing that was suspect: the crates were much too heavy for the oranges they seemingly contained. On closer investigation cannabis was found hidden behind false bottoms and walls of the orange crates. Later the drug was also found in cargoes of onyx and woodcarvings, other imports of the same company. All in all the company had imported millions of guilders' worth of cannabis and had distributed the drug to warehouses. Almost 2,000 kilograms of hashish had been smuggled in the orange crates alone.[96] The size of this operation dwarfed the amounts that could be handled by sailor and hippie smugglers.

The Pakistani smuggling operation was not new in itself. A similar cargo of around 40 kilograms of hashish hidden in orange crates on a flight from Pakistan had been seized by British customs in 1967. Pakistani immigrants had built up smuggling networks between Britain and Pakistan, using immigrants' underground banking networks to buy cannabis in Pakistan, smuggle it to Britain through Lahore airport, and send back consumer goods.[97] It seems that the Pakistani networks now made use of the possibilities created by the surging demand for cannabis and had expanded their operations to the Netherlands.

Dutch criminal entrepreneurs

However, since the bulk of hashish was so much heavier than that of heroin, for instance – another drug that became increasingly popular at the time and was smuggled in by plane (see Chapter 5) – smuggling by sea offered better business opportunities, especially for imports of hashish from Morocco and Lebanon. Criminal entrepreneurs and opportunists started to grab these openings, moving from smuggling by plane to maritime smuggling by using their relations with maritime networks. The background of these adventurers was not so much the counterculture (although most of them were young enough to have some sort of association with this culture), nor were they carrying on the traditions of the sailor smugglers (despite making use of maritime networks). Their background was the criminal underworld of the larger Dutch cities, especially in the western part of the country. (In the south of the country kindred criminal opportunists started to move in at this time on amphetamine smuggling – see Chapter 8.) To them, the profits of the illegal drug trade were highly enticing.

These criminals were not always big guns or even successful in their operations. A minor example was the 39-year-old unemployed administrator Nicolaas J.M.V. from Voorburg, a suburb of The Hague, who had a criminal record (or, according to one newspaper account, a 'difficult youth'). He was also in possession of a pilot's licence. With financing from a café owner in the city of Terneuzen Nicolaas flew a sports aircraft to Beirut and Morocco to buy hashish. The Terneuzen bar connection demonstrates how such a criminal opportunist could embed his operations in existing networks and places. The city, a port town on the Dutch–Belgian border, had a long-standing reputation as a smuggling centre. The embeddedness of cannabis smuggling in maritime networks showed when Nicolaas, on not receiving financial compensation for his flights, went to Terneuzen to confront the bar owner and received from him 50 kilograms of hashish that had been brought to the bar by sailors. Unfortunately for Nicolaas he was then caught in possession of the hashish by police detectives in Amsterdam, and this terminated his career.[98]

Operating on a bigger scale were three 'businessmen' from Rotterdam who in September 1972 were given jail sentences of eighteen months (for two of them) and nine months (for one) for smuggling hashish. These sentences were the results of a year of judicial struggle in which the court of The Hague finally decided that hashish was prohibited under the Opium Act, even when it could not be proven that the stuff was made of the dried tops of the cannabis plant. The case of these businessmen concerned the seizure of 110 kilograms of hashish in 1971, the largest seizure at the time.[99] The newspapers were quick to dub this group the 'Great Hashish Conspiracy'. A seizure of this size would soon be considered small fry; however, it was a first visible example of how the criminal underworld was moving in on the profitable cannabis trade.

Three traders and one sales representative from Rotterdam, aged between 26 and 32, developed an ingenious method in which they flew hashish in planes from Morocco and Libya to the Netherlands. The hashish was hidden among other goods that were meant for transit through the harbour of Rotterdam, such as wooden horses from Iceland, or machine components. The paperwork was in order. During the transport by car from the airport to the Rotterdam harbour the crates were changed for identical-looking ones, but without the drugs. On 27 April 1971 the trick did not work any more, and customs intercepted the drugs and arrested four people. They were part of an international network; the broker of the drugs was a Dutchman living in Beirut. The drugs were flown to the airports of Amsterdam and Rotterdam via Belgium and West Germany to evade suspicion. By the time of the arrests at least 330 kilograms had been smuggled into the Netherlands, at that time more than had ever been caught in any year by customs and police. The drugs were distributed in the Netherlands by an extensive network, including a café owner in Rotterdam and a contact on the other side of the country, in Venlo near the German border. The Venlo contact redistributed the stuff to West Germany and other parts of Europe, which showed that the Netherlands was developing into a transit hub for the illegal hash trade. The businessmen were part of Rotterdam criminal circles: one of them was a former boxer and now organizer of boxing matches. During the trial fights erupted on the public gallery between visitors who clearly had some scores to settle.[100]

Former boxer 'Aadje V', by then in his early thirties, was the connecting person between investors, smugglers, and producers. During the trial Aadje showed himself unruffled by this temporary setback. He even suggested, to loud cheers of his friends on the gallery, a solution to the whole problem of the illegal drug trade: legalization of soft drugs, which would earn the Dutch state at least 450 million guilders each year.[101] Aadje was, however, not so much a representative of an alternative counterculture as this proposal suggests; rather he was a representative of the criminal milieu of Rotterdam, born and bred in the working-class quarter of Crooswijk. He and other criminal opportunists were starting to link demand and supply.

A similar development was occurring in Amsterdam, where Blonde Greet had started out by buying hashish from sailors on the ships to and from Indonesia. To meet demand she needed bigger supplies, and she started working with the husband of one of her friends, a leading figure in the criminal underworld of Amsterdam's harbour district around the Nieuwmarkt and the Zeedijk. Simon Adriaanse was known in those circles as Frits van de Wereld. He belonged to a select group of criminal entrepreneurs who around 1965 more or less controlled the Zeedijk district. In the words of the stepson of one of them, this made the district (until the heroin epidemic of 1972) a 'safe and self-regulating neighbourhood with hardly any trouble for the police'.[102] Frits was a typical entrepreneur who liked to diversify his activities. Not only a smuggler but also a pimp and the owner of illegal gambling houses in the red-light district, he was keen to move in on the expanding cannabis market and had funds to invest in bigger operations than those possible for the old small-scale smugglers. The start of Frits's criminal career was connected to the introduction of a new drug during the Second World War, or rather of a new form of consuming an existing drug: *shagtabak*, tobacco rolled and smoked in cigarette papers, a cheaper way of consumption that became very popular in the Netherlands. The war had made the import of tobacco from the colonies and South America problematic. Dutch indigenous tobacco cultivation had mostly disappeared by 1900, but in Belgium, where shag was introduced in 1942, indigenous tobacco cultivation still survived. Smuggling of food and soap from the Netherlands to

Belgium existed on a grand scale. Now the smuggling went the other way as well: tobacco was transported from Belgium to the Netherlands, often by or with the assistance of German soldiers. (After the Allied liberation of Belgium and the south of the Netherlands Allied soldiers took the smuggling over from the Germans.) An extensive network of tobacco distribution in the Netherlands came into existence, 'protected' by the upperworld: German military and Dutch police officers. Rotterdam, because of its close geographical location to Belgium and because of its logistical infrastructure, became a nucleus in the illegal distribution, but the smuggling spread all over the country, including to Amsterdam. In 1946, after the liberation, an estimated 125,000 smugglers were operating in the illegal distribution of tobacco. Government institutions were especially worried because 'many youngsters became used to earning a lot of money without having to do any real work'.[103]

Frits van de Wereld was one of these youngsters. Born in 1927 in a typical working-class neighbourhood in the north of Amsterdam, he had already been arrested several times for food theft during the war and shortly after. He worked all kinds of jobs in the Amsterdam harbour (including cleaning ships) and moved as a doorman to the red-light district. According to the daughter of Blonde Greet he then started tobacco smuggling. He told stories of how by the 1950s he imported vans full of cigarettes. Once, when receiving a tip that customs officers were on the trail of one of his cargoes, he exchanged the tobacco for cow dung. Frits's activities were socially embedded in the red-light district when in 1956 he bought his own café on the Zeedijk. The café was called *De Wereld* (The World), hence his nickname in the criminal milieu: Frits of the Wereld. The bar was frequented by other criminal entrepreneurs. In the rooms above Frits had prostitutes working for him, while the bar also became a centre for dealing in tobacco and later cannabis smuggling. It was a small step from the one to the other.

Frits and his generation clearly enjoyed the game. He and likeminded entrepreneurs invested money in a new way of operations: ships that were specifically chartered by smugglers to transport contraband. The *Scheveningen 36*, one of the first cutters carrying drugs into the Netherlands to be seized, was carrying fifteen small containers of hashish fastened to the bottom of the outside of the hull when it was stopped in 1973 by a customs surveillance boat in the port of

Amsterdam. Through a simple mechanism the containers could be unfastened and dropped to the sea bottom, where divers could bring them up later.

By using his own ships Frits was able to import batches of 3,000 kilograms that associates picked up in the harbours of Zeeland in the south of the country and that middlemen such as Blonde Greet sold for him. He was further involved in the famous *Lammie* case of 1974, in which the Dutch navy pursued the eponymous fishing boat with 10,000 kilograms of hashish from Lebanon on board. Chased and shot at by a naval vessel and about to be boarded, the captain sank the *Lammie* himself. The *Lammie* transport had been organized by Frits with the help of fish trader Jacques Stroek, exemplifying the connection between criminal and maritime networks in the expansion of cannabis smuggling.[104] Frits van de Wereld's activities were not restricted to cannabis smuggling. He also acted, again using Blonde Greet, as a broker for Chinese networks in the heroin trade with Malaysia.[105] Later Frits van de Wereld became the mentor of Klaas Bruinsma (see Chapter 6).[106]

As Frits moved from tobacco to cannabis, another criminal entrepreneur from Rotterdam moved from human smuggling to cannabis. In the 1950s he had transported illegal Pakistani migrants through the Netherlands into the UK. His existing network enabled him to move from Pakistani men to Pakistani hashish: 2,000 kilograms of hashish imported by him and two of his colleagues were found by the police in a warehouse in Schiehaven in the Rotterdam harbour.[107]

Yet another typical case of a consortium of opportunists smuggling cannabis was only discovered in 1980. Five men from the cities of Groningen and Utrecht had pooled resources to buy the coastal vessel *Total*, with the Lebanese flag, in southern Europe for 600,000 guilders. The Utrecht merchant who had bought the ship went aboard, together with an ex-coxswain from Groningen, who became the captain, and two bar owners and a taxi driver from the same city, who formed the rest of the crew. In Lebanon 5,000 kilograms of hashish were bought and stowed on the *Total*. The ship then set course to the Wadden Sea, off the north coast of the Netherlands. There the cargo should have been loaded on motorboats and smuggled into the country. But things went wrong. Passing the harbour of Rotterdam the ship's engine broke down and the vessel had to be towed into the port. Here police and customs, tipped off by an informer on the island of Cyprus where the ship had touched on its way to the Netherlands, seized the *Total* and its cargo. A Rotterdam police commissioner remembered that at the time of the seizure a well-known figure from the Rotterdam underworld nicknamed 'Dog Face' was hanging around in the harbour – possibly a coincidence, but more likely because he had been asked by the smugglers to help move the contraband elsewhere.[108]

Containerization

By the early 1970s the scale of smuggling operations was changing decisively. The seizure of the *Scheveningen 36* in 1973 led to vehement American reactions. Two members of the US Congress designated Rotterdam and Amsterdam key transit hubs for the smuggling of drugs from Indochina to the United States, and as key suppliers of the US military in West Germany. The Rotterdam police were quite restrained in their reaction to these allegations. That the Rotterdam harbour was an important transit hub for drug smuggling was nothing new to them, and not surprising considering the harbour's size and the importance of the maritime traffic through the port. But they could not make an estimate of the exact volume of this smuggling.[109]

The container revolution in the maritime industry that started in the 1960s contributed to the expansion of cannabis smuggling, in combination with the existence of criminal networks already operating in the harbours. Containerization gave criminal entrepreneurs new chances, to which they responded in innovative ways. Theft of cargo, 'lost', 'damaged', or 'fallen' during transport or loading, was a common and time-honoured practice in the harbours. Containerization offered new chances in this area, since one could now 'hijack' a whole container or truck with its contents. In 1974 the hijacking of cargoes of cigarettes, whisky, electronics, clothing, and food with a value of more than 6 million guilders was reported to the Rotterdam police. The problem had become so intense that the police organized a special 'container team' to fight the hijacking.

Rotterdam police commissioner Blaauw described the general structure of the groups behind the hijacking: the typical flexible network structure of the underworld, in the words of Blaauw, was organized in a 'primitive' way.[110] This 'primitive' organization, embedded in the social environment of the harbours and drawing on the social capital, knowledge, and relations of its participants, worked rather smoothly.

According to Blaauw there was one key actor in the network who took the initiative and was in most cases the 'boss'. Other actors had specialized functions: for a small price one participant delivered the information about containers and trucks that could be hijacked; a second actor was the truck driver; a third organized a hide-out for the hijacked cargo, preferably in a farm shed close to the Belgian border; a fourth arranged the sale of the cargo to fences (so-called 'vultures'). The methods of the hijackers were very similar to the smugglers that had been (and still were) operating between Rotterdam and Belgium earlier in the century. These operators were, moreover, prepared to use violence to solve internal conflicts (casting doubt on later notions of the non-violent and 'romantic' period of smuggling before the 1980s) – they had to, since they could not take recourse to legal means.

A typical example of a key player in a hijacking group was the Rotterdam café owner 'Jan B' who was born in 1941 or 1942. His café was the meeting place for him and his associates, the place where their operations were socially embedded. He also received unemployment benefit from the Rotterdam municipality. Jan worked together with a Belgian group that was caught by the Belgian police in 1974; in the trial against this group Jan was also a defendant, but he did not show up for the case. The Belgian public prosecutor called him a 'hard gangster' who had intimidated the other defendants, and he was sentenced in his absence to four years. This did not stop his operations. A year later he stood trial in Rotterdam. One of the charges was that he had again been involved in container theft. Together with two associates he had stolen a trailer full of meat, worth 300,000 guilders. The second charge was that he had defrauded the city of Rotterdam of 46,000 guilders unemployment benefit while he did have an income. But most importantly Jan B had expanded his business and taken an interest in the cannabis trade. According to the police he had imported hashish from Morocco, Lebanon, and India, and exported the drug to Belgium and Germany, and was now setting up distribution lines to the United States and Canada. What had undone Jan B was a deal he had made at the end of 1974 in Teheran, whereby, with the assistance of corrupt Iranian military and (rumour had it) a bent official from Interpol, he had arranged for a military transport of 1,600 kilograms of hashish from Afghanistan (retail value several million guilders) to Teheran. Here the hashish was loaded in a truck and driven by a Dutch driver and associate of Jan to the Netherlands. Unfortunately the Rotterdam police already had their eye on this transport and followed the route of the truck by tapping phone calls from the driver to Jan. The police seized the truck and its cargo in a warehouse in the Netherland, and Jan was (after appeal) sentenced to six years in prison.[111]

Conclusion

In its first phase, illegal cannabis smuggling in the Netherlands occurred on a very small scale. It was partly based on traditional small-scale smuggling by sailors, and partly on the needs and drives of a new generation of countercultural activists with anti-establishment views and the need to supply drugs to themselves and their friends. However, by 1971 the illegal cannabis market had become an increasingly interesting and profitable business for more commercially minded smugglers; so interesting indeed that criminal entrepreneurs moved in. Pakistani entrepreneurs used planes for larger deliveries to Europe. Dutch criminal entrepreneurs embedded in the working-class neighbourhoods and harbour districts of the big cities used their skills, their funds, and their contacts with transporters (e.g., fishermen) in the Netherlands' maritime trading culture and with retailers, to develop the import of cannabis from producing countries on a scale that had not previously been witnessed. This flexible organizational model that the police saw as 'primitive' proved to be quite successful when transferred to the illegal drug trade. Containerization of the world's shipping offered further possibilities for smuggling drugs in bulk that would be more fully utilized after 1976 (see Chapter 6).

Dutch smuggling entrepreneurs and networks connected quite easily with counterparts in areas such as the Moroccan Rif mountains and the Lebanese Bekaa Valley. Here, in response to Western demand, cannabis cultivation and trade became a profitable economic sector more or less protected by political authorities and basically left alone by the state.

The strategies of the Dutch state to control the flow and use of cannabis had given rise to the tactics and ways of operation of an underground or shadow economy that undermined the very power of this state. Ironically the cultural and criminal deviance that lay at the foundation of Dutch cannabis smuggling would make possible the normalization of cannabis use in the Netherlands after 1976 (see Chapter 6). Dutch maritime and criminal traditions had come together in a powerful setting of criminal anarchy; we may agree with the words of Dutch poet and cannabis user Simon Vinkenoog that the illegal cannabis trade 'was just fitting in the whole Dutch pirate smuggling ethos'.[112]

Notes

1. On the early history of cannabis use in the Netherlands, see N. Maalsté, *Het kruid, de krant en de kroongetuigen. De geschiedenis van hennep van 1950 tot 1970* (Utrecht: Stichting WGU, 1993); M. de Kort, *Tussen patiënt en delinquent. Geschiedenis van het Nederlandse drugsbeleid* (Hilversum: Verloren, 1995), pp. 163–71; S. Snelders, 'Het gebruik van psychedelische middelen in Nederland in de jaren zestig. Een hoofdstuk uit de sociale geschiedenis van druggebruik', *Tijdschrift voor Sociale Geschiedenis* 21 (1995) 37–60.
2. See *Pharmacopoea Amstelredamensis, of d' Amsterdammer apotheek, in welke allerlei medicamenten, tot Amsterdam in 't gebruik zynde, konstiglyk bereyd worden,* 7th edn (Amsterdam: Jan ten Hoorn, 1714).
3. T. Blom, *Opiumwetgeving en drugsbeleid* (Deventer: Wolters Kluwer, 2015), pp. 20–1.
4. J. Sayer and D. Botting, *Nazi Gold: The Story of the World's Greatest Robbery and its Aftermath* (London: Granada, 1984), pp. 242–7.
5. Nederlandsche Centrale tot bestrijding van den smokkelhandel in verdoovende middelen (hereafter Nederlandsche Centrale), annual report 1947, part 1, in Ministry of Foreign Affairs Code Archive 1945–1954, National Archive, The Hague, inv. no. 205.117 (hereafter NA/FAII), 26301.
6. Nederlandsche Centrale, annual report 1947, part 2, NA/FAII, 26302.
7. Minutes of Pharmaceutical Inspectorate 18 November 1948, in archive of Pharmaceutical Inspectorate 1921–1961, National Archive, The Hague, inv. no. 2.15.39 (hereafter NA/PI).
8. Information sheet, Nederlandsche Centrale on arrest, 27 July 1955, NA/FAII, 6037.
9. D. J. Korf and M. de Kort, 'Drugshandel en drugsbestrijding' (University of Amsterdam, Bonger Institute of Criminology, 1990), p. 51. The immediate reason for doubling the section to four detectives in 1966 was the prohibition of LSD: Bureau Verdovende Middelen, annual report 1966, in archive of Municipal Police of Amsterdam (Gemeentepolitie

Amsterdam) 1957–1993, City Archive Amsterdam, inv. no. 5225A (hereafter GPA), 5146.
10 de Kort, *Tussen patiënt en delinquent*, pp. 163–71.
11 E.g., GPA, 5147.
12 Annual report 1965, GPA, 5146.
13 Archive of Ministry of Foreign Affairs 1955–1964, National Archive, The Hague, inv. no. 2.05.118 (hereafter NA/FAIII), 26033.
14 NA/FAIII, 26033.
15 NA/FAIII, 26069.
16 NA/FAIII, 26069.
17 de Kort, *Tussen patiënt en delinquent*, pp. 113–14; public prosecutor G. van der Burg in *De Telegraaf* 10 April 2018.
18 D. J. H. N. den Beer Portugael, *De Marechaussee grijpt in* (Utrecht: A. W. Bruna, 1954), p. 170.
19 Delpher digitized newspaper archive (ww.delpher.nl/nl/kranten, hereafter D): *NRC Handelsblad* 1 May 1971.
20 J. A. Blaauw, *Narcoticabrigade. De eindeloze strijd tegen drugshandelaren* (Baarn: De Fontein, 1997), p. 163.
21 J. A. Blaauw, 'De bestrijding van de georganiseerde misdaad in Nederland', *Algemeen Politieblad* 123 (1974): 228–36, on p. 229.
22 H. Cohen, 'Psychologie, sociale psychologie en sociologie van het deviante drug-gebruik. Een tussentijds rapport' (Instituut voor Sociale Geneeskunde, University of Amsterdam, 1969), p. 42.
23 *Aloha* 29 January 1971; report by Rotterdam Youth Council in Simon Vinkenoog Archive, International Institute of Social History, Amsterdam, inv. no. ARCH01561, 004.52.
24 I. Gadourek and J. L. Jessen, 'Prescription and acceptance of drug-taking habits in the Netherlands', *Mens en Maatschappij* 46 (1971) 376–410, on p. 389.
25 [L. H. C. Hulsman], *Ruimte in het drugbeleid. Rapport van een werkgroep van de Stichting Algemeen Centraal Bureau voor de Geestelijke Volksgezondheid* (Meppel: Boom, 1971), pp. 22–3. Remarkably, this report denied the existence of an organized illegal drug market: see p. 27.
26 W. Buikhuisen, H. Timmerman and J. De Jong, 'De ontwikkeling van het druggebruik onder middelbare scholieren tussen 1969 en 1973' (Criminologisch Instituut, University of Groningen, n.d.); de Kort, *Tussen patiënt en delinquent*, p. 186.
27 de Kort, *Tussen patiënt en delinquent*, p. 314.
28 E. Leuw, 'Het gebruik van cannabis onder leerlingen van voortgezet onderwijs: een poging tot interpretatie', *Nederlands Tijdschrift voor Criminologie* 14 (1972) 243–74.
29 de Kort, *Tussen patiënt en delinquent*, p. 182.

30 H. Cohen, 'De hasjcultuur anno 1980: een overlijdensbericht', in C. J. M. Goos and H. J. van der Wal (eds), *Druggebruiken: verslaving en hulpverlening* (Samsom: Alphen aan den Rijn, 1981), pp. 13–24.
31 'Abu Ali, age 88, a Lebanese farmer from the Bekaa Valley [...] claims to be the first to grow hashish plants in the Bekaa Valley (in 1935), from seeds smuggled from India inside of the walking stick of his friend Naif Ali Abbas', R. C. Clarke, *Hashish!* (Los Angeles: Red Eye Press, 1998), p. 153. There is a photograph of Ali Abbas at www.gettyimages.nl/detail/nieuwsfoto's/lebanese-farmer-abou-ali-who-was-the-first-to-plant-nieuwsfotos/55756926 (accessed 7 August 2020).
32 J. V. Marshall, *The Lebanese Connection: Corruption, Civil War, and the International Drug Traffic* (Stanford: Stanford University Press, 2012), pp. 16–18; Clarke, *Hashish!*, pp. 39, 153–64; M. Booth, *Cannabis: A History* (London: Bantam Books, 2004), p. 182; C. Schayegh, 'The many worlds of 'Abud Yasin; or, what narcotics trafficking in the interwar Middle East can tell us about territorialization', *American Historical Review* 116 (2011) 273–306.
33 Marshall, *Lebanese Connection*, pp. 2–3.
34 Marshall, *Lebanese Connection*, pp. 15–24.
35 H. Ram, 'Hashishophobia and the Jewish ethnic question in Mandatory Palestine and the state of Israel', in J. Mills and L. Ritchert (eds), *Cannabis: Global Histories* (Cambridge: MIT Press, 2021); on the Mossad affair: Booth, *Cannabis*, p. 330.
36 Booth, *Cannabis*, p. 329.
37 Marshall, *Lebanese Connection*, pp. 26–8.
38 For details on Lebanese hashish production see Clarke, *Hashish!*, pp. 154–64.
39 Clarke, *Hashish!*, pp. 175–83; K. Afsahi, 'Cannabis cultivation practices in the Moroccan Rif', in T. Decorte, G. Potter, and M. Bouchard (eds), *World Wide Weed: Global Trends in Cannabis Cultivation and its Control* (Farnham: Ashgate, 2011), pp. 39–54; Booth, *Cannabis*, pp. 320–2; H. Driessen, 'Smuggling as a border way of life: A Mediterranean case', in: M. Rösler and T. Wendl (eds), *Frontiers and Borderlands: Anthropological Perspectives* (Frankfurt am Main: Peter Lang, 1999), pp. 117–27.
40 C. Alverson, 'Ketama: Morocco's hash capital', *Rolling Stone* 5 Augustus 1971.
41 L. Cherniak, *The Great Book of Hashish*, vol. 1, book 1 (Berkeley: And/Or Press, 1979), p. 45.
42 Afsahi, 'Cannabis cultivation', pp. 41–7; Clarke, *Hashish!*, pp. 184–98.
43 Clarke, *Hashish!*, pp. 184–5.
44 D. Seddon, *Moroccan Peasants: A Century of Change in the Eastern Rif 1870–1970* (Folkestone: Dawson, 1981), pp. 156–7; Driessen, 'Smuggling'.

CANNABIS, COUNTERCULTURE, AND CRIMINALS 107

45 Driessen, 'Smuggling', pp. 122–4.
46 Driessen, 'Smuggling', p. 124.
47 Driessen, 'Smuggling', pp. 124–5; F. Bovenkerk and C. Fijnaut, 'Georganiseerde criminaliteit in Nederland: over allochtone en buitenlandse criminele groepen', Parlementaire Enquêtecommissie Opsporingsmethoden, Tweede Kamer der Staten-Generaal, 1995–1996, 24 072 (hereafter PEO), 17, pp. 112–22.
48 On Afghan cannabis cultivation and production of cannabis: Clarke, *Hashish!*, pp. 115–45.
49 C. J. Charpentier, 'The use of haschish and opium in Afghanistan', *Anthropos* 68 (1973) 482–90, on p. 482.
50 Charpentier, 'Use of haschish and opium'; J. Bradford, 'Linking East and West: How hash helped to globalize the Afghan drug trade' (unpublished paper, for the Cannabis: Global Histories conference, Strathclyde University, Glasgow, 19–20 April 2018).
51 Prices mentioned in S. Tendler and D. May, *The Brotherhood of Eternal Love: From Flower Power to Hippie Mafia* (London: Cyan Books, 2007), pp. 105; Charpentier, 'Use of hashisch and opium', p. 484; Bradford, 'Linking East and West'. United States Senate Committee on the Judiciary, *Hashish Smuggling and Passport Fraud: "The Brotherhood of Eternal Love"* (Washington: US Government Printing Office, 1973), p. 13, mentions a price of 15 dollars per pound.
52 Tendler and May, *Brotherhood*, pp. 105–8.
53 International Narcotics Control Board, annual reports and documents, (incb.org, hereafter INCB), annual report 1971, p. 24.
54 Bradford, 'Linking East and West'.
55 Charpentier, 'Use of hashisch and opium', p. 484.
56 Bradford, 'Linking East and West'.
57 Bradford, 'Linking East and West'.
58 Charpentier, 'Use of haschish and opium', p. 482.
59 Clarke, *Hashish!*, p. 134.
60 Charpentier, 'Use of haschish and opium', p. 484; L. Albert, 'Afghanistan: A perspective', in L. Dupree and L. Albert (eds), *Afghanistan in the 1970s* (New York: Praeger Press, 1974), pp. 249–59; Bradford, 'Linking East and West'.
61 H. Marks, *Mr Nice* (London: Vintage, 1998), pp. 73–5, 84–7, 107.
62 N. Schou, *Orange Sunshine: The Brotherhood of Eternal Love and Its Quest to Spread Peace, Love, and Acid to the World* (New York: Thomas Dunne Books, 2010), pp. 249–50, 270–1; Bradford, 'Linking East and West'.
63 Booth, *Cannabis*, pp. 327–8.
64 Alfred W. McCoy, *The Politics of Heroin: CIA Complicity in the Global Drug Trade*, rev. edn (Chicago: Lawrence Hill Books, 2003), pp. 505–7.

65 Clarke, *Hashish!*, pp. 146–8.
66 Clarke, *Hashish!*, p. 120.
67 S. Aftab, 'Post 2014: The regional drug economy and its implications for Pakistan' (Barcelona: CIDOB, 2014).
68 Aftab, 'Post 2014'.
69 D. Buddenberg, in L. Tullis, *Unintended Consequences: Illegal Drugs and Drug Policies in Nine Countries* (Boulder: Lynne Rienner, 1995), p. 83.
70 'The plight of the fishermen along Makran coast', PakVoices, 8 July 2015, www.pakvoices.pk/the-plight-of-the-fishermen-along-makran-coast/ (accessed 7 August 2020).
71 Tullis, *Unintended Consequences*, p 83.
72 Aftab, 'Post 2014'.
73 Booth, *Cannabis*, pp. 327–8, 415–16.
74 N. Dorn, K. Murji, and N. South, *Traffickers: Drug Markets and Law Enforcement* (London: Routledge, 1992), pp. 3–41.
75 Maalsté, *Kruid*, p. 117.
76 Archive of Ministry of Foreign Affairs 1965–1974, National Archive, The Hague, inv. no. 2.05.313 (hereafter NA/FAIV), report for 1966, 24354.
77 H. Cohen, *Drugs, druggebruikers en drug-scene* (Alphen aan den Rijn: Samsom, 1975), pp. 73, 118.
78 Cohen, *Drugs*, pp. 82–3, 123.
79 GPA, 5148.
80 Cohen, 'Hasjcultuur', p. 18.
81 D: *Trouw* 13 November 1972.
82 D: *Het Parool* 23 November 1972.
83 D: *De Volkskrant* 10 April 1972.
84 D: *De Volkskrant* 12 February 1972.
85 D: *De Volkskrant* 4 August 1972.
86 E.g., S. Snelders, *The Devil's Anarchy: The Sea Robberies of the Most Famous Pirate Claes G. Compaen and the Very Remarkable Travels of Jan Erasmus Reyning, Buccaneer* 2nd rev. edn (Brooklyn: Autonomedia, 2014), pp. 1–47.
87 Driessen, 'Smuggling', p. 120.
88 L. Fielding, *To Live Outside the Law: A Memoir* (London: Serpent's Tail, 2012), pp. 107–17, 183, 210, 232–4.
89 O. Prakash, *The Dutch East India Company and the Economy of Bengal, 1630–1729* (Princeton: Princeton University Press, 1985), p. 154.
90 W. Klooster, *Illicit Riches: Dutch Trade in the Caribbean, 1648–1795* (Leiden: KITLV Press, 1998), pp. 68–9.
91 Personal communication Hans Plomp (cannabis user), 29 March 2017.
92 Annual report 1966, GPA, 5146.

93 D: *Het Parool* 3 February 1972.
94 B. Middelburg, *De Godmother. De criminele carrière van Thea Moear, medeoprichter van de Bruinsma-groep* (Amsterdam: Pandora, 2004), pp. 24–5.
95 As they would in the 1990s for the distribution of Colombian cocaine: see D. Zaitch, 'From Cali to Rotterdam: Perceptions of Colombian cocaine traffickers on the Dutch port', *Crime, Law & Social Change* 38 (2002) 239–66.
96 D: *Trouw* 10 November 1972.
97 Booth, *Cannabis*, pp. 379–80.
98 D: *NRC Handelsblad* 22 August 1972; *De Telegraaf* 22 August 1972.
99 Blaauw, *Narcoticabrigade*, p. 162.
100 D: *Het Vrije Volk* 30 April 1971, 25 May 1971, 8 September 1971, 16 October 1971, 29 October 1971, 5 November 1971; *De Telegraaf* 14 May 1971, 11 June 1971, 8 September 1971, 15 September 1971, 16 October 1971; *Nederlands Dagblad* 23 October 1971.
101 D: *Het Vrije Volk* 16 October 1971.
102 B. van Hout, *De jacht op 'de erven Bruinsma' en de Delta-organisatie: hoe de CID-Haarlem het IRT opblies* (Amsterdam: PS, 2000), pp. 29–30. See also G. Meershoek, 'Terug naar de burgers. Wijkteams en buurtregie 1965–2004' in P. de Rooy (ed.), *Waakzaam in Amsterdam, Hoofdstad en politie vanaf 1275* (Amsterdam: Boom, 2011), pp. 517–55, on p. 539.
103 H. A. M. Klemann, *Nederland 1938–1948. Economie en samenleving in jaren van oorlog en bezetting* (Amsterdam: Boom, 2002), pp. 331–7.
104 Middelburg, *Godmother*, pp. 29–31; P. P. H. M. Klerks, *Groot in de hasj. Theorie en praktijk van de georganiseerde criminaliteit* (Antwerp: Samsom, 2000), pp. 99–100; 'De jacht op de Lammie', Andere Tijden, www.anderetijden.nl/aflevering/402/De-jacht-op-de-Lammie (accessed 7 August 2020).
105 Middelburg, *Godmother*, pp. 24–6.
106 van Hout, *Jacht*, p. 30.
107 Blaauw, *Narcoticabrigade*, p. 163.
108 Blaauw, *Narcoticabrigade*, pp. 165–7.
109 Blaauw, *Narcoticabrigade*, pp. 163–4.
110 Blaauw, *Narcoticabrigade*, p. 190.
111 D: *Het Parool* 27 July 1976; Blaauw, *Narcoticabrigade*, pp. 190–200. 'Wouter Koops' in Blaauw's account is Jan B.
112 Maalsté, *Kruid*, p. 114.

5

Global perils II: Chinese triads, Turkish families, and heroin

In the interwar period the introduction and implementation of the drug regulatory regime had led to opium smuggling becoming embedded in Chinese communities in the Netherlands. Suppression of smuggling proved impossible. However, a certain degree of tolerance of the Chinese opium markets by Dutch law enforcement in a kind of co-management with Chinese mutual aid societies did assist in containing the problem.

This chapter investigates how after 1970 heroin smuggling to and through the Netherlands successfully evolved and led to the proliferation of groups and networks connecting supply and demand. The containment of the opium market turned out to have been dependent on the limited demand for opium and opiates among native Dutch and other non-Chinese consumers. This demand started to surge after 1971 and burst the containment of the opium market. While opium trade and consumption among the Chinese in the Netherlands had dwindled after the war, existing networks morphed into new connections with suppliers in Hong Kong and Singapore to fuel the heroin epidemic of the 1970s and 1980s. This took place in a context of international developments. The Vietnam War stimulated the expansion of the heroin market among American soldiers and in the United States. Since other routes for heroin from Asia to the USA had been cut off, the Netherlands became an ideal transit hub for Chinese smuggling networks. These networks were embedded in the Chinese communities in the country, and moreover the Netherlands had excellent logistical connections around the globe. Heroin started to flow through the Netherlands and became as a side effect available to a growing group of users of Dutch and other ethnic backgrounds in the country.

Chinese heroin supply by air was extended, while criminal anarchy manifested in increasing rivalry and armed violence between Chinese groups. In this fragmented situation Turkish and Kurdish crime families took over dominance of the heroin trade after 1980. These groups connected opium production in Afghanistan with heroin manufacture in Turkey and consumption in the Netherlands and elsewhere. They made use of the geographical and historical position of Turkey as a transit hub for trade between Asia and Europe by road. The drug regulatory regime became faced with insurmountable problems of how to control the drug traffic on the European motorway system expanding from the 1970s onwards, and how to control the Turkish and Kurdish families and criminal networks embedded in migrant communities in the Netherlands.

Chinese opium smuggling, 1940–1970

The German occupation of the Netherlands in the years 1940 to 1945 disrupted international maritime traffic and communication with supply sources of opium in the Middle East. Immediately after the end of the war, police reports started to mention seizures of opium again. In 1951 opium seizures reached their highest post-war level of 60 kilograms. Almost all of the seizures concerned opium from Iran, most of it seized in Rotterdam. Nearly all involved Chinese seamen, with a few Dutchmen involved.[1] After 1951 Chinese seamen continued to be arrested occasionally in Dutch ports or in the Dutch colonies in the West Indies such as Curaçao, but the numbers of seizures and arrests started to dwindle. Opium smuggling, or at least its detection, decreased significantly in the 1950s. After 1952 total annual seizures of opium were almost always less than 10 kilograms. In the report of the Centrale for 1957, the drug trade was presented as more or less finished: after that year the unit was disbanded.[2]

It was not only Chinese people who were involved in opium smuggling. One notorious smuggler was a native Dutch woman named by the newspapers 'Cora S'. She and her husband lived in Huijbergen, a village close to the Belgian border situated on the railway connection between Antwerp and the border city of Roosendaal. Cora was known to the police and a suspect because she had travelled in India and

Great Britain. In September 1967 she and her husband were arrested by the police for involvement in an attempt by a sailor to sell 2.5 kilograms of opium with a retail value of 5 to 7.5 guilders per gram, for 6,000 guilders in a Rotterdam café.³ In spite of this, involvement of native Dutch was rare, especially on this scale.

In 1968 there was a little peak again in the seizure of opium: 13 kilograms.⁴ The focus of the Dutch authorities had by then moved to the smuggling of cannabis. In 1971, on the eve of the heroin epidemic, only 2 kilograms of opium were seized. The number of arrested drug users, dealers, and smugglers had by then exploded to the unprecedented figure of 1,401, but only sixteen of them were Chinese.⁵

Had opium use and smuggling among the Chinese significantly decreased between 1951 and 1971, or had it been given less attention by the police? It is impossible to give a definitive answer to this question. One important group in which opium smoking was embedded – the seamen working on the shipping companies – had slowly decreased in size since the Second World War. The economic crisis of the 1930s had already reduced the demand for Chinese seamen. The decolonization of Indonesia in 1949 led to the demise of the profitable shipping routes and the operations of the shipping companies to the Far East in the next decade. Moreover, after the Communist victory in the Chinese Civil War in 1949 it became difficult for Chinese workers to bring over family members from Guangdong or Fujian to Europe. The traditional Chinese communities grew older and were primarily male: many Chinese men married Dutch women. Predictions about a disintegration of these communities were not fulfilled, however. A new source of migration became Hong Kong: according to one estimate, at the end of the 1970s there were more than 50,000 Chinese in the Netherlands, including Hong Kong Chinese with a British passport and illegal migrants, but not including Chinese migrants from the former Dutch colonies. Restaurants became a new profitable economic basis for Chinese migrants and their families. Especially after 1965 the number of Chinese restaurants in the Netherlands increased: by 1982 there was one for every 7,500 inhabitants of the country.⁶ The embeddedness of the Chinese in Dutch society and their direct contacts with Hong Kong and the Far East did not disappear, but were reconstituted. A new chapter in Chinese drug smuggling was waiting for a new kind of demand.

A global heroin market

In 1971 the heroin epidemic in the Netherlands took off. In November of that year the Amsterdam police arrested two Chinese traffickers in the possession of opium, heroin, and morphine base. The possession of heroin was remarkable at the time. In the same month a Dutchman was found dead in his squat in the centre of Amsterdam. Cause of death: a heroin overdose, the first that the police had ever observed.[7] These two events were the first signals of a new drug problem that took on explosive dimensions in the following years. From 1971 the use of opiates increasingly spread among native Dutch people. Seizures of heroin multiplied.[8] Estimated numbers of opiate users outside medical settings rose from a few hundred opium smokers in 1970 to 1,500 heroin users in Amsterdam alone in 1973, and 4,000 to 5,000 nationwide in 1975, 10,000 in 1977, and 30,000 in 1983.[9]

Even more disturbing were the shocking visible side effects of illegal heroin use: certain areas of Amsterdam and other cities became 'no-go' areas for the citizens and hotbeds of street crime, prostitution, drug use, and trafficking, geographical spaces where the authority of state and police was challenged.[10]

By 1977 foreign observers were in general agreement that Amsterdam had become the heroin capital of Europe.[11] According to the DEA, by the mid-1970s 'overseas Chinese traffickers, using the Netherlands as a main importation and distribution area, virtually controlled the heroin market in Europe'.[12] The global context of this development is well known, especially because of the work of American historian Alfred J. McCoy. In 1971 the US Army started to withdraw from Vietnam and addicted American GIs returned to their country. The Chinese groups who had supplied the American soldiers in Southeast Asia now needed to devise tactics to bring their heroin into the United States. For this the American military stationed in West Germany were an ideal springboard. West Germany's neighbour the Netherlands had been an important transit hub for the international illegal drug trade for half a century: the Amsterdam drug market had started to receive visiting American soldiers on leave since the Second World War, travelling from Germany to the Dutch capital to buy cannabis and other drugs. The Chinese communities living in the ports of Amsterdam and Rotterdam were very well situated to perform a pivotal role in the redirection of the international heroin trade.

Ironically, one of the other causes of the new business opportunities for the Chinese heroin trade was the very success of the DEA and the French police in the fight against the heroin trade from Turkey through Marseilles into Europe and the United States (of which the pre-war Greek smuggling networks had been a part). This trade was brought to an end in the early 1970s, but McCoy shows how the reinforcement shield of the DEA succeeded only in deflecting rather than stopping the flow of heroin from Asia into Europe and Australia. Already by 1968 contacts were made between Italian criminal groups in Florida and Chinese facilitators of heroin supply in Saigon, Hong Kong, and Singapore.[13]

A key role in the deflection of the heroin flow was played by Chinese Chiu chow networks. The Chiu chow (as it is pronounced in Cantonese) originally came from eastern Guangdong, one of the areas of origin of Chinese labour migrants in the Netherlands. In the nineteenth century many of the Chiu chow moved to Singapore, inaugurating a diaspora of the group to other parts of Southeast Asia. In the early 1860s Chiu chow groups were already fighting other Chinese groups over the control of the opium trade in Singapore.[14] Chiu chow also played an important role in the opium trade in Shanghai until they were overshadowed by other groups after the First World War. The Communist takeover of China, the end of the colonial opium monopolies after the Second World War, and the start of decolonization profoundly changed the international opiates market and created new opportunities for Chiu chow and their international networks. These networks were based on shared ethnicity, language, and culture, and embedded in cities in Asia as well as in Europe. After the Communist victory in China thousands of gangsters fled to Hong Kong. Here the Chiu chow took over control of the illegal import of opium into the colony.

Partly because of the end of the Western colonial opium monopolies after the war, opium from Iran, India, and China disappeared from the markets. From the 1950s onwards, opium cultivation in the Golden Triangle (the highlands of northeastern Burma, Laos, and Vietnam) increased significantly. Itinerant Chinese caravan traders, the descendants of Chinese Muslim traders from neighbouring Yunnan province in China who had smuggled opium and tea to Southeast Asia since the mid-nineteenth century, brought the opium from the villages in the highlands to heroin laboratories on the Thai–Burmese border.

From there the heroin was exported and smuggled throughout the world by the Chiu chow networks. Some of the Chinese merchants in the Triangle developed into powerful warlords: for instance the infamous Khun Sa, whose caravans after the harvest of 1977 held enough opium to supply all illicit demand in the United States. In the Golden Triangle warlords were connected to the Chinese nationalist Kuomintang movement and could operate with the tacit support of the American CIA, who assisted the nationalists.[15]

Hong Kong was an important hub in the heroin trade. Suppression of opium use, opium dens, and opium trade in the city by the British police had by the early 1960s led to a decisive shift from opium to heroin use. From smoking opium, users shifted to the smoking or injecting of heroin no. 3, made available by Chinese traders. Heroin no. 3 consisted of high-quality, low-cost greyish or white chunks of opium powder of 40 or 50 per cent purity. Too expensive for the average user in Hong Kong was heroin no. 4, a generally white powder of 80 to 99 per cent purity that was four or five times diluted with caffeine or lactose for use, producing a heroin that dissolved easily in water and was shot directly in the veins with a syringe. Heroin no. 4 became the drug of choice for most American and European addicts.

In 1970 there were an estimated 100,000 addicts in a total population of 4 million in Hong Kong, making it the country with the highest percentage of illegal drug users in the world. From the mid-1960s onwards the Chiu chow controlled the import, retail trade, and export of heroin in Hong Kong. By that time a small fleet of fishing trawlers smuggled raw opium and morphine bricks from Thailand to Hong Kong. Turned into heroin no. 4 in one of the illegal laboratories on the island, the drugs were then brought by couriers on planes to Europe or Australia, where after a stopover the drugs were further transported to the USA. Profits were huge: one could sell 1 kilogram of heroin, bought in Hong Kong for 1,600 US dollars, for 34,000 US dollars in the United States.[16] Criminologists estimated the value of the illegal heroin market in the USA by 1980 to be 30 billion dollars, and the number of addicts there at 1 million.[17]

In the analysis of McCoy, an important factor in creating a heroin epidemic was the aggressive marketing of heroin by the Chinese to American soldiers in Vietnam. In this narrative Chinese master chemists supervised the introduction of the final ether precipitation process that enabled the production of heroin no. 4 in the laboratories in the

Golden Triangle in 1968 or 1969. This production took place quite close to the consumer market of American soldiers. In 1971 a survey of GIs concluded that 11 per cent of them used heroin; in 1973 another survey even came to an estimate of one-third. Heroin seemed to be, next to alcohol, cannabis, and amphetamines, in common use in the US Army. However, these figures need to be taken with some caution. Analysis of urine samples from repatriated soldiers in 1971 showed a user percentage of 'only' 5.5 per cent. Of the detected users 90 per cent smoked, rather than injected, heroin. Heroin no. 4 was expensive and its destination market was the United States and Europe, rather than the soldiers in Vietnam.[18]

To realize the potential high profits of the heroin trade the Chiu chow needed access to the affluent markets and consumers in the developed countries: the USA, Western Europe, Japan, and Australia. However, as part of President Nixon's declared 'war on drugs' the DEA set up a successful programme to target the heroin trade flows from Southeast Asia (and especially Thailand) into the USA. By 1975 the availability of Southeast Asian heroin had decreased significantly on the US streets. This, together with the eradication of opium in Turkey, only led to increased availability of heroin from Mexico. The Chinese had to find new methods to reach the American market – through Europe.[19] For this, the Netherlands as an important geographical trade hub, as a country with an excellent logistical infrastructure, and with a Chinese community with a background in the same southern provinces as the Chiu chow and with half a century's tradition of opium smuggling, was ideal.

Demand for heroin in the Netherlands

In November 1971 the moment had arrived when global flows of trade and consumption between Southeast Asia and Western Europe burst the barriers of containment that had been in place since the introduction of national, international, and colonial drug regulation regimes more than half a century before. A side effect of this redirection of global trade was that heroin flowed into the Netherlands and made new consumption patterns possible.

Although the Amsterdam and Rotterdam police forces had been well informed of the location of opium dens in their respective cities, they had often turned a blind eye to them, preferring co-management of the drug problem with the Chinese rather than a policy of zero tolerance. This tolerance of Chinese deviance ended when opium use crossed from the Chinese to native Dutch. In 1949 the Amsterdam police were upset at the behaviour of a Chinese dealer who had allowed a Dutchman to smoke opium, at the cost of 3 guilders a pipe.[20] Opium use remained relatively rare among Dutchmen. Around 1970 Frank Baas, an addicted user living in Rotterdam, was advised by his general physician to visit an opium den. The room was full of Chinese people reclining on straw mats and smoking water pipes with opium. The Dutchman felt that he was the first native to enter the den, bought 5 grams for 15 guilders, and left. The supply was enough to keep him going for two weeks.[21]

Heroin changed the scene. On 22 November 1971 the Amsterdam police arrested two Chinese in possession of 610 grams of opium, 50 grams of heroin, and 700 grams of morphine base, a product used for the manufacturing of heroin. Though these seizures entailed only relatively small amounts, it was the first time Chinese traffickers were arrested with heroin. More ominously, five days later a native Dutchman named Ronnie Pieterman died of an overdose of heroin in a squat in the centre of Amsterdam.[22] By 1972 heroin was generally available in the capital.

In a detailed analysis of heroin users in the Netherlands, based on fieldwork and published in 1982, criminologists Otto Janssen en Koert Swietstra constructed a typology of users that shows the social and cultural context in which heroin use developed in the early 1970s. As with cannabis, for many users the intake of heroin was part of their cultural rebellion against society. For instance, three of the interviewed users, born between 1952 and 1956, had already used illegal drugs in 1970 when they were only between 14 and 18 years of age. All three came from the middle or upper classes. In 1972 they immediately took to heroin.[23] Dependence on heroin was for this type of user often a conscious choice, an imitation of cultural icons that had entered their imagination well before the drug was available to them. These users took their drug from the Chinese, but the cultural context and consumption patterns from their American heroes such as the writer William Burroughs. The oral history project of Dutch historian Gemma Blok interviewing survivors of this group of heroin users indicates that pioneers among them started to inject smokable opium even before heroin was available – although smokable opium is not meant for injection because of the toxic side effects.²⁴ These kinds of experiment by inexperienced users might account for early deaths, such as that of Pieterman.

Not all users could be classified as middle-class dropouts or heirs of a hippie counterculture. Another type of user could be found among the working classes. Typically having started their use of drugs with amphetamines (which, even when not easily available, were not regulated under the Opium Act until 1976), these users needed drugs for purposes of relaxation or stimulation after a boring and hard working day and when going out at the weekend. Often these users became involved in petty crime and hooliganism. The illegal structure of the heroin scenes in the cities from 1972 onwards were actually not new, but grew from similar amphetamine scenes with their traditions of theft and fencing of stolen goods. Heroin offered this second type of user a new kick. Moreover, the use of heroin and amphetamines complemented each other: one drug used for relaxation, the other for stimulation. One could even combine the drugs in a so-called 'speedball' that was considered very cool. Heroin use offered relaxation after the intense stimulation caused by the use of amphetamines, and was also a method of self-medication to kick the amphetamine habit. Since amphetamines were injected as well, users took easily to the rituals of heroin injection. These users were not typical hippies: for instance they considered LSD too 'cerebral' a drug.²⁵

Heroin also became popular among a third type of user: the socially marginalized, unemployed youngsters thrown out of their parents' home, and the homeless. Furthermore, from 1973 the ranks of the heroin users were swelled by a fourth category: migrants from Suriname. This Dutch colony would become independent in 1975, and many Surinamese opted for migration to the Netherlands in order to keep their Dutch citizenship and to further their economic opportunities. The Bijlmer, a newly built district in the south of Amsterdam, became almost a Surinamese ghetto. However, not all Surinamese migrants succeeded in adapting to life in the Netherlands or in finding employment. Many of them fell into a lifestyle of cannabis smoking and 'hustling', whether legal or illegal, to earn money. Heroin smoking (rather than injecting) became part of their way of living.²⁶ While the native Dutch consumers were positioned at the lowest levels of the heroin market, dependent on their dealers, these Surinamese users stood a little higher in the hierarchy of the heroin market, closer to the small retail dealers (the '7-gram dealers' so named for the size of their supplies) who were often Surinamese users themselves. Among the 7-gram dealers interviewed by Janssen and Swietstra we find a Surinamese Chinese, a descendant of Chinese migrants to Suriname, who had joined a triad in the Netherlands and started dealing as middleman for one of his nephews. But on the whole the contacts of the 7-gram dealers with the 'big boys' behind the heroin trade, positioned on the highest levels of the market in the wholesale trade, was limited. All these types of user started from 1971 to meet, deal, and use in public spaces (train stations, bars, social centres) and drug squats, some of them also resorting to violence (such as robberies of and gunfights with Chinese dealers) in order to finance their habit and lifestyle.[27]

It took some time for public authorities, law enforcement, health care, and social work to catch up, but in the summer of 1972 the first warnings were sounded in Amsterdam and Rotterdam. Estimates of drug users at the time differed wildly, however: for instance, in Amsterdam the figure varied between 500 and 3,000. Use of heroin was stimulated by reduced availability of amphetamines and of opium. There was also increased police attention to dealing in the traditional Chinatowns in the city centres. At first opium became more expensive and because of the increased risks it was no longer sold in small packages of 10 guilders' worth but in larger quantities for 100 guilders. Then opium became less available. The dark chunks of smokable opium disappeared from the market. Chinese suppliers shifted from opium to the more profitable heroin. The drug scene in Amsterdam was in turmoil because of this transition and (unsubstantiated) rumours abounded: that the new heroin dealers would inform on the older opium dealers to the police, or that heroin dealers gave free samples of their merchandise to potential clients to get them addicted. User Frank Baas did receive free samples of heroin in small matchboxes from a Chinese in a bar on the Zeedijk, courtesy of a 'Mister Wo'.

There was at first among the users some unwillingness to shift to heroin; however, there was not much choice. Other opiates such as morphine, or the synthetic opioid Palfium (dextromoramide), were only available when stolen from pharmacies and could not be supplied in sufficient quantities to meet the rising demand. Users therefore needed an alternative and found it in brown Hong Kong heroin, at first available in good quality and sold by a few Chinese and Dutch retail traders. From the deviant subcultures whose members scored their drugs in the inner cities heroin use expanded throughout the town, to bars, dance clubs, and youth centres. Frank Baas started with smoking granules of heroin in a cigarette, which made him feel better and also did not give him the nausea which opium smoking produced. However, withdrawal symptoms when not smoking were more severe. After a few months, prices of heroin went up.[28] In Amsterdam Chinese dealers carried out retail sales to the heroin users while guards kept watch on police activities. The Zeedijk in the oldest part of the town was known as the 'Chinese street': Tung Yan Kai.[29]

While seizures of opium had increased from 1970 to 1973 they became dwarfed by the seizures of heroin: zero grams in 1970, 50 grams in 1971, more than 2 kilograms in 1972, and over 25 kilograms in 1973.[30] Similar developments to those in Amsterdam occurred in other cities. Until 1973 only small amounts of heroin had been seized by the Rotterdam police: 20 grams in 1964, in a house 'frequented by seamen and coloured people'; an incidental high amount of 380 grams in 1967; 2 grams in 1972 – but 126 kilograms were seized in 1977.[31] Police seemed powerless against the expansion of the trade, even when the drugs unit of the Amsterdam police received considerably greater resources and expanded to fifty officers.[32]

As a consequence of the increased popularity, prices of heroin rose: from 25–60 guilders per gram to 100–125 guilders, while quality went down. In 1976 the price of a gram was up to 200 guilders, and by the end of the 1970s it had gone up to as much as 300 guilders.[33] As mentioned above, estimated numbers of opiate users outside medical settings rose dramatically.

The shift from opium to heroin was partly connected to the advantages of the new product for producers and traders. A semi-synthetic drug, it could be made more profitably than opium and transported in much smaller bulk. Trade could be embedded in existing networks of trafficking. Most importantly, there now existed a demand that was much larger than the traditional Chinese demand, in a completely changed cultural environment. Users did not need an opiate to get through their working day, as had Chinese coolies and sailors, but were anxious to drop out of society, embracing the anti-bourgeois morality of the counterculture. The Chinese responded by giving them their drug, even when this meant an end to the tacit agreement of co-managing the drug problem with the police.

Smugglers: the 14K

To connect supply and demand, the heroin networks made use of new transport methods. The favoured mode of transport became the passenger airlines flying between Asia, Europe, and the United States. Methods of smuggling, however, resembled those of the opium smugglers on the steamships. The amounts smuggled were generally small, up to 10 kilograms, that could fit into a suitcase. Bottles, rice cookers, clothing, boxes, anything that could be used was utilized to hide heroin. Couriers, Chinese people as well as Europeans and Americans, brought the drugs in suitcases or hidden on their bodies in planes from Hong Kong, Singapore, or Malaysia to Europe. Inventiveness was high: two white girls carried heroin hidden in plastic penises. Once or twice a year smugglers chanced the transfer of significantly bigger amounts of 200 kilograms or so. Travelling on the same planes were the Chinese controllers, who watched the couriers – who did not know them – and did not themselves run any risks. This did not mean that smuggling on freighters had become totally obsolete: in 1990 a cargo of 40 kilograms was seized in the Amsterdam harbour on board a ship coming from Bangkok.[34]

By 1973 the Amsterdam police began to pay closer attention to the organizations behind the smuggling: the Chinese triads. The most important triad responsible for the introduction of heroin in the Netherlands was the Hong Kong-based 14K. The 14K (or the Sap Sie Kee, the 'fourteen carat') had its origins in Canton (Guangzhou). It was a pro-nationalist society whose members were among those fleeing to Hong Kong after the Communist takeover in 1949. The origins of the 14K were therefore in the same regions and districts that had spawned the Bo On. Membership of the society (which did not have a central leadership) gave essential social and cultural capital to take part in the illegal trade. In his study of the Hong Kong triads, criminologist Yiu Kong Chu has described the 14K in Hong Kong as a loose network of independent gangs, each of them operating in its own territory with its own leader and a nucleus of fifteen to twenty members. Personal connections between gang members were much more important than institutional ones. On the retail level, local gangs in Hong Kong affiliated to the 14K offered protection to street dealers. On an international level affiliation to the 14K and knowledge of its rituals facilitated operating within the networks of the Chiu chow in other countries. However, the different chapters in the diaspora of the 14K were not necessarily connected to each other.[35]

British and Dutch police officials emphasized the ritual nature and structure of societies such as the 14K. On the one hand they acknowledged that the 14K in Hong Kong was not a society with a central leadership, but consisted of at least twenty-one factions; on the other hand they highlighted the hierarchical nature of these groups, with a 'godfather' (*cho kuen*) at their head and local district bosses (*tai ko kai*) beneath them.[36] The police accounts are rather confusing: R. Weijenburg, deputy chief of the drugs department of the CRI, claimed in 1997 that the 14K had 80,000 members worldwide, implying that they were all somehow involved in criminal activities.[37] Hong Kong police officials were sceptical about the global influence of the triads. One of them doubted whether the gangs in Hong Kong could control other gangs overseas since all of them were primarily driven by local dynamics.[38]

Nevertheless, Dutch and other national and international police forces in the 1970s–1980s were quite convinced of the 'Yellow Peril' of the secret societies. The British lawyer and author Fenton Bresler interviewed a number of policemen around the globe between 1978 and 1980; among his informers were Jan van Straten, chief of the Dutch CRI, and the Amsterdam police commissioner and chief of the Amsterdam drugs unit Gerard Toorenaar. While policemen in Hong Kong, Singapore, and Macao expressed their doubts whether one could really speak of an international conspiracy of the triads and discounted this as a narrow outlook, Bresler constructed on the basis of his interviews with their colleagues in the West an image of the triads' heroin trade as 'the greatest potential threat to law and order on the international front for the 1980s'.[39] According to him every Chinese person involved in the drug trade was a member of a triad.

There are conflicting accounts of when the 14K moved to the Netherlands. According to Dutch criminologists, who based their reports on police information, the 14K was already active in Amsterdam before the Second World War and ran two gambling houses and one brothel.[40] Another account mentions operations by the 14K in Amsterdam in 1951.[41] Chung Mon, aka Chen Hsien, aka Fo Kee Lun (the 'Unicorn'), the man held responsible by police and public media for the heroin epidemic and named the 'Godfather of Amsterdam', was reputed to have joined the 14K at the end of the 1960s. He personifies the continuities between Chinese smuggling in the interwar period and the 1970s. Chung was, according to DEA accounts, a Hakka Chinese, born in 1920 (or 1918) in Ba' On, the place of origin of the pre-war Bo On group. At the age of 18 he was forcibly recruited as a soldier for the nationalist army of the Kuomintang. Within a year Chung had deserted, fled to Hong Kong, and enrolled on a steamship to Rotterdam. He then stayed in the Netherlands, undoubtedly assisted by contacts in the Bo On group. He is found again in Amsterdam, where he is supposed to have worked as an informer for the Gestapo (the German secret police) during the German occupation. Chung Mon married a Dutch girl, became a father after the war, and lived with his family in an apartment on the second floor in a working-class neighbourhood in the north of Amsterdam – not exactly the place where one expects a godfather to live.

There is mention of Chung Mon staying some time in Düsseldorf in 1968, and this might be where the alliance between the remnants of the Bo On and the 14K was forged and where Chung Mon became a member of the latter society. Returning to Amsterdam, he directed a small business empire in the Amsterdam harbour district: a Cantonese restaurant, a gambling house, an import company, and a travel agency. He was the chairman of the chapter of the Chinese Overseas Association.[42] It is likely that he also provided protection services. Chung Mon had followed the footsteps of the leaders of the Bo On from the interwar period, and his conglomerate of companies, associations, and personal relations was perfectly suited to implement the shift from opium to heroin smuggling. He was an essential figure in both the international Chiu chow network and the Chinese community in Amsterdam, and he directed the ideal infrastructure for smuggling drugs into and through the Netherlands, and for stocking and hiding the drugs (in Chinese restaurants, for instance). Moreover, given his location in the Amsterdam harbour district, he could easily supply the retail trade with the new group of consumers that arrived in the 1970s. Last but not least, Chung Mon had, again as an inheritance from his interwar predecessors, contacts with the local police in a tradition of co-management of crime in the district.

The 14K and law enforcement: co-management of crime?

In 1976 the *Rijksrecherche*, the internal investigation unit of the Dutch police, started to investigate practices of corruption in the Amsterdam police force. In April the next year, eight police officers, working with the force in the notorious district bureau in Warmoesstraat (in the red-light area), in the immigration police, and in the CRI were arrested and charged with accepting presents such as brandy and cigars as well as money from Chung Mon. One chief inspector told a journalist that it was quite normal for an officer to accept a little 'money for luck' (25 or 50 guilders) in a Chinese gambling house. A former collaborator of Chung Mon told a journalist that he had delivered fruit baskets in which money was hidden to high-ranking police officers. Newspaper articles leaking details of the internal police investigation spoke of presents of up to 500 guilders, biweekly paydays in a Chinese gambling house, dinners, trips abroad, and visits to sex clubs all paid for by the Chinese. However, as a result of the investigation only five of the charged officers were fined, and all of them kept their positions.[43]

Gerard Toorenaar, the chief of the *Bijzondere Zaken* (Special Investigations) unit of the Amsterdam police responsible for dealing with serious crime including drug trafficking, walked a fine line in his dealings with Chung Mon. This led to accusations of corruption and his transferral from the unit to one of the city's precincts in 1979. Toorenaar claimed he was not aware of the involvement of Chung Mon himself in the drug trade, but that he used him as an informer. There were suspicions about the dealings between the commissioner and the Chinese 'restaurant owner' – for instance, when Chung Mon's expensive white Mercedes was seized carrying heroin, but returned by the commissioner to its owner. However, the rumours about and allegations against Toorenaar were never substantiated.[44]

Working together and possibly accepting presents from Chinese entrepreneurs in the inner city might be construed as a kind of corruption: in this view, acceptance of the Chinese practice of gifts (*guanxi*) puts the police officer in a position where he has to return the favour somehow.[45] These kinds of practice were not unlike the ones in

Rotterdam in the 1920s examined in Chapter 3. On the other hand these practices can be seen not as out-and-out corruption but as oiling the kind of co-management needed to exert some sort of control over the illegal drug trade. From this point of view, police officers merely continued the tradition of dealing with Chinese communities that had existed in Amsterdam since the First World War. However, the world had changed and there were new problems about the co-management of crime by police and the Chinese. The profitability and the size of the illegal heroin trade decisively shifted the configuration. No longer did the Chinese limit their trading to their compatriots, as was clear from 1972 onwards. Moreover, from 1975 their internal wars were fought in the streets and under the public gaze. For the first time since the early 1920s Chinese drug trafficking had become part of a major public order problem that could not be ignored by the city government and its police force.

The second and third Chinese wars

In a record heroin bust in 1973 four Chinese traffickers were arrested by the Amsterdam police: three were born in Hong Kong, one in Canton.[46] The Guangdong area (Canton, Hong Kong, Macao) had traditionally been the place where Chinese smugglers and migrants in the Netherlands had come from. After 1973 a shift occurred: in 1976 eleven smugglers were arrested, but almost all of them came from Malaysia.[47] This signified the arrival of competitive Chinese networks.

The 14K was, like its predecessors the Bo On and the Three Fingers, a 'power syndicate' not only facilitating the drug trade but providing other 'services' such as protection. This, rather than the drug trade, led to attacks on the position of the 14K from within the Chinese community. According to the police, Chung Mon started to increase his 'fees' for protection to the Chinese gambling houses in the city. Some of them looked for an alternative and made contact with another group from the Chiu chow diaspora, this time from Singapore: Ah Kong (literally 'The Company'). A hit man from Ah Kong went over to Amsterdam in 1975 to kill Chung Mon.[48]

An account by an Amsterdam journalist related the murder of Chung Mon to a conflict with yet another triad, the Wo Lee Kwan. Chung Mon reneged on a deal with the Wo allowing them to operate a gambling house of their own. The Wo had opened their casino anyway, following which Chung Mon cut off the supply of heroin to the Wo. On 3 March 1975 Chung Mon was shot and murdered in the harbour district on the steps of his amusement house and casino, almost exactly one of the spots where in the 1920s the first Chinese war had been fought. The murder of Chung Mon sparked the second Chinese war in Amsterdam, fought for control not only of the drug trade but of the geographical infrastructure of the Chinese community in the capital in which the drug trade was socially, culturally and historically embedded. In May ten members of the Wo attacked a 14K gambling house, but two of them were shot.[49] Both parties imported hitmen from the Far East to participate; according to the police there were five murders in 1975 and six in 1976.[50]

The international involvement of Far East Chinese in the war was facilitated by developments in international transit and the availability of air travel . It was also a signal that the Amsterdam trade was of international rather than local importance. Police officers in various countries claimed that at least one-third of the heroin smuggled into the Netherlands had as destination the USA, Canada, or Mexico. The 'Red Rod' or leader of the fighters of the 14K was said to have visited Suriname in an attempt to set up a transit point on the route from the Netherlands to the USA there among the local Chinese community. West German authorities claimed that most of the heroin in their country was brought in through the Netherlands.[51]

According to the DEA, Ah Kong was 'a modern adapted form of the Triad Society', with local chapters in Singapore and Malaysia, and later in European cities: Amsterdam, Hamburg, Copenhagen. The Ah Kong gangs were organized like the triads, with chiefs, treasurers, counsellors, martial arts experts and five or so fighters, and ten to thirty ordinary members. Unlike more traditional triads they did not have any secret initiation rituals. Migrant sailors and two refugees from a gang war in Singapore in 1969 brought the social and cultural capital of Ah Kong with them to Europe. As other societies, Ah Kong was a power syndicate, offering protection, involved in loan-sharking but also in legal businesses such as restaurants, night clubs, and the distribution of martial arts movies from Hong Kong.[52] They therefore fitted in a continuous tradition of Chinese societies from southern China and Southeast Asia coming to the West.

In 1975–1976 Ah Kong, according to the police, was victorious in its power struggle with the 14K, at least in Amsterdam; there were still reports on 14K activities in Rotterdam and The Hague later in the decade. Some of the defeated Chinese fled abroad. Control of the heroin trade was part of the spoils. Amsterdam became the centre of Ah Kong's import and transit trade in Europe. Heroin was bought through middlemen in Bangkok from the Chinese producers in the interior. Couriers, often recruited and poor Asians in need of income, smuggled the drugs on planes to Europe, while their Ah Kong controllers kept an eye on them, travelling on the same planes. For security reasons the heroin was not flown directly to Amsterdam, but brought to the Netherlands using stopovers in Scandinavian countries, for instance. Ah Kong chapters in Hamburg and Copenhagen were important in the network and transit relations with Amsterdam. Members of Ah Kong were only interested in smuggling and wholesale and left the retail trade in the streets to Dutch and Surinamese dealers.[53]

The position of Ah Kong turned out to be as fragile as that of the 14K, another sign of the fluidity of the Chinese networks but also of their relative powerlessness. Intensified persecution by international police forces combined with internal conflicts to undermine the central Chinese position in the heroin trade. The period of the second Chinese war also witnessed record numbers of arrested and extradited Chinese. The number of illegal Chinese in the Netherlands had grown. According to Toorenaar, the Chinese population in Amsterdam grew from 1,500 (500 families) in 1970 to 7,000 in 1976, of whom 5,000 had no passport.[54] In 1970 Toorenaar's unit had arrested eight Chinese people. In 1975 the figure rose to 122 and in 1976 to 225. Hereafter the figure went down again, to fifteen in 1981. For a short period this strategy succeeded in disrupting, at least to some extent, the flow of heroin. Wholesale prices went up to 1,000 guilders per kilogram.[55] However, Turkish, Kurdish, and Pakistani smugglers quickly arranged for new sources of supply (see below).

The success of the Chinese heroin trade at the same time heralded its demise, since the transit lines with the Far East were relatively extended and smuggling by air was easier to detect than smuggling in maritime traffic. Moreover, the leader of Ah Kong in Copenhagen estranged his collaborators through his gambling addiction, which led to incidents of violence. The Ah Kong leader in the Netherlands was caught and received a sentence of four years in prison. The Dutch police also arrested members of the 14K in various cities. By the end of the 1970s the supreme position of the Chinese in the heroin trade was over: the fragility of the networks and the transport connections were such that they lost the competition to Turkish and Pakistani heroin traders.

This did not mean that their activities were at an end. On the contrary: Chinese criminal anarchy continued to operate and took new forms. In 1984 a new society had become active in the Netherlands: the Dai Huen Jai (the 'Big Circle Boys'). This was not a traditional society; it was fairly new, formed by former Red Guardists and Red Army commandos who after the end of the Cultural Revolution in the People's Republic had fled to Hong Kong. It did not have any central command. According to the Dutch police, 'cells' of the Dai Huen Jai started to operate as a power syndicate in the Netherlands. They had a similar fluid organization to those of the more traditional societies, consisting of a leader with two close collaborators and six to ten followers with specialized activities. The Dai Huen Jai were involved in extortion, protection, credit card fraud, money laundering, and heroin smuggling. They were also involved in human smuggling (by the 1990s there were 20,000 illegal Chinese migrants in the Netherlands) and cross-border armed robberies.[56]

By 1987 the CRI believed that the Dai Huen Jai had gained a dominant position within the heroin trade in the Netherlands, but that the other Chinese groups were not prepared to accept a subservient role and that a violent confrontation was to be expected.[57] The 14K was still active and prepared to defend its position against both Chinese and Turkish syndicates. War broke out between the Dai Huen Jai and other Chinese societies such as Ah Kong: the 'third Chinese war'. In 1990 the police found two dead Chinese men in a creek, killed because they could not deliver to their clients since their heroin had been seized by the police. In 1991 the body count of the war was four, in 1992 there were three murders of Chinese, in 1993 six, and in 1994 one Chinese and one Cambodian were assassinated.[58] Just as the first two Chinese wars, the third was not purely about the heroin trade, but also about control of loan-sharking and gambling houses. Nevertheless, despite the war, the Chinese heroin trade continued to occupy its own niche in the national and international drug markets, even when its importance was now overshadowed by the Turkish and Kurdish heroin trade: while in 1992 6 per cent of all heroin in the Netherlands still came from Southeast Asia, by then the import and transit of heroin was mainly in the hands of Turkish and Kurdish groups.[59]

New sources of supply

For a short time the second Chinese war had endangered the supply of heroin to the Netherlands. However, an alternative source of supply and alternative suppliers was quickly found among Turkish, Kurdish, and Pakistani smugglers.[60]

Pakistani smugglers had already been active in the Netherlands since at least the end of the 1960s when they started to supply illegal cannabis. In the 1970s Pakistani smugglers started to supply Western European markets with Afghan opium refined to heroin in the tribal areas and brought to the smugglers in Karachi and Islamabad. Pakistani wholesale dealers flew from the Netherlands to these cities to place their orders. To deliver the heroin Pakistani smugglers had several options. The first was to smuggle small supplies of 4 to 5 kilograms to cities such as Brussels and Copenhagen, and then bring the drugs by public transport to their customer – for example in the Bijlmer district in Amsterdam – who would sell to the retail dealers. Since many Nigerians lived in Pakistan (both Pakistan and Nigeria had been part of the British Commonwealth) use was often made of them as couriers. Other methods were by ship, or by post.[61] The importers were individuals or small groups of two to four people: enterprise syndicates rather than power syndicates, more reminiscent of the Greek smugglers of the interwar period than of the Chinese triads or later of the Turkish crime families.[62] Through family and tribe they were related to the middlemen in Pakistan. The smugglers in the Netherlands had constantly to devise new methods and were also not assured of a stable demand.[63] Violence and liquidations did not take place or did not come to the attention of the police, unlike the case of the Chinese and the Turks.[64]

The Pakistani attempt to move into the heroin market was trumped by Turkish and Kurdish groups, who were much more deeply embedded in Dutch society.[65] The geographic position of Turkey between the supply markets of Asia and the demand market in Europe, facilitating transport by road, explains how Turkish and Kurdish smugglers were able to triumph over the competition of Pakistani smugglers after the setbacks to the Chinese networks in the second half of the 1970s, although Pakistani and Chinese heroin kept a niche on the market. In the 1990s there was still Pakistani heroin seized, but in very varying quantities: 193 kilograms in 1990, only 38 kilograms in 1991.[66]

By 1979 large amounts of Turkish heroin were supplied to the Dutch market, of a substantially better quality and purity than Chinese heroin. This led on the one hand to an increase in the number of deaths due to overdose, especially among drug tourists not used to such purity. On the other hand, retail prices went down from 1,000 to 250–300 guilders per gram: a substantial decrease, though the price was still three times the price of the early 1970s.[67] In the 1980s and 1990s Turkish heroin continued to dominate the market. According to the CRI, in 1993 85 per cent of all heroin seized in the Netherlands came from Turkey.[68] By the early 1990s annually on average 500 kilograms were seized, suggesting a total import of 5 tonnes each year. Since the Dutch share in the total volume of trade was disproportionate to the number of addicts in the country, this meant the existence of a thriving transit trade.[69] Smugglers paid at that time around 7,500 US dollars, or 14,000 Dutch guilders, for a kilogram in Turkey.[70] Profits were sizeable, even where wholesale prices for middlemen in demand countries had gone down from 21,060 US dollars in 1983 to 16,695 dollars in 1993.[71]

The heroin Silk Road

Starting point for the heroin production for Pakistani, Turkish, and Kurdish smugglers was opium from Afghanistan. Since the 1960s production of both cannabis and opium had significantly increased there, as seen in the previous chapter. The increase in opium production was stimulated by a number of factors. While demand for heroin in the West increased, production in other countries situated on the traditional trade routes from Asia to Europe was under attack. American pressure and diplomacy led to an official halt to opium production in Turkey in 1971 (which started again but only for the medical market under strict government control in 1974). In Iran after the Islamic revolution of 1979 and in US ally Pakistan opium production was under attack by the governments as well. In Afghanistan the political situation remained more conducive to opium production. After the Soviet invasion large tribal areas were controlled by insurgent mujahideen, for whom the drug trade was an important financial and economic resource. Opium became a significant source of income for farmers: in the early 1990s they could make around 430 US dollars on an annual production of 7 kilograms, ten times as much as could be made with other, legal, crops.[72]

The harvesting of opium spread throughout different Afghan provinces and the crop was smuggled over the border into the mountain areas and autonomous tribal zones of Pakistan.[73] After the withdrawal of the Soviet forces in 1989, opium production in Afghanistan multiplied: from 1,200 tonnes in 1989 to between 2,500 and 3,000 tonnes annually in the 1990s, with extreme peaks in 1994 (3,544 tonnes) and 1999 (4,574 tonnes). With a conversion rate of opium into heroin and morphine of 1:10, it meant a potential annual production of 250 to 300 tonnes of heroin available for the world market.[74] Afghanistan's share of world opium production rose from 19 per cent in the 1980s to 52 per cent in 1995 and 79 per cent in 1999. By 2002 according to the calculations of the UNODC, the value of Afghanistan's opium export corresponded to roughly half of the country's GDP.[75] The Taliban who took over the country between 1994 and 1999 did not impede opium trade in any way although they were not so heavily involved in it as the mujahideen had been. In 2000 they promulgated an opium ban, for reasons that are still debated but possibly to further their political legitimacy. However, the ban was hardly enforced.[76] By the time of the opium ban around 15,000 Afghan traffickers were involved in the opium trade: smugglers of opium out of the country; small seasonal traders in the countryside; shop owners in the cities who traded quite openly in opium as a sideline to other economic activities; and a small group of large-scale traffickers with considerably higher profits.[77]

Chain networks linked farmers in Afghanistan to consumers in Western Europe, involving Afghan tribes and Turkish and Kurdish smugglers. Historically Turkey was a key transport hub linking Europe and Asia on the so-called Silk Road. The Silk Road still functioned in the heroin trade: opium was grown in Afghanistan and turned into morphine base; the morphine base was transported to Turkey and refined into heroin in small laboratories or 'kitchens' close to the Turkish–Iranian border (in traditional smuggling areas such as the Kurdish town of Lice) or in Istanbul. The European chemical industry itself was also involved, since it delivered the main precursor chemical for the refinement of heroin, acetic anhydride, to the producers, even after the introduction of a permit system. 'In 1996 a Dutch van driver was arrested at the border with Turkey with an entire lorry full of acetic anhydride without the necessary permits.'[78]

The expansion of the trans-European motorways since the 1970s considerably eased traffic by road – including illegal traffic. By the end of the twentieth century more than 1.5 million trucks, a quarter of a million coaches, and 4 million cars crossed the Turkish border each year transporting industrial and agricultural products, in addition to the flow of migrants going to Europe and returning to visit their families.[79] It was (and is) impossible for police and customs to control traffic on this route completely. Criminologists touring the motorways going from Turkey through Bulgaria, Romania, and Hungary into Western Europe in 2000 wrote:

> As an outsider, you see very little of all the illegal activity along the route [...] simple restaurants line the roads. Young ladies come from the villages in the area to offer the drivers sexual favours for payment. We struck up conversations with restaurant owners and Turkish travellers (without residence permits) everywhere, in an attempt to gain some information. Participant observation in this way generates nothing, however.[80]

The Turkish route had one great advantage over the Chinese route: in trucks cargoes of dozens of kilograms could be transported, rather than the around 10-kilogram maximum that could be flown in as passenger luggage on an plane. This gave the Turkish smugglers the advantage of economies of scale, while smaller cargoes could be transported by couriers in smaller automobiles.[81] The drugs were hidden anywhere in the cars: in the fuel tanks, in spare wheels, in the chassis, in the bulkhead, between the load or in the luggage of the driver, in tubes of luggage racks on top of vans, or in hollowed rear axles – sometimes without the knowledge of the driver. If the police focused searches on Turkish drivers from certain areas, the smugglers would start to use Western European drivers. Just as the Chinese sent controllers on the planes with the actual smugglers, the Turks sent controllers in cars behind the trucks with the cargoes. This did not mean that the Turkish smugglers limited themselves to transport by motorway. Part of the routes were also crossed by sea: for instance, from Istanbul to the Romanian port of Constanza. Sometimes couriers with small cargoes went by plane, and international trains were also used.[82] In short, the methods were so diffuse and the possibilities so extensive that no matter the size of the seizures, police and customs could not control heroin smuggling from Turkey. The aforementioned criminologists wrote:

> The bag of tricks is big. With a substantial transport the organisation [of smugglers] can decide to sacrifice a small quantity of drugs in order to distract the attention from the real shipment crossing the border at the same moment. Drivers can work together by driving one behind another and letting the one behind know if checks are being carried out. If that does happen, the one following can feign a breakdown and wait with his bonnet open until the coast is clear.[83]

An essential element that enabled the smooth working of operations was bribery:

> 'Actually, it doesn't work without bribery', one of the larger Dutch drug barons told us. More than ten years previously, he had worked as a driver in Turkey. He always took several tens of thousands of German marks with him for on the way and, if a customs officer didn't trust him, he took out his wallet. Fortunately for him, that always worked, although he always had to wait and see whether the bribe would be accepted.[84]

The drugs were transported to all countries with a large Turkish community, such as Germany and Italy. Heroin that was smuggled into the Netherlands for an important part went out again, to the UK, Belgium, France, and Spain.[85]

Of primary importance in the Turkish smuggling operations by road was the connection between underworld and upperworld. Without the involvement of Dutch transport companies the Turkish heroin trade would have been far less successful. These connections were once again flexible and heterogeneous, as becomes evident from a number of case studies undertaken by the Dutch police in the 1990s. In one case the smugglers' method was highly structured; it was an operation by four Kurdish brothers who sent morphine base by a Turkish transport company to a heroin laboratory in Macedonia. A Macedonian transport company delivered the heroin to Kurdish contacts in the Netherlands. In most cases there was great use of Dutch transport companies, which reduced the chance of detection by customs and police. The key role in providing the connections was in these cases not so much performed by the 'leaders' of the organizations involved; most essential were the facilitators or 'intermediaries' who arranged for the trucks or cars in which the heroin was transported, the cargoes in which it was hidden, and the personnel who undertook the transport (the chauffeurs, the suppliers of the vehicles and other material, and the controllers who followed the transports). In one case telephone taps by the police divulged that the facilitator here was more or less an independent contractor. He was 'not very respectful' to the 'leader' of the organization transporting the drugs to the Netherlands. This leader himself was not truly representative of the traditional Turkish crime family leader, as he was married to a Dutch woman and was quite integrated in Dutch culture, according to the police report. His right hand was also Dutch. The facilitator arranged the transport from a stash in Romania to the Netherlands and from there transit on to the UK, where he ran a distribution scheme. The execution of the transport was undertaken by two small Dutch firms: one of them was specialized in refrigerated transport. One of the trucks from the latter company was found in Portugal with a cargo of 1,500 kilograms of hashish, suggesting that the company was used by more drug smuggling rings. Part of the heroin in this case was supplied to a Dutch criminal entrepreneur in the southern province of North Brabant who in his turn distributed and exported the drugs on his own account. The case shows a very diverse and opportunistic way of operation where Turkish and Dutch entrepreneurs easily found each other.

Not all entrepreneurs operated quite so professionally. In a second case investigated by the police an owner of a transport company that normally transported household goods from Romania agreed with a facilitator to pick up heroin in Romania. The owner was then clumsily caught at Dutch customs because he was too careless to do the paperwork properly to avoid alerting the officers.

In both these cases legal transport companies worked opportunistically for facilitators. More rare was a case where a legitimate transport company (with over a hundred drivers) was used without knowing that heroin was hidden in its cargoes.[86]

Turkish and Kurdish smugglers

Who were the smugglers? It took the Dutch police some time to catch up with the activities of Turkish heroin traffickers in the

Netherlands. Focused investigations of Turkish organized crime did not start before 1985. Until 1987 no official cooperation of the Dutch police with Turkish authorities was possible because in Turkey drug dealers and smugglers could be sentenced to death, and this meant that the Dutch police were not supposed to exchange information with their Turkish colleagues. Turkey abolished this penalty only in 1990, but nevertheless already in 1987 a Dutch liaison officer was stationed in Turkey. In that year the Dutch national drugs unit had been resurrected under the name *Landelijke Verdovende Middelenteam* (National Narcotics Team), a branch of the CRI. From then onwards Turkish heroin trafficking was a primary target of the Dutch police, leading to a new record seizure of 99 kilograms of heroin in 1988. In the early 1990s as many as twenty special police taskforces investigated Turkish crime. In 1991 the CRI estimated that there were thirty-six Turkish criminal groups active in the Netherlands, making up 6 per cent of all so-called 'organized crime groups'. These groups were in competition, stealing each other's heroin and fighting each other. In 1992 nine Turks were murdered within a four-week period.[87]

The investigations of the CRI showed that the pioneer of Turkish organized crime in the Netherlands was what was called the 'Oflu syndicate'. Members of this syndicate originated from Of, a small town on the Black Sea coast in the northeast of Turkey. According to the analysis of the police and their graphic representations of relations within the Of syndicate, this was primarily an extended family organized in what the police called 'cells'.[88] In fact, it was a group centred around Ismail Hacisüleymanoğlu, a man from Of and therefore known as Oflu Ismail. He was a son-in-law of one of the most important gangster bosses in Istanbul and well connected to the Bulgarian authorities (he was also involved in tobacco smuggling from Bulgaria to Turkey). With support of the Bulgarian government, who offered the assistance of Bulgarian banks in money laundering in the hope of gaining foreign currency, Oflu Ismail attempted to delineate spheres of influence between different Turkish smugglers in the early 1980s, claiming the Netherlands (where he had been active as early as 1977) for himself.[89] By the later 1990s observers thought that there were around twelve to fifteen of these families, or 'clans', but not too much should be made of this number since families could endlessly be sub-divided in 'cells', and personal, ethnic, and familial contacts do not necessarily point to any high density of organization.[90]

In extended families such as that of Oflu Ismail smuggling and criminal behaviour were passed down from one generation to the next; the close relationships within the families were essential prerequisites for crime to function.[91] Included in the transmission process was acquiring a skill essential to successful smugglers: *köylu kurnazligi*, craftiness, a mindset that enabled flexible responses to changes in police strategies and the development of new opportunities within systems of control.[92] The Turkish criminals had, just as the Chinese and other criminal groups such as the Japanese yakuza and the Italian Mafia, Camorra, and 'Ndrangheta, their own Robin Hood kind of mythology of 'men of honour' (in Turkish *kabadayi* – literally 'crude uncle'). These were criminals with their own code of conduct who defended the poor and fought authority. Although the Turkish men of honour and their mountainous rebel bandit cousins the *efe* now belong to the realms of mythology, 'smugglers of drugs, especially heroin [...] try to convey the ethos of the traditional *kabadayi*'.[93]

Central in the criminal family networks were the *babas*, the fathers; a name that came into vogue after the release of the movie *The Godfather* that created a new self-image for gangsters worldwide.[94] One should perhaps not make too much of these self-images. Family and ethnic ties remained important, providing connections, closure, and more security for criminal groups. The traditional baba, however, changed. By the end of the century, according to criminologist Mark Galeotti, 'the typical new gang leader [had become] younger, less interested in traditional status within a clan and more of an entrepreneur interested in profit and the trappings of success but much less about traditions, ancient feuds, ethnic identity and custom.'[95] In other ways, they more closely resembled the Dutch criminal entrepreneurs that they allied with. But this cultural shift did not change the basic structure of the Turkish criminal networks.

The babas could straddle the lines between upper- and underworld, making money in the latter, being benefactors and increasing their social status in the former. For instance, drug smuggler Halil Havar, who was caught in the Netherlands and was the first to escape from a Dutch prison by helicopter (in 1991), was according to criminologists Frank Bovenkerk and Yücel Yesilgöz chairman of the Turkish football club Gaziantepspor.[96]

The extended families could be quite large. On the basis of telephone taps the Dutch police reconstructed one network of heroin smugglers consisting of three families in the east of Turkey. One of them, which financed operations and supplied the heroin from Pakistan, had sixty or seventy members. The second family, which took care of transport to Europe, consisted of only a father with his two sons, while a third family more or less supervised the activities in Europe. A legal transport company in the Netherlands from which transit of heroin to the UK took place was part of the network, as was a group of nine Turkish and Dutch criminals who transported the drugs (not always successfully) to the UK, and supplied part of it to a group of five Turkish and Pakistani smugglers to France. Although it was clear who were the babas of the families, it was not always obvious who performed the specialized activities: in one case a baba had to accompany transport and chauffeur to the Netherlands and was arrested. Other networks did not show much planned organization either: there were many members doing things more or less as they came along. Although the organization model of these networks was fluid and horizontal, the position of the heads of the families in the local context was decisive. These heads had the resources to impose discipline and sanctions. For instance, one female head of a Turkish family in Germany, who cooperated in the transit trade with a family in the Netherlands, did not hesitate to have the girlfriend of a customer who was behind payment locked up until her friend had paid his debts.[97]

As with the Chinese, the police complained that it was hard to fight against these extended family networks. Officers compared them to octopuses: it did not matter how many arms one chopped off, they would always grow back again. Following the Of group, the police identified dozens of other 'syndicates', organized along the same lines and with members of their families migrated to Western Europe. These networks came not only from Of but also from other places with traditions in the smuggling or the opium trade, such as Izmir on the west coast, across the Aegean Sea from Greece and an important source of opium for the Greek smuggling networks of the interwar period.[98] At the end of the century most arrested smugglers came from traditional smuggling areas in the southeast of Turkey: the province of Diyarbakir and especially the district of Lice; the areas of Van and Gaziantep and particularly the small town of Kilis near the Syrian border; the province of Hakkari and the city of Yüksekova on the Iranian border; and Palu and Tunceli in the province of Elazig. Here, after the end of the Ottoman Empire, tobacco and alcohol were routinely smuggled across borders.[99] Kurdish tribes such as the Harki and the Pizhdar seasonally crossed over the border with their sheep, at the same time smuggling salt from Iran to Iraq and bringing wheat from Iraq back to Turkey. The frontiers were permeable.[100] These smuggling cultures were not unlike those in the southeast of the Netherlands. Smugglers were connected with Kurdish family members and others in Western Europe, one example being the migrants that in the 1960s had moved to the city of Arnhem, close to the Dutch–German border, to work in the chemical and other industries. Arnhem became an important transit point for the drug trade. According to criminologists Gerben Bruinsma and Henk van de Bunt, the heroin trade was set up there in the early 1980s by an unemployed textile labourer. His two sons extended the business and, with four other Kurdish families, the family became pivotal in the heroin trade in the region.[101]

Kurdish drug smuggler Hüseyin Baybasin, who was presented by criminologists Bovenkerk and Yesilgöz in their book on Turkish organized crime as a typical example of a Turkish smuggler and was interviewed by them in 1996 in a Dutch prison, came from Lice and was born there in 1956. According to his own testimonies his landowning family became rich by trading in crude Turkish opium. Baybasin's grandfather and uncle were the *aga* or leaders of their extended family, of which many members had a criminal record. They were also connected to the upperworld of their town:

> Baybasin always strives to make plain that the underworld would never survive without the government [...] He talks of his uncle as one of the people who 'were supported'. Gentlemen such as he constituted a governmental link with the state, which was represented in the village by the police and lower-ranking army officers. The symbiosis with the state was also reflected in the many connections his uncle had with senior state officials.[102]

This did not prevent the family becoming embroiled in gunfights with the local gendarmerie, probably over smuggling issues. As a youngster Baybasin was already involved in small-scale smuggling over the Syrian border. When he came of age he went to Istanbul, became involved in criminal gangs in the capital, and then went back to Lice where he agreed to work as an agent provocateur for the police. Another uncle of his was already smuggling drugs, and Baybasin now joined the group of Mahmut 'the Anarchist', smuggling heroin in coaches and fishing boats to Greece and the rest of Europe. Baybasin claimed that the Turkish army, navy, and plane companies were involved in arranging transport for the heroin trade, and in bringing tonnes of water and chemicals needed for heroin production to the clandestine laboratories.[103]

In 1979 or 1980 Mahmut the Anarchist started to smuggle small amounts of heroin into Arnhem. The Arnhem area would grow into a major heroin trafficking hub, especially between 1986 and 1994.[104] Networks like those of Mahmut imported opium from Iran, Lebanon, Pakistan, or Afghanistan, refined it into heroin in small laboratories in Istanbul or the east of Turkey, and smuggled it into Western Europe. But, just as for the Chinese societies, the drug trade was for them only one of a range of illegal activities that also included the weapons trade and money laundering.[105] The Baybasin clan consisted of around forty people centred around Hüseyin and his three brothers. The clan was designated one of the most important criminal Turkish clans and dominant within the narcotics trade.[106] Hüseyin was convicted in 2002 in the Netherlands for murder, kidnapping, and illegal drug trading. He claimed that he actually worked for the Turkish government. In fairness to Baybasin, we must refer here to the work of Dutch philosopher Ton Derksen, who deconstructed the evidence against Baybasin, which was primarily based on telephone taps, and concluded that Baybasin was innocent.[107] Hüseyin's brothers Abdullah and Siri were arrested in London and Abdullah was convicted in 2006 and sentenced to twenty-two years in prison; however, in 2019 he was found on appeal not guilty.[108]

Turkish criminal anarchy manifested in chain networks that were independent of each other. In their totality they resembled what one criminological analysis characterized as a 'heroin bazaar'.[109] The groups in these networks cooperated with each other as much as they fought each other. A particular spectacular gang war in Rotterdam in 1991 and 1992 between a Kurdish family from Lice and their nephew, also from Lice, led to a body count of eleven.[110] There was little continuity in these groups: lists of crime bosses in the early 1970s show no overlap with those of the 1980s. The position of the babas was fluid and temporary, based on status as much as on social or cultural capital. Directing and negotiating operations from their Turkish and Kurdish coffee houses, they were not so much 'running' a crime group as taking the responsibility for its functioning.[111] The fluidity of Turkish criminal anarchy led by 1995 to a *Turken-moeheid* (Turks fatigue) among the specialists and investigators of the Dutch police: one could put groups or individuals behind bars after years of investigation, but new ones would immediately appear to take their place.[112]

Political connections

Smugglers, both Turkish and Kurdish, were thought to have connections with militant and terrorist organizations such as the extreme right Grey Wolves connected to the Turkish state, the Marxist Leninist Devsol, or the *Partiya Karkerên Kurdistan* (PKK – Kurdish Labour Party), and with Turkish government officials and state personnel. There has been much rumour and speculation about these ties: profits from the drug trade were used to finance political operations, but much of these reports were based on newspaper articles and informants, and not proven in court.[113] If we look at the drug trade as networks of different families and groups, one should see these cross-overs as more on a personal than on an organizational level. Individual criminal entrepreneurs were involved in political action or violence, for example Oflu Ismail, who subsidized the political party allied to the Grey Wolves.[114]

Apart from corruption, political powers might look the other way when the illegal drug trade could have profitable side effects for themselves. For instance, it was thought by the Turkish police that much profit from the drug trade went to finance the PKK's armed struggle for independence. This group was founded in 1978 in Diyarbakir and in 1984 started a guerrilla warfare against the Turkish government from the Lebanese Bekaa Valley, where civil war raged.[115] According to journalists, by the later 1990s the PKK was supposed to earn 300 million US dollars annually by charging criminal groups for using opium fields in PKK-controlled territories and for using these territories as safe transit hub. At the same time the Turkish government supported 'village guards' that were using the same methods. The PKK was also thought to extort Kurdish legal and illegal entrepreneurs.[116] The PKK in the Netherlands was said to intimidate Kurdish entrepreneurs to give financial contributions to their movement.

The Turkish government itself assisted the illegal drug trade by not only turning a blind eye to money laundering, but actually stimulating it. Since labour migration to Western Europe had started in the 1960s, money had flowed to the poorer parts of Turkey where the migrants came from and invested in housing, shops, hotels, and amusement parks. Drug money went the same route, and the Turkish government was unwilling to stop it. But drug money also financed the activities of the PKK. In 1995 the Turkish parliament therefore passed a law against laundering criminal money – too late to stop the illegal heroin trade in its infancy.[117]

Embeddedness in Dutch society

Unlike the Pakistani smugglers, the Turkish and Kurdish smugglers were as embedded in society in the Netherlands as the Chinese. Turkish labour migrants had come to the Netherlands since 1960, establishing a sizeable presence: between 1964 and 1974 (when an economic crisis ended recruitment) 65,000 migrants had moved to the country. In 1994 200,000 Turks lived legally in the Netherlands; one-third of them were born in the country.[118] The number of Kurds living in the Netherlands with a legal permit was 5,000 in 1995.[119] In the city of Amsterdam the Turkish community made up more than 4 per cent of the total population and was the fourth largest ethnic community, after the native Dutch, the Surinamese, and the Moroccans.[120] Like the Chinese, Turkish migrants in the Netherlands lived together and organized themselves according to regional background.

Turkish coffee houses, bars, and restaurants were the meeting places where the drug trade was socially embedded. Turkish transport enterprises, import/export companies, sewing shops, and catering businesses were used as covers for money laundering. The retail drug trade was left to dealers of other ethnic backgrounds, mostly Moroccans. In 1993 Amsterdam police raided five coffee shops and one restaurant in a district where many Turkish migrants lived, in the west of the city. Four 'organizations' with import and export companies were caught, 235 people were arrested (of whom 116 were prosecuted), and the year's largest single seizure of heroin took place in a town in the south of the country: 302 kilograms brought by truck from Turkey through Greece and Italy. The gangs did not only deal in heroin: around 9,500 kilograms of hashish was found as well, and forty-six guns.[121]

The social basis of people involved in the heroin trade (including the couriers, stash keepers, and money runners, but also the collaborators from legal enterprises, the money collectors, and even those who earned money by robbing the drug traffickers) was considerably extended by the economic crisis of the 1980s. The crisis led to high rates of unemployment and loss of social status among Turkish labour migrants: in 1994 31 per cent of Turkish labourers were unemployed, compared to 7 per cent of the native Dutch.[122] However, a study of the Spijker district in Arnhem, a hotbed of the illegal heroin trade, concluded that it was not necessarily the 'underprivileged' (migrants with unemployment benefit or illegal migrants) who were involved, but increasingly 'well-educated' people were making an income on the side in the drug trade. Most of them did not become wealthy, but some of the organizers did. The illegal heroin trade, according to these studies, was deeply embedded within the Turkish and Kurdish communities.[123] A Turkish university student claimed in an interview that: 'family from the village we came from started a couple of years ago [with heroin trafficking]. They think it's normal; they are not even ashamed of it.'[124]

In a controversial conclusion to their research into Turkish organized crime in the Netherlands – undertaken in close collaboration with Dutch police forces – Bovenkerk and Yesilgöz claimed:

> Drug trafficking was so integrated into the daily life of Turkish men in the neighbourhoods that traffickers and those who were not involved simply sat next to and in the midst of one another. When a heroin shipment was expected, or when people decided to invest in an upcoming shipment, the hat was passed round fairly openly and everyone put in his few hundred or thousand. Import and export companies could serve as a place for unloading the drug shipments and loading money transports and the company itself could serve for laundering money [...] Garages in both neighbourhoods [i.e., two streets in the Mercator district in the west of Amsterdam, a traditional working-class-district where 10 per cent of the population was Turkish, and another 10 per cent Moroccan] are used for preparing hiding places for drugs in cars and for deploying cars brought in for repair for drug transports [...] Some Turkish travel agencies organize trips for the dealers and couriers.[125]

Bovenkerk testified in September 1995 to the parliamentary commission investigating the involvement of the Dutch police in the drug trade. He claimed that thousands of Turks and Kurds in Amsterdam, about 20 to 40 per cent of their total population there (*enkele tientallen procenten*) was involved in the drug trade, but, confronted with public outrage at this estimate, he had to tone the percentage down.[126]

Different research methods – quantitative analyses based on seizures, police investigations using telephone taps and observations, or ethnographic methods – could and can only give us indications, not certainties. Another Dutch criminologist, Richard Staring, criticized the research of Bovenkerk and Yesilgöz (who had based their study on police investigations and ethnographic studies, and had used newspaper articles for their analysis of Turkish and Kurdish organized crime) on methodological grounds and doubted the validity of their conclusions. Staring himself – as well as other researchers – had found no indications in their fieldwork that the illegal drug trade had a central place in Turkish communities in the Netherlands.[127]

Conclusion

The Chinese Chiu chow networks spanning the globe from the Far East to Western Europe were ideally suited to reconstitute the global heroin market in the 1970s. Law enforcement proved incapable of containing, let alone controlling, the expansion of this market. Similar factors were at play as in the cannabis markets investigated in Chapter 4. Most importantly a new public demand for heroin turned to the illegal market to satisfy its needs. The Chinese networks could flexibly connect supply and demand based on their social embeddedness in Chinese communities in Dutch society, and building on the networks that had come into existence since the First World War. From the perspectives of geography and logistical infrastructure the Netherlands was an ideal transit hub for the heroin trade. While the favourite mode of transport shifted from steamships to planes, organization and methods of smuggling remained traditional, with Chinese supervisors overseeing couriers of various national and ethnic backgrounds.

The flexibility and global networks of Chinese heroin smuggling did not lead to monopolization of the market. While power syndicates such as the 14K, which was connected to Hong Kong, dominated the market in the first half of the 1970s, criminal anarchy resulted in increasing competition and gang wars with newcomers such as Ah

Kong, connected to Singapore, and the Dai Huen Jai. The Chinese societies were as unable to control the heroin market as the Dutch state. Another weakness of the Chinese trade was the extended supply lines by air, which meant that only relatively small amounts of drugs could be smuggled at any one time.

In the 1980s dominance (but not control) of the market was taken over by Turkish and Kurdish groups. They connected opium production in Afghanistan with demand for heroin in Western Europe, using the time-honoured transport system by road through Asia and the trans-European motorway system that had been developing since the 1970s. Like the Chinese, these groups were embedded in migrant communities in the Netherlands. The economic crisis of the 1970s–1980s made participation in activities connected to smuggling within these communities more attractive. As with Chinese heroin smuggling, Turkish and Kurdish smuggling developed out of longer criminal traditions, embodied in crime families – with a baba at the centre – in which criminal behaviour and smuggling skills were transmitted from one generation to the next. These were not centralized organizations; the networks and groups involved were as temporary, fluid, and opportunistic as those of other criminal groups in the drug markets. They were involved in a constant shifting of alliances and conflicts with each other and with Dutch entrepreneurs. Their successful functioning furthermore depended on making alliances in an 'upper-world' of transport companies and corrupt customs officials facilitating the transport through Europe.

Chinese and Turkish/Kurdish smuggling was organized in extensive international networks of facilitators, experts, and specialists, held together by personal ties, rituals, and shared language and culture, but also by personal authority and charisma and when necessary (the threat of) violence. Embedded in migrant communities, situated on historically important transport routes and with connections to the upperworld, these fragmented but powerful manifestations of criminal anarchy defied the control of the state.

Notes

1 Nederlandsche Centrale tot bestrijding van den smokkelhandel in verdoovende middelen (hereafter Nederlandsche Centrale), annual report 1951, in Ministry of Foreign Affairs Code Archive 1945–1954,

National Archive, The Hague, inv. no. 205.117 (hereafter NA/FAII), 26306.
2   Annual reports, Nederlandsche Centrale, NA/FAII, 26307; archive of the Ministry of Foreign Affairs 1955–1964, National Archive, The Hague, inv. no. 2.05.118 (hereafter NA/FAIII) 260378.
3   Delpher digitized newspaper archive (ww.delpher.nl/nl/kranten, hereafter D): 'Partij opium in beslag genomen', *De Volkskrant* 19 September 1967; 'Echtpaar voor handel in opium gearresteerd', *Algemeen Handelsblad* 19 September 1967.
4   Report 'Onderafdeling Opsporingsbijstand namens het Hoofd Afdeling Criminele Zaken van het Ministerie van Justitie' to United Nations 1968, NA/FAIII, 25354.
5   Report 'Onderafdeling Opsporingsbijstand namens het Hoofd Afdeling Criminele Zaken van het Ministerie van Justitie' to United Nations 1971, NA/FAIII, 25354.
6   G. Benton and H. Vermeulen (eds), *De Chinezen* (Muiderberg: Dick Coutinho, 1987).
7   Narcotics Department, annual report 1971, in archive of Municipal Police of Amsterdam (Gemeentepolitie Amsterdam) 1957–1993, City Archive Amsterdam, inv. no. 5225A (hereafter GPA), 5148.
8   Report to International Narcotics Control Board, 3 November 1974, in archive of Ministry of Foreign Affairs 1965–1974, National Archive, The Hague, inv. no. 205.313 (hereafter: NA/FAIV), 24848.
9   G. Blok, *Ziek of zwak. Geschiedenis van de verslavingszorg in Nederland* (Amsterdam: Uitgeverij Nieuwezijds, 2011), p. 6; 'Editorial', *Tijdschrift voor Alcohol, Drugs en Andere Psychotrope Stoffen* 1 (1975), p. 1. After 1983 the number decreased. J. van Limbeek, M. C. A. Buster, and G. H. A. van Brussel, 'Epidemiologie van drugsverslaving in Nederland', *Nederlands Tijdschrift voor Geneeskunde* 139 (1995) 2614–18, estimated 22,000 users around 1985. In the 1990s the number stabilized at 30,000, half of whom were from 1993 onwards in the heroin treatment programmes sponsored by the Dutch government. See L. Paoli, L., V. A. Greenfield, and P. Reuter, *The World Heroin Market: Can Supply Be Cut?* (Oxford: Oxford University Press, 2009, p. 59.
10 See for example G. Meershoek, 'Terug naar de burgers: Wijkteams en buurtregie, 1965–2004', in P. de Rooy (ed.), *Waakzaam in Amsterdam. Hoofdstad en politie vanaf 1275* (Amsterdam: Boom, 2011) 517–55.
11 E.g., F. Bresler, *The Trail of the Triads: An Investigation into International Crime* (London: Weidenfeld & Nicolson, 1980), p. 7.
12 Quoted in A. W. McCoy, *The Politics of Heroin: CIA Complicity in the Global Drug Trade*, rev. edn (Chicago: Lawrence Hill Books, 2003), p. 396.

13. McCoy, *Politics of Heroin*, p. 76. See also D. Valentine, *The Strength of the Wolf: The Secret History of America's War on Drugs* (London: Verso, 2006).
14. C. A. Trocki, 'The rise of Singapore's great opium syndicate, 1840–86', *Journal of Southeastern Studies* 18 (1987) 58–80.
15. McCoy, *Politics of Heroin*, especially pp. 93–6, 262–71, 386–9; Paoli et al., *World Heroin Market*, pp. 130–42.
16. McCoy, *Politics of Heroin*, pp. 269–82. On different kinds of heroin see also Bresler, *Trail of the Triads*, pp. 13–15; R. Weijenburg, *Drugs en drugsbestrijding in Nederland. Een beschrijving van de aanpak van het gebruik en misbruik van en de (illegale) handel in verdovende middelen* (The Hague: VUGA Uitgeverij, 1996), pp. 18–21. On the anti-corruption offensive in Hong Kong and the shift from opium to heroin see also Y. K. Chu, *The Triads as Business* (London: Routledge, 2000), p. 84.
17. A. A. Block and W. J. Chambliss, *Organizing Crime* (New York: Elsevier, 1981), p. 33.
18. McCoy, *Politics of Heroin*, pp. 222-3, 256–8, 286–7. On drugs and the US Army in Vietnam see also J. Kuzmarov, *The Myth of the Addicted Army: Vietnam and the Modern War on Drugs* (Amherst: University of Massachusetts Press, 2009).
19. McCoy, *Politics of Heroin*.
20. Nederlandsche Centrale, annual report 1950, NA/FAII.
21. D: 'Opium moest ik in m'n thee gooien, dat was zo lekker', *Het Vrije Volk* 1 December 1987.
22. Amsterdam police, annual report 1971, GPA, 5148.
23. O. Janssen and K. Swietstra, 'Heroïnegebruikers in Nederland. Een typologie van levensstijlen' (Kriminologisch Instituut Rijksuniversiteit Groningen, 1982), pp. 122–31.
24. G. Blok, '"We the avant-garde": A history from below of Dutch heroin use in the 1970s', *BMGN – Low Countries Historical Review* 132 (2017) 104–25; personal communications with Gemma Blok. Blok focuses on the self-understanding of heroin users as social and cultural rebels.
25. Janssen and Swietstra, 'Heroinegebruikers', pp. 173–81.
26. Janssen and Swietstra, 'Heroinegebruikers', pp. 414–41.
27. Janssen and Swietstra, 'Heroinegebruikers', pp. 489–90.
28. Janssen and Swietstra, 'Heroinegebruikers', pp. 247–52, on a user in the year 1971; [Anon.], 'Het heroïngebruik in Amsterdam. Een signalement', in Erik Fromberg Archive, in International Institute of Social History, Amsterdam, no. ARCH 03137 (no inventory); D: interview with Frank Baas in 'Opium moest ik in m'n thee gooien, dat was zo lekker'. *Het Vrije Volk* 1 December 1987; M. de Kort, *Tussen patiënt en delinquent*.

Geschiedenis van het Nederlandse drugsbeleid (Hilversum: Verloren, 1995), pp. 229–30; G. F. van de Wijngaart, 'Competing perspectives on drug use: The Dutch experience' (Ph. thesis, Utrecht University, 1996), p. 321 on Chinese dealers.
29 Weijenburg, *Drugs en drugsbestrijding*, pp. 33–4.
30 Telex from Ministry Foreign Affairs, 3 November 1974, NA/FAIV, 24848.
31 J. A. Blaauw, *Narcoticabrigade. De eindeloze strijd tegen drugshandelaren* (Baarn: De Fontein, 1997), p. 174.
32 According to police commissioner G. Toorenaar, quoted in M. Booth, *The Dragon Syndicates: The Global Phenomenon of the Triads* (London: Bantam, 2000), pp. 48–9.
33 Amsterdam police, annual report 1976, GPA; van de Wijngaart, 'Competing perspectives'; Blok, *Ziek of zwak*, p. 185.
34 Smuggling methods: Bresler, *Trail of the Triads*, pp. 18–23; Weijenburg, *Drugs en drugsbestrijding*, pp. 29–32.
35 Y. K. Chu, *International Triad Movements: The Threat of Chinese Organised Crime* (London: Research Institute for the Study of Conflict and Terrorism, 1996); Chu, *Triads as Business*.
36 M. J. Winterton, 'The collation of crime intelligence with regard to Chinese triads in Holland', *Police Journal* 54 (1981) 34–57; Weijenburg, *Drugs en drugsbestrijding*, pp. 50–3.
37 Weijenburg, *Drugs en drugsbestrijding*, p. 55.
38 Chu, *International Triad Movements*, p. 5.
39 Bresler, *Trail of the Triads*, p. 6.
40 F. Bovenkerk and C. Fijnaut, 'Georganiseerde criminaliteit in Nederland: Over allochtone en buitenlandse criminele groepen', Parlementaire Enquêtecommissie Opsporingsmethoden, Tweede Kamer der Staten-Generaal, 1995–1996, 24 072 (hereafter PEO), 17, p. 137.
41 Booth, *Dragon Syndicates*, pp. 430–1.
42 Bresler, *Trail of the Triads*, pp. 137–43 (based on accounts of Dutch journalists and police officers, and a 'profile' given to him by the DEA); Booth, *Dragon Syndicates*, pp. 430–6.
43 D. J. Korf and M. de Kort, 'Drugshandel en drugsbestrijding' (University of Amsterdam, Bonger Institute of Criminology, 1990), pp. 56–8; B. Middelburg, *De mafia in Amsterdam* (Amsterdam: De Arbeiderspers, 1988), pp. 46–8. On police work in the Warmoesstraat precinct: M. Punch, *Policing the Inner City: A Study of Amsterdam's Warmoesstraat* (London: Macmillan, 1979).
44 Bresler, *Trail of the Triads*, pp. 140–1; Korf and de Kort, 'Drugshandel', p. 57. For accusations in the press, e.g., D: Henry Korver and Ron Govers, 'Portret van een omstreden politiecommissaris', *De Telegraaf*

4 November 1978. Toorenaar defended himself in P. R. de Vries, *Uit de dossiers van commissaris Toorenaar* (Baarn: Fontein, 1985).
45 Cf. J. Knotter, D. J. Korf, and H. Y. Lau, *Slangekoppen en tijgerjagers. Illegaliteit en criminaliteit onder Chinezen in Nederland* (The Hague: Boom, 2009), pp. 18–19.
46 Amsterdam police, annual report 1973, GPA, 5150.
47 Amsterdam police, annual report 1976, GPA, 5155.
48 Bresler, *Trail of the Triads*, pp. 115–19.
49 Middelburg, *Mafia in Amsterdam*, pp. 12–14.
50 F. Robertson, *The Triangle of Death: Inside Story of the Triads* (London: Corgi, 1978), pp. 48–9.
51 Robertson, *Triangle*, pp. 48–52.
52 Bresler, *Trail of the Triads*, pp. 115–19; Chu, *International Triad Movements*; Chu, *Triads as Business*.
53 On Ah Kong see Fijnaut and Bovenkerk, 'Georganiseerde criminaliteit', PEO, 17, p. 137; Weijenburg, *Drugs en drugsbestrijding*, pp. 35–6; Chu, *International Triad Movements*; Chu, *Triads as Business*.
54 Bresler, *Trail of the Triads*, p. 133.
55 Korf and de Kort, 'Drugshandel', p. 53.
56 R. van der Roer, 'Inbreng geld en geweld bepalen leiderschap van de Tai Huen Chai', in C. J. C. F. Fijnaut (ed.), *Georganiseerde misdaad en strafrechterlijk politiebeleid* (Lochem: Van den Brink, 1989), pp. 91–5; Weijenburg, *Drugs en drugsbestrijding*, pp. 38–46; Chu, *International Triad Movements*, pp. 15–16; B. Lintner, *Blood Brothers: Crime, Business and Politics in Asia* (Chiangmai: Silkworm Books, 2002), pp. 374–5.
57 Centrale Recherche Informatiedienst (CRI), annual report 1987, pp. 22–3.
58 P. C. van Duyne, *Het spook en de dreiging van de georganiseerde misdaad* (The Hague: Sdu, 1995), p. 67; Weijenburg, *Drugs en drugsbestrijding*, pp. 41–6.
59 CRI, annual report 1991, pp. 22–3; CRI, annual report 1992, p. 10. See also overview of seizures in the 1980s in CRI, annual report 1989, p. 96.
60 Korf and de Kort, 'Drugshandel', p. 56.
61 Weijenburg, *Drugs en drugsbestrijding*, pp. 71–5. Around 1990 the Chinese also made use of Nigerian couriers, see pp. 42–3.
62 Korf and de Kort, 'Drugshandel', pp. 79–81.
63 P. C. van Duyne, R. F. Kouwenberg, and G. Romeijn, *Misdaadondernemingen. Ondernemende misdadigers in Nederland* (The Hague: Sdu, 1990), pp. 60–2.
64 Weijenburg, *Drugs en drugsbestrijding*, p. 75.

65 Bovenkerk and Fijnaut, 'Georganiseerde criminaliteit', PEO, 17, p. 107.
66 CRI, annual report 1991, pp. 22–3; CRI, annual report 1992, p. 10. See also overview of seizures in the 1980s in CRI, annual report 1989, p. 96.
67 Korf and de Kort, 'Drugshandel', p. 56.
68 Bovenkerk and Fijnaut, 'Georganiseerde criminaliteit', PEO, 17, p. 107.
69 O. F. Akinbingöl, 'De Zwarte Driehoek. Politie, politici en de drugsmaffia in Turkije', *Justitiële Verkenningen* 26 (2000) 45–57, on p. 47.
70 Bovenkerk and Fijnaut, 'Georganiseerde criminaliteit', PEO, 17, p. 108. I recalculated the prices according to the exchange rate of guilder and dollar in 1993: 1 US dollar = 1.85 Dutch guilders, from www.measuringworth.com/datasets/exchangeglobal (accessed 7 August 2020).
71 G. K. Farrell, K. Mansur, and M. Tulis, 'Cocaine and heroin in Europe 1983–93', *British Journal of Criminology* 36 (1996) 255–81, on p. 264. Average retail prices for users went down from 59 US dollars per gram in 1983 to 34 in 1993. (Farrell et al., 'Cocaine and heroin', p. 263.)
72 van Duyne, *Het spook en de dreiging*, p. 65.
73 For the rise of opium production in Afghanistan see McCoy, *Politics of Heroin*; Paoli et al., *World Heroin Market*, pp. 118–30.
74 Paoli et al., *World Heroin Market*, p. 44; on properties of opium production: pp. 53–7.
75 Paoli et al., *World Heroin Market*, p. 118.
76 Paoli et al., *World Heroin Market*, pp. 70–1, 125–6.
77 Paoli et al., *World Heroin Market*, pp. 121–2.
78 F. Bovenkerk and Y. Yesilgöz, *The Turkish Mafia: A History of the Heroin Godfathers* (Wrea Green: Milo Books, 2007), p. 48.
79 Bovenkerk and Yesilgöz, *Turkish Mafia*, pp. 56–9.
80 Bovenkerk and Yesilgöz, *Turkish Mafia*, pp. 56–7.
81 van Duyne et al., *Misdaadondernemingen*, pp. 41–2.
82 Bovenkerk and Yesilgöz, *Turkish Mafia*, pp. 58–9.
83 Bovenkerk and Yesilgöz, *Turkish Mafia*, p. 60.
84 Bovenkerk and Yesilgöz, *Turkish Mafia*, pp. 60–1.
85 van Duyne, *Het spook en de dreiging*, pp. 66–7.
86 'Turkse heroïnesmokkel over de weg' (report IRT Noord- en Oost-Nederland Nijverdal, 1997).
87 Weijenburg, *Drugs en drugsbestrijding*, pp. 66–9. Police analysts tried to identify assassinations occurring in conflicts between criminal groups in the period 1989–1995 in Amsterdam. According to the analysis,

at the lowest count the murders of eight Turks, five Yugoslavs, two Colombians, one Moroccan and one Chinese could be regarded as assassinations in this period. See C. Fijnaut and F. Bovenkerk, 'Georganiseerde criminaliteit in Nederland. Een analyse van de situatie in Amsterdam', PEO, 20, p. 23.
88 The information collected by the CRI seems to have been based for an important part on phone taps. See R. van der Roer, 'De Turkse mafia', in Fijnaut (ed), *Georganiseerde misdaad*, pp. 81–90; Weijenburg, *Drugs en drugsbestrijding*, p. 70. Dutch privacy laws prevent access to police files and in principle decrees their destruction after five years.
89 Bovenkerk and Yesilgöz, *Turkish Mafia*, pp. 111–13, 151.
90 Cf. M. Galeotti, 'Turkish organized crime: Where state, crime and rebellion conspire', *Transnational Organized Crime* 4 (1998) 25–41, on p. 26.
91 Bovenkerk and Fijnaut, 'Georganiseerde criminaliteit', PEO, 17, p. 102.
92 Bovenkerk and Yesilgöz, *Turkish Mafia*, p. 63.
93 Bovenkerk and Yesilgöz, *Turkish Mafia*, p. 91.
94 Bovenkerk and Yesilgöz, *Turkish Mafia*, p. 102.
95 M. Galeotti, 'Turkish organized crime: From tradition to business', in D. Siegel and H. van de Bunt (eds), *Traditional Organized Crime in the Modern World: Responses to Socioeconomic Change* (New York: Springer, 2012), pp. 49–64, on p. 50.
96 Bovenkerk and Yesilgöz, *Turkish Mafia*, p. 103; 'Deze ontsnappingen met een helicopter lukten wél', *Het Parool* 12 October 2017.
97 van Duyne, *Het spook en dedreiging*, pp. 69–73.
98 van der Roer, 'Turkse mafia'.
99 Bovenkerk and Yesilgöz, *Turkish Mafia*, pp. 59, 100.
100 D. McDowall, *A Modern History of the Kurds* (London: Tauris, 1996), p. 8.
101 G. Bruinsma and H. van de Bunt, 'Georganiseerde criminaliteit in Nederland: Een analyse van de situatie in Enschede, Nijmegen en Arnhem', PEO, IV, 20, p. 200.
102 Bovenkerk and Yesilgöz, *Turkish Mafia*, p. 224.
103 Interview with Baybasin: Bovenkerk and Yesilgöz, *Turkish Mafia*, pp. 222–52.
104 Bovenkerk and Yesilgöz, *Turkish Mafia*, p. 259.
105 van der Roer, 'Turkse mafia'.
106 Galeotti, 'Turkish organized crime', pp. 26–7.
107 T. Derksen, *Verknipt bewijs. De zaak-Baybasin* (Leusden: ISVW Uitgevers, 2014).

108　On the Baybasins in London see T. Thompson, 'Heroin "emperor" brings terror to UK streets', *Observer* 17 November 2002; Galeotti, 'Turkish organized crime', pp. 51–2.
109　van Duyne et al., *Misdaadondernemingen*, pp. 58–60.
110　Bovenkerk and Fijnaut, 'Georganiseerde criminaliteit', PEO, 17, p. 110.
111　Bovenkerk and Yesilgöz, *Turkish Mafia*, pp. 122–7.
112　Bovenkerk and Fijnaut, 'Georganiseerde criminaliteit', PEO, 17, p. 107.
113　van der Roer, 'Turkse mafia'; Bovenkerk and Fijnaut, 'Georganiseerde criminaliteit', PEO, 17, pp. 100–1; Bovenkerk and Yesilgöz, *Turkish Mafia*.
114　Bovenkerk and Fijnaut, 'Georganiseerde criminaliteit', PEO, 17, p. 100.
115　D. Nieuwboer, 'De gewelddadige vrijheidsstrijd van de PKK', *Historisch Nieuwsblad* 7 (2007), www.historischnieuwsblad.nl/nl/artikel/6964/de-gewelddadige-vrijheidsstrijd-van-de-pkk.html (accessed 7 August 2020).
116　Galleotti, 'Turkish organized crime', p. 27–8.
117　Bovenkerk and Fijnaut, 'Georganiseerde criminaliteit', PEO, 17, p. 95; Bovenkerk Yesilgöz, *Turkish Mafia*, pp. 65–6.
118　Bovenkerk and Fijnaut, 'Georganiseerde criminaliteit', PEO, 17, p. 104.
119　Bruinsma and van de Bunt, 'Georganiseerde criminaliteit in Nederland', PEO, IV, 20, p. 200.
120　Figures from Fijnaut and Bovenkerk, 'Georganiseerde criminaliteit in Nederland: Een analyse van de situatie in Amsterdam', PEO, 20, p. 14.
121　Weijenburg, *Drugs en drugsbestrijding*, pp. 69–71; Y. Yesilgöz, A. Lempens and F. Bovenkerk, 'Georganiseerde misdaad als buurtprobleem', *De Gids* 159 (1996) 644–54, on p. 646.
122　Bovenkerk and Fijnaut, 'Georganiseerde criminaliteit', PEO, 17, p. 106.
123　Bovenkerk and Yesilgöz, *Turkish Mafia*, pp. 266–9.
124　Quoted in Bovenkerk and Yesilgöz, *Turkish Mafia*, p. 271.
125　Bovenkerk and Yesilgöz, *Turkish Mafia*, p. 263. See also Yesilgöz et al., 'Georganiseerde misdaad'.
126　Yesilgöz et al., 'Georganiseerde misdaad', pp. 651–2.
127　For the discussion between Staring and Bovenkerk/Yesilgöz see R. Staring, 'Het criminologische tekort. Turkse migranten en georganiseerde drugscriminaliteit', *Migrantenstudies* 14 (1998) 191–7; F. Bovenkerk and Y. Yesilgöz, 'Antwoord aan Richard Staring', *Migrantenstudies* 14

(1998) 198–202; R. Staring, 'Nawoord', *Migrantenstudies* 14 (1998) pp. 203–4. See also F. Bovenkerk (ed.), *De georganiseerde criminaliteit in Nederland. Het criminologisch onderzoek voor de parlementaire enquêtecommissie opsporingsmethoden in discussie* (Deventer: Gouda Quint, 1996), and especially the criticism in D. J. Korf, 'De octopus en de mier', in Bovenkerk (ed.), *Georganiseerde criminaliteit in Nederland*, pp. 101–8.

6

The expansion of the cannabis trade after 1976

Illegal cannabis use increased enormously in the Netherlands from the mid-1960s onwards, as we have seen in Chapter 4. Strategies of the state notwithstanding, a thriving Dutch international trade in cannabis had come into existence by the mid-1970s, supplying the Netherlands as well as other countries. This successful supply made further increase of demand possible. In response to this increase, the strategies of the Dutch state shifted. The country changed from a staunch upholder of the international regime of drug prohibition into an international idiosyncrasy. The 1976 revision of the Opium Act decriminalized individual possession of small amounts of cannabis of up to 30 grams for personal use. Though legally still a civil offence punishable with a sentence of up to one month in prison, in practice possession for own use has since been tolerated. At the same time, however, Dutch policymakers left the supply side of the cannabis market unregulated. The new regulatory regime of 1976 had unintended consequences, such as the tolerated concentration of retail in the so-called 'coffee shops' and their expansive growth in the 1980s, and the cultural transformation of cannabis use as an act of resistance into an act of everyday consumption.

Even before the liberalization of Dutch cannabis policies in 1976, smuggling cultures and networks had been expanding. After 1976 the demand for cannabis continued to grow in a political climate of liberal attitudes to consumption of the drug. These liberal attitudes did not encompass the production, smuggling, and wholesale distribution of cannabis. By the end of the 1980s police attention increasingly directed its focus at the supply side of the cannabis market. Nevertheless, more and more traders and smugglers of various nationalities and ethnic backgrounds observed and took their chance to enter the cannabis market. While the supply side of the market came to be dominated by entrepreneurs with a criminal background, idealism did not disappear completely. The influence of the Sixties counterculture was paramount in the development of extensive Dutch indoor cultivation of marihuana, the so-called nederwiet, although criminal entrepreneurs quickly entered this cultivation as well.

By 1995 the Netherlands was considered the most important country in the European distribution of cannabis.[1] In that year one report estimated the annual value of the import of cannabis in the Netherlands at 2.2 billion Dutch guilders (at the time 1.2 billion US dollars). By comparison, the value of the consumption of tobacco in the Netherlands in 1993 was 4.9 billion guilders, with alcohol worth 5.1 billion guilders, and coffee 1 billion. The value of the cannabis trade had become greater than that of the coffee trade, despite the widespread everyday use of coffee in the country. Smugglers had contributed decisively to the normalization or naturalization of cannabis use and trade in Dutch society. The cultivation of nederwiet had developed into a successful export industry, estimated at 1.8 billion guilders (1 billion US dollars) in 1995. In addition the turnover of the *transit* trade of cannabis from other supply countries through the Netherlands was estimated at 3.9 billion guilders (2.2 billion US dollars). The global scale of the operations of Dutch cannabis smugglers had changed. Not only were they involved in a transit trade in which the Netherlands was a hub for transport and distribution to other countries, Dutch smugglers also transported drugs directly from the country of production to the country of consumption without touching the Netherlands, with an estimated turnover of 12.5 billion guilders (6.8 billion US dollars).[2] These successful global operations functioned in a setting of criminal anarchy in which groups and networks of different background became involved.

Demand

The revision of the Opium Act in 1976 was basically a legal codification of existing practice. The Dutch police had more important worries than consumers in possession of small amounts of cannabis for their own use. In the larger cities the heroin epidemic was in full swing and of much more importance to the everyday operations of law enforcement officials. The first 'coffee shops' doing retail trade in cannabis were already in operation before 1976; for instance in Amsterdam the Mellow Yellow (founded in a squat in 1972), the Bulldog, and Rusland. Although involved in illegal activities, these coffee shops were more or less tolerated by the police, as were the so-called 'house dealers' of cannabis in youth centres.[3] From a law and order perspective the migration of retail from the streets, parks, and other public spaces to specific indoor places had its advantages, since it curbed street dealing, often by heroin addicts, with its attendant nuisances. Nevertheless the police were at first uncomfortable with the coffee shops, even after 1976. For instance in 1981 the Amsterdam police regularly raided them, arrested dealers, and seized cannabis. With one exception the seizures were very small, since coffee shop owners were keen not to have too much stock.

In the course of the 1980s the Amsterdam police decided to adopt a more tolerant attitude towards the coffee shops, co-opting them in a kind of co-management of the drug problem. In 1987 the police sent a letter to all the coffee shops in the city announcing that they would not interfere on condition that the shops did not openly advertise their products (for instance, by displaying a large cannabis leaf on the shop window), that there was no dealing in other drugs on the premises, that there was no public nuisance (such as noise disturbances), and that an age limit of 16 years for customers was upheld. The coffee shops agreed. This agreement with the police assisted their expansion. Street dealing in cannabis disappeared, as did the house dealers in youth centres. Retail of cannabis became as 'normalized' as the use of the drug. In 1980 there were twenty to thirty coffee shops in Amsterdam, which was a centre for drug tourism; in 1990 this number had grown to between 250 and 300.[4] In 1995 the number of coffee shops in Amsterdam had increased to 362, alongside 108 other places where cannabis also could be obtained. In the Netherlands as a whole there were by then 1,500 to 1,700 coffee shops and 700 to 2,200 dealers who sold from their own homes and 500 to 1,000 dealers in community centres. A conservative estimate of the total annual turnover of the coffee shops in that year came to 333 million guilders.[5] By the 1990s one estimate of the number of regular cannabis users in the Netherlands was 600,000 to 800,000: a multiplication by at least twenty of the estimates of regular users twenty years before. Total estimated demand of these users was between 31 and 80 tonnes. Half of this demand was supposed to be cultivated by indoor growers in the Netherlands, leaving demand for between 15 and 40 tonnes to be smuggled in.[6]

Supply

The expansion of demand created new puzzles for suppliers to solve. Although it was fairly easy to contact suppliers in countries such as Morocco, Lebanon, Pakistan, Afghanistan, and Nepal, the continuity and quality of the supply was dependent on the harvests. Neither could be guaranteed. Meteorological conditions could vary extremely, influencing the quality of the product. Good-quality cannabis was relatively rare and therefore expensive. According to cannabis researcher and user Herman Cohen, the import from Pakistan especially and to some degree Lebanon was of an inferior quality in the 1970s. In Cohen's analysis suppliers had problems in producing good-quality cannabis at guaranteed intervals in the quantities the market demanded – in the order of shipments of 1,000 to 2,000 kilograms. By 1980 a kilogram of cannabis of inferior of average quality could be bought by wholesale distributors for anything between 2,500 and 6,000 guilders; cannabis of good quality would cost between 7,000 and 10,000 guilders. As a consequence good-quality cannabis was only imported in small cargoes. Most consumers were not that interested in the more expensive high-end good-quality products that had to be smuggled in from Afghanistan or Nepal. They were perfectly happy with what connoisseurs such as Cohen and Wernard Bruijning, one of the founders of Mellow Yellow, considered to be inferior products.

This commodification of cannabis made it more interesting for large-scale smugglers to bring in cannabis of medium or low quality. The time of the small-time smuggler bringing in 5, 10, or at most 20 kilograms of cannabis back from the hippie trail or smuggled on ships and planes was slowly dying out. Wholesale distributors who bought their supplies from the smugglers, according to Cohen, sold with relatively little profit – around 3.5 to 5.5 per cent – to middlemen who in their turn sold to the retailers in the coffee shops, where prices for the user were one-third higher than the purchase price for the retailers. Distributors and middlemen were no longer driven by countercultural aspirations, but lived in middle-class housing areas and were often not even full-time traders. To Cohen this commercialization of the market was symbolic for the end of his beloved 'hashish culture' in the Netherlands, a culture that by 1980 had become, he felt, quite bourgeois.[7]

But if the 'hashish culture' might be dying, cannabis trade in the Netherlands did not become a completely bourgeois affair. On the contrary, in the 1980s and 1990s it further developed into an underground economy in which smugglers thrived. In 1995 the total estimate of cannabis smuggled into the Netherlands was somewhere between 146 and 359 tonnes, of which 80 per cent was in turn exported. Around 70 to 75 per cent of all foreign-grown cannabis on the Dutch market was estimated to be hashish from Morocco, while 25 to 30 per cent was 'black hashish' (from Pakistan and to some extent from Nepal and Afghanistan), 5 to 10 per cent 'red' or 'yellow' Lebanese hashish, and 5 to 10 per cent Colombian weed, while small cargoes came in from Jamaica and Nigeria. The sum of these percentages is more than 100 per cent, which shows the uncertainty of the estimates. Distribution lines from Morocco were stable: an estimated 2,000 to 5,000 kilograms were smuggled in each week, on average 182 tonnes each year. Cannabis from other countries was smuggled in more irregularly, and sometimes came in large cargoes in the order of tens of thousands of kilograms. Black hashish from Afghanistan, Nepal, or Pakistan was even smuggled in cargoes of 30,000 to 40,000 kilograms, taking a year or two to sell in small amounts on the market and incurring extra costs for storage and security, making profit margins more or less the same. Marihuana from Colombia, Nigeria, and sometimes Jamaica or Ghana was meant either for transit or for an interior niche market of Surinamese and Antillean users in the Netherlands.[8]

Smugglers continued to charge wholesale distributors twice the cost price when selling their contraband in the Netherlands. For instance, the costs of buying and smuggling 1 kilogram of hashish from Morocco to the Netherlands was approximately 1,500 Dutch guilders, but the sale price to distributors in the Netherlands was 3,000 guilders. Transit from the Netherlands to other demand countries was even more profitable. For instance, transit to the UK doubled the costs of smuggling 1 kilogram to 3,000 guilders, but the drugs were sold to distributors for 6,000 to 9,000 guilders, two to three times the price they fetched in the Netherlands. In Sweden prices were even six to eight times as high.[9]

Dutch people were conspicuously present among cannabis smugglers arrested outside the Netherlands. According to Interpol, in 1991 thirty cargoes were intercepted in Morocco with fifteen Dutchmen among the fifty-one transporters arrested. The Dutchmen were responsible for 11,000 kilograms out of a total of 21,700. In the same year Dutch people were involved in almost a third of all seizures of cannabis in the UK, and in more than 60 per cent of all seizures in Denmark. In 1992 British customs officers seized various cargoes of over 100 kilogram of hashish from Southwest Asia transported by Dutch companies. In that year, of a total of 194 tonnes of hashish seized outside the Netherlands, 185 tonnes were on their way to the country.[10]

By the early 1990s indoor cannabis cultivation in the Netherlands troubled law enforcement agencies as well. In 1990 five indoor growing operations were raided by the police and cannabis seized. What particularly gave cause for concern was that the cannabis grown indoors was more potent than that smuggled in from abroad. While the average THC content was only 7 per cent in cannabis from abroad, in indoor nederwiet it was 12 to 23 per cent. However, indoor cultivation was not yet in the hands of criminal organizations, according to the police.[11] Nevertheless, more and more police resources went into the raiding of indoor growing operations. In 1991 71,000 plants were seized, and twenty indoor growing operations raided with at least 500 plants in cultivation. In 1992 almost twice as many operations (thirty-seven) were raided, and the number of seized plants had risen to 313,000, yielding 15,650 kilograms of nederwiet.[12] In 1993 the number was 194,000 plants, and 237 indoor growing operations had been discovered. These figures might indicate a dispersal into smaller cultivation operations of between 200 and 1,000 plants in order to decrease the chance of detection.[13]

Smugglers

Until 1986 the smuggling of cannabis had a low priority for the Dutch police compared to the heroin trade. But by 1986 the Dutch police became convinced that 'organized crime' was the driving force in cannabis supply, and that cannabis supply in its turn stimulated the growth of organized crime.[14] The concept 'organized crime' was still a hard one to understand for Dutch policymakers and law enforcement personnel. In two memorandums to the attorney general, written in 1985 and 1986, and in his inspector's thesis at the Police Academy in 1990, Cees de Bruyne claimed that the Netherlands had developed more and more into a distribution centre for cannabis in Western Europe – especially to the UK, France, and Scandinavia. The profit margin on 1 kilogram of hashish was equal to that of 1 kilogram of heroin, but since priority was given to the fight against the heroin trade, the chances of getting caught were much lower for a cannabis smuggler. According to De Bruyne (who became chief inspector and coordinator of the fight against the cannabis trade at the CRI) and to other police officers cannabis smuggling was controlled by a 'top ten' of professional criminals. By 1990 the police accorded high priority to fighting the cannabis trade. Following De Bruyne's first memorandum the police inaugurated several investigations into wholesale importers and dealers, leading to an increase in seizures. As mentioned in the introduction, an analysis of the CRI listed more than 260 'drug gangs', most of them also involved in other criminal activities.[15] In contrast to their neighbours in Germany, the Dutch police left small consumers alone, in accordance with the revised Opium Act of 1976. Where in Germany in 1990 tens of thousands of users were still arrested for the possession of only a few grams, in the Netherlands the around 1,000 traffickers who were arrested were on average in possession of 100 kilogram of cannabis.[16]

The entrepreneurs of the 1980s further developed the methods pioneered by the smugglers of the early 1970s. For instance, in 1990 a UNODC report sounded alarm bells over the continuing importance of maritime drug smuggling.[17] Seizure records showed increases in the smuggling of drugs concealed on commercial carriers with a legal cargo, and in clandestine transports of drugs as sole shipment on private vessels. From 1983 onwards Dutch police and customs also noticed increased smuggling of cannabis in containers: by 1986 80 per cent of all seizures of cannabis were made on inspection of containers.[18] Use of containers significantly increased supply. In 1993 most of the marihuana seized by Dutch law enforcement was seized in the port of Rotterdam, on transit from Africa to countries such as the UK, Poland, and Switzerland.[19] In 1990 43 tonnes of hashish were seized in the port of Rotterdam, at that time one of the three largest ever seizures of cannabis worldwide.[20] Maritime smuggling did not do away with transport by road, however. Cannabis hidden in secret compartments – for instance in the isolation layers of refrigerated trucks – travelled throughout Europe.[21]

Foreign groups increasingly decided to enter the market, using the excellent geographical position and logistical infrastructure of the Netherlands. In 1976 the police seized almost 1,300 kilograms of hashish smuggled into the Rotterdam harbour on a Turkish ship, and arrested four Turks.[22] In 1985 the Rotterdam police seized 1,000 kilograms of hashish hidden in a container with flowerpots sent from Colombia.[23] Santa Marta marihuana, also known as 'Colombian Gold', had been an important Colombian export product since the 1960s and was now entering Europe in the wake of cocaine.[24] New associations between Dutch and Colombian entrepreneurs came into existence. In 1988 the French coastguard hailed the *Salton Sea*, a freighter flying the flag of Honduras, in the Straits of Dover. The freighter tried to flee and was chased and shot at by the French ship. Finally the *Salton Sea* ran into British waters and was captured by British customs. On board the ship was found, apart from four Dutchmen and four Colombians, 10,000 kilograms of Colombian marihuana hidden under the ballast tanks. Destination of the ship: Rotterdam.[25]

Changes in scale: the example of Klaas Bruinsma

The 1970s had seen the entrance of the Dutch underworld into the lucrative cannabis trade. We have shown that these were loose-knit groups, often with one individual acting as a central broker, organizer and financer, using his network of personal contacts to recruit specialists, to arrange transport, to find suppliers and buyers. While to the new generation of smugglers coming of age in the 1970s this older generation of smugglers, represented by established criminals such as Frits van de Wereld, was seen as too romantic and unprofessional, and often incautious and careless (for instance, when using telephones), the essential structure of 'criminal anarchy' remained the same even when the scale of the illegal trade considerably expanded in the 1980s.[26] To illustrate this we will take a closer look at the most publicized case of a 'drug kingpin' and his 'organization' from that decade: Klaas Bruinsma.

Bruinsma became from 1988 the primary target of the investigations of the Dutch police when they decided to focus on dismantling the illegal drug trade by challenging the major key players in international smuggling. That year he was portrayed in an Amsterdam newspaper, with little historical sense, as the leader of the 'largest and most violent, Mafia-like organization in the Netherlands'.[27] In the parliamentary inquiry of 1994–1996 that followed the debacle of a police investigation involving undercover operations in which the police facilitated the smuggling of XTC and other illegal drugs, the influential criminologist Cyrille Fijnaut held up Bruinsma as a prime example of the rise and danger of organized crime in the Netherlands.

In the 1970s Bruinsma had grown to prominence in the illegal Dutch cannabis trade, smuggling supplies from all over the world and – at least according to some observers – becoming for a short period in the 1980s the biggest cannabis trader in the world. He had connections with the main suppliers of cannabis in Morocco, Lebanon, and Pakistan. He had links with ships and sailors who transported cargoes of drugs from these suppliers and brought them to the Netherlands (sometimes via Spain and Portugal), where they were offloaded in one of the harbours or transported via speedboats to the coastal beaches. Bruinsma's operations were not limited to cannabis: he sidelined in heroin (smuggled in from Afghanistan through the Soviet Union, Pakistan, or Thailand) and cocaine (from Colombia). He maintained a highly visible profile in the city of Amsterdam, living in luxury hotels, and was – together with a 'hard core' of ten of his associates – involved in various violent incidents and in at least three assassinations. Furthermore he expanded into real estate, becoming an important power in the Amsterdam red-light district (a centre of gambling and prostitution), and he laundered his drug money with the help of financial and legal advisors from the upperworld. In short, Bruinsma was the closest the Netherlands had ever come to producing a crime boss in the mould of Al Capone.[28]

This appraisal of Bruinsma is problematic. Rather than directing a hierarchical organization, bound in obedience to him, he was continually negotiating (even if at times using threats or violence) his position on the criminal markets. He did not control the market; the police would later acknowledge that their strategy of targeting key players was ineffective in enforcing regulation on a market that was relatively open. Bruinsma and his associates (the three leading ones were, as his 'successors', the target of a judicial investigation called 'Octopus' after he was murdered in 1991) were easily replaced when in prison or dead. Even the image of Bruinsma as a leading mafia boss has been challenged. According to one account by a journalist who was close to the criminal milieu of Amsterdam, Bruinsma had lost most of his influence already by the end of the 1980s before his death. In any case the members of his group or 'organization' did not work exclusively for him. Rather than a new phenomenon in Dutch crime and Dutch society, Bruinsma was a more evolved example of the criminal entrepreneur typified by Frits van de Wereld and his contemporaries, except that, more than Frits, Bruinsma helped to shape a globalizing underground economy in which rising demand went together with increasing availability of supply in developing countries. Bruinsma and other criminal entrepreneurs of the 1980s could become crucial links in supply chains because their 'disorganized' structure kept them flexible and difficult to control for law enforcement.

In Bruinsma a number of aspects of the new drug underground economy came together. He did not come from a criminal background himself – in other words he was not 'culturally determined' to become a criminal. His father was a director of a well-known soda company. According to Bruinsma it was the conflicts with his father that led him into a life of crime and violence. Born in 1953, as a youngster in school Klaas came under the influence of the underground culture, and especially of its rebelliousness and its drug use. At school he was already dealing in cannabis and he was a heavy everyday user. He was arrested by the police for the first time in 1970, but was not prosecuted. Thereafter he continued dealing and was expelled from school. In 1976 he was arrested in Copenhagen, where he had delivered hashish and amphetamines. His father was allowed by officers at the police station to beat him up, after which he was set free. Back in Amsterdam Bruinsma and two associates continued working in the cannabis trade: he and a man called *De Snor* (the Moustache) took care of smuggling, and their female friend Thea Moear of distribution. By now Klaas was closely connected to the criminal milieu of Amsterdam: Thea was the daughter of Blonde Greet, the associate of Frits van de Wereld in his drug dealings (see Chapter 4).[29] A rebellious youngster from the middle class had allied himself to the members and families of the underworld. The Moustache was a streetwise criminal and the alliance with him was essential for Bruinsma to operate in the underworld of Amsterdam, where it was difficult for him to be accepted because of his background and also because of his appearance: he was always wearing a suit and his continual verbal expostulations earned him the nickname *De Dominee* (the Vicar).

Early in her criminal career Thea had started dealing cannabis. Access to this market was easy because of her family connections. Her husband worked as a doorman in discotheques around the Leidseplein square (a centre of Amsterdam's nightlife and of drug dealing), supplying customers with amphetamines and cannabis. Later he moved on to dealing in Chinese heroin. Thea herself started to work for a middleman named Black Peter in the bars and cafés around the Leidseplein, buying a piece of cannabis from him for 15 guilders, selling it to a retailer for 25 guilders, and splitting the profits. All small fry compared to what her mother and Frits van de Wereld were doing, but nevertheless her distribution network grew in an emerging market that worked through personal contacts and communication.[30] In this market there existed no monopolization or territorialization by individual dealers. Thea and her associates worked from the same bar as two other dealers, one of whom was Klaas Bruinsma, then operating under a false name as *Lange* (Big) Frans van Arkel. The cannabis trade was socially embedded in this bar, and it was here that Bruinsma, the Moustache, and Moear started working together.

So far their operations were rooted in the general distribution system that had existed since the 1960s and was basically a form of 'waiting for my man': buyers could not rely on their dealers to be accessible or present in bars or apartments, but had to find them somewhere; dealers would not always be supplied with merchandise. Here the triumvirate started to make decisive innovative steps that ultimately spiralled Bruinsma to his position of notoriety. They restructured the whole chain of supply and distribution in order to ensure customers of continuity and certainty. Their 'firm' could be reached at any time of day at an apartment rented by Bruinsma in the centre of the city, contacted even by telephone and even in the morning. A strict and reliable sales system was offered. Customers who called asking for '10 (or 20) kilograms black', meaning black Pakistani hashish, could be quite certain that it was available. Professional drivers in rented vans delivered consignments to clients. The triumvirate also became active on the retail side. Inspired by the Mellow Yellow, the coffee shop opened by idealistic hippies, Moear opened a coffee shop of her own called the Buggie in the west of Amsterdam. Not only did this provide a retail outlet, it was also useful in laundering the profits of the drug trade.

The most decisive innovations concerned the extent to which Bruinsma and his associates expanded the scale of import and smuggling. At first the trio were reliant on other importers and wholesale distributors. They were supported by Frits van de Wereld who, because of his relationship with Moear, sold them his smuggled cannabis for lower prices and connected them to customers. An important other supplier was a Pakistani middleman named Mustapha Malik who lived in Amsterdam (and, if we may believe a journalistic account of the time, was also an informer of the Amsterdam police and therefore to some degree 'protected').[31] Later Bruinsma and the Moustache started their own smuggling operations. At first they transported small cargoes of cannabis from Pakistan of up to 15 kilograms in suitcases by plane. Then they entered the world of maritime smuggling, again with the assistance of Frits van de Wereld. Their first adventure, in which they took a share in smuggling a few thousand kilograms on a vessel organized by Frits, was a failure (the consignment was almost immediately seized), but this was only a temporary setback, as was the arrest of Bruinsma with 100 kilograms of cannabis in Amsterdam which led to him doing three months in prison in 1976. After his release Bruinsma travelled to supply countries (Pakistan, Morocco, Lebanon, Syria) to test the merchandise and arrange for the deliveries. In 1977 the triumvirate could celebrate earning their first million guilders.[32]

Moear remembered that Bruinsma started to deal directly with the bigger merchants in Pakistan and Morocco, bypassing the middlemen as well as the other importers in the Netherlands like Frits van de Wereld and Mustapha Malik. The most important supplier in Pakistan, she told a journalist, was an elderly, distinguished male Pakistani. 'Between ourselves we always called him *de Ouwe* (the Old Guy). He was then one of the biggest [traders] in Pakistan. I always went along with him quite well.'[33] The most important smuggling method went back to the 1920s. A company in the country of supply, often only existing as a front company, sent cargoes with official paperwork for legal goods to the clients in the Netherlands. These clients were real companies, often in financial problems and therefore susceptible to making a little extra profit by looking the other way while the hashish was hidden in containers with legal goods sent to them. The cooperation between under- and upperworld made smuggling feasible. Stocks were stashed in houses with a garage, inhabited by discrete families without criminal records or any observable connection with the triumvirate. From there the triumvirate distributed the drugs in smaller stashes of 100 kilograms, mostly concealed in buildings in busy market neighbourhood so the drivers could pick up their deliveries without attracting much notice, but also without them knowing of the bigger stashes.[34]

If something went wrong with the smuggled goods and the consignment was seized, the Bruinsma firm still paid the supplier, if the problem had occurred because of a mistake on the Dutch side. Moear also claimed that customs officials needed to be bribed, but, she added, there was no pressure involved and it was made clear from the start that the smugglers would make use of the same officials only two or three times because of the high risks involved for all parties. Sometimes, Moear claimed, seized hashish turned up on the Amsterdam market anyway, sold – so she suggested – by corrupt police officials.[35]

Again according to Moear, in the first years of the triumvirate most hashish was smuggled in from Lebanon and Morocco, with occasional more exclusive consignments coming in from Afghanistan (through Pakistan) or Nepal.[36] The latter consignments were more rare and more difficult to sell because they came in larger quantities. Wernard Bruijning of the Mellow Yellow coffee shop therefore complained about the general quality of the Bruinsma supplies.[37] The triumvirate, however, wanted to serve all ends of the market, and most of it came to be dominated by the low-quality Moroccan hashish of the 1980s. To handle larger consignments Bruinsma lent technical expertise and equipment to his suppliers. For instance, it was far more convenient to smuggle hashish in smaller and more compact blocks. At the beginning of the 1980s Bruinsma sent a hydraulic press to different hashish producers in the Rif. The hashish was pressed by the machine into *zepies*, pieces of the size of a block of hand soap.[38]

The size of the consignments grew exponentially. In 1979 Bruinsma was arrested for involvement in smuggling 1,500 kilograms of Pakistani hashish sent overland through Syria and Germany. He was given eighteen months in prison, of which he served twelve. Out again in 1980, he was already smuggling consignments of 8,000 kilograms in containers through the port of Antwerp.[39] The first 'mega transport' of more than 10,000 kilograms, consisting of four containers each with 4,000 kilograms of Pakistani hashish, was seized in 1981 in Antwerp. Nevertheless the operations continued.[40]

Next to the import business Bruinsma developed a transit trade in partnership with the Englishman Roy Adkins, also known as the 'Fat Man'. Adkins came from a British criminal environment. He had started out with armed robbery, then decided that there was a more profitable future in the illegal drug trade. Bruinsma and Adkins began smuggling small consignments of 50 kilograms on ferries from the Netherlands (Hook of Holland) and Belgium (Ostend) to the UK. The consignments were kept small since it was considered more difficult to bribe customs officials in the UK than in the ports of Amsterdam and Rotterdam. Larger consignments went to other Western European countries: Belgium, Germany, Scandinavia, and France.[41]

The Bruinsma–Moear combination also started to innovate in another way: apart from the import and transit trade, they began to use their networks to create an international flow of cannabis that did not pass through the Netherlands at all. By the end of the 1970s Pakistani middlemen supplied Bruinsma with consignments of around a few thousands kilograms of hashish, and Bruinsma smuggled these consignments directly to buyers in Canada.[42]

Because of the size of their operations and the assured continuity of their operations Bruinsma and Moear could afford to set their own prices and to give their clients huge discounts without jeopardizing their profits. Moear remembered that in the early 1980s she sold 1 kilogram of black Pakistani hashish for 3,500 guilders, with a discount of up to 200 guilders per kilogram for the purchase of 100 kilograms. On an ordinary day, she claimed (with perhaps some exaggeration), she sold 200 kilograms; on some days this could be as much as 500 kilograms. Even if up to two-thirds of the sales price went on expenses – half to pay for buying and smuggling (including bribing of customs officials) and another 15 per cent or so to other expenses (the rent of safe houses, the payments for the drivers distributing the contraband – which was initially 25 guilders per kilogram and later became 75 guilders; 1,000 guilders per week for the bodyguards), this would make for sizeable profits.[43] When in 1982 the Moustache decided to quit he was bought out by Bruinsma and Moear for 2.5 million guilders. Then, after Bruinsma had served three years in prison for killing someone in a shoot-out, Moear withdrew from the business as well in return for a retirement pension of 12,000 guilders per month.[44] The Dutch tax authority estimated Bruinsma's income in 1989 to be 25 to 30 million guilders.[45] In 1990 a study sponsored by the Ministry of Justice estimated the annual profits of the Bruinsma group to be 10 to 20 million guilders, including other activities such as loan-sharking.[46] One of his bodyguards considered it to be at least ten times as high, between 100 and 200 million guilders per year.[47]

These were gross income levels the Dutch underworld had not known before but it has to be taken into account that smuggling, although it was the basis of Bruinsma's criminal enterprise, was not his sole source of income. Bruinsma was involved in a number of separate criminal operations, the 'divisions'. Drug smuggling, now including heroin and cocaine, was one of these divisions in which Adkins became increasingly important. Laundering drug money with the assistance of financial and legal advisors was another division. In 1983 Bruinsma started investments in real estate and became the director of an 'architectural firm' as a legal cover for these operations. Private limited liability companies were established on the Bahamas. They gave fake loans to newly established 'real estate companies' in the Netherlands. These companies invested the loans in real estate, and then went bankrupt, and the real estate, by then often with maintenance overdue, was sold again, laundering the drug money.[48]

A third division was the exploitation of slot machines. The porn trade was a fourth outlet and very useful for laundering money. In 1990 associates of Bruinsma also opened three coffee shops in the Amsterdam red-light district. Other coffee shops were pressured to offer only hashish and slot machines from the Bruinsma group. This attempt by Bruinsma to make the transition from an 'enterprise syndicate' to a 'power syndicate' increased his conflicts with other criminal entrepreneurs. These conflicts finally led to his assassination in 1991.[49]

Criminal anarchy in the cannabis trade

After the death of Bruinsma the police tried to hunt down a new triumvirate that had supposedly taken over his 'organization', consisting of his Surinamese bodyguard Etienne Urka, the former Bruinsma lawyer and *consigliere* John Engelsma, and a businessman in pornography and real estate named Charles Geerts. Analyses by the CRI reinforced an image of an 'octopus' that had spread its tentacles throughout the

Dutch underworld. From 1987 onwards an interregional police investigation unit (IRT) had tried to target the presumed leaders of the illegal drug trade in the Netherlands. To catch Urka and his associates, the IRT made use of someone inside the organization: an importer of Colombian marihuana. The IRT facilitated the smuggling of an estimated 500 tonnes of cannabis and 15 tonnes of cocaine into the Netherlands, the import of precursor chemicals for the production of XTC, and the export of XTC into the UK. This led to a public scandal known as the 'IRT affair' and to the resignation of the responsible ministers of justice and of interior affairs in 1994.[50]

However, researchers associated with the WODC of the Ministry of Justice developed a completely different image of the involvement of 'organized crime' in the illegal drug trade. In a study of police files, published in 1990, Petrus C. van Duyne, R. F. Kouwenberg, and G. Romeijn pioneered an analysis of organized crime groups in the Netherlands as 'crime enterprises'.

In fact the enterprise of Bruinsma totally puzzled the researchers, who had started to doubt whether one could speak of an actual enterprise or organization in any sense, and even whether Bruinsma was the facilitator of all activities associated with his 'enterprise' or only involved as a silent partner. On the one hand the researchers disagreed with the police that Bruinsma was involved in or behind all these activities. On the other hand the study did identify a small core consisting of Bruinsma, of a 'manager' (Etienne Urka, like Bruinsma and all other criminals, presented in the report under a false name), of an expert in commercial enterprises, and of a tax expert. Then there were a few bodyguards in the group, some specialists hired on a temporary basis, and network contacts with other criminal entrepreneurs. What characterized this motley group above all was flexibility.[51]

A journalist with close connections in the Amsterdam underworld described Bruinsma as an underworld broker or matchmaker, someone who connected people on an ad hoc basis, a spider in the web of the 'Dutch Network'.[52] Significantly, even Bruinsma's associates did not know how large this network was. One associate remembered around thirty people who were available on short notice in Amsterdam; if one counted all associates within and outside of the Netherlands, including lawyers and tax advisors, Bruinsma's network might have covered between 100 and 200 people.[53] Bruinsma worked with various specialists: importers, transporters, exporters, people who on request organized a safe place or a half-container for storage and transport, and businessmen from the upperworld who liked to invest. Interviews with former associates of Bruinsma made it clear that the structure of the network was flexible and that there was not a strict hierarchy in the group. According to Bruinsma's accountant Edwin S, it was primarily a collaboration of mates and acquaintances from the world of cannabis trafficking, people who encountered each other again and again in different situations. Participants in the networks, from Adkins and Urka to the bodyguards and drivers, all had their own business ventures that were not related to Bruinsma.[54] Although never proven it was also considered likely that he had his contacts within the police and justice departments. According to police officers, he had a book of photographs of police officials in compromising situations, and at the end of the 1980s some essential files disappeared from the police headquarters.[55]

The study by Van Duyne et al. identified a number of importers working together with Bruinsma but not subordinated to him. They all worked on their own account and included his own tax advisor and a man from Pakistan as well as smugglers spread over the country, from a man running a scrap-metal yard in a village in a traditional smuggling area on the border between Limburg and Belgium to a group of fishermen in the cities of Monnickendam and Marken to the north of Amsterdam with contacts in Spain. The wholesale distributors who bought the contraband, the financiers who bankrolled operations, the tax experts and money-launderers, and the actual smugglers, the transporters and seamen – they were all basically independent, associating with each other in temporary operations.[56] Then there were the contacts with the upperworld of security in the ports, supervisors in the ports, security experts, warehouse employees. They were also not part of an organization, but were associated on a temporary basis.[57]

An example of a Bruinsma associate was Karel Vosseveld. Born in the Caribbean, he had started his criminal career as an armed robber, then went on to cigarette smuggling and in his twenties moved to the cannabis trade. He smuggled hashish from Lebanon and Morocco into the Netherlands and from there into the rest of Europe. According to Vosseveld one never got caught when one had the right contacts. At the end of the 1980s he started to work with Bruinsma, but not exclusively. Vosseveld took care of logistics and was a specialist in container transports of consignments of more than 10,000 kilograms. His fee was 500 to 1,500 guilders per kilogram. Until his arrest in 1985 he had a whole car park of thirty trucks transporting 'oranges' from Morocco and Spain. According to Vosseveld, 'nothing fitted together' in the Bruinsma group: 'The people who participated all had their own little companies.'[58] There were also vast cultural differences and mindsets between the participants. Vosseveld with his laissez-faire 'Caribbean mindset' did not like the use of violence, nor having to attend meetings, while Bruinsma did.[59]

Apart from Bruinsma, in the 1980s there were more large-scale international facilitators operating from Amsterdam, such as Stanley Karel 'Kai' Esser, an Antillean from the island of Curaçao who had moved from cigarette smuggling to hashish smuggling in the 1970s, and who is said to have supplied as much as 40 tonnes per year at the time of his arrest in 1984; and the Englishman Howard Marks, arrested on Mallorca in 1988 and extradited to the United States.[60] The landscape of cannabis smuggling was more diverse than the image of Bruinsma as drug kingpin suggested.

Nederwiet

By the end of our period it was not only foreign cannabis that was smuggled out of the country, but Dutch cannabis as well. Nederwiet production originated in a period of crisis, as an additional means of subsistence for an unemployed underclass, but was so successful that it became a profitable line of business. Technical expertise was essential to the successful evolution of Dutch indoor production. Indoor cultivation of cannabis was pioneered in the United States, where the 'war on drugs' and increased surveillance and the spraying of toxic chemicals on outdoor cultivation areas under the Reagan administration made alternative cultivation methods a necessity. As cannabis historian Nick Johnson writes: 'The importance of this shift in cannabis growing cannot be overstated. Forcing growers indoors not only made it harder for federal and state authorities to enforce prohibition, but it also inspired the innovation [that] yielded indoor-adapted varieties of cannabis with bigger flowers and more potent resin.'[61] One of the pioneers of the Dutch coffee shops, Wernard Bruijning, went to the American western states California and Oregon in 1979 for a research visit to growers working on genetic manipulation of the cannabis plant. These were sparsely populated states where covert cultivators, who viewed themselves as outlaws, had found space to create a thriving cannabis cultivation industry.[62] They supplied marihuana of good quality for cheaper prices than in Europe.

Enthused for both idealistic and commercial reasons, Bruijning and his friends in the Netherlands invited an American grower nicknamed 'Old Ed' to come over and teach them the art of growing cannabis. Their aim was to turn the Netherlands into what they called the 'Jamaica of Europe'. First cultivating outdoors on a farm in the north of the country, the group turned to indoor cultivation in increasingly bigger safe houses. The Lowlands Seed Company of Bruijning and his friends also started to disseminate knowledge about cultivation.[63] Other American pioneers travelled to the Netherlands and networked with Dutch producers and enthusiast at events such as the annual Cannabis Cup.

In 1990 the police dismantled five operations in which use was made of hydroculture. Plants were grown without using soil, but using rock wool and a water solvent, improving results by climate control, and 'fooling' the plants into flowering by turning off the light (received from high-powered lamps) for twelve hours a day. Growers could now have several harvests a year and got rid of male plants (only the females produce psychoactive sinsemilla). Indoor growing is energy intensive and far from sustainable, but has yielded by now more than 2,000 hybrid strains with higher THC content (held responsible for the psychoactive 'high') and particular smell, taste, and reported effects. By 1990 the Dutch police reported increases of THC to at least 12 or 13 per cent, where 'traditional' cannabis has a content no higher than 7 per cent.[64]

As with other elements of the illegal drug trade, indoor nederwiet cultivation had to be socially and culturally embedded. In a series of police operations in different parts of the Netherlands from 1996 onwards, indoor plantations were discovered and raided in neighbourhoods with a high percentage of unemployment and cultural traditions in which respect for the law was low. These included neighbourhoods of cities as well as camps where the so-called *kampers* ('campers') lived, though not always in trailers since some of them had built houses. People on unemployment benefit and with criminal records cultivated 250 plants in one room, using advanced hydrocultural techniques and illegally tapping off electricity from the city network.

The police suspected that these operations were financed and controlled by kampers involved in the illegal drug trade.[65] The kampers would exert considerable pressure on unemployed people to force them to work the indoor plantations. Other researchers concluded that the exertion of pressure by criminal entrepreneurs was relatively rare. While cannabis cultivation became professionalized (growers were no longer always users), most indoor cultivators worked independently, or had their operations financed by friends, relatives, or neighbours. Most of the cultivators did not illegally tap off electricity.[66] Large-scale production was not a general characteristic of modernized cultivation, but small-scale profitability.[67] The world of indoor cultivation was as fragmented as the world of drug smuggling, organized in criminal anarchy rather than directed by crime syndicates.

Kampers

Who were the kampers? The first permanent camps of caravans or mobile homes in or near Dutch cities appeared around 1900. The inhabitants were members of farmers' families who had drifted into a precarious existence and travelled around earning a living – for instance, by offering to sharpen scissors, or by holding fairs. Their ambulant lifestyle made them suspect to the authorities, especially after a law was passed in 1918 with the intent of limiting the size and number of camps. The camps were moved to rather unattractive places where a specific culture came into existence that was tolerant of criminal behaviour directed against the outside world and defiant of authority. These were places where criminal anarchy was potentially embedded. In 1968 the government decided to concentrate the mobile camps in fifty centres. Seven years later this decision was reversed, but by then major social damage had been done. The decision of 1968 had led to large camps in which inhabitants had to compete to earn a living, and to impoverishment. In some of the camps arms trafficking, fencing of stolen goods, and defiance of police expanded. Kampers became involved in armed robberies, thefts, insurance swindle, and finally the illegal drug trade, and some of the camps became 'no-go' areas for the police. In 1983 a permanent police post was installed in a camp in Utrecht; in 1985 in a camp in Den Bosch. By 1995 almost all of the 30,000 inhabitants of the camps claimed unemployment benefit.[68]

THE EXPANSION OF THE CANNABIS TRADE

In the smaller camps criminals were socially prominent, and a culture of 'us against them', anti-statist feelings, and traditional criminal values of not informing and mutual solidarity gave structure to life in the camps. This did not mean that all kampers turned to criminality: in fact, many of them disliked the criminal operations and turned to other strategies for survival.[69] Nevertheless a social and cultural environment existed in the camps in which the illegal drug trade could be embedded, while the structures of criminal anarchy were in place and there were sufficient profits from earlier criminal enterprises available to finance the smuggling of illegal drugs.

In 1995 the parliamentary investigation into organized crime aired the views of criminologist Cyrille Fijnaut about the importance of the camps as criminal hotbeds.[70] From the following year, mobile camps increasingly became targets of police operations against indoor cultivation, as did lower-class neighbourhood districts of cities.[71] Fijnaut in his testimony for the parliamentary commission mentioned at least five cannabis smugglers from the camps, some of them actively involved in disrupting the strategies of the authorities against them by counter-observing their observers, intimidation, and corruption.[72]

When in 1979 the police raided the mobile camp at the Doolplein square in the city of Eindhoven in Brabant (where, according to one police commissioner, 'only rats lived'), the spokesman of the kampers Grad van Wesenbeeck threatened to form armed gangs to fight the police.[73] In the 1990s Grad turned from scrap dealing to the illegal trade in nederwiet. His son Janus (nicknamed 'Harry Potter' because of his reading glasses) subsequently developed in what one journalist called 'one of the largest drug dealers of Europe', smuggling cannabis, XTC, and amphetamines.[74] 'Drug barons' such as Janus and Johan Verhoek, aka the *Hakkelaar* (the Stutterer) combined the cultural criminal traditions of the camps and the precarious economic existence of many of the kampers to develop successful criminal enterprises.

The Hakkelaar was born in 1954 in a camp in the city of Leidschendam in the west of the country. He first worked as a used-car dealer in a petrol station near the highway called De Hackelaer: this is one hypothesis about the origin of his nom de guerre. In the 1980s he became involved in drug trafficking. The Hakkelaar was initially a broker, connecting different specialists, supply, and demand. He had contacts in the world of the kampers who could take care of the storage and the distribution of contraband cannabis. Another connection was Ad Karman, a garage owner in the working-class neighbourhood of the Jordaan in Amsterdam which was another geographical space in which many criminal entrepreneurs were embedded. Karman could arrange for the boats, the containers, and the cranes needed for the transport of drugs by sea. The collaboration started in 1987 with the smuggling of 16 tonnes of hashish on the ship *Volendam*. In the following years the Hakkelaar smuggled tens of thousands of kilograms by ship, part of it with Canada as destination. The biggest consignment was one of 115 tonnes transported on the *Pacific Tide 5*. Part of it was sunk to the sea floor near the Azores for storage, but the Canadians seized part of the consignments and the rest was brought to the surface by divers from the Dutch navy. Ultimately the Dutch police, public prosecutor, and fiscal investigation service succeeded in arresting Karman and a Pakistani middleman and turning them into witnesses against the Hakkelaar. The latter was arrested in 1996 and in 1997 sentenced to six years in prison, on appeal reduced to five and a half years and a 1 million guilder fine.[75] His connections made the Hakkelaar a 'spider in the web', but he did not *control* the web as a drug kingpin.

In a detailed case study of one 'criminal organization' in which kampers were involved, criminologist Peter Klerks concluded that this kind of enterprise could not be seen as *one* criminal enterprise, but as combinations of cooperating and opportunistic merchants based on close networks.[76]

A fragmented landscape

By 1990 the amounts of cannabis seized in the Netherlands, destined for the country or for transit, were significantly higher than in neighbouring countries. There was plenty of space available for people to move into the cannabis market. A survey by criminologists in Amsterdam in 1991 that included interviews with traffickers showed their diversity, as they ranged from the 'old guard' of the hippie era to entrepreneurs with a criminal background.[77] Although one still encountered smugglers in one-man operations involving a very limited amount of good-quality hashish, the bulk of the hash market was by now supplied by larger networks, capable of the financial investments needed for the import of tonnes of hashish. Another report described four of these groups that had their own boats, some of them decrepit, but others were yachts worth millions of guilders. The groups used other methods of transport as well: regular freight ships, with a bought crew and the hashish hidden in legal cargo, and containers. All these methods needed big investment and the participation of twelve to thirteen people.[78] One of these groups had a whole armada of eight vessels at its disposal and eight or so smugglers who brought in tens of tonnes of hashish.[79]

The demand for illegal drugs was such that there was plenty of room for different distributors and producers, while regulation and law enforcement stimulated structures of criminal anarchy on the supply side of the market. In 1991 one police report identified 262 groups active in the cannabis trade; 162 of these groups were also active in other forms of crime, 165 groups had fewer than ten core members. Of the groups 60 per cent were purely native Dutch, 31 per cent were of mixed composition, and there were six Turkish, six Moroccan, and three Surinamese groups, and finally one Pakistani group.[80] Several of these groups were dismantled; for instance, in 1992 one group that was smuggling tens of tonnes of Moroccan hashish into the Netherlands, and from there hundreds of kilograms to the UK and Canada. This group was also active in the production, distribution, and export of XTC. In 1993 one group was dismantled that had smuggled hashish from Pakistan and stashed it near the Azores in underwater container terminals. Divers recovered the contraband when needed. Another investigation led to the arrest of twenty employees from Amsterdam airport, and directors and drivers of transport companies involved in cannabis smuggling. Yet another investigation led to the dismantling of a Turkish criminal group involved in smuggling and distributing Moroccan hashish – and so forth and so on. What especially struck the police was that the criminals now started to counter-operate against the investigation, by threatening officials and prosecutors, by placing their own telephone taps, and by hacking computers of the police and justice departments.[81]

Whereas Bruinsma, the son of a wealthy factory owner, was in many ways atypical of the criminal environment in which he rose to greater glory or notoriety, other more typical smugglers came from criminal cultural backgrounds. We have seen that the Hakkelaar came from a kamper family.[82] Steve Brown, whose 'youth clubs' in Amsterdam sold cannabis and made an estimated annual turnover of 50 million guilders, and who also turned his hand to the heroin trade, was from De Pijp, a working-class neighbourhood in Amsterdam characterized by flexible attitudes to the borders between legal and illegal behaviour.[83]

There was definitely some overlap in the trade in different drugs, but it was limited. Of nineteen illegal enterprises analysed by Van Duyne et al. in 1990, only five smuggled both cannabis and other drugs. The entrepreneurs smuggling both cannabis and other drugs were all native Dutch with one exception who was an immigrant from New Guinea in the former Dutch East Indies. The majority of the entrepreneurs smuggling other drugs were native Dutch, but with a large minority of smugglers with different ethnic backgrounds present: Turkish, Pakistani, Chinese, West Indian, and Colombian.[84]

All these 'enterprises' had the same kind of flexible structure as the Bruinsma group, whatever their background. To give two examples out of the nineteen: the cannabis smuggling group led by the man from New Guinea that was active in the smuggling of heroin as well was a big operation with an estimated annual turnover of 6 million guilders. Apart from its 'leader' it was composed only of native Dutchmen. The group consisted of an inner circle of seven or eight specialists (for transport, storage, money, and legal advice) who were in almost daily contact with each other, and an outer circle of six to nine persons who were available for temporary jobs when needed. For supply there were direct contacts with cannabis suppliers in India, Syria, and Lebanon, and with a cocaine supplier in Uruguay.[85]

The second example dealt only in cannabis, smuggled to the UK and to Scandinavia with the contraband fastened to the outside of the keel of a ship. This group was basically a network around a 'leader', with a contact to a money launderer, three associates who arranged for boats and transport, two who took care of the transit of the drugs through the Netherlands, two seamen (one British, one American) to sail the ships, one contact in North Africa, two assistants for small jobs, and three wholesale buyers/distributors in the Netherlands. The 'leader' of the network here made use of legal front enterprises and bank accounts, but this was not the case for all of the enterprises analysed in the report.[86]

Contacts with the maritime industry were of crucial importance; for instance, for three years in the early 1990s one group of three Dutch associates ran a smuggling empire that with eight ships and around eighty helpers and specialists imported according to a conservative police estimate 50,000 kilograms of cannabis per year. To organize maritime smuggling operations the trio collaborated closely with a German who bought and sold the contraband and managed ship maintenance and repairs, and with a Dutchman who managed communications with the ships and the payment for repairs. An office in Rotterdam with a manager and two accountants functioned as the legal front. There were eight captains and a large number of seamen from various nationalities, considered by the police as 'seasoned veterans of smuggling', to sail the ships. The fleet was actually the weak point in the operations, since the ships that were used were hardly seaworthy and their engines often failed within the sight of the harbour and under the eyes of customs officials.[87]

Truck transport companies were also important for cannabis smuggling. One transport company used its eight trucks to transport Moroccan hashish through Spain to the Netherlands and from there to Scandinavia and the UK. The truck drivers, who had no criminal records, received between 10,000 and 25,000 guilders for each run.[88] Another transport company had a long history in smuggling. Three times in the early 1980s cargoes of hashish were discovered by customs and the police in trucks of this company in the Netherlands and Germany. A few years later the company started to work with the smuggler and migrant from New Guinea. One and a half million guilders were invested to procure container trucks with hidden storage spaces. The trucks transported subtropical fruit from Morocco for legal customers, and Moroccan hashish destined for transit to the UK.[89] Smugglers could also transport cannabis in trucks from transport companies who were not aware of the involvement of their drivers in the trade, or they could transport cannabis hidden in cargoes without the knowledge of the drivers.[90] According to a report, in 1995 40 per cent of the hashish imported from the largest supply country, Morocco, was smuggled by sea and another 40 per cent by land through Spain in cargoes of 1,000 to 1,500 kilograms. There were still small-scale smugglers active, such as Moroccans living in the Netherlands who would take 10 or so kilograms with them, or people smuggling that kind of amount in by plane. Profit margins were still similar to those of the 1980s: one could buy a kilogram of hashish in Morocco for 500 to 800 guilders, depending on how much one bought in total, and smuggle it for an further 1,300 to 1,800 guilders to the Netherlands. There one could sell the drugs to wholesale distributors for at least 5,300 guilders, double the cost price. The chance of being caught was estimated at one in three, and most groups supported the families of arrested members. Profits were not so high for the associates on the lower rings of the smuggling group, but they were recruited from the unemployed, giving them at least some income.[91]

Violence

The early 1980s started to witness the first 'rip deals' in which criminals who were not averse to violence preyed on weaker traders. For instance, Steve Brown, who started to build his own Happy Family coffee shop empire in Amsterdam, was ripped of 100 kilograms of hashish and needed the assistance of Bruinsma to get the drugs back at gunpoint.[92] When Bruijning admonished Bruinsma that he should not be carrying a gun, the smuggler answered that carrying one was necessary in order not to get ripped when delivering merchandise.[93] Since the architecture of the drug trade made it impossible for traders to solve business conflicts by court, personal violence and the threat of personal violence became the ultimate appeal. This meant that criminals were needed with expertise in this area. The police estimated that Bruinsma was responsible for at least ten murders; the Amsterdam journalist and 'Bruinsma watcher' Bart Middelburg thought it was more. But most of these killings were never proven.[94] Violence also entered the world of the coffee shops. Benny 'Pukkel' Mulch, cocaine trafficker and owner of coffee shop The Buddha in the centre of Amsterdam's red-light district, was shot dead in 1985 when on Christmas leave from prison.[95]

Although Bruinsma himself did not originate from a violent criminal milieu he entered one. His English business associate Roy Adkins is said to have ordered the killing of one of the former gang members behind the famous Great Train Robbery who was supposed to have crossed him in a drug deal. This concerned the 1988 'Perestroika Bust', in which a container of Afghan hashish was seized in the UK. Adkins' involvement in this failed deal led to his own liquidation in Marbella, Spain, in September 1990.[96] Half a year later, on 27 June 1991, Bruinsma was also murdered – according to some by or on assignment for Yugoslav professional criminals with whom he had had a conflict over a cargo of cocaine. Bruinsma was said to have had one of the Yugoslavs murdered, and was murdered himself by a former policeman and friend of the Yugoslavs. According to other testimonies the killing of Bruinsma took place on the orders of the Hakkelaar.[97]

In 1996 two journalists interviewed a cannabis dealer who called himself 'Joe' and who had been active in the 1980s. According to Joe, as late as the early 1980s cannabis smuggling was still something thrilling and romantic: making secret hideouts for his stash in the petrol tank of his car, earning a large profit even with small turnovers. But in the middle of the 1980s this changed when the kampers entered the market. In 1986 Joe experienced a rip-deal when kampers picked up an ordered 35 kilograms of hashish with drawn guns and without payment.[98]

However this was not a general characteristic of the cannabis trade. The publications of Van Duyne et al. repeatedly report on the analysed enterprises: scarcely any mention of internal violence.[99] When there is a mention, it seems to be largely a matter of personal predisposition and not always a rational policy. One Dutch smuggler who later died of a heart attack in prison liked to brandish a gun but his police files never mentioned violence against anyone, apart from one attempt at intimidation of an associate from whose warehouse a large consignment of cannabis had disappeared.[100] After his death this smuggler's activities were carried on by three of his associates, one of whom was especially noted for his violent behaviour. For instance, when someone went back on a agreement to sell a ship to the group of three (not knowing that he was dealing with drug smugglers), they went to his house together with four other gang members armed with Kalashnikovs, pistols, and knives, destroyed the house and left the victim in hospital. This was not only rather pointless, since they still did not get the ship, it also put the police on their trail.[101] In the 1990 report of Van Duyne et al. only one group, a family of Antillean smugglers, is mentioned for extreme violence: one registered murder, several rumoured murders, the long-term disappearance of a courier, a Swedish captain who wanted out of the business intimidated, rip deals. But this family dealt in cocaine and amphetamines, not in cannabis.[102]

The idea that the underworld was becoming more and more violent and assassinations were increasing was prevalent by 1995. For criminologists this was an important indication of the growth of organized crime.[103] The anthropologist Mattijs van de Port has, however, deconstructed the use of the word *liquidatie* (as assassination is referred to) by police officers as a factual description. When testifying before parliament on organized crime in 1996, eminent criminologist Cyrille Fijnaut spoke of 'dozens' of assassinations, but in the same testimony he also said that their occurrence was hard to establish even for the police. Sometimes the police had lost track of a criminal, maybe even for years, and it was hard to say if he was murdered or had disappeared with enough money to settle somewhere else.[104] In Van de Port's readings of police files on assassinations, emotional factors such as fear, anxiety, and stress are at least as important as more practical factors, while one hardly encounters any cold-blooded murders by professionals for purely business reasons. Criminals were not simply economic actors or criminal entrepreneurs; they were emotional and volatile. Use of violence to monopolize a market or control a territory was actually not a general characteristic of the illegal drug trade in the Netherlands, more prevalence of violent quarrels leading to murders notwithstanding.

Conclusion

After the liberalization of the Opium Act in 1976 the cannabis market further expanded. By the 1980s cannabis use was not primarily limited to youth and others with countercultural aspirations, but almost 'normalized' in large sections of the Dutch population. Illegal cannabis supply succeeded in adapting to the necessity of increasing and more standardized demand, in particular for cannabis of cheaper varieties. Klaas Bruinsma and his associates evolved from small-scale dealers in a criminal underworld to large-scale international entrepreneurs. They made use of contacts in the maritime transport industry, in countries of supply, and within an upperworld of small business enterprises and families with no criminal associations that were used for covers and stashes. Bruinsma and his associates offered regular supply and even regular business hours to their clients. They profited from the containerization of shipping to smuggle cannabis in bulk. Bruinsma also attempted to turn himself into the leader of a power syndicate controlling Amsterdam's red-light district.

In all this, however, and contrary to the perspective of law enforcement officers and possibly the aspirations of criminals, the supply side of the cannabis market remained fragmented. The networks around Bruinsma never evolved into a permanent structured organization. Supply remained characterized by flexibility, with different entrepreneurs and specialists working in shifting alliances. The police started to hunt for the presumed kingpins in the drug networks at the end of the 1980s, but literally hundreds of groups had entered the market by 1990. They originated from various social and ethnic backgrounds, although they were for the most part dominated by native Dutch. While violence between groups seemed to increase as a response to business disagreements in the market, it remained – with some exceptions – still very much a matter of personal predisposition rather than a rational element of business operations. Kamper communities became an important locus of embeddedness of the cannabis trade. Various groups of smugglers succeeded in establishing crucial alliances in supply countries and within the maritime and truck transport industries. They also moved from trade to production and took a share in the indoor cultivation of nederwiet that had been set up by former hippie idealists.

By 1995 the cannabis market had evolved significantly. Turnover from the sale of cannabis within the Netherlands had become higher than that of coffee, the favourite intoxicant of Dutch society. Dutch smugglers were involved in an extensive and profitable international and transit trade, supplying wholesale on a global scale. This market was messy and resisted attempts by the state to map and control it. Just at the moment that the police intensified their activities against the cannabis trade, it seemed that the point of no return and the possibility of the regulatory regime to control the production, distribution, and consumption of drugs had passed. The new focus of law enforcement agencies directed at the cannabis trade, new ways of gathering and sharing information in cooperation with other countries, and the use of informers and infiltrators certainly offered results, as witnessed by the capture and sentence of the Hakkelaar. However, while battles could be won, the war against drugs continued to go badly. Criminal anarchy was too embedded in Dutch society and too ideally placed to connect supply in countries such as Morocco, Lebanon, Afghanistan, and Pakistan, or the Netherlands itself, with demand in the West, to be overcome by the strategies of the state authorities. Centralized strategies were ultimately deficient against decentralized tactics in a climate of demand for illegal drugs. The asymmetry between these strategies and tactics benefited the smugglers and not the state.

Notes

1. P. C. van Duyne, *Het spook en de dreiging van de georganiseerde misdaad* (The Hague: Sdu, 1995), p. 49.
2. P. Boekhoorn, A. G. van Dijk et al., 'Softdrugs in Nederland. Consumptie en handel' (Amsterdam: Van Dijk, Van Someren & Partners, 1995), p. 60.
3. See A. Nuijten, 'Regulating Paradise: The rise and fall of the housedealer' (paper for the conference, Cannabis: Global Histories, University of Strathclyde, Glasgow, 19–20 April 2018).
4. D. Korf and H. Verbraeck, 'Dealers en dienders. Dynamiek tussen drugsbestrijding en de midden- en hogere niveaus van de cannabis-, cocaïne-, amfetamine- en ecstasyhandel in Amsterdam' (University of Amsterdam, Bonger Institute of Criminology, 1993), pp. 63–5. For the 1980s cannabis market see A. C. M. Jansen, *Cannabis in Amsterdam. Een geografie van hashish en marijuana* (Muiderberg: Dick Coutinho, 1989).
5. Boekhoorn, et al., 'Softdrugs in Nederland'.
6. Most conservative estimate: Boekhoorn, 'Softdrugs in Nederland'. Higher estimates: R. Weijenburg, *Drugs en drugsbestrijding in Nederland. Een beschrijving van de aanpak van het gebruik en misbruik van en de (illegale) handel in verdovende middelen* (The Hague: VUGA Uitgeverij, 1996), p. 175.
7. H. Cohen, 'De hasjcultuur anno 1980: een overlijdensbericht', in C. J. M. Goos and H. J. van der Wal (eds), *Druggebruiken: verslaving en hulpverlening* (Alphen aan den Rijn: Samsom, 1981), pp. 13–24, on pp. 18–22. For the retail prices of cannabis (between 2,500 and 5,000 guilders per kilogram) see also B. Middelburg, *De dominee. Opkomst en ondergang van mafiabaas Klaas Bruinsma* (Amsterdam: L. J. Veen, 1993), p. 39. Quality of cannabis confirmed in personal communication with Wernard Bruijning.
8. Boekhoorn, 'Softdrugs in Nederland'.
9. Weijenberg, *Drugs en drugsbestrijding*, pp. 172–3.
10. van Duyne, *Het spook en de dreiging*, p. 49.
11. Centrale Recherche Informatiedienst (CRI), annual report 1990, p. 86.
12. Based on an average yield of 50 grams per plant. I have taken the figures from CRI, annual report 1992, p. 12 – other CRI reports sometimes give slightly different numbers. See also M. A. M. H. Weijenburg, 'De opsporing van softdrugs in Nederland', *Justitiële Verkenningen* 19 (1993) 60–76, on p. 66. If one takes an average yield of 40 grams, as in CRI, annual report 1993, p. 11, the estimated yield is one-fifth lower.

A. C. M. Jansen, 'De Nederlandse marihuanasector', *Economisch-Statistische Berichten* 78 (1993) 294–6, suggests even lower yields. In the Netherlands cultivation of five cannabis plants or fewer is not prosecuted. See T. Blom, *Opiumwetgeving en drugsbeleid* (Deventer: Wolters Kluwer, 2015), p. 201.
13 CRI, annual report 1993, p. 11; Jansen, 'Nederlandse marihuanasector'.
14 CRI, annual report 1987, p. 25.
15 CRI, annual report 1991, p. 20.
16 CRI, annual report 1988, p. 52; CRI, annual report 1989, p. 91; CRI, annual report 1990, p. 85; CRI, annual report 1991, p. 27; Korf and Verbraeck, 'Dealers en dienders', pp. 57–9; M. van den Eerenbeemt and M. Kruijt, 'Opmars der onderwereldeconomen', *De Volkskrant* 30 November 1996, www.volkskrant.nl/mensen/opmars-der-onderwereld-economen~b82e3539 (accessed 7 August 2020); J. A. Blaauw, *Narcoticabrigade. De eindeloze strijd tegen drugshandelaren* (Baarn: De Fontein, 1997), p. 173.
17 B. R. Aune, 'Maritime drug trafficking: An underrated problem' (Vienna: UNODC, 1990), www.unodc.org/unodc/en/data-and-analysis/bulletin/bulletin_1990-01-01_1_page008.html (accessed 7 August 2020).
18 Weijenburg, *Drugs en drugsbestrijding*, p. 173.
19 CRI, annual report 1993, pp. 10–11.
20 Weijenburg, *Drugs en drugsbestrijding*, p. 174.
21 Weijenberg, *Drugs en drugsbestrijding*, pp. 173–4.
22 Blaauw, *Narcoticabrigade*, p. 165.
23 Blaauw, *Narcoticabrigade*, p. 169.
24 See Chapter 7.
25 Aune, 'Maritime drug trafficking'; Weijenburg, *Drugs*, p. 172; D: *Leeuwarder Courant* 8 September 1988; *Nieuwsblad van het Noorden* 9 September 1988.
26 Jacques, 'Frits van de Wereld', at www.documentairenet.nl/nieuws/frits-van-de-wereld (accessed 7 August 2020); B. Middelburg, *De Godmother. De criminele carrière van Thea Moear, medeoprichter van de Bruinsma-groep* (Amsterdam: L J. Veen, 2000), pp. 102–3.
27 Middelburg, *Dominee*, p. 91.
28 C. Fijnaut, 'Georganiseerde criminaliteit in Nederland: de rol van autochtone criminele groepen', Parlementaire Enquêtecommissie Opsporingsmethoden, Tweede Kamer der Staten-Generaal, 1995–1996, 24 072 (hereafter PEO), 17, pp. 22–5. See also C. Fijnaut and F. Bovenkerk, 'Georganiseerde criminaliteit in Nederland. Een analyse van de situatie in Amsterdam', PEO, 20, pp. 37–41. For an earlier study of Bruinsma by researchers associated with the Ministry of Justice see P. C. van Duyne, R. F. Kouwenberg and G. Romeijn, *Misdaadondernemingen*.

Ondernemende misdadigers in Nederland (Gouda: Quint, 1990), pp. 64–73. Bruinsma is called 'Nicodemus Narcissus' in this study. For the accounts of journalist and 'Bruinsma watcher' Bart Middelburg, who portrayed Bruinsma as a criminal godfather, see his works *Dominee* and *Godmother*. For an opposite view from another journalist: B. van Hout, *De jacht op 'de erven Bruinsma' en de Delta-organisatie: hoe de CID-Haarlem het IRT opblies* (Amsterdam: PS, 2000).

29 Middelburg, *Dominee*; van Hout, *Jacht op de erven Bruinsma*.
30 Middelburg, *Godmother*, pp. 49–67.
31 Middelburg, *Dominee*, p. 38.
32 Middelburg, *Dominee*, pp. 36–7, 58; *Godmother*, pp. 67–82, 110–11, 125.
33 Middelburg, *Godmother*, p. 121.
34 Middelburg, *Godmother*, pp. 121–5.
35 Middelburg, *Godmother*, pp. 131–2, 136–7.
36 Middelburg, *Godmother*, pp. 119–20.
37 Personal communication from Wernard Bruijning to author.
38 Middelburg, *Godmother*, pp. 119–20.
39 Middelburg, *Dominee*, pp. 56–7.
40 Middelburg, *Godmother*, p. 117.
41 Middelburg, *Dominee*, pp. 58–9; *Godmother*, p. 108.
42 Middelburg, *Godmother*, p. 108.
43 Middelburg, *Godmother*, pp. 126–31.
44 Middelburg, *Godmother*, pp. 141–3, 175–178.
45 Middelburg, *Dominee*, p. 183.
46 van Duyne et al., *Misdaadondernemingen*, p. 72.
47 Middelburg, *Dominee*, pp. 81–2.
48 Middelburg, *Dominee*, pp. 55–6, 59–60.
49 Middelburg, *Dominee*, pp. 163–72, relates his assassination to his malfunctioning in directing his criminal operations. For the view that the heydays of Bruinsma were long gone at the time of his murder: van Hout, *Jacht op de erven Bruinsma*.
50 B. Middelburg and K. van Es, *Operatie Delta. Hoe de drugsmafia het IRT opblies*, 3rd rev. edn (Amsterdam: L. J. Veen, 1996); H. Schutten, *De jacht op Octopus. Hoe Nederlandse drugscriminelen greep kregen op de bovenwereld* (Amsterdam: Meulenhoff: 1996); A. B. Hoogenboom, *Schaduwen over Van Traa* (The Hague: Koninklijke Vermande, 2000); van Hout, *Jacht op de erven Bruinsma*.
51 van Duyne et al., *Misdaadondernemingen*, pp. 43, 64–73.
52 van Hout, *Jacht op de erven Bruinsma*, p. 32.
53 Middelburg, *Dominee*, pp. 79–81; expansion of operations: pp. 101–60.

54 van Hout, *Jacht op de erven Bruinsma*, p. 32–3.
55 Middelburg, *Dominee*, p. 181–2.
56 van Duyne et al., *Misdaadondernemingen*, pp. 65–70.
57 van Duyne et al., *Misdaadondernemingen*, pp. 62–3.
58 van Hout, *Jacht op de erven Bruinsma*, p. 77.
59 van Hout, *Jacht op de erven Bruinsma*, p. 69–79.
60 Middelburg, *Dominee*, pp. 85–8.
61 N. Johnson, *Grass Roots: A History of Cannabis in the American West* (Corvallis: Oregon State University Press, 2017), pp. 136–7.
62 On the growth of the cannabis industry in California and Oregon: Johnson, *Grass Roots*, pp. 122–7.
63 Personal communication from Wernard Bruijning to author.
64 CRI, annual report 1990, p. 86.
65 F. Bovenkerk, *Misdaadprofielen* (Amsterdam: Meulenhoff, 2001), pp. 197–215.
66 N. Maalsté, 'Nieuw licht op ontwikkelingen in de Nederlandse cannabissector', in: T. Decorte (ed.), *Cannabisteelt in de Lage Landen. Perspectieven op de cannabismarkt in België en Nederland* (Leuven: Acco, 2008), pp. 29–48.
67 Jansen, 'Nederlandse marihuanasector'; A. C. M. Jansen, 'Prijsvorming in de Nederlandse marihuana-sector 1990–1995. Een beleidsperspectief', *Economisch-Statistische Berichten* 81 (1996) 257–9; A. C. M. Jansen, 'Een halve eeuw productie en consumptie van cannabis in de westerse wereld', in Decorte (ed.), *Cannabisteelt*, pp. 17–28, on pp. 20–2.
68 C. Fijnaut, 'Georganiseerde criminaliteit', PEO, 17, pp. 17–18; J. C. A. M. Cottaar, 'Kooplui, kermisklanten en andere woonwagenbewoners. Groepsvorming en beleid 1870–1945' (PhD thesis, VU-University Amsterdam, 1996); A. Cottaar, L. Lucassen, and W. Willems, 'Woonwagenbewoners en georganiseerde criminaliteit', *Contrast* 14 (25 April 1996) 4–5; S. Khonraad, *Woonwagenbewoners, burgers in de risicomaatschappij* (Utrecht: Jan van Arkel, 2000); Bovenkerk, *Misdaadprofielen*, p. 253; S. van der Poel, 'De vulkanische relatie tussen overheid en woonwagenbewoners', *Tijdschrift voor Crminologie* 40 (1998) 235–56; S. van der Poel, 'De herovering van een no-go area', *Sociologisch Tijdschrift* 25 (1998) 128–30; S. van der Poel, 'Onder en boven de wet: woonwagenbewoners in Noord-Brabant', in M. Moerings, C. M. Pelser, and C. H. Brants (eds), *Morele kwesties in het strafrecht* (Deventer: Gouda Quint, 1999), pp. 75–99.
69 Khonraad, *Woonwagenbewoners*.
70 Fijnaut, 'Georganiseerde criminaliteit', PEO, 17, pp. 17–18.
71 Bovenkerk, *Misdaadprofielen*, pp. 197–215.

72 Fijnaut, 'Georganiseerde criminaliteit', PEO, 17, p. 21.
73 'Only rats lived': P. Tops, J. van Valkenhoef et al., *Waar een klein land groot in kan zijn. Nederland en synthetische drugs in de afgelopen 50 jaar* (The Hague: Boom, 2018), p. 124. On Grad van Wesenbeeck: Delpher digitized newspaper archive (ww.delpher.nl/nl/kranten, hereafter D) : *Nieuwe Rotterdamsche Courant* 2 May and 4 May 1979.
74 J. van der Aa, 'Opkomst en ondergang van een Brabantse misdaadbaas: Janus van W.', in K. Scharrenberg and J. van der Aa, *Georganiseerde misdaad in de Lage Landen* (n.p.: Just Publishers, 2011), pp. 77–97; 'Ondergang van het rijk van Janus', CrimeSite, 20 September 2011, www.crimesite.nl/de-ondergang-van-janus/ (accessed 7 August 2020); P. Tops and J. Tromp, *De achterkant van Nederland. Hoe onder- en bovenwereld verstrengeld raken* (Amsterdam: Balans, 2017), pp. 124–6.
75 M. Husken, *Deals met justitie. Van infiltrant 'Haagse Kees' tot kroongetuige Peter La S.* (Amsterdam: Meulenhoff 2000), pp. 72–3, 131–42.
76 P. P. H. M. Klerks, *Groot in de hasj. Theorie en praktijk van de georganiseerde criminaliteit* (n.p.: Samsom, 2000), p. 334.
77 Korf and Verbraeck, 'Dealers en dienders', pp. 72–3.
78 van Duyne et al., *Misdaadondernemingen*, pp. 40–1.
79 van Duyne et al., *Misdaadondernemingen*, pp. 51–3.
80 Eight criteria were formulated for the grade of organization: a hierarchical structure; active for three or more years; active in more than one criminal business; use of cover companies; money laundering; use of intimidation and violence; corrupting contacts in public and private sectors; sanctions against its own members. Weijenburg, 'Opsporing van softdrugs', pp. 70–1.
81 Weijenburg, *Drug en drugsbestrijding*, pp. 178–180.
82 Middelburg and van Es, *Operation Delta*, pp. 28–9.
83 S. Brown, *Drugsbaron in spijkerbroek. De opzienbarende biografie van een rechtenstudent* (Rijswijk: Elmar, 2001).
84 van Duyne et al., *Misdaadondernemingen*, pp. 39–40.
85 van Duyne et al., *Misdaadondernemingen*, pp. 43–51.
86 van Duyne et al., *Misdaadondernemingen*, pp. 51–3.
87 van Duyne, *Het spook en de dreiging*, pp. 51–3.
88 van Duyne, *Het spook en de dreiging*, p. 55.
89 van Duyne, *Het spook en de dreiging*, p. 60.
90 van Duyne, *Het spook en de dreiging*, p. 61.
91 Boekhoorn et al. 'Softdrugs in Nederland'.
92 Middelburg, *Godmother*, p. 123.
93 Personal communication from Wernard Bruijning to author.
94 Fijnaut, 'Georganiseerde criminaliteit', PEO, 17, p. 22; Middelburg, *Dominee*, pp. 182–5.

95 Fijnaut, 'Georganiseerde criminaliteit', PEO, 17, p. 22; Middelburg, *Dominee*, pp. 182–5.
96 Middelburg, *Dominee*, p. 170
97 Middelburg, *Dominee*, pp. 172–2; Middelburg and van Es, *Operatie Delta*, pp. 27–8.
98 van den Eerenbeemt and Kruijt, 'Opmars der onderwereldeconomen'.
99 van Duyne et al., *Misdaadondernemingen*, pp. 47, 55–6; van Duyne, *Het spook en de dreiging*, p. 55.
100 van Duyne et al., *Misdaadondernemingen*, pp. 47–8.
101 van Duyne et al., *Het spook en de dreiging*, pp. 51–3.
102 van Duyne et al., *Misdaadondernemingen*, pp. 51–6.
103 See the first WODC-Monitor of 1998, quoted in M. van de Port, *Geliquideerd. Criminele afrekeningen in Nederland* (Amsterdam: Meulenhoff, 2001), p. 56.
104 van de Port, *Geliquideerd*, p. 43.

7

Global perils III: Colombian syndicates and cocaine

While cannabis became the most important illegal drug of choice in the Netherlands, in the 1980s demand for other illegal drugs started to expand significantly as well. These included cocaine and synthetic drugs such as amphetamines and XTC. New supply lines and new networks of supply came into existence. This chapter investigates the rise of cocaine smuggling to and through the Netherlands. In the United States restrictive policies regarding amphetamine production had stimulated the demand for a substitute stimulant, cocaine. Colombian entrepreneurs supplying this demand expanded their trade into Europe.[1] In the 1980s cocaine became popular among a very heterogeneous group of users. For instance, criminologists estimated the number of cocaine users in Amsterdam by the early 1990s at around 10,000. These were mostly native Dutch city dwellers in their mid-twenties to late thirties, among them a sizeable percentage of Surinamese.[2] In the course of the 1990s populations of cocaine users became more and more diverse, ranging from middle-class users to marginalized individuals in the large cities such as the homeless and poor youth, to clubbers and ravers.[3]

To supply this new demand cocaine smuggling had to be embedded in society and ways of operation to link production and supply had to be found. In the 1980s and 1990s cocaine was supplied by networks who were, like the Greek networks of the interwar period, not embedded in Dutch society to the extent of the Chinese and the Turks, but who were capable of allying themselves with groups that were embedded. Interwar period cocaine had been produced by the pharmaceutical industry in European and other industrialized countries. The network chains that supplied cocaine to European consumers in the 1980s and 1990s connected farmers and producers in Colombia, Peru, and Bolivia to suppliers of precursor chemicals, and to smugglers and criminal entrepreneurs overseas. Next to Spain the Netherlands became the most important transit hub for a European cocaine trade that was perceived as a global peril threatening Western society – a South American variant of the opiate peril from Asia. The volume of seizures of cocaine in the Netherlands increased from the mid-1980s onwards and reached unprecedented heights after 1990 (see Figure 5 in the Appendix).

As in the case of cannabis, the strategies of the Dutch state to enforce the drug regulatory regime failed. Even where after 1989 the cargoes of cocaine that were seized by law enforcement agencies became larger and larger, supply never became scarce. Once again it proved impossible for the Dutch state to control transport routes by sea and air, whether from Colombia, from former Dutch colonies in South America, or from elsewhere.

Producing cocaine

In the first half of the 1960s the growing of coca, its processing into cocaine, and the smuggling of the drug had become increasingly a systematic and extensive criminal enterprise in Latin America. US policies driving Bolivian coca farmers into the lowland jungles, in effect making cultivation uncontrollable, contributed to this development.[4] The central role of Colombians in the cocaine trade started after 1970 in reaction to increased American and European demand. Before moving into cocaine trafficking Colombian smugglers of alcohol, cigarettes, and fabrics in the 1960s had taken up the smuggling of Santa Marta marihuana ('Colombian Gold') into the USA. Smugglers encouraged farmers in Colombia to increase cannabis cultivation. After the 1973 military coup in Chile, Colombia took over from this country as a transit hub for cocaine, since the Chilean military dictatorship rewarded the USA for its support by handing over several drug traffickers to the Americans. Producers of and traders in illegal cocaine moved their operations to Colombia, linking their ways of operation to the existing culture of smuggling in the country. Peru and Bolivia also developed into cocaine exporting countries.[5]

Various steps are needed in the process of turning the agricultural crop coca into the end product cocaine. The processes involved are low tech and not capital intensive, so ideally suited for less-developed countries. Refinement takes place in a laboratory called the 'kitchen', or '*cocina*'. The cocaine molecule is extracted from dried coca leaves to make a coca paste by adding chemicals and pressing and filtering the mixture. The first steps in the process are relatively simple and take place close to the cultivation fields, obviating the need for bulk transports of coca leaves. To produce the end product, cocaine hydrochloride or powder cocaine (which again can be converted in crack or freebase), more extensive refinement and 'cooking' is needed, done in laboratories in rural areas with the necessary infrastructure (landing strips, communication technologies, militarized security) or hidden in cities.[6]

Cocaine, as heroin and cannabis, was basically a product of a neo-colonial structure, with cheap producers in low-cost less-developed countries and its profit mainly going to a group of entrepreneurs. The drug contributed considerably to the Colombian economy. A fall in the world's cocaine prices in the mid-1980s meant that the drug's contribution to the revenues of Colombian exports decreased from 70 per cent to 30 per cent, and its percentage of the GDP from 7 to 2 or 3 per cent. Nevertheless in the 1990s the Colombian illegal drug industry (including the trade in marihuana and heroin) annually generated between 2.5 billion and 3 billion US dollars.[7]

Coca farmers in Peru and Bolivia received around 2.5 US dollars for a kilogram of coca.[8] The costs of coca paste needed to produce 1 kilogram of cocaine came to 800 dollars in 1995; 1 kilogram of cocaine could be bought in Colombia for 2,000 dollars.[9] Even when the prices of cocaine dropped, overall profits of the industry remained huge. Wholesale prices of a kilogram of cocaine in the Netherlands went down from 35,100 US dollars in 1983 (or 100,000 Dutch guilders) to 18,550 US dollars (or almost 35,000 Dutch guilders – the dollar had by then lost almost a third of its value) in 1993, and then up again to 25,000 US dollars (46,000 Dutch guilders) in 1995.[10] In 1993 Dutch smugglers claimed that they could buy a kilogram of cocaine in Colombia for prices of 800 to 1,350 dollars. Wholesale distributors who bought a kilogram from the smugglers for 20,000 to 27,000 dollars sold it on to retail dealers for 30,000 to 55,000 dollars (or 55,000 to 100,000 guilders).[11] Despite rising demand, the costs of cocaine for consumers did not rise. Taking into account the fluctuating exchange rates between US dollars and guilders, the retail price of a gram of cocaine on the Dutch market sank from 200 guilders (70 US dollars) in 1983 to 160 guilders (50 dollars) in 1984, and then went to between 85 and 175 guilders (46 to 95 US dollars) in 1993, and at least 75 guilders (48 dollars) in 1995.[12] As we will see in this chapter, criminal anarchy ensured segmentation and competition in the market, countervailing the effects of rising demand and the risks of illegality on price levels.

Economist Francisco Thoumi has identified a complex of factors to explain the success of the Colombian cocaine industry: political (operating in a weak state), geographical (Colombia is located between the coca-producing countries Bolivia and Peru and the North American market, with easy access to the transit hub of the Caribbean), and socio-economic (long-term expertise in smuggling activities, an entrepreneurial culture focused on high short-term returns, and a large illegal migration of Colombians to the United States embedding cocaine trafficking).[13] Moreover, the illegal drug trade thrived in a cultural environment with institutions that do not impose behavioural controls and that tolerate and condone deviant behaviour.[14] The Colombian drug industry was embedded in society and based on historical traditions of smuggling and deviance.

For export, contacts in the demand countries were essential but they were also essential for importing the precursor chemicals necessary to produce powder cocaine, such as potassium permanganate, acetone, ethyl ether, methylethylketone (MEK), and toluene. For the production of 1 kilogram of cocaine approximately 590 litres of gasoline or kerosene, and 16 to 25 litres of other precursor chemicals are needed.[15] The United States was at first the most important supplier of these precursors, but after 1990 European companies took an increasing share of the market in a process of corporate non-compliance with the international drug regulatory regime. The import of these chemicals was often diverted in illegal channels by different methods: 'adulterated invoices; fictitious loans, transactions, returns or losses; duplicated licenses or permits; use of false clients or suppliers [...] authorised import by trade names linked to cocaine producers, with valid permits'.[16] By these operations the restrictions imposed by the United Nations Convention against Illicit Traffic in Narcotic Drugs and Psychotropic Substances of 1988 were circumvented.

In 1994 the Colombian National Council for Narcotic Drugs withdrew the permit of the Dutch company Holland Chemical International (HCI), or Holanda Colombia, for the distribution of chemicals and raw materials (including kerosene) in Colombia. Subsequently throughout the country eight offices and distribution centres of HCI were raided by the Colombian police, including those in the cities of Medellin, Cali, and Barranquilla, seizing 1,753 tonnes of chemicals, including MEK and toluene. The Colombian police claimed that a severe blow had been dealt to the illegal cocaine industry. Journalists were shown photos of illegal cocaine laboratories in the jungle raided by police or army: in nine out of ten of the photos, drums with the legend HC (Holanda Colombia) were visible.[17] Trade in MEK was quite profitable: its price had gone up in a few months from 220,000 pesos (260 US dollars) to 1.3 million pesos (1,540 US dollars).[18] A year earlier the police had also seized supplies from HCI destined for cocaine production.[19]

Founded in 1920 in the Dutch city of Dordrecht as J. & W. Wegman, under the name Holanda Colombia, the company had established itself the next year in Barranquilla in Colombia, located near to the Caribbean Sea and close to the Guajira peninsula: a traditional smuggling area that in the 1980s became an important transit point for the illegal cocaine trade. In its beginnings Holanda Colombia functioned as a distributor of the products of the Shell oil refinery on the Dutch island of Curaçao close to the coastline of Venezuela and Colombia. Under the directorship of Amsterdam-born Gerry Staartjes, Holanda Colombia opened offices in Ecuador, Peru, Venezuela, and Brazil, and became the largest distributor of chemicals and raw materials for the chemical industry in Latin America, changing its name again to Holland Chemical International.[20]

Unsurprisingly after the police raids HCI denied its involvement in the cocaine industry. The company claimed that the drums with its labels had been stolen or sold to apparently bona fide clients, even although there was sometimes something wrong with the latter's permits. According to HCI the trade in MEK accounted for only 4 per cent of its revenues. Police experts acknowledged that the chemicals could have been stolen, but considered this a purely theoretical possibility when looking at the enormous quantity of the chemicals involved, in the range of 100,000 litres. Nevertheless the company was not prosecuted. Economic interests were too great since HCI supplied chemicals to most of the Colombian chemical industry.[21]

The 'cartels'

In the popular imagination the central players in these operations were drug lords such as the infamous Pablo Escobar, who was murdered in 1993 but whose image can still be found on t-shirts in European cities. Escobar's group, the so-called Medellin 'cartel', and his competitors from the so-called Cali 'cartel', have been portrayed in similar ways to the Chinese triads in the 1970s: as hierarchical and closely organized societies under strict leadership and with their tentacles spreading around the globe, held together by (the threat of) violence. In contrast to this popular view academic researchers such as Thoumi and Damiàn Zaitch have stressed the fluidity and flexibility of the Colombian cocaine trade, and its heterogeneous character. Rather than viewing the Colombian cocaine trade within the context of sensational reporting on octopus-like cartels, they should be seen as specific manifestations of criminal anarchy. Experts have long expressed their doubts even about applying the word 'cartel' to the Colombian drug industry. A 'cartel' in an economic sense controls raw material production and most distribution systems, so effectively controlling the price of a good. This has not been the case in the Colombian drug industry, which can be understood better as 'chain networks'.[22] Thoumi prefers to describe the Colombian 'cartels' involved in the production of the refined product (cocaine) and its distribution and export to other countries, where it is taken up for the retail trade by other links in the chains, as 'export syndicates'.[23]

Decisive in the evolution of these syndicates was the development of large-scale smuggling methods in the 1980s. While the volumes of post-war cocaine smuggling started out rather small, in the early 1980s one innovator began to smuggle cocaine in planes to the United States, having established his own airport on a Caribbean island.[24] In order to minimize the high risks of the cocaine export and to maximize profits, producers and smugglers started to band together. By funding and exporting combined cargoes and accepting the loss of a certain percentage of these cargoes because of seizures by customs and police, they created economies of scale that ensured a high level of profits. These syndicates bought cocaine paste in Bolivia and Peru, organized their refinement into cocaine in laboratories in Colombia, and exported and made wholesale transactions of their products in the United States and elsewhere. They also created money-laundering systems and ensured social support among wealthy Colombians by letting them buy a share in the exports. Other elements of their support networks included politicians, guerrillas, paramilitaries, police and army personnel, and suppliers of precursor chemicals.

However, the whole structure of the illegal cocaine industry remained too precarious for these syndicates either to develop into more bureaucratized organizations or even to be able to control the drug trade. Thoumi writes:

> The illegal drug industry comprised a diverse group of participants: peasants, chemists, various types of suppliers, purchasers and intermediaries, pilots, lawyers, financial and tax advisers, enforcers, bodyguards, front men [...] and smugglers that helped launder profits. They were tied to the central cartels in different ways. Some were directly part of the cartels, but many were loosely tied to them and acted more like independent contractors that sold their services for a fee. This arrangement was frequently preferred by the cartels, because when law enforcers captured subcontractors, they could provide only minimum information about the cartel's structure and leadership.[25]

Even the famous Medellin cartel of Pablo Escobar, who at a certain point took up the fight against the Colombian state, was not a formalized organization at all. Escobar had a close collaborator organizing the transport of cargoes, while other 'lieutenants' undertook other specific tasks in production and distribution. Specialists (chemical engineers, financial experts etc.) worked on specific assignments, and an indeterminate number of 'foot soldiers' were available for different less important tasks. Enforcement and the execution of violence were outsourced to professional killers or *sicarios* from the slums. The organization was not formal and division of labour was flexible, the personal authority of the boss based on charisma, personal relations, and fear.[26] To present this kind of flexible organization in an organogram, as is often done, is rather misleading, suggesting a tightness of operations that is exaggerated.

The export syndicates came from six different regions of Colombia that all had their own traditions of smuggling. One was the area on the northern Caribbean coast involved in the marihuana trade, with the peninsula of La Guajira and the port of Barranquilla. Another was the Antioquia region with its capital Medellin. Here Pablo Escobar had become an apprentice in the trade as bodyguard of a famous 'king of smuggling'.[27] Descriptions of the business mentality of the population of Antioquia show remarkable similarities to the business mentality often accorded to another population with a long-standing tradition of smuggling: the Dutch. In the words of a journalist: 'They are known as hard workers, thrifty, with an astute sense of business and an exaggerated affinity for money and material gains and furthermore not too picky about *how* the money is made.'[28]

Cocaine smuggling also developed in the central region of Boyacá and Cundinamarca with its rich tradition of illegal exploitation of emerald mines; in the low-profile centres Cucuta and Bucaramanga in the eastern region closest to the Venezuelan border; and in the southern region of the Cauca Valley on the Pacific coast with its centre in the industrial city of Cali. The small cities in the northern Cauca Valley – where after the imprisonment of leaders of the Cali syndicate a younger generation of small and independent groups and entrepreneurs came to the fore in associations with Mexican groups – became of importance after 1995.[29]

The CRI was bewildered by the rapid changes in the cocaine market. It reported that the global cocaine trade was 75 per cent controlled by two large-scale criminal organizations (the Medellin and Cali 'cartels'). At the same time it sub-divided these cartels in eight families that operated from Colombia and Venezuela, and emphasized that the situation could be totally different again within a few months.[30] US intelligence analysts identified ten to fourteen large organizations running the cocaine export to the US and Europe in the early 1990s. The most important of them, the 'Cali cartel', was said to control 80 per cent of the export to the USA. However, many independent groups continued to operate. These groups also worked as independent contractors for the larger syndicates in a proliferation of criminal anarchy that made effectuation of law enforcement policies extremely difficult. It was impossible for any single syndicate to control the drug trade; it remained relatively easy for small producers and smugglers to enter the market. Moreover the syndicates did not control the production of raw materials or the systems of distribution. The decrease in prices mentioned above and a stagnating North American market, combined with increased activities of Colombian and Peruvian governments against production and traffic, led to the demise of the Medellin syndicate and the imprisonment of leaders of the Cali syndicate. Paramilitary and guerrilla organizations became increasingly involved in protecting drug production and trade, fuelling political struggles for the profits. The two main consequences were the further proliferation of the drug industry into many small 'cartels' or '*cartelitos*', and the search for new markets in Europe.[31]

Cocaine to Europe

However, unlike the situation in the United States, in Europe there was not a sizeable Colombian presence in which smuggling and distribution of cocaine could be embedded. To enter the illegal European drug markets Colombians had to copy the Greek smugglers of the interwar period who had succeeded in making alliances with native criminal groups. Contacts were established between the Colombian drug industry and Italian criminal groups, with Sicilian migrants in Venezuela as intermediaries. For instance, the Sicilian Cuntrera-Caruana family had ties with legitimate enterprises all over the world, including an investment company on the Dutch Caribbean island of St Maarten.[32]

Seizures of cocaine in Europe increased significantly in the mid-1980s: 0.8 tonnes in 1985; 1.4 tonnes in 1986; 5.3 tonnes in 1988; 13 tonnes in 1990.[33] In northwestern Europe (the Netherlands, Germany, the UK, Belgium, and Denmark) the volume of all seizures combined multiplied a hundredfold, from 80 kilograms in 1981 to 8 tonnes in 1990. After the fall of the Berlin Wall traffic was furthermore diverted through Eastern European countries. For instance, in 1991 more than 200 kilograms of cocaine destined for the Netherlands and the UK were seized in the Czech Republic and in the Polish port of Gdansk.[34]

In the 1990s Spain and the Netherlands were the main countries of import from South America.[35] Of these Spain was the most important import destination point in Europe. Importers and dealers interviewed by criminologists in Amsterdam explained in the early 1990s that cocaine was sent 'in bulk' (thousands rather than hundreds of kilograms) to Spain and then moved in smaller quantities throughout Europe.[36] The shared language made Spain a convenient destination for the Colombian drug industry. Most import was arranged for by traditional Galician smuggling groups from fishing communities, who moved from the smuggling of cigarettes to hashish and cocaine. Their activities were often facilitated by corruption among police and customs, and links were forged with Italian crime groups.[37]

Cocaine and the Netherlands

Of a total of 17 tonnes of cocaine seized in northwestern Europe in the 1980s, almost half was seized in the Netherlands.[38] In the port of Rotterdam in April 1989 100 kilograms were seized on a Colombian ore carrier; later that year 330 kilograms on a Surinamese ship, the *Paramaribo*. In May 1991 200 kilograms were seized, again on board the *Paramaribo*. In February 1991 650 kilograms were found in a hangar in the village of Oudenhoorn, smuggled from Trinidad to Rotterdam. Other cargoes came from Curaçao. Such large cargoes were probably meant for onward transit into other European countries.[39] In 1995 1 tonne was found in a Rotterdam storehouse. Rotterdam, however, was not the only point of entry of cocaine into the Netherlands. In 1990 2.7 tonnes were found in a harbour warehouse in IJmuiden, a fishing port on the west coast; in 1994 3 tonnes in another smaller harbour, Zeewolde. In Amsterdam in 1992 1 tonne was found in a Colombian van, and in 1994 again 1.1 tonne. The Dutch harbours were part of a whole group of North Sea ports, including Antwerp and Hamburg, that were points of entry for the cocaine trade.[40]

In interviews that Zaitch held between 1996 and 1999 with Colombians involved in the drug trade with the Netherlands, he found that they were very positive about the Dutch harbours and considered them safe points of transit. Not only Rotterdam but Amsterdam, IJmuiden, and Vlissingen were also considered quite safe and convenient. One Colombian wholesale distributor operating in Amsterdam told Zaitch that 'sometimes you lose something [but] what is good in Rotterdam is that it goes fast, you take the thing and you sleep elsewhere [the cocaine container or bulk can be quickly moved to stash]'.[41] Police, customs, and port authority officers in the Rotterdam harbour interviewed in 1994 considered the port impossible to control. In the early 1990s 32,000 ships carrying around 35 million containers docked at the port each year. The ships were lying at anchor spread over a quay of 58 kilometres. A few dozen customs officers with four or five dogs were able to check only three or four ships each day. Customs estimated that 1 per cent of all ships carried illegal drugs; this percentage was based on multiplying by ten the figure of thirty-two ships on which contraband had actually been seized. Even with refined methods of selecting the ships to search based on the country of origin and on information from the CRI and other law enforcement investigations, customs thought they could at most catch 30 per cent of illegal cargoes – an acceptable risk for smugglers.

Cocaine was expertly hidden by the Colombian exporters. In one police operation cocaine was found in vessels with frozen and concentrated passion-fruit juice, soldered and sealed; sniffer dogs could not smell the drugs. Cocaine was also found in cargoes of shoe heels and engine parts, tars and cokes, or in false bottoms and walls of containers and on the outside of freighters bringing fruit into the European harbours. Import-export and transport companies, either front companies or bona fide enterprises unaware of what they were transporting, could bring the cocaine into the port and from there the excellent Dutch infrastructure made it possible to reach 80 per cent of Western Europe within twenty-four hours.[42]

Caribbean connections

Smaller cargoes of cocaine came in through the airport of Schiphol, carried by couriers. Schiphol had excellent connections to other airports in Latin America and Europe, but also with the Dutch Antilles islands in the Caribbean and the former Dutch colony of Suriname. The islands of Curaçao and Aruba, close to the coast of Venezuela, were meeting points for Colombian drug entrepreneurs. On Aruba there lived a sizeable Colombian community.[43]

Suriname had become independent in 1975. In 1980 the military staged a *coup d'état* and took over control in the country until civilian government and free elections returned in 1987. During the military regime a guerrilla war of the Maroon peoples of the interior of Suriname against the government broke out. With the country isolated, economically vulnerable, and in need of foreign exchange, the illegal cocaine trade offered excellent opportunities for Surinamese entrepreneurs. Suriname had, because of its former colonial status and the presence of a large Surinamese migrant community of 250,000 people in the Netherlands, strong logistical and social ties with its former colonizer. Dutch and US law enforcement agencies tried to gather intelligence in Suriname and reported on the presence there of Colombians, Peruvians, and Bolivians.[44] Witnesses testified to the CocaïneParamaribo (COPA) team – a special team of the Dutch judiciary and police that in the 1990s investigated the Surinamese involvement in the cocaine trade – that the Surinamese military was already in 1982 facilitating the transit of cargoes of 100 to 150 kilograms of cocaine through the country. In 1983 the first tip-offs of Surinamese cocaine smuggling reached the CRI. In that year the president of the Surinamese national bank resigned because he did not wish to facilitate a loan with dubious Colombian origins.[45] The native Tucajana tribe in the interior was armed by the military and not only fought against the Maroon insurgents, but was actively involved in the cocaine trade.[46] There was much speculation about the involvement of the Surinamese military regime in the cocaine trade, about the use of airstrips in the interior of the jungle, and about the establishment of cocaine laboratories for production. If we believe the witness statements to the COPA team, military dictator Desi Bouterse operated a cocaine laboratory in the interior of Suriname, 10 kilometres from the border with Guyana. Coca paste was flown in using small planes from Colombia, Bolivia, and Brazil, and landed on an airstrip near the laboratory, where the paste was refined. Witness accounts spoke of more than one cocaine laboratory, and of assassinations of Colombians and native people who guarded the laboratories and needed to be silenced. Cocaine was sent to Paramaribo in armoured military cars. From there the drug was exported by planes and boats. Bouterse was in charge of a fleet of four or five ships that transported the cocaine hidden in frozen fish.[47] Cocaine was also transported by boats on the Amazon to the city of Belém in Brazil and from there the cocaine, transferred to other ships or motorboats, and sometimes to trucks, was brought to French Guyana using traditional smuggling routes. From Guyana the cocaine was flown to Europe, to Schiphol or to airports in France and Belgium, from where the cocaine was transported by trucks to the Netherlands. Another route was through West Africa, by boat or by plane courier.[48]

In 1986 Bouterse's second-in-command was arrested in Miami by DEA undercover agents when he tried to sell free passage through the Surinamese airspace to traffickers. In 1994 the son of Bouterse was arrested for involvement in the drug trade.[49] He was released when witnesses withdrew their statements, but was finally convicted in 2005 and served three of his eight-year prison sentence. In 2013 he was again arrested, in Panama, and extradited to the United States where in 2016 he was sentenced to sixteen years in prison. In 1990 a Colombian plane with 1,000 kilograms of cocaine and a Cuban refugee and possible arms trader on board had to make an emergency stop in a small mining town in the interior of Suriname that was occupied by Maroon insurgents, the so-called Jungle Commando. The leader of the Commando, Ronnie Brunswijk, then in peace negotiations with the Surinamese state (civil authority was restored in 1987 but Bouterse was still supreme commander of the military), handed the drugs over to the police. Bouterse was so angered that he led Brunswijk into a trap and had him arrested. Two of the latter's bodyguards were shot dead. Under pressure from the Surinamese judiciary, the USA, and the Netherlands, Brunswijk was released. Later it turned out that not only the military but also the Maroon Jungle Commando were involved or at least facilitated the illegal drug trade. In 1999 Brunswijk was sentenced in absentia to eight years in prison by a Dutch court; in 2000 this sentence was reduced to six years on appeal.[50] Bouterse himself did not escape prosecution by Dutch law enforcement either. A special police unit investigated his involvement in the cocaine trade to the Netherlands, and in 1999 he was sentenced in absentia as well. The court at The Hague gave him a sentence of sixteen years in prison and a fine of 4.6 million euros; in appeal the sentence was reduced to eleven years. The court considered Bouterse's involvement in the smuggling of 474 kilogram of cocaine to the Netherlands proven; his connection to five other transports not.[51] Despite this sentence Bouterse was elected president of Suriname in 2010 and held the office until 2020.

In the media Bouterse was presented as the leader of a 'Suricartel', although in the court case the prosecution could not prove his involvement in a criminal organization. From the perspective of criminal anarchy it is more correct to see him as a facilitator and as a participant in an export syndicate. Surinamese state officials and high-ranking military officers had developed into criminal diversifiers, facilitating the cocaine trade and laundering drug money, but also involved in many other affairs of corruption and dubious economic transactions. The link between the underworld and the upperworld here became so close that it was hard to see where one started and the other ended.

Involvement in the cocaine trade went through all classes of society and involved not only the military. It went from wealthy Hindustani businessmen providing capital and laundering profits to poor Maroons operating as couriers to Europe.[52] One example of a Surinamese smuggling operation is that of a family and its assistants who, with help from customs officers and the military in Suriname, sent smaller cargoes of cocaine (of up to 50 kilograms) by couriers with suitcases on planes, as well as larger amounts (of up to 250 kilograms) also by air through a transport company to the Netherlands. The family worked together with an export syndicate from Medellin and could operate because of corruption among personnel at both Paramaribo and Schiphol airports. Part of the cocaine was meant for transit to the United States. An import-export company trading in cacao and coffee acted as a front for the cocaine trade and also imported ether for cocaine production into Suriname.[53]

In 1997 the Surinamese police estimated that annually 26 tonnes of cocaine were sent to Europe through Suriname, with an export value of 1 billion US dollars – about as much as that of the most important export sector of Suriname, bauxite mining.[54] In 1989 one-quarter of all cocaine (392 kilogrammes) seized at Schiphol airport came from Suriname; in 1990 it was half, with a volume of 900 kilograms.[55] In 1991 36 per cent of all cocaine seized in the Netherlands came from Suriname; in 1992 it was half.[56] In 1996 one-quarter of all cocaine couriers arrested in the airport came from Paramaribo.[57] The route from Colombia through Suriname had become an import entry point for Colombian cocaine.

Another route from Colombia was through Venezuela and Curaçao. In its report of 1987 the CRI concluded there were unlimited amounts of cocaine on the Dutch Antilles islands. In 1986 2,000 kilograms were seized on Curaçao alone. Through couriers or sent by post, the drugs went by plane to the Netherlands.[58] Weekly cargoes of cocaine from Curaçao were seized at the airport. In 1992 9 per cent of all cocaine seized in the Netherlands came from Curaçao, some of it by ship.[59] In 1993 11 per cent of all seized cocaine came from Suriname and 11 per cent from the Dutch Antilles.[60] These percentages fluctuated each year, and could be disproportionate because of the relatively strict surveillance at the airport (including searching all passengers on direct flights from Suriname, Curaçao, and Aruba) compared to other routes of entry. The vast majority of cocaine from South America reached the Netherlands and Europe by sea.

Smuggling cocaine and the Netherlands

The connections with Suriname and the Dutch Caribbean contributed to making the Netherlands second major entry point for Colombian cocaine in Europe, after Spain. The cultural climate in the Netherlands was furthermore congenial to Colombian entrepreneurs. Some of them told Zaitch that they greatly valued the business mentality in the Netherlands – characterized by pragmatism, efficiency, and professionalism – and the many import-export companies proliferating in the 1990s, as conducive to the cocaine trade. Moreover, since trade is international it was quite convenient that one could easily meet and make deals with contacts from many different nationalities. Bars and coffee shops were places where meetings and deals were socially embedded. One entrepreneur told Zaitch:

> I meet people from places I never imagined before. The owners of the coffee-shop [where he meets them] are Dutch, they did time in Spain. [Another guy] is from Venezuela. Then you find Surinamese, Antilleans and Moroccans, all trying to get something when you enter and tell you are a Colombian. [X] sells to Germans, and so on. It is fantastic, so many people, I learnt a lot in Amsterdam, I don't want to leave.[61]

Although Colombians such as this entrepreneur were involved in the import and wholesale distribution of cocaine in the Netherlands (but not so much in the retail trade) as couriers, envoys, importers, or in an opportunistic adventure, the most important importers were Dutchmen and Surinamese.[62] A modest migration of Colombians to the Netherlands had started in the 1980s (by the end of the century there were around 6,500 Colombian residents in the country, and 3,000 to 4,000 illegal migrants), but this never led to the formation of an ethnic and cultural conclave comparable to the Chinatowns or to the Turkish communities. Most of the migrants in the 1980s were young women married to native Dutchmen, or working as cleaners or prostitutes.[63] Zaitch found it impossible to determine how many of the Colombian migrants were involved in the cocaine business when he did his research in the late 1990s, but felt it likely that only a small number of them were.[64]

Heterogeneity characterizes the classification of smugglers that Amsterdam criminologists Dirk Korf and Hans Verbraeck produced on the basis of interviews with cocaine traders in the Netherlands. This classification was based on a limited number of interviews and the criminologists did not claim to offer a definitive analysis of the smuggling of cocaine. Their analysis, however, was basically confirmed by other studies (see below). Smuggling cocaine to the Netherlands was not controlled by any Colombian 'cartel'. The Colombian export syndicates performed a key role in the whole chain of production, distribution, and consumption in Europe by supplying a refined product ready for export, but the actual process of smuggling was undertaken by independent groups and individual entrepreneurs that succeeded in establishing contacts with the suppliers in South America. Korf and Verbraeck mention four types. (a) Individual traders who worked alone, with contacts and networks in South American countries where they bought the cocaine that they subsequently smuggled back into the Netherlands themselves. (b) Individual traders who went to South America to purchase cocaine, but intermittently used South American couriers for the actual smuggling operations. (c) Groups of smugglers active in the import of various drugs, of which individual members fetched supplies in South America and had them smuggled into the Netherlands by couriers. (d) Dutchmen married into South American families and cooperating with these families' smuggling operations.[65] Multinational enterprises were rare and while import and distribution definitely became professionalized, it remained the province of loosely organized groups without closely structured hierarchical organization, often undetected by the police.[66]

Nevertheless, the role of the small-scale smugglers bringing a kilogram or so of cocaine hidden on their own bodies to the Netherlands, for personal use and to share it with or sell it to friends and acquaintances had by 1990 become completely overshadowed by that of the large-scale traders: Dutch intermediaries who bought dozens of kilograms from the Colombian suppliers and sold it on the Dutch market to wholesale distributors.[67]

There is evidence that with the increase in cocaine imports the relations between the actors in the market became more hostile towards each other. One Dutch cocaine importer left the business at the end of the 1980s because too many guns were around, at least so he claimed. Since most of the trade in cocaine was done on credit, this was the only mechanism to ensure the honouring of business arrangements.[68]

Finding allies in the Netherlands

In the search for buyers in Europe the Colombian export syndicates sent envoys to Europe.[69] Two participants who turned police informers gave more details on the resulting networks in popular publications authored by criminologist Bovenkerk and published in the mid-1990s. Although these accounts are not to be taken at face value they do give us more insights into the forging of Colombian–Dutch connections. Bovenkerk wrote a book on the cocaine trade based on his interviews with one of the envoys named Bettien Martens, a female Dutch go-between for the Colombian syndicates who was arrested by Italian police in Rome in 1992 and immediately turned witness for the prosecution and cooperated with Italian, American, and Dutch law enforcement agencies.[70] Martens told the police and Bovenkerk stories of how the 'Cali cartel' from 1988 onwards attempted to set up business relationships with Klaas Bruinsma, but Bruinsma preferred to work with other suppliers. Martens' stories confirm analyses of the heterogeneity and relative accessibility of the cocaine market. She told Bovenkerk of her attempts to find buyers in the Netherlands for large cargoes of cocaine sent by members of the Cali syndicate:

> How did the drug world [in the Netherlands] precisely look from the perspective of Colombia and working for the cartel? The only real group that I could find was that of Klaas Bruinsma. I had direct contact with around ten men around Klaas and around them were some shadowy figures and people who occasionally worked for him [...] there were some dealers here and there who knew and watched each other, but that was mostly local. There was a person of importance in [the city of] Vianen, there were a few big guys in Eindhoven, in Venlo there was something and in Heerlen there was a man running a boxing gym in Belgium who worked with Klaas, and Maastricht was more or less in Turkish hands. In Rotterdam there were a few groups, there was a well-organized Jewish organization and there was something in Nijmegen. In the north of the Netherlands I knew strangely enough absolutely nobody.[71]

To Martens the Dutch drug market was fragmented and rather opaque at the level of importers and wholesale dealers, confirming our notions and images of criminal anarchy. Contacts were made on the basis of a network of personal relationships; meetings took place where the drug trade was socially embedded, such as the Buggie coffee shop in Amsterdam owned by Bruinsma.[72]

Cali smugglers did not succeed in making a deal with Bruinsma, but because of the heterogeneity of the market it turned out not to be very problematic to make contacts with other Dutch smugglers. Another envoy sent to the Netherlands was a Colombian from Cali named Londoño who had spent four years in a Spanish prison for smuggling. He was sent by the Grajales family, owners of a vast business empire that included plantations, coalmines, a chain of department stores, and the largest Colombian winery. The plantations were connected to a fruit juice production and export business. Containers of fruit juice were excellently suited for smuggling cocaine into the US and Europe. The Grajales business empire was a front for cocaine trade and money laundering. The family was based in the Cauca Valley near the city of Cali, and hence closely associated with other Cali entrepreneurs such as 'Gentleman' Pedro Filipe Villaquiràn, who in 1992 would be arrested by the Italian police together with Bettina Martens.[73] The Grajales envoy lived in the Netherlands for four years, travelling back and forth to the UK and Colombia and forging alliances with Dutch partners. The Grajales family had legitimate business contacts in the Netherlands, and approached various Dutch firms (a producer of shoeshine machines, a seed cultivation enterprise, and a tree cultivator) for cooperation. It is not clear whether these enterprises knew that they would be used for the smuggling of cocaine but the deals were not closed.

Therefore in 1987 the envoy established an import-export company with the assistance of a Dutch contact, owner of a kickboxing gym in Haarlem. 'Closely following instructions from Colombia, he financed and organized the Dutch import from store, rented the warehouse in IJmuiden, recruited the other Colombians involved, and monitored, especially through the Dutch partners, money transfers and debts from wholesalers.'[74] Three Dutch partners were recruited: the native Dutchman who was the official founder of the import-export firm, a Surinamese 'hustler' (and possibly at some point police informer), and his Dutch girlfriend. The cocaine was hidden in containers of passion-fruit juice and shipped to Rotterdam, from where it was transported by a legitimate company to the warehouse in IJmuiden.

From there the drugs were supplied to the wholesale trade. Payments were then sent by money orders through Thomas Cook to Panama, where they were cashed in by the Grajales family. In 1988 and 1989 seventeen cargoes of passion-fruit juice were sent by the firm Comercializadora de Frutos Tropicales in Cali to its Dutch business associates. Four or five successful runs had been made before the police raided the warehouse in February 1990, seized more than 2.5 tonnes of cocaine with an estimated wholesale value of 270 million guilders and a retail value of more than 1 billion guilders, and arrested the three Dutchmen and five Colombians, including a man called 'Vilas' who turned out to be Pedro Filipe Villaquiràn. Those arrested received prison sentences of between seven and sixteen years, but the three major Colombian partners, who all received sixteen years, escaped within the next two years from Dutch prison, possibly aided by Dutch and Antillean criminals.[75]

Holle Vaten (Empty Vessels), as the police operation leading to the seizure in IJmuiden was called, showed the heterogeneity and accessibility of the illegal cocaine market. The smuggling line set up by the Grajales family and its envoy in the Netherlands was not the result of cooperation between two smooth-functioning international drug cartels, one Colombian, and one Dutch. In fact, another envoy had failed to set up cooperation between the two reputedly most powerful smuggling organizations, the Cali cartel and the Klaas Bruinsma group. The Dutch participants in Holle Vaten were called by criminologist Bovenkerk (who published an article on Holle Vaten based on an informer's story) 'third-rate criminals'. They did not form an organized crime group; inexperienced, they made all the mistakes they could that drew attention to them, such as in turning into big spenders, buying a house using a falsified certificate of employment, giving away the emptied vessels for free, dumping the juice in sewers and so alerting the authorities.[76] Criminal anarchy is by its nature opportunistic and offers chances that are taken up by many with insufficient experience and intelligence to evade detection by law enforcement agencies.

Native Dutch professional criminals started to get involved in the cocaine trade. In January 1994 15 kilograms of cocaine were seized on a Colombian fruit ship in Amsterdam harbour. A well-known Dutch criminal involved in the operation, who had been one of the kidnappers of beer magnate Freddy Heineken, started shooting and killed a customs officer, for which he received a life prison sentence.[77]

Other smuggling operations show similarities with the operation discovered by Holle Vaten, with Colombian supervisors in the Netherlands working for an export syndicate and with a few collaborators in the Netherlands (native Dutch, Surinamese, or other nationalities) who assisted in getting the merchandise into the country and delivering it to wholesale dealers. In two other cases we notice a similar lack of competence and a clumsiness that compares well with those in the Holle Vaten operation. In one case the windows of the warehouse where the cocaine was stashed were very obviously blinded, and data of the operation logged on personal computers that could easily be hacked by the police. In another case the receivers of the cargo were too late in collecting: the cocaine had already been sent with the legitimate cargo on a truck to Switzerland.[78]

Operation Swagger

Criminal entrepreneurs from different countries and cultures succeeded with surprising ease in forging alliances and making cocaine smuggling work. An interesting example of how foreign entrepreneurs could benefit from the role of the Netherlands as a transit hub was researched by British crime journalist Graham Johnson: Operation Swagger.

Operation Swagger concerned two criminal entrepreneurs from Liverpool known as 'Kaiser' and 'Scarface': both typical 'villains' from the city's criminal culture involved in various illegal money-making activities and prone to violent behaviour. In 1988 they relocated to Amsterdam (known among British smugglers as 'the Dam') to export illegal drugs (cannabis, heroin, cocaine) from that city to the UK. This was not unusual: by that time smuggling groups from various nations – at least twenty, according to Johnson's sources – had made their headquarters in Amsterdam. Wishing to expand their operations, they searched for a supplier of 1 tonne of cocaine. This was then reputedly the biggest amount of the drug ever smuggled into Britain. To locate the supplier they used their personal network: old friends in Jamaica brought them into contact with a facilitator who gave them introductions to contacts in Bogotá, the capital of Colombia. Chance was of paramount importance. When the contacts were reluctant, Kaiser and Scarface approached gangster-looking types in a local bar and, amazingly, received an invitation to visit a ranch that turned out to be run by a cocaine trafficker connected to the Grajales family. Apart from contacts and chance, social skills were also decisive. Although Kaiser and Scarface usually posed as heavies and manipulated the fear of others in Amsterdam and London, in Colombia they left this act behind. As Johnson writes: 'The reason they got on with South Americans [a witness said] is that they were friendly and family oriented – much like the people back home.'[79] The Colombians agreed to supply the cocaine for a deposit of 25,000 pounds sterling on the final payment.

The next step was to organize the transport. Kaiser and Scarface flew back to Amsterdam and recruited four collaborators: one Dutchman to sail a yacht with the cocaine from Venezuela to the Caribbean and from there to Europe; two Germans to organize the logistics (buying and testing the boat, planning the route, and taking care of paperwork, a van, and a safe storehouse); and one South American as translator and assistant.

From this point on the saga of Operation Swagger, as Kaiser and Scarface dubbed their operation, takes on even more adventurous dimensions. In true pirate style Scarface decided to sail the yacht himself, together with the Dutchman and the South American. After a test run with the yacht from Amsterdam to Cape Verde and back again in June 1989 the yacht set sail from Amsterdam to Venezuela: on the way in the Caribbean the South American was replaced by another Dutchman. In a three-month round trip the yacht picked up its cargo in Venezuela and sailed back via Curaçao and the southern Caribbean, trying to evade the Dutch navy, the US coastguard, and the DEA. At one point they were hailed by a US coastguard cutter with DEA officers on board but managed to talk themselves through. The biggest ordeal had yet to come, since Scarface decided to sail the yacht into the port of Amsterdam with its heavy maritime surveillance and set course between the enormous container ships. Amazingly he was not stopped by customs or the river police. After finding its way through Amsterdam's canals the ship arrived at the safehouse. From there cargoes were shipped by mules to Liverpool and sold; money was brought back in cash and the Colombian suppliers, who had flown representatives to Amsterdam, were paid off and the other revenue laundered in the city's exchange bureaux. The total turnover was 20 million pounds, of which 5 million went for payment to the suppliers.[80]

Conclusion

The cocaine economy was predatory, laissez-faire capitalism in which traditional coca cultivation was transformed to meet Western demand. In this market small producers profited the least and the chain of production and distribution lined the pockets of smugglers, middlemen, facilitators, corrupt officials, and wholesale and retail dealers. Colombian smugglers succeeded on a grander scale in what had been pioneered by the Greek smugglers of the interwar period: forging alliances within Dutch society in order to link supply and demand. Colombian cocaine smuggling was not embedded in Dutch society to the extent Chinese or Turkish and Kurdish heroin smuggling was. Nevertheless it proved as successful. A number of factors explain these successes. To start with, the geographical location of the Netherlands, its logistical infrastructure connecting transport arriving from overseas expediently with Britain and the rest of Europe, and the congenial business climate for international trade, were excellently suited for smuggling. The logistical infrastructure and the transport routes by sea and air were impossible for Dutch law enforcement agencies to close off. A bonus, but not essential, advantage was the connection of the Netherlands with its former colonies in South America, and especially in the independent state of Suriname, where the regime facilitated the cocaine trade.

Another essential factor was the way of organization and operation of the smugglers. Contrary to what media images suggest, smuggling was not directed by strictly organized Colombian cartels controlling the chain of coca cultivation to distribution. Export syndicates were fragmented, temporary, and shifting in their constitution. Most of them were quite small and they are better characterized as chain networks. Envoys from the syndicates had to establish personal relationships in the Netherlands to further their trade, as had the Greeks in the interwar period. Their business associates were often 'third-rate criminals' rather than criminal masterminds. Nevertheless, despite the successes of some police operations, the very fragmentation and flexibility of the smuggling networks ensured that supply was never threatened and never was monopolized.

Notes

1. P. Gootenberg, *Andean Cocaine: The Making of a Global Drug* (Chapel Hill: University of North Carolina Press, 2008), p. 307; R. Davenport-Hines, *The Pursuit of Oblivion: A Social History of Drugs* (London: Weidenfeld & Nicolson, 2001), pp. 348–9.
2. D. Korf and H. Verbraeck, 'Dealers en dienders. Dynamiek tussen drugsbestrijding en de midden- en hogere niveaus van de cannabis-, cocaine-, amfetamine- en ecstasyhandel in Amsterdam' (University of Amsterdam, Bonger Institute of Criminology, 1993), pp. 108–9.
3. See B. Bieleman, A. Diaz et al (eds), *Lines across Europe: Nature and Extent of Cocaine Use in Barcelona, Rotterdam and Turin* (Amsterdam: Swets and Zeitlinger, 1993); P. Cohen, 'Cocaine use in Amsterdam in non deviant subcultures' (University of Amsterdam, Department of Human Geography, 1989); P. Cohen and A. Sas, 'Ten years of cocaine: A follow-up study of 64 cocaine users in Amsterdam' (University of Amsterdam, Department of Human Geography, 1993); T. Nabben and D. Korf, 'Cocaine and crack in Amsterdam: Diverging subcultures', *Journal of Drug Issues* 29 (1999) 627–52; D. Zaitch, *Trafficking Cocaine: Colombian Drug Entrepreneurs in the Netherlands* (The Hague: Kluwers, 2002), p. 79.
4. Gootenberg, *Andean Cocaine*, p. 247.
5. F. E. Thoumi, *Political Economy and Illegal Drugs in Colombia* (Boulder: Lynne Rienner, 1995); P. L. Clawson and Rensselaer W. Lee III, *The Andean Cocaine Industry* (Houndmills: Macmillan, 1996); J. Orlando Melo, 'The drug trade, politics, and the economy: The Colombian experience', in E. Joyce and C. Malamud (eds), *Latin America and the Multinational Drug Trade* (Houndmills: Macmillan Press, 1998), pp. 63–96; Zaitch, *Trafficking Cocaine*, pp. 29–42; F. E. Thoumi, *Illegal Drugs, Economy, and Society in the Andes* (Washington: Woodrow Wilson Center Press, 2003); Gootenberg, *Andean Cocaine*, pp. 273, 301–6; Davenport-Hines, *Pursuit of Oblivion*, p. 349; A. Camacho-Guizado and A. López-Restrepo, 'From smugglers to drug lords', in C. Welna and G. Gallón (eds), *Peace, Democracy, and Human Rights in Colombia* (Notre Dame: University of Notre Dame Press, 2007), pp. 60–89; M. Kenney, 'The evolution of the international drugs trade: The case of Colombia, 1930–2000', in F. Allum and S. Gilmour (eds), *Routledge Handbook of Transnational Organized Crime* (London: Routledge, 2012), pp. 201–17.
6. On the refinement process: Zaitch, *Trafficking Cocaine*, pp. 41–2.
7. Zaitch, *Trafficking Cocaine*, p. 48.
8. Korf and Verbraeck, 'Dealers en dienders', p. 125.
9. Zaitch, *Trafficking Cocaine*, p. 46.

10 G. Farrell, K. Mansur, and M. Tulis, 'Cocaine and heroin in Europe 1983–93', *British Journal of Criminology* 36 (1996) 255–81, on p. 264. For 1995: Zaitch, *Trafficking Cocaine*, p. 31.
11 Korf and Verbraeck, 'Dealers en dienders', p. 125.
12 Farrell et al., 'Cocaine and heroin', p. 263. For 1995: Zaitch, *Trafficking Cocaine*, p. 31. These are the prices of cut grams which have around 60 per cent purity. These are average prices: in Amsterdam in 1993 one could pay 120 to 175 guilders (65 to 95 US dollars) for a gram, according to Korf and Verbraeck, 'Dealers en dienders', p. 125 – conceivably this product had a higher purity. I recalculated the prices in this paragraph according to the exchange value rates of guilder and dollar in 1983 (1 US dollar = 2.85 Dutch guilders), 1985 (1 US dollar = 3.2 Dutch guilders), 1993 (1 US dollar = 1.85 Dutch guilders), and 1995 (1 US dollar = 1.6 Dutch guilders), from www.measuringworth.com/datasets/exchangeglobal/ (accessed 7 August 2020).
13 F. E. Thoumi. 'The rise of the two drug tigers: The development of the illegal drugs industry and drug policy failure in Afghanistan and Colombia', in F. Bovenkerk and M. Levi (eds), *The Organized Crime Community* (n.p.: Springer, 2007), pp. 125–48. For a discussion see Zaitch, *Trafficking Cocaine*, pp. 35–9.
14 Quoted in Zaitch, *Trafficking Cocaine*, p. 37.
15 International Narcotics Control Board, annual reports and documents, at incb.org (hereafter INCB): 1998 report, 'Precursors and chemicals frequently used in the illicit manufacture of narcotic drugs and psychotropic substances: Report of the International Narcotics Control Board on the implementation of Article 12 of the United Nations Convention against Illicit Traffic in Narcotic Drugs and Psychotropic Substances of 1988'.
16 Zaitch, *Trafficking Cocaine*, p. 43.
17 Delpher digitized newspaper archive (ww.delpher.nl/nl/kranten, hereafter D): 'Politie Colombia verdenkt Nederlands bedrijf al jaren', *Volkskrant* 28 May 1994.
18 D: 'Holanda Colombia verdacht van banden met cokekartels', *Volkskrant* 28 May 1994.
19 D: 'Grondstof cocaïne uit Nederland. Bedrijf ontkent relatie laboratoria', *Het Parool* 12 March 1994.
20 'Holland Chemical International BV', Bloomberg company information at www.bloomberg.com/research/stocks/private/snapshot.asp?privcapid =12828692 (accessed 7 August 2020); 'Beursgang HCI brengt Gerry Staartjes weer in Amsterdam', *Volkskrant* 18 October 1997, www.volkskrant.nl/economie/beursgang-hci-brengt-gerry-staartjes-weer-in-amsterdam~be226dd4 (accessed 7 August 2020). 'G. Staartjes (66), topman

Holland Chemical International', *Trouw* 1 November 1997, www.trouw.nl/home/g-staartjes-66-topman-holland-chemical-international~ab714f53 (accessed 7 August 2020).

21 D: 'Politie Colombia verdenkt Nederlands bedrijf', *Volkskrant* 28 May 1994.
22 M. Kenney, 'The architecture of drug trafficking: Network forms of organisation in the Colombian cocaine trade', *Global Crime* 8 (2007) 233–59.
23 Thoumi, *Illegal Drugs, Economy, and Society*, p. 94.
24 N. Verbeek, *Pablo Escobar. De zoektocht naar de man achter de mythe* (n.p.: Pandora, 2008), pp. 91–2.
25 Thoumi, *Illegal Drugs, Economy, and Society*, pp. 96–7.
26 Verbeek, *Pablo Escobar*, p. 72.
27 Verbeek, *Pablo Escobar*, pp. 72–81.
28 Verbeek, *Pablo Escobar*, p. 61.
29 Zaitch, *Trafficking Cocaine*, pp. 51–6.
30 Korf and Verbraeck, 'Dealers en dienders', p. 105.
31 For a synthesis of the development of the Colombian illegal drug industry see Thoumi, *Political Economy and Illegal Drugs*, chapter 3; Thoumi, *Illegal Drugs, Economy, and Society*, pp. 97–108; Zaitch, *Trafficking Cocaine*, pp. 27–71; Gootenberg, *Andean Cocaine*. The situation is rather similar to the present one in Mexico. A 2019 report on the illegal fentanyl trade concluded: 'The reconfiguration of these criminal groups is near constant. And while it is easy for crime analysts, law enforcement, and prosecutors to place them in large groups, the truth is that these are fluid relationships subject to a large number of changing variables. In fact, over the last several years, it is clear that the traditionally hierarchical drug trafficking organizations in Mexico have been replaced by flatter, more nimble organizations that are loosely networked. Within this framework, it is likely that Sinaloa and the CJNG outsource aspects of production and trafficking to smaller criminal groups. Sinaloa, in particular, is believed to operate with an increasingly horizontal structure in which local and regional gangs that specialize in particular operations are subcontracted for their services' (S. Dudley, D. Bonello et al., 'Mexico's role in the deadly rise of fentanyl' (Washington: Woodrow Wilson Center, Mexico Institute, 2019)).
32 Clawson and Lee, *Andean Cocaine Industry*, p. 74.
33 Data of the INCB, quoted in V. Ruggiero and N. South, *Eurodrugs: Drug Use, Markets and Trafficking in Europe* (London: UCL Press, 1995), p. 74.
34 Ruggiero and South, *Eurodrugs*, pp. 74–5.
35 Zaitch, *Trafficking Cocaine*, p. 94.

36 Korf and Verbraeck, 'Dealers en dienders', p. 113.
37 Zaitch, *Trafficking Cocaine*, p. 87; N. Carretero, *Snow on the Atlantic: How Cocaine Came to Europe* (London: Zed Books, 2018).
38 Korf and Verbraeck, 'Dealers en dienders', pp. 105–7.
39 Korf and Verbraeck, 'Dealers en dienders', pp. 111–12, 118. See for example www.nrc.nl/nieuws/1991/05/21/politie-van-rotterdam-neemt-700-kg-cocane-uit-suriname-6967587-a1287748 (accessed 7 August 2020).
40 Zaitch, *Trafficking Cocaine*, pp. 95–6.
41 Zaitch, *Trafficking Cocaine*, p. 102.
42 G. Hofland and J. Remie, 'De haven van Rotterdam. Volledig vrije doorgang?' (thesis Willem Pompe Institute for Criminology, Utrecht University, 1994), cited in F. Bovenkerk, 'Cocaïnesmokkelaar in Colombiaanse dienst', *Vrij Nederland* 15 April 1995.
43 Zaitch, *Trafficking Cocaine*, pp. 101–7. On the overrepresentation of cocaine from Suriname and the Dutch Antilles see also R. Weijenburg, *Drugs en drugsbestrijding in Nederland. Een beschrijving van de aanpak van het gebruik en misbruik van en de (illegal) handel in verdovende middelen* (The Hague: VUGA, 1996), pp. 116–21.
44 M. Haenen and H. Buddingh', *De Danser. Hoe de drugshandel Nederland veroverde* (Amsterdam: De Arbeiderspers, 1994), pp. 130–50; F. Bovenkerk and C. Fijnaut, 'Georganiseerde criminaliteit in Nederland: Over allochtone en buitenlandse criminele groepen', Parlementaire Enquêtecommissie Opsporingsmethoden, Tweede Kamer der Staten-Generaal, 1995–1996, 24 072 (hereafter PEO), 17, p. 85; J. van den Heuvel, *De jacht op Desi Bouterse. Hoe het Suri-kartel de Nederlandse drugsmarkt veroverde* (The Hague: BZZTôH, 1999); M. Haenen, *Baas Bouterse. De krankzinnige jacht op het Surinaamse drugskartel* (Amsterdam: Sirene, 2000).
45 van den Heuvel, *Jacht*, p. 122; Haenen and Buddingh', *Danser*; H. Buddingh', *De geschiedenis van Suriname* (n.p.: Nieuw Amsterdam, 2012), p. 347.
46 Buddingh', *Geschiedenis*, p. 392.
47 van den Heuvel, *Jacht*, pp. 60–72.
48 Bovenkerk and Fijnaut, 'Georganiseerde criminaliteit', PEO, 17, pp. 86–7; Weijenburg, *Drugs en drugsbestrijding*, p. 109.
49 Bovenkerk and Fijnaut, 'Georganiseerde criminaliteit', PEO, 17, p. 86.
50 F. Hirschland, *Dossier Moengo '290' uur* (The Hague: Cast Publishing, 1993); 'Brunswijk veroordeeld tot acht jaar cel', *NRC Handelsblad* 3 March 1999; Buddingh', *Geschiedenis*, p. 435.
51 Cited in Buddingh', *Geschiedenis*, p. 393.
52 Buddingh', *Geschiedenis*, pp. 380–2, 393–4; Bovenkerk and Fijnaut, 'Georganiseerde criminaliteit', PEO, 17, p. 87.
53 van Duyne et al., *Het spook en de dreiging*, pp. 85–6.

54 Buddingh', *Geschiedenis*, pp. 394. See also Haenen, *Baas Bouterse*, pp. 51–2.
55 Centrale Recherche Informatiedienst (CRI), annual report 1990, p. 84.
56 CRI, annual report 1991, p. 24; CRI, annual report 1992, p. 29.
57 Zaitch, *Trafficking Cocaine*, p. 140.
58 CRI, annual report 1987, p. 24; CRI, annual report 1989, p. 86.
59 CRI, annual report 1990, pp. 84–5; CRI, annual report 1992, p. 11.
60 CRI, annual report 1993, p. 9.
61 Zaitch, *Trafficking Cocaine*, p. 106.
62 Zaitch, *Trafficking Cocaine*, pp. 156–64.
63 Zaitch, *Trafficking Cocaine*, pp. 112–17.
64 Zaitch, *Trafficking Cocaine*, pp. 133–6.
65 Korf and Verbraeck, 'Dealers en dienders', pp. 121–2.
66 Ruggiero and South, *Eurodrugs*, p. 74; Zaitch, *Trafficking Cocaine*, p. 87.
67 Korf and Verbraeck, 'Dealers en dienders', pp. 113–15.
68 Korf and Verbraeck, 'Dealers en dienders', pp. 110, 131–3.
69 See also van Duyne et al., *Het spook en de dreiging*, p. 83.
70 F. Bovenkerk, *La Bella Bettien. Het levensverhaal van een Nederlandse go-between voor de Colombiaanse drugskartels* (n.p.: Pandora, 2008 [1995]).
71 Bovenkerk, *Bella Bettien*, p. 108 (author's translation). The 'Jewish organization' was the Jewish family 'E' that owned currency exchange offices in Amsterdam and was involved in money-laundering as well as cocaine smuggling. See D: S. van der Hoek, 'Tot vijf jaar celstraf geëist in Gouden Kalf-zaak', *Volkskrant* 13 June 1994.
72 Bovenkerk, *Bella Bettien*, p. 113.
73 Bovenkerk, *Bella Bettien*, pp. 145–6; Zaitch, *Trafficking Cocaine*, pp. 159–60; G. Johnson, *The Cartel: The Inside Story of Britain's Biggest Drugs Gang* (Edinburgh: Mainstream Publishing, 2013).
74 Zaitch, *Trafficking Cocaine*, p. 160. The envoy is here called Jairo; in Bovenkerk, 'Cocaïnesmokkelaar', he is called 'Londoño'.
75 D: 'Cocaïne land in gekomen via bedrijf bij Rotterdam', *Het Vrije Volk* 2 March 1990; Bovenkerk, 'Cocaïnesmokkelaar'; Bovenkerk, *Bella Bettien*, p. 145; Zaitch, *Trafficking Cocaine*, p. 305.
76 Bovenkerk, 'Cocaïnesmokkelaar'.
77 Zaitch, *Trafficking Cocaine*, p. 307.
78 van Duyne et al., *Het spook en de dreiging*, pp. 82–3.
79 Johnson, *Cartel*, p. 72.
80 Johnson, *Cartel*, pp. 70–95.

8

The floodgates of criminal anarchy: Synthetic drugs and subverting the state

Cannabis, heroin, and cocaine markets prospered despite the attempts of the Dutch state to control them. The state's problems with drug markets only further increased as, from the mid-1960s, the drug regulatory regime was extended to other, synthetic drugs: hallucinogens, amphetamines, and MDMA and other substances known as XTC or Ecstasy. The prohibition of amphetamines and later of XTC especially offered new chances for criminal entrepreneurs. Moreover, criminal and chemical expertise combined to create a thriving underground economy of drug production and export trade. This in turn led to substantial worries among policymakers, politicians, law enforcement officers, and journalists about the subversion of the democratic Dutch state by organized crime.

This chapter investigates the rise of this underground economy. As had been the case with cannabis, both countercultural idealists and criminal entrepreneurs reacted to and took the opportunities offered by the prohibition of illegal drugs. This prohibition itself was not so much a reaction by the state to domestic drug problems as a consequence of the international relations policies of the Dutch state. Amphetamine production first became the target of regulation because of the smuggling of amphetamines from the Netherlands (where they were still legal) to Sweden (where they were already illegal). LSD and other hallucinogens were prohibited in the context of a wave of similar prohibitions in Western countries in 1965–1966. Consumption, however, significantly increased only after prohibition. A similar dynamic to that of LSD characterized the prohibition of MDMA and related compounds at the end of the 1980s. Strategies by the state not only failed to stop the distribution of all these drugs, it also failed to hinder the development of an underground chemistry industry, in which the expertise of countercultural idealists and criminal entrepreneurs came together.

As a consequence of these failures of the drug regulatory regime, fears about the subversion of the democratic state and the rule of law are widespread in the Netherlands. All over the country there is production of and trade in nederwiet as well as XTC and other synthetic drugs, notwithstanding police raids on indoor growing operations and illegal laboratories. Illegal dumping of chemical waste from these laboratories, violent conflicts between rival criminals, and extensive laundering of illegal drug money are spectacular characteristics of the underground drug economy.

Fears about subversion centre on the southern provinces of the Netherlands, especially North Brabant and Zeeland. A series of violent incidents led in 2010 to the creation of a special police taskforce, 'Brabant-Zeeland', which combined regional police forces, municipalities, the fiscal investigation unit (FIOD) and customs, collaborating closely with public prosecutors and the national police. The taskforce's aim of halting subversion in the south resulted in hundreds of arrests, raids on clandestine laboratories, investigations of more than eighty criminal groups, and the seizure of hundreds of firearms.[1] Academics and journalists have discussed the existence of a 'parallel society' in Brabant in which criminal smuggler families together with Turkish organized crime groups and outlaw motorcycle gangs defy the authorities and make large fortunes in the illegal indoor cultivation of and trade in nederwiet. It is postulated to be a 'criminogenic structure' – that is, culturally determined by traditions of deviance and anti-government attitudes in the province.[2] Deviance and criminal behaviour have been traced in successive generations of criminals and drug traffickers.[3] However, the nucleus of this criminogenic structure in Brabant is supposed to be quite small, consisting of only ten to fifteen persons, mostly native Dutchmen with a sprinkling of Turkish and possibly Moroccan men. These people entered the illegal drug trade in the 1990s and since then have supposedly led discreet lives invisible to the public eye (although a few of them have had a media presence, having been arrested, sentenced, and/or physically attacked by rivals).[4]

This idea of a small group ruling a criminal underworld that ran the illegal drug industry was already paramount among the police forces twenty years ago. Then it concerned the country as a whole and was estimated at around twenty to thirty people.[5] This chapter will discuss a more complex historical reality, tracing the social and cultural embeddedness of the underground economy and its composition to a long-term tradition of criminal anarchy in Dutch society, in the south and elsewhere.

Amphetamines

Amphetamines, a class of stimulant compounds based on the structure of its parent compound amphetamine, entered the medical market in the 1930s and 1940s and quickly became popular in the public domain as well. At first they were not perceived as 'drugs' or 'narcotics' with the attendant negative connotations. In the Netherlands it took until 1976 before these drugs were scheduled in the Opium Act.

Amphetamine was commercially developed in 1929 in the USA and appeared on the American pharmaceutical market in 1933 as an inhaler under the brand name Benzedrine. Later in the 1930s the use of pills became popular. Historian Nicolas Rasmussen estimates that by 1945 half a million Americans regularly used the drug; this while already in 1935 publications pointed to side effects of excessive use such as sleeping disorders, cardiovascular disorders, and excitability.[6]

Negative images of amphetamine were present in Dutch media and professional journals as early as 1937, before the drug was actually available on the Dutch market.[7] This did not hinder the Dutch pharmaceutical company N. V. Koninklijke Pharmaceutische Fabrieken v.h. Brocades-Shteeman to develop its own amphetamine, introduced in 1939 under the brand name Pharmedrine. Suggested indications for use were reduced mental activity and depressions.[8] Dutch newspapers quoted the claim of the well-known British scientist J. B. S. Haldane that he always used amphetamine when he had to drive for more than eight hours.[9] In 1941 Brocades-Shteeman followed up its production of amphetamine with that of methamphetamine, originally a German analogue of amphetamine marketed under the brand name Pervitin, and brought by Brocades-Shteeman on the Dutch market as Neo-Pharmedrine.[10]

The arrival of the amphetamines tested the borderlines between everyday intoxicants (such as alcohol or tobacco), medicinal drugs, and illegal narcotics. The war and the German occupation led to an enormous reduction in the availability of coffee, tea, chocolate, and tobacco. With the exception of beer (which was in high demand among German soldiers of the occupation forces) the production of everyday intoxicants (coffee, tea, chocolate, sugar, distilled liquor, cigars, and cigarettes) plummeted during the war, leading among other things to extensive tobacco smuggling from Belgium.[11] Use of amphetamine or methamphetamine offered an alternative intoxication. A few historians have emphasized the use of methamphetamine in the Nazi war machine, to keep the German Panzer troops going in the Blitzkrieg or on the Eastern Front, but methamphetamine was not a secret weapon of war.[12] Amphetamines filled a gap in the availability of stimulants in everyday life. They were not yet generally perceived as dangerous narcotics, even though the influential *Nederlandsch Tijdschrift voor Geneeskunde* (Dutch Journal of Medicine) described them in 1941 as dangerous and addictive.[13]

Their use in that period is impossible to quantify, but there are indications (especially from contemporary warnings about their use) that they were not uncommonly used, not only by the military but by doctors, nurses, students, housewives, and others in the Netherlands and in Germany. Negative images of health risks and the danger of addiction did circulate in medical journals and among the pharmaceutical inspectors. The latter noted an increased addiction to methamphetamine in the Dutch population.[14] However, this did not deter people from regular use of the new drugs.[15] Use by the higher educated and scandals such as a the affair of a medical student who gave three Pervitin pills to a 21-year-old girl to seduce her into sexual contact did not change the position of the drug as a valued ingredient of everyday life.[16]

Use expanded in the post-war period. By 1951 amphetamines (by then often prescribed for eating disorders and for losing weight) were firmly present in the Netherlands. For that year one researcher calculated a legal use of 7.3 million dosage units, on a total population of 10.2 million people. This use was small compared to the 126.35 million dosage units of barbiturates (tranquillizers) that were prescribed annually, but surpassed the number of 4.5 million dosage units of morphine.[17] In 1961 the Ministry of Public Health considered amphetamine use a 'social danger'; the number of amphetamine addicts was thought to be larger than that of opiate addicts. However, use of amphetamines was at that time too 'normalized' to make illegalization a policy option.[18] How normalized amphetamine use was is shown in the 30 million prescriptions (for the most part for dextroamphetamine or Dexedrine) financed by state health insurance in 1968 alone.[19] According to a 1967 newspaper article, youngsters bought pills for 50 cents or 1 guilder and consumed them when going out at the weekends.[20]

It took until 1 April 1968 before amphetamines were regulated under the *Wet op de Geneesmiddelenvoorziening* (Medicine Supply Act), restricting trade to licensed companies and prohibiting sale to users without medical prescription. A year later, the *Wekaminenbesluit* (Stimulants Decree) made possession of and trade in amphetamines without prescription liable to a maximum sentence of six months in prison or a 500-guilder fine.[21] Perhaps the restriction on non-medical use was responsible for the 15 to 18 per cent increase in use on medical prescription between early 1968 and early 1969. Illegal trade blossomed. The government's public health council (*Gezondheidsraad*) was especially concerned about the extent of abuse in the world of sport, where the drugs were supplied by doctors but also by illegal traders and from abroad. An Amsterdam addiction treatment centre considered abusers of amphetamines one of the largest problem groups among its clients.[22]

By 1970 two fundamental conditions for the successful evolution of an illegal drug trade were met: the limitation of competing sources of supply by regulatory policies, in particular of legal supplies and of 'leaks' from the legal pharmaceutical industry; and the rise of a demand side in existing drug subcultures in the Netherlands as well as abroad. Amsterdam social workers noticed that a new group of amphetamine users consisted of young workers from lower social backgrounds and working-class districts. Their number rose until 1972, when heroin became more easily available and many of these users switched to the heroin habit.[23] In 1972 the *Wet op de Econonomische Delicten* (Law on Economic Offences) placed a maximum sentence of six years in prison on the import and export of amphetamines without licence: two years more than the maximum sentence provided for by the Opium Act at the time.[24] It took until 1976 for the scheduling of amphetamines in the Opium Act.

This scheduling stimulated the development of a clandestine amphetamine industry. However, although before 1968 amphetamines could legally be obtained in pharmacies, there is evidence of an illegal trade even then. Was there a kind of self-regulating mechanism that made pharmacists hesitant in selling amphetamines to young users without prescription? In 1949 an Amsterdam apothecary explained that pharmacies almost only ever sold amphetamine on prescription, even although this was not necessary under the law. This explains why a young woman tried to obtain Pharmedrine from a pharmacy with a false prescription that year.[25]

Demand was so large that it offered business opportunities for illegal producers to manufacture their own pills, possibly undercutting the prices of the pharmaceutical industry and avoiding the difficulties of obtaining the drugs in pharmacies. Amphetamines were the first drugs manufactured by a clandestine chemistry operation. In 1963 the police discovered a laboratory in the city of Haarlem, to the west of Amsterdam. It was run by two men from Amsterdam, employees of, respectively, a wholesale dealer in chemicals and a pharmaceutical laboratory. They had stolen equipment and chemicals from their employers.[26] Clandestine manufacture was a realistic and profitable option since amphetamine is relatively easy to produce and the necessary equipment rather low tech (see below). Regulation provided an impetus for the development of clandestine chemistry. In 1977, only one year after the amphetamines were scheduled in the Opium Act, five illegal amphetamine labs were discovered by the police.[27]

LSD

Although amphetamines were introduced in society earlier than another new synthetic drug called LSD, the latter was regulated at an earlier stage. In February 1966 LSD and eighteen other hallucinogens were scheduled in the Opium Act. Although at that time only a very limited group of LSD users existed in the Netherlands outside of medical psychiatric settings, the drug had become a favourite of the international counterculture next to cannabis. In Amsterdam LSD was used on a limited scale by beat-generation-inspired artists, students, and dropouts. The immediate occasion for the regulation in 1966 was the threat of the anarchist Provo group that they would disturb the wedding of the Crown Princess by dosing the police horses with LSD. This led to a small panic among the authorities and the scheduling of February 1966.[28]

Making LSD illegal had little effect on its use. In the Netherlands, as in Western countries in general, LSD became a fashionable drug in the counterculture, especially after the celebrated Summer of Love of 1967. While the number of cannabis users increased by the early 1970s to tens of thousands, that of LSD users might have grown into thousands.[29] This created a demand for illegal supply. At first LSD use outside medical settings had been a spillover from the production of pharmaceutical company Sandoz in Switzerland (and possibly of production in Czechoslovakia behind the Iron Curtain). Steve Groff, an American psychedelic enthusiast and associate of LSD guru Timothy Leary, took some of the last remnants of Sandoz LSD to the Netherlands, where it was distributed in psychedelic circles.[30] In the early 1960s idealistic enthusiasts for the mind-expanding properties of LSD and other psychedelic drugs started to produce their own versions. By 1963 underground chemists in the USA distributed a 'green LSD' that was only 60 per cent pure and contained adrenaline and other substances.[31] While the production by Sandoz was terminated in the mid-1960s, clandestine manufacturing improved and began producing pure LSD. Since LSD is active in doses of only 100 micrograms or more, global distribution and smuggling was far from difficult. For instance, in 1964 one could get fifty-five dosage units of LSD by sending 55 pounds sterling to a man named O'Dwyer in England. The LSD was sent in a return envelope by post.[32]

Even before the scheduling of LSD in the Opium Act, LSD manufacturing was set up in the Netherlands, not by criminal entrepreneurs, but by idealists from the Amsterdam drug scene. A first attempt in someone's home laboratory produced only a moderately effective liquid but the process was perfected by Onno Nol, an idealistic student of first medicine and later physics. Nol believed in what he called the 'Message': use of LSD was the panacea to solve the world's problems. For instance, if the Russian and American leaders would take LSD they would never start a nuclear war. Nol recruited investors for his lab from the Amsterdam beatnik and drug scene and first succeeded with a trial run producing a test tube containing a liquid with fifty to eighty dosage units. Three months later Nol's lab produced a bottle containing 40,000 dosage units of LSD that were dripped with a pipette onto sugar cubes. The LSD cubes were made available for 5 to 10 guilders in the bars and other locations in Amsterdam where the alternative youth and drug scene gathered. LSD production and distribution was at first embedded not in a criminal environment but among rebelling middle-class youth. Nol's LSD was possibly also a major source of supply for the underground UK market. His lab had to discontinue operations, however, since Nol was a major consumer of his own product, taking a staggeringly high dose of 900 micrograms each day for a period of eight months. He became completely paranoid and went to Germany.[33]

Clandestine production was not extremely difficult technically. With some chemical expertise and equipment one could start manufacture in one's own basement. Precursor and other chemicals needed were easily available at chemical supply companies until well into the 1980s.[34] Ergotamine, ergine, and ergonovine (derived from ergot fungus on rye) are naturally occurring alkaloids that contain the lysergic acid molecule. Lysergic acid is synthesized and then combined with diethylamine to give LSD.[35] Ergotamine and lysergic acid were legally available at chemical companies abroad. Ideally 25 kilograms of ergotamine can give 5 or 6 kilograms of LSD crystal, enough for 100 million dosage units.[36] Still, as one underground manual for LSD production cautions, there is a little more skill needed for the production of LSD than for that of amphetamines.

> The synthesis of LSD is not a task to be undertaken lightly by the novice wannabe drug chemist. It requires a level of skill roughly double than needed to produce more conventional drugs such as methamphetamine. A person contemplating this task should be well trained prior to beginning the attempt, as learning 'while on the job' is likely to lead not only to failure, but also the probable poisoning of the said wannabe drug chemist.[37]

This is because of the nature of the drug as well as of the production process. LSD is extremely potent in minute amounts: 1 gram can give 10,000 effective doses. It is also easily absorbed by the skin. In converting the basic material for LSD many an aspiring chemist 'cooked himself over' or poisoned himself with the drug – as in fact happened to its first inventor, Albert Hofmann, in 1943, who thus inadvertently discovered the mind-affecting properties of the drug. Furthermore LSD and lysergic acid are fragile molecules vulnerable to light, air, and heat. Producing LSD is, moreover, a time-consuming process: it takes two to three days to produce 30 to 100 grams of LSD crystal. LSD production is therefore mostly in small batches that go a long way to supply the market. Some of the problems in setting up a clandestine LSD lab can be learned from the adventures of English producer Peter Simmons, who in 1968 obtained a partial recipe for LSD, then gained access to a complete one through a friend at the London Patents Office. The costs for equipping his first lab, in a caravan outside of the city, were 1,000 pounds, a substantial amount at the time. The second lab was located in a house in Kent and the first production run produced liquid LSD, but the chemists were not able to make it solid enough to crystallize and had to sell the liquid in bottles. In the second run they did manage to produce capsules. However, because of their inexperience they mishandled the LSD, got dosed and were high most of the time.[38]

While expertise and experience are needed, LSD manufacture can hardly be called a high-tech or high-skilled venture. This is an important factor contributing to the success of the illegal drug trade. Although serious laboratory equipment is needed (such as a rotary evaporator, distilling kit with ground glass joints, a vacuum desiccator, and a vacuum pump), it can be installed in one's basement or attic. Some academic education in organic chemistry and the use of chromatography for isolating biological substances from complete mixtures is essential, but one does not need to hold a PhD in chemistry. The famous manufacturer of underground LSD such as Orange Sunshine in the 1960s, the American Augustus Owsley Stanley III has been described as having 'little training and a smart wife'.[39]

By 1970 clandestine LSD manufacture had become increasingly efficient. One British underground chemist claimed to have improved on the synthesis from ergotamine and to have made LSD that was more pure than the original Sandoz drug.[40] The illegal labs in the 1970s were almost invisible to the police. The major production facility of LSD in that decade was located in the UK. The products of two underworld labs, one in London, the other in Wales, supplied the international market from 1969 onwards and were dismantled in a major British police operation (Operation Julie) in 1977. Up to the beginning of 1976 these labs had produced in total 18 million LSD dosage units, solving the problem of standardized dosage by the invention of the production of microdots. According to police estimates the labs produced 60 per cent of the world supplies of LSD. The Netherlands was an export destination for this product as well as a pivotal transit hub. By 1977 100,000 LSD pills were smuggled to Amsterdam each month and delivered to a man named Vincent (the police never learned his family name). From Amsterdam they were distributed into the European markets. Amsterdam was also the transit hub for the ergotamine needed for production and purchased from chemical companies in Germany and Switzerland.[41] Amsterdam performed this role because of its geographic location and infrastructure and the embeddedness of the LSD trade in the city's alternative culture.

The LSD production and distribution busted by Operation Julie had begun with characteristic 1960s idealistic intentions. Chemist Richard Kemp 'had wanted to turn on the world [...] producing kilos of acid [LSD], enough for tens of millions of trips'.[42] But by 1970 the process was increasingly professionalized in response to police strategies. The 1960s happy-go-lucky attitude was replaced by the safety measures of a secret organization wishing to survive, complete with hideouts and covert stashes, procedural protocols, and passwords. The belief in the acid revolution started to dwindle during the 1970s. Distributor Leaf Fielding described how his belief faded and how he started a health food company, but continued to be involved in the LSD trade since it was good business.[43]

LSD smuggling mostly escaped the notice of the police. In the Netherlands in the early 1970s the numbers of seized LSD dosage units increased: 4,440 in 1970; 7,765 in 1972; 12,209 in 1974. But there were no arrests of large-scale smugglers in that decade. In 1970 two men were arrested who tried to smuggle a test tube containing 1 gram of LSD wrapped in a newspaper into the Netherlands. They received a twelve-month prison sentence.[44] In the 1980s blotting paper sprinkled with LSD became the major form of consumption of the drug on the illegal market, priced at around 10 guilders per dosage unit. The blotting paper was marketed with names and symbols: the Pink Panther, strawberries, Gorbachev, Garfield, red micro dots, penguins, 'conan el barbaro', the Superman logo, the Chinese yin-yang symbol, or a red 'Arabic sign' (as the police called it; it was probably the Indian letter 'aum'). LSD also became available in pills in the later 1980s. However, not everything that was sold as LSD turned out to be LSD.[45]

The first LSD laboratory discovered by the police in the Netherlands, in 1985, was located in the attic of an apartment in Amsterdam. The paper lubricated with LSD from which the dosage units would be cut was still hanging to dry and a Dutch clandestine chemist and his wife were arrested. According to the police the production was mainly meant for export, in particular to France. The chemists had taken the formula for LSD from the university library; the precursors necessary for production were bought from a chemical supply company in Antwerp. The papers were sold to retail dealers for 1 guilder each. The chemist and one of his associates received sentences of eighteen months in prison.[46]

The discovery of the LSD lab occurred only half a year after the Dutch government had denied allegations from the International Narcotics Control Board (INCB) that the Netherlands was the largest and possibly the sole distribution centre of LSD in Europe. LSD use was not even popular in the Netherlands, so the government claimed.[47] This rather conflicted with the suspicions of Dutch and other European police officers, circulating since 1982, that a major clandestine LSD lab existed in the Netherlands. This suspicion was probably aroused by the uncharacteristically high quantities of LSD seized in 1982 by the Dutch police: almost 50,000 dosage units. However, apart from the 1985 bust the Dutch police did not find any LSD labs in the Netherlands in the 1980s.[48]

The police found connections between the LSD trade in the Netherlands and the seizures of LSD blotting paper in neighbouring countries Belgium, West Germany, and France, and as far as South Africa and later New Zealand.[49] More than half (54 per cent) of all LSD seized in Europe between 1988 and 1992 came from the Netherlands, while the place of origin could not be established from 36 per cent.[50] In 1993 a German travelling to Chile was arrested at Schiphol airport with 9,482 pieces of blotting paper hidden in his underwear, which he said he had received in Amsterdam from a Spaniard and had to deliver to a Bolivian in Santiago. It is not clear whether this was transit trade or whether the Spaniard had bought the LSD in Amsterdam.[51] In the early 1990s seizures suddenly started to multiply: from a little more than 1,600 dosage units in 1991 to 50,000 in 1992 and 187,000 in 1993.[52] The second largest bust of a clandestine LSD lab in the Netherlands took place in 1993. Information from the German police, who had become suspicious because of the ordering of large amounts of chemicals from German companies, led their Dutch colleagues to a house in the north of Amsterdam where they discovered a clandestine American chemist and his Dutch girlfriend in a laboratory capable of producing both LSD and amphetamines. The American turned out to have a criminal record in the United States, having received a ten-year prison sentence for earlier manufacture of LSD. The police also found two guns and ammunition: the underground LSD industry seemed to have hardened as well.[53]

Smuggling in the south: historical backgrounds

Of much greater concern to the police was the development of the illegal amphetamine trade after 1968. By 1971 the attention of law enforcement agencies and media focused on a German trafficker named Kalle Pauksch who settled in Limburg and was considered the mastermind behind the organization of amphetamine smuggling to Sweden.[54] The real driving forces behind the smuggling, however, were native Dutch criminal networks in Limburg that laid the foundations of the synthetic drugs industry in the south. Clandestine chemistry in Limburg was from the outset connected to existing traditions of smuggling and built on the infrastructure of the illegal production of distilled liquor to evade excise duties. In the illegal distilleries chemical and other know-how was present that could be turned to the production of illegal drugs.

In the 1930s smuggling, in itself a phenomenon of all ages, took new shapes in Limburg. According to police officers and journalists, it became organized crime. Sugar, butter, and other goods were smuggled into Belgium by unemployed labourers while tobacco and rolling papers, and guns and ammunition went the other way. According to one account, 'each night a few hundred smugglers crossed the borders'.[55] The military police or *marechaussee* responsible for guarding the borders spoke of the organization of professional smugglers in a network controlled by unknown bosses.[56] Their operations were socially embedded in local towns and villages; the smugglers were not unpopular among the population of the border areas. The organizers remained invisible. It was very much an exception when in 1964 twenty Dutch so-called 'smuggler kings' were sentenced by a court in Antwerp to sentences of four months to two years in prison and heavy fines.[57]

In the 1930s the scale of operations expanded and technological innovations were introduced. From around 1932 smugglers used automobiles to cross the border. When shot at or confronted with roadblocks they progressed to the use of armoured cars. After the Second World War smugglers produced spikes that were thrown onto the road to discourage pursuers. The two decades between 1949 and 1969 were the peak of operations for the butter smugglers. Demand came from the Belgian butter trade, who placed orders with Dutch intermediaries. In 1961 a Belgian newspaper made a distinction between financers, who on a temporary basis pooled resources to finance operation (these financers at one point even included the mayor of a border town), and the professional Dutch smugglers who had their own (armoured) cars and other tools (spikes and smoke bombs to deter pursuing law enforcement officers) and resources (drivers and lookouts or scouts on bikes) available.[58] Between 1959 and 1966 police and marechaussee seized no less than 289,000 kilograms of smuggled butter, but this was considered only a fragment of the total that was smuggled before the development of a common European agricultural policy ended the steep Belgian import taxes on butter and did away with the incentives for butter smuggling.[59] Entrepreneurs now moved to the illegal manufacture and smuggling of alcohol.[60]

Smuggling in the south had a centuries-old background. However, in the nineteenth and the first decades of the twentieth century one could still hardly say there was organized smuggling. Smuggling occurred on a small scale and was performed by individuals from villages close to the border. Some of these villages, especially in Brabant (such as Zundert, Rucphen, Hilvarenbeek, and St Willebrord), developed a reputation as 'smuggler villages'. Sometimes smuggling ran in families over generations.[61] This did not mean that everybody in the village was involved in smuggling operations. Even when in the years around the Second World War police officials, sociologists, and criminologists identified towns and villages such as Oss, Goirle, and St Willebrord in Brabant as hotbeds of criminal behaviour, their research actually identified few smugglers.[62] An example is Goirle, a village to the south of Tilburg in Brabant, on the Belgian border. The village was the subject of a sociological study shortly after the Second World War. The researcher characterized morals in the village as deviant. Youngsters, boys as well as girls, showed rowdiness and mendacity. The researcher also deplored their fondness for sweets. Parents were in his view too tolerant. According to him, during the German occupation entrepreneurs had made more money than ever on the black market, while fondness for sweets developed into addiction to tobacco, and disrespect for authorities further increased.[63]

However, while smuggling was an economic activity in this kind of border village that was not particularly disapproved of, it was not a core activity in the economic system. The deviant morals of the inhabitants of Goirle did not necessarily culturally determine them to smuggling. Market changes and opportunities did stimulate smuggling among some of the inhabitants – in particular during the Second World War and its aftermath – but it is unclear exactly how many people were involved. As mentioned in Chapter 6, the government estimated the number of smugglers of Belgian (shag) tobacco in the country direct after the war to be no less than 125,000, more than 10 per cent of the whole population, but on the basis of which data is unclear.[64] In the years after the war only ten smugglers were identified in the village of Goirle, and these were for the larger part married unemployed labourers who took to the economic opportunities of smuggling.[65]

Historian Florike Egmond has shown that criminal traditions can be discerned in some of the 'smuggler' towns and villages such as Oss and St Willebrord as far back as the eighteenth century.[66] In 1999 the Dutch police arrested John H, a well-known member of the St Willebrord village community, because of his involvement in the illegal trade of hundreds of thousands of XTC tablets manufactured in two illegal labs and partly exported to the USA. John H was on the one hand a disreputable figure in the village: his source of income was nefarious, he lived in a grand villa, drove expensive cars, and was known for his rowdy behaviour in the local pub. On the other hand he was a benefactor who gave generous financial support for the restoration of the Catholic church. One of his suspected accomplices was a public servant working in the legal department of the municipality of Rucphen, of which St Willebrord was a part.[67] It would be too facile to postulate a direct genealogical descent between the robbers and thieves' gangs of the eighteenth century and twentieth-century smugglers such as John H. For instance, the above average level of criminal behaviour in Oss actually disappeared after police interventions in 1935.[68] The recurrence of similar family names among criminals in different centuries is not conclusive either.[69]

What did continue to exist was a cultural tradition of smuggling in the Brabant and Limburg smuggling villages that shows affinities with those of, for instance, the Kurdish villages on the eastern Turkish border; John H shows a distinct resemblance to the Baybasin smugglers from Kurdistan (see Chapter 5). In this sense, smuggling was socially and culturally embedded in the villages, revived when new opportunities arose. This was not unique to Brabant and Limburg; historically the seeds of criminal anarchy are also found in other border communities in the Netherlands or in the working-class districts and underworlds of Amsterdam and Rotterdam. Take the example of Terneuzen in Zeeland. Police and prosecutors kept their eyes on smugglers there who transported opium and cannabis since at least 1954. The officers could only arrest small-scale smugglers but considered them to be links in larger networks. The drugs were smuggled by ship from Antwerp to Terneuzen and from there distributed by couriers to Rotterdam and Amsterdam.[70] The end of the lucrative butter smuggling at the end of the 1960s increased incentives for smugglers to find new contraband.

One of these men was Sjefke Faas. Faas grew up in a place where smuggling was socially and culturally embedded: the café of his father just outside of Terneuzen. He became one of the flamboyant butter smugglers, driving his armoured car across the border and evading police bullets. To the local community he was a well-dressed, friendly, and modest person who did not flaunt his wealth, except that he lived in an ostentatious house. When meeting customs officials in the local restaurant he generously paid for their wine in a gesture of sportsmanship. From butter smuggling Faas diversified into setting up an illegal gin distillery in Brabant and in smuggling Pakistani migrants into the UK on his trawler. He also imported hashish from Lebanon and Morocco. According to rumour, a tipoff from one of his underworld colleagues led to his arrest in 1976, when he was 35, with 2,500 kilograms of Lebanese hashish (worth 12 million guilders) in his car.[71] Sjefke Faas fell into the same category of romanticized smugglers as Frits van de Wereld and, as did Frits, he took his opportunities in the illegal drug trade using the networks and contacts from his earlier operations. Smuggling was embedded in cities and villages throughout the Netherlands.

Moving into amphetamines

As criminal entrepreneurs from Amsterdam and Rotterdam had reacted to the economic opportunities of the illegalization of cannabis, southern entrepreneurs did likewise after the illegalization of synthetic drugs. One of the pioneers of the XTC industry in the 1990s, the reputed drug kingpin Robbie van L, came from Einighausen, a small village in the province of Limburg to the northwest of Heerlen.

This was territory well known to the drug smugglers of the interwar period (see Chapter 2). Robbie started his criminal career in a gang of safebreakers in the province, at that time considered a kind of criminal elite. The leader of the gang, Anno Mink from the city of Heerlen, had earned himself the nickname of the 'Robin Hood of the South'. The safebreakers only robbed banks and wealthy corporations, reputedly did not use violence against bystanders or ordinary citizens, and showed the kind of daring and cunning that gained them the admiration and envy of more law-abiding people. The successes of the safe-breaking gang led to increased police surveillance: by 1972 all members were regularly observed by both the Dutch and the Belgian police forces. The criminal entrepreneurs of Heerlen and the surrounding villages gathered in their own bars, where (as in the interwar period) their activities were embedded. The Cranen café in the centre of Heerlen and the Palma Bar, a nightclub in the city, were meeting points and drinking-holes for the criminal milieu. When increased security measures to protect the banks led Anno and his associates to consider other sources of income, in these bars foundations were laid for new operations. One of the scouts of the gang, nicknamed 'little Rat', set himself up in the amphetamine trade, and others followed.[72]

Smuggling to Sweden turned out to be highly profitable. Phenmetrazine (brand name Preludin) was a substitute amphetamine compound that was highly popular, especially in Sweden, where its use had been banned in 1965 and where there were an estimated 10,000–20,000 users.[73] A Limburg family of car dealers in the village of Schinveld, to the north of Heerlen, supplied the Swedish market with at least 300,000 amphetamine pills, but one of the sons was caught in Sweden in 1969 and received a three-year prison sentence.[74] Anno Mink and two other gang members were arrested in 1970 on the ferry to Sweden in Helsingborg in their Jaguar with 3,500 pills.[75] Mink spent until 1975 in a Swedish prison.[76]

It must be said that not all Limburg criminals embraced the new operations in the amphetamine trade. Another master safecracker, Lei Mooten, disapproved of drugs and did not hide his opinions. According to some he had given the police the tip leading to the arrest of Mink. Whether this was true or not, one member of the Mink gang tried to blow up Mooten in his car in December 1970 but failed.[77]

At first the amphetamine traders smuggled drugs obtained from countries abroad, especially Italy. The next step was producing them. In a number of villages changing combinations of an estimated total of forty to forty-five people were involved in the illegal liquor industry. These cooperations switched to amphetamine manufacture. For instance, Eersel, a small town in Brabant, was once a centre of butter smuggling. There was also an illegal alcohol distillery located in the town, financed – according to the finance police – by butter smugglers. Both smuggling and clandestine chemistry were therefore embedded in Eersel when Peerke S, the son of one of the operators of the distillery, set up a synthetic drug lab to supply entrepreneurs and smugglers such as Robbie van L and Peter van D, another reputed drug 'kingpin'.[78]

Amphetamine laboratories

As mentioned above, the necessary equipment for the production of amphetamines and later of XTC is quite small and low tech, which is ideal for a kind of 'guerrilla production': manufacturing batches of the product in one place, then quickly moving to another. This outlaw production needed some chemical expertise (for instance of a chemistry student looking for some money), chemical apparatus (obtainable at wholesale dealers without too many questions asked), a space invisible to police and law-abiding citizens (the laboratories were hidden and socially embedded in the agricultural landscape of Limburg or Brabant), and raw materials and precursor chemicals (in the 1980s obtainable over the border in Germany or Belgium).[79] While amphetamine production is less complicated than that of LSD, some experience is helpful in making the manufacturing process as efficient as possible. Interviews with amphetamine producers in this period showed that beginner chemists could expect to have 60 per cent wastage from raw chemicals and more experienced chemists would have 40 per cent wastage.[80] The manufacture of amphetamines and later of XTC is not without risks. Now and then accidents happened. A police report from 1992 mentions producers in a clandestine lab in the city of Zandvoort (on the west coast) who had left the lab because they were unsure what to do with a barrel containing a liquid that was suddenly bubbling and boiling. In another lab personnel started to vomit when one of the barrels of chemicals began to leak. Two years later a chemical reaction in an illegal XTC lab led to the emission of ammonia. Neighbours had difficulties breathing and were admitted to hospital.[81]

Robert Hollemans was the kind of underground chemist whose expertise was useful for the successful functioning of illegal production and smuggling operations. In the late 1970s he ran a wholesale chemicals company in Terneuzen. Hollemans took the chemical formula for the production of amphetamine from a textbook or journal and succeeded in manufacturing pills for the illegal market. In 1982 this led to a prison sentence of two and a half years. In 1984 he was given another sentence, of one and a half years in prison, for divulging the formula to another manufacturer, even though the formula itself was in the public domain. Irritated, Hollemans explained the procedure for producing amphetamine in the national magazine for prisoners, so educating other would-be producers in the process.[82]

According to police information, in 1985 seven amphetamine labs were active for short or longer periods. These labs were not, it seems, in permanent operation. They were set up in unobtrusive locations such as farms and were used to produce significant batches and then dismantled again – as, for instance, one abandoned laboratory discovered by the police in 1985 in the countryside to the north of Amsterdam. The batches produced could be stored, for example the 216 kilograms discovered by the police in 1992 buried in the woods near Baarle-Nassau, close to the Belgian border and a traditional smuggling area. Of the seven labs discovered in 1985 and 1986, four were located in Brabant, and three were in the west of the country: the abandoned lab mentioned above, one in Amsterdam, and one in The Hague.[83] Most of the labs raided by the police in 1990 were located in the countryside: four in Limburg but others in other provinces, while there were also labs discovered in the cities of Amsterdam and Utrecht.[84] This suggests that by this time the amphetamine industry had expanded beyond the southern provinces and was now taken up by criminal entrepreneurs from the west of the country as well. In the Zeeland–Brabant–Antwerp triangle products and expertise were exchanged across the border. Two Dutchmen were involved in operating an illegal distillery in Essen near Antwerp that in 1981 switched over to the production of amphetamines. Six years later the Belgian police discovered in Weelde, again a village near Antwerp, an illegal distillery with next to it an amphetamine lab.[85] In 1987 the police, having noticed increased amphetamine use in Zeeland, arrested four people in the cities of Vlissingen and Middelburg. They were in possession of 90 kilograms of amphetamine, with a retail value of 2.25 million guilders, and of a large supply of chemicals. This was the biggest catch in the fight against the amphetamine trade so far.[86] In the decade of the 1980s a total of twenty-five labs were dismantled, which suggests there was a much larger number of labs throughout the country.[87] One of the largest of the amphetamine smuggling groups was thought to have produced 9,500 kilograms between 1983 and 1989.[88]

The organization of manufacture and trade

In 1991 criminologists investigated three amphetamine labs. In their interviews with manufacturers we notice that the organization was basically anarchic and based on shared commercial interests and personal relations, and not on hierarchical power structures. Wholesale dealers and smugglers took batches of between five and a few dozen kilograms from the clandestine labs and sold them to whoever they wanted. They perceived themselves as *vrije jongens* (free men) beholden to no one and living outside the law. The labs themselves were of necessity very well organized with a clear division of labour. In one group there was a partnership of a 'brain' behind the operation and a manager responsible for location, equipment and chemicals, and distribution, working with a financer (who received his investments back plus a provision for every kilogram sold), and a chemist (who also received a provision for every kilogram sold). Specialization involved knowledge on a need-to-know basis. The brain did not know to whom the drugs were sold, nor where the manager bought his chemicals and equipment – only that the latter used a false passport to obtain them, suggesting they were imported from abroad. The manager and the financer had never met the chemist. In another lab there were five people involved in a kind of cooperative endeavour, although one of them was the organizer and had founded a legal front company (a decorating business) for the purchase of chemicals.[89]

The amphetamine industry was not so much an integrated organization as a network connecting entrepreneurs throughout the country. One example of how such a network functioned was given by the criminologist Fijnaut. Two clandestine chemists operated with the assistance of three or four others an amphetamine lab in a business premises in a medium-sized city in Brabant. Parts of the production process took place at other locations in order to spread the risk of detection. Chemicals were supplied by five other persons, one of whom was also involved in the arms trade. The chemicals were obtained from companies in the Netherlands or Belgium, or in Eastern Europe. Between January 1994 and April 1995 hundreds of kilograms of amphetamine were produced. Ten kilograms were sold (at least on one occasion) for 32,000 guilders, making a net profit of 10,000 guilders. The lab supplied amphetamine to different customers: to a local dealer, to a family of five who sometimes completed the production process by making the capsules and who sold the product in Amsterdam, to a wholesale dealer, and to a group of Hell's Angels who in their turn exported the drug to the UK. Some of the people involved invested in a new lab in the south of the country, but because of internal differences (occasioned by the quality of the product being low) and because of police interventions this new operation failed. This network was diverse, flexible, and fluid. Differences of opinion were sometimes settled by (the threat of) violence, which is why the illegal possession of firearms was not uncommon among participants. Violence was, however, internal, and never directed at law enforcement personnel, although there was some pressure exerted by a male member of the group on one female police officer to give him access to confidential information. One member of this network liberated a friend arrested by the police and taken to prison at gunpoint.[90]

Amphetamine production was mainly a native Dutch affair. The police thought that in 1991 80 per cent of all core members involved were Dutch.[91] A non-native Dutch group involved were the Antillean cannabis smugglers with a reputation for violence mentioned in Chapter 6, who also worked an amphetamine line to Sweden, in cooperation with Yugoslav criminals.[92] Amphetamine smuggling became a sideline for groups trading other drugs. One example is a criminal family of five, consisting of the father, his wife, his brother-in-law, his daughter, and his son-in-law, living in a village on the Belgian border with a rich tradition of smuggling. This family organized smuggling ventures of mainly cocaine and cannabis, but also started to work in amphetamines. In the network were Colombian suppliers of cocaine (through Argentina), producers of both nederwiet and amphetamines, suppliers of precursors, and regular customers. All the people involved were native Dutch. It was a flexible network in which everybody acted with a large measure of independence. This was one of the larger smuggling groups, with an estimated revenue in 1990 of 2 to 5 million guilders.[93] A smaller group based in Limburg with a core of five people had a supplier of cannabis from Spain and smuggled cannabis and amphetamines, and a little heroin, to Germany and Scandinavia. Their network contained a manufacturer of amphetamines, customers in Germany and Sweden, a transporter, and couriers. Their activities were barely noticeable to the police, in part because they did not use a bank for monetary transactions.[94]

There was little common structure in all of these groups. Two Dutch veteran drug smugglers living in Utrecht and The Hague teamed up with a retired physician from Luxembourg. They first smuggled cannabis to the UK, and later expanded into XTC and amphetamines. The doctor took care of the supply of chemicals for production. For every single task (production, storage, drugs transport, smuggling, money transport) specialists were used who had no contact with each other; forty people in total.[95]

Smuggling into Europe

Profits were to be made, especially when smuggling the drug for export out of the country. Around 1990 1 kilogram of amphetamine sold to wholesale dealers in the Netherlands for between 2,000 and 3,500 guilders (depending on the total amount purchased by the client). The wholesale dealer sold again to middlemen or retailers for between 6,000 and 10,000 guilders; the retail price for the user was 25 to 35 guilders per gram or 100 guilders for 4 to 6 grams.[96] For producers it was far more profitable to export to Sweden, where in 1989 the wholesale price of 1 kilogram of amphetamine was at least five times as high as in the Netherlands, or to Norway, Denmark, or Germany.[97]

Smugglers primarily used transport by road. The memoirs of a Swedish police detective give more insights into their ways of operation in the 1980s. Robbie van L made use of a truck driver who drove a container with amphetamines hidden in a false compartment among cargoes of plastic to Sweden. The driver used the regular traffic route by the highway through Germany and Denmark and there took the ferry to Helsingborg in Sweden. From Helsingborg the truck drove to an illegal laboratory in Skåne, where the drugs, delivered with a purity of 90–100 per cent, were cut to 50 per cent purity and then distributed on the retail market. The greatest risks were for the truck driver, a 40-year-old man who was caught by the Swedes with 42 kilograms of amphetamines in his container (street value at the time almost 17 million Swedish kronor – more than 48 million kronor in today's values, or 5.5 million US dollars).[98] He turned out to have participated in at least four smuggling operations and received a prison sentence of nine years.[99] Driving amphetamines to Sweden was not the only method of smuggling. For instance, a Greek shipowner in Piraeus organized transport from Rotterdam to Stockholm.[100]

Germany was an important transit hub en route to Scandinavia as well as a demand country. The average annual seizure of amphetamines at the German border multiplied from 21 kilograms in the years 1982 to 1985, to 83 kilograms in 1986–1992. On the UK border annual seizures went from 58.8 kilograms in 1984 to 420.7 in 1991.[101] The UK market became another important customer for illegal Dutch amphetamines. In 1988, of 213 kilograms of Dutch amphetamine seized in Europe, 65 were seized in Sweden, 55 in the UK, and 54 in Germany. In 1994 of 717 kilograms of amphetamine seized by British law enforcement when smuggling into the UK, 60 per cent (430 kilograms) was of Dutch origin. The same methods were used as for transport to Scandinavia: the amphetamines were hidden in trucks and transported in ferries, in this case through Dover.[102]

In 1989 the amphetamine profiling project of the Swedish police concluded on the basis of a study of amphetamine pills seized in Europe between 1985 and 1989 that almost 80 per cent of all the pills had been produced in the Netherlands. Half of these pills came from the same laboratory. In September 1989 the Dutch police found this laboratory, the largest it had so far discovered, on a turkey farm in the village of Heythuysen in Limburg. Raids were carried out in nine other places and fourteen people were arrested, most of them in different places in Limburg and a few in the west of the country. Twelve kilograms of amphetamines (street value 400,000 guilders), supplies of precursor chemicals, and a few guns were seized. According to the police the lab had a production capacity of 20 kilograms per day. The manager of the lab, a 49-year-old man from Limburg named E. Moerman, would later be sentenced to six years in prison.[103]

This seizure did little to stop smuggling to Sweden. Robbie van L's group expanded its market share and was thought by the Swedes to produce one-quarter of all Dutch amphetamines. In 1982 Van L had been arrested in Germany and extradited to Sweden, where he received a ten-year prison sentence. But in December 1986, not long before Christmas, a fast car with two armed men appeared before the walls of the Swedish prison where Van L served his time. A ladder was thrown over the wall, shots were fired to scare off the jailers and the other prisoners, and Robbie and one of his mates climbed over the wall and disappeared in the car. A few days later he was back in the Netherlands and could not be extradited to Sweden.[104]

In 1987 an IRT was established in Heerlen with the aim of putting Van L and others out of operation.[105] To catch Van L the police employed a new strategy: the use of pseudo buyers. Ironically, one of the buyers who secretly worked for the police and attempted to ensnare Van L was Kalle Pauksch. However, it was not Pauksch but two English pseudo buyers from Scotland Yard who successfully set a trap for Van L. One year after the Heythuysen raid, a similar police action involving 140 officers raided two drug labs in Brabant and Limburg, arrested nine people, and again seized drugs, precursor chemicals, weapons, and cash. Some of the people involved had been arrested earlier in other raids.[106] The use of pseudo buyers was considered by the Dutch courts to be an unacceptable provocation by the police.[107] In 1990 Van L was arrested in the raid on his drug labs and after a lengthy procedure that took years was sentenced to five years in prison. Three years later, thirty officers were again involved in the 'dismantling of a major drug operation', raiding places in Heerlen (the home base of the Arno Mink gang) and the nearby village of Schinveld (where Mink's brother-in-law lived and at whose place the police had found a money chest from a safe cracked by Mink in 1968), arresting eight people and once again seizing drugs, equipment, and money.[108]

The floodgates of criminal anarchy had opened and there was no way to stop the wave. Another smuggler who followed in Van L's footsteps and who earned the nickname 'drug baron of the south' in the popular press was Peter van D from Schinveld. The Swedish police considered him and his brother Harrie the leaders of a major drug syndicate.[109] At the end of the 1980s Peter van D would become a pioneer in the production of and trade in XTC. Peter associated in

Schinveld with 'Fat Billy' P, who worked at a garage and as car dealer and who had worked with Mink. Later Billy became involved in illegal amphetamine production.[110] In Brabant the Denis brothers, criminal entrepreneurs from the Vogeltjesbuurt district in the city of Tilburg, turned their attention to amphetamines in the early 1990s. According to their son and successor in the business they built the foundations for a successful illegal drugs enterprise.[111]

The arrival of XTC

The dominant Dutch position in the illegal amphetamine market could not be maintained. The fall of the Iron Curtain opened the way for competition from Eastern Europe, especially from Poland. In 1989 75 per cent of all amphetamines seized in Germany came from the Netherlands, and 25 per cent from Poland, but in 1990 the percentages were 50–50. In 1989 7 per cent of amphetamines seized in Scandinavia came from Poland. In 1991 this was 21 per cent.[112] However, at the same time a new opportunity opened up for the Dutch synthetic drug industry: the XTC market.

3,4-methylenedioxy-n-methylamphetamine or MDMA (also known by street names such as Ecstasy, XTC, acid, or Adam) was patented by Merck in Germany in 1912 but never distributed by the company on the market. It took another sixty years before use of the drug as a stimulant appeared in the public domain. At that time MDMA was not a fashionable drug, but this slowly started to change when American pharmacologist Alexander Shulgin rediscovered and synthesized the drug, shared it with his friends, and gave it to psychotherapists who discovered its therapeutic potential. Under the influence of MDMA their patients opened up and became more accessible for therapeutic interventions, giving new perspectives on their problems. By the end of the 1970s a growing network of psychotherapists administered the still legal drug in their practice.[113] Fearful of the adverse publicity that had led to the demise of LSD-assisted therapies, they did not publish their results and tried to keep MDMA out of public attention. Over the next decade this attempt failed; in the 1980s the drug became popular in the Bhagwan movement of the followers of the Indian guru Shri Rajneesh. In hippie enclaves such as Goa in India the drug was used as a party drug, provoking an ecstatic dance trance. In the United States house culture was born, quickly spreading around the world, while XTC use spread from the Bhagwan communes in Oregon to Europe in the second half of the 1980s. The Spanish island of Ibiza became a hub where partygoers went, experiencing house culture, and taking it back to their home countries. Under the stimulating influence of XTC, house music, light shows, and stroboscopes, users participated in nightlong dance sessions. The name used in the hippie underground for LSD, acid, was now transferred to MDMA, as exemplified in the iconic t-shirt with the smiley symbol and the text: 'The House that Acid Built'. In the Western world 1988 became a new 'Summer of Love' reminiscent of that of 1967. In 1988 an Amsterdam dealer estimated the total consumption of XTC in the city to be 1,000 tablets each week. Among regulatory authorities and in public media, house culture and dance parties started to raise new concerns about drug abuse.[114]

In the United States in 1986 MDMA was placed in Schedule 1 of the Controlled Substances Act, as a drug with 'no medical value' and a 'high abuse potential', and its production, distribution, and use consequently prohibited. Other countries followed suit. In the same year the United Nations Commission on Narcotic Drugs scheduled MDMA, as well as related substances from the group of phenyl amphetamines, in the International Treaty on Psychotropic Substances (the 1971 convention that listed all substances of which use had to be controlled). The Netherlands had still not ratified this treaty in 1986 because it also included substances that had an extensive medical use in the Netherlands such as tranquillizers. Use of MDMA was at that time still unknown in the country, and Dutch regulatory authorities were under the impression that MDMA was an amphetamine and so already scheduled in the Dutch Opium Act. MDMA was also confused with related substances such as 3,4-methylenydioxyamphetamine (MDA), which was scheduled in the Opium Act in 1986. When in 1988 newspaper reports came out detailing the involvement of the Netherlands in the production of MDMA, the reputation of the country was at stake and MDMA and five related drugs were scheduled in the Opium Act.[115]

Clandestine manufacture of XTC

Producers of illegal amphetamines took their expertise to the new market for XTC. Before the regulation of 1988 Robert Hollemans, on the invitation of his former associates in the amphetamine trade, had already set up an XTC laboratory on a farm in the east of the country. He had found the formula for XTC in the library, as he had done with the formula for amphetamine. Raw materials and precursor chemicals needed for production were still freely available. A raid by the police looking for illegal amphetamines was useless since MDMA was still legal.[116] Hollemans was one example of the kind of chemist with expertise one needed to operate a clandestine laboratory, switching from amphetamine to the manufacture of MDMA and related compounds (see below), and who affiliated with criminal entrepreneurs. Another example was the Belgian Danny Leclère who came from Belgian Limburg, just over the border with the Netherlands, a pharmacist who had worked in an apothecary but decided to try his hands on more profitable ventures.[117]

In the late 1980s there was also a spillover from the German pharmaceutical industry available on the market. In Amsterdam 900,000 so-called 'Stanleys', white XTC tablets manufactured by the Immhausen company, were discovered by the police.[118] Once MDMA became illegal, clandestine manufacture had to develop in order to supply a growing market. In the early days many underground producers were themselves users and at first produced the drug for friends and acquaintances; later they expanded and used intermediaries to distribute their drugs in the house scene. Idealism was of importance in clandestine production in this early stage, as it had been in early cannabis smuggling and in clandestine LSD manufacture. Twice, in 1989 and again in 1991, the Dutch police took in for questioning a retired professor of chemistry at the Free University of Amsterdam who had produced MDMA. The clandestine lab in his house was discovered the first time after a fire alarm.[119] More successful than this professor were two idealistic producers who in 1986 had met an American supplier of XTC from California. Although enthusiastic about the effects of the drug, they did not at first succeed in getting their friends and acquaintances in the Amsterdam nightlife to share their enthusiasm. XTC was not yet in fashion. The two idealists did have the right contacts in the American XTC manufacturing world to obtain the necessary knowledge and expertise for developing their own clandestine lab when the house phenomenon struck the Netherlands in 1988, but it took until 1990 before the lab was functionally operating. By

1992 the duo were full-time XTC producers and worked in tandem with a salesman, producing batches of 1 to 2 kilograms of MDMA (10,000 to 20,000 tablets) every two months. The two claimed that the profit motive had only been secondary when they started out; their primary motive was the lack of good-quality XTC available on the market. Investment had been so high that it took at least a year before profits were made. On the other hand, by then the profits were huge.[120]

At the time of writing, clandestine chemists have easy access to the formula and preparation methods of MDMA through the Internet. Around 1990 they were dependent on formulas from textbooks, journals, or underground publications with titles such as *Psychedelic Chemistry* or *The Whole Drug Manufacturer's Catalogue*. MDMA is rather simple and cheap to produce, although not so easy as amphetamine. Its structure is relatively less stable, which can lead to its conversion into a more toxic product and a more limited shelf life. The necessary laboratory equipment is not high tech and includes distillation apparatus, a thermometer, a hotplate, a magnetic stir bar, a water aspirator, glass container/bottles, and a set of scales. Chemical suppliers, pharmacies, or even photo shops and groceries were potential suppliers for the chemicals needed in the production process.[121] The same methods needed to produce MDMA and related compounds are used in amphetamine production, only using other raw materials and precursor chemicals. For instance, while the precursor PMK (piperonal methyl ketone) is a key chemical for the manufacture of MDMA and related compounds such as MDA and MDEA (3,4-methylenedioxy-n-ethylamphetamine, also called MDE), the precursor benzyl methyl ketone (BMK) is key in the production of amphetamine and meth-amphetamine. In general, 10 litres of precursor chemicals are needed to produce 5 kilograms of MDMA oil or base, which when crystallized, dried, and ground is mixed with caffeine or lactose to produce pills. One kilogram of base can give 10,000 pills of 100 milligrams.[122]

To set up clandestine production one needed investment money. Expensive equipment was required, such as an autoclave or pressing chamber and a tablet machine. Apart from this basic equipment, one could make the lab as expensive as one wished: one police estimate from 1996 calculated that the equipment of a clandestine lab could cost anything between 10,000 and 3,000,000 guilders, depending on the measure of professionalism one aimed for.[123] In the beginning idealistic producers would choose the cheaper options out of necessity. Furthermore, the clandestine chemist needed a location out of sight of police and neighbours, and a place to dispose chemical waste (although in the early days one could still deliver the waste to chemical companies for processing). Two early idealists, an unemployed photographer and his American financer, produced 1.5 kilograms of MDMA base in their lab in the photographer's attic. It took them two months of hard work and an investment of 35,000 guilders: 30,000 guilders went on equipment and 5,000 guilders on chemicals. The investment paid off: they sold their final MDMA for 90,000 guilders to a distributor in Amsterdam, making a net profit of 55,000 guilders.[124]

Operating a clandestine lab was not without risks. In November 1990 six people received prison sentences of ten months to three years for attempting to set up a lab.[125] Dismantling one operation did not stop the growth of others. After the scheduling of MDMA in the Opium Act, underground production only started to proliferate. Profits were so high that the drug became of interest to criminal entrepreneurs as well as to idealistic producers.

A number of small-scale XTC laboratories were discovered by the police in early January 1989.[126] However in 1988 and 1989 most tablets were still being imported rather than produced in the Netherlands. In the early stages of house culture in Amsterdam what were consumed were the Immhausen pills or capsules with a yellow powder or little pink tablets, both imported from Spain, or drugs that did not contain any XTC: amphetamines and fake pills. However, by 1990 XTC production in the Netherlands was well underway and started exporting to the rest of Europe. Clandestine labs were found in the south of the country, in Brabant and Limburg, in the west, in and around Amsterdam, and in the centre, in Utrecht. They were found in all kinds of locations: in apartments, basements, houseboats, warehouses, and barns.[127]

The tablets became more professional-looking, evidence of the spread of the use of tablet machines in the labs. In 1991 there were already dozens of different kinds of tablets available on the market. The supply market became segmented as well and economies of scale started to operate. The costs of producing a tablet were only 25 to 40 cents, while a single tablet usually fetched in the retail trade to users anything between 15 and 40 guilders, depending on the location (the lowest prices were in Amsterdam); prices of 10 and 70 guilders are also mentioned.[128]

XTC that is not MDMA

To evade the strategies of the drug regulatory regime one tactic of producers was the development of so-called *designer drugs*. Designer drugs were compounds with a slightly altered molecular structure resembling (homologues of) illegal drugs such as MDMA, but not yet scheduled themselves in any drug law. The first XTC lab raided by the Dutch police in Utrecht in 1989 did not produce MDMA but MDA.[129] It turned out that the lab had been producing MDA for a decade, well before its prohibition in 1986. This was a kind of idealistic venture, minimally commercially driven and producing for self-use by a small group of friends and acquaintances of the chemist.[130] Clandestine MDA production did not end here. In 1992 the Dutch police seized two and a half million tablets that contained MDA rather than MDMA.[131]

MDEA was not scheduled in the Opium Act until 1993. While the effects of MDEA are slightly different from those of MDMA, it is probable that most partygoers who obtained a pill containing 'XTC' would not have realized the difference. Shorter-acting than MDMA (three instead of six hours), 'the effects of MDE are similar in many ways [...] but there are believable differences. The particular magic, and affective transference, does not appear to be there. There is a stoning intoxication [...] and the properties of unusually easy communication and positive self-viewing of MDMA seem to be absent,' a chemist wrote.[132] In 1990 Hollemans started production of MDEA on a houseboat in Maastricht in the south of Limburg. His lab was raided by the police, but despite the seizure of 188,400 tablets he could not be prosecuted since his operations were not yet illegal. Nevertheless, to take the heat off, Hollemans moved to Hungary where he continued the production until new legislation made this illegal, and 54 kilograms of MDEA, produced as a veterinary drug under the name Edma Hol Fantasia, were seized.

Hollemans's brother continued (at least according to Hollemans himself) the production facility in Maastricht and forged new alliances with illegal traders in the province.[133] One of them was an entrepreneur named Pelzer living in the small town of Landgraaf near to Heerlen.

In 1992 Pelzer was arrested with a kilogram of cocaine, a supply of XTC pills, a firearm, and a large amount of money in cash. He was released because of an error in the subpoena. Pelzer now innovated. He founded a company E-xpress, which took orders from consumers for at least four XTC pills (containing MDEA) and delivered them to their homes. E-xpress advertised via leaflets in discotheques and at house parties, and on the side of a double-decker touring parties. Due to the activities of entrepreneurs such as Hollemans and Pelzer the market for MDEA increased. Tests on illegal drugs showed that whereas in June 1992 only 6 per cent of all tested XTC pills contained MDEA, in December this percentage had risen to 59 per cent. They were marketed with the legend 'EVA'. In 1993 three clandestine labs were raided where MDEA was produced, but the manufacturers could not yet be prosecuted. The success of this production was also its undoing, because MDEA was scheduled in the Opium Act in that year. The next year a successor to EVA called Abeltje was already available on the market.[134]

XTC could be any kind of drug. A random sample of twenty-seven tablets analysed in 1989 and 1990 showed that only about half (thirteen) really contained MDMA, and three contained MDA. The dosage of MDMA in the tablets varied between 60 and 116 milligrams (120 milligram is a strong effective dose). Two tablets actually contained LSD, five were amphetamine, and four of the tablets did not contain any active drug at all. Another analysis of eighty-one tablets conducted in Amsterdam in 1991 showed almost 60 per cent of the pills to contain MDMA, with an average dose of 90.5 milligrams. Seven contained amphetamine and in the other tablets all kinds of substances were discovered: opiates (methadone or codeine), and even paracetamol or yeast.[135]

Organizing resources

The major problem for clandestine production was the availability of the precursor chemical PMK. By 1992 the chemical industry had to issue an end-user statement on supplying chemicals and to inform the CRI if there was any suspicion of bad intentions. PMK was used in the decorating and cleaning industry, so one way of obtaining the chemical was by using a front company in one of these branches. Another way was to go abroad: end-user statements also needed to be issued by chemical companies in other countries, but they were less attuned or sensitive to any dubiousness of orders from the Netherlands. When intensified attention by the police made the purchase of precursors in the Netherlands more of a risk to the secrecy of operations, chemicals were obtained in neighbouring countries Germany and Belgium, and increasingly in Eastern Europe – for instance in Slovakia. The legal market was the cheapest option. In the early 1990s 1 litre of PMK was priced at 300 German marks, while on the black market prices were three to ten times as high. Other necessary chemicals were brought through legal fronts or in small supplies from different companies in the Netherlands. These included dealers in chemicals, apothecaries, and veterinary pharmacists. Another problem in clandestine production was the purchase of a tablet machine. They were not only expensive (a new one could cost tens of thousands of guilders) but one needed a legal front company to purchase one. However, with the right contacts in the chemical industry one could always find ways around difficulties. One manufacturer bought a second-hand tablet machine in Eastern Europe and smuggled it to the Netherlands.

A large part of the chemicals used in the clandestine labs that were dismantled by the police in the early 1990s had been purchased from well-known chemical firms in the Netherlands, Belgium, and Germany, while the hardware and laboratory equipment came from Dutch and Belgian factories and companies. As criminologist Fijnaut reported to parliament: 'The manufacture of synthetic drugs is – from an economic perspective – a more normal activity than would appear at first sight.'[136]

The relative ease with which illegal producers could get their hands on chemicals and equipment was shown in the testimonies of a police informer. Entrepreneur Peter van D assigned one his associates, 'Anton B', to obtain a supply of dimethylformamide, a solvent used in the synthesis of MDMA. Anton knew – through other acquaintances in the criminal milieu – of a garage owner in the city of Zandvoort called 'Rob J', nicknamed the 'Snail'. As a garage owner the Snail could easily order chemicals. The Snail in his turn contacted a wholesale supplier of chemicals: Bechem Chemie in Haarlem. This company now started to supply the Snail, and through him the underground laboratories of Peter van D with first dimethylformamide and then all kinds of chemicals needed for drug production. What neither

Anton B nor Peter van D nor Bechem Chemie knew was that the Snail was a police informer who at the same time alerted his handlers in the police. What the director of Bechem Chemie did know was that it was extremely unlikely that a garage owner needed the chemicals ordered by the Snail. But, in another example of the kind of corporate non-compliance characteristic of other representatives of the chemical industry seen in earlier chapters, the director kept his suspicions for himself. In fact, he took advantage of the opportunity and increased the price of dimethylformamide by a factor of almost eight: from 4.5 guilders per litre to 35. Questioned later by the police about his way of operation, the director testified that 'he had slowly become suspicious about the frequent remit of his products. And he hated drugs. Therefore he had asked more money for his merchandise.'[137] The flexible attitude of this company should not have surprised the police. In 1990 the company was raided for another non-compliant activity: exporting triethanolamine, a chemical used in the production of mustard gas, to Iran.[138] The Snail also took care of repairs of the tablet machine used by the operation of Van D and of the supply of high-pressure boilers. His information was vital in the dismantling of Van D's clandestine production in 1993 by an IRT team.[139]

The UN Convention against Illicit Traffic in Narcotic Drugs and Psychotropic Substances, which obligated surveillance of the international trade in precursor and other essential chemicals, the European Community ordinances of 1990 and 1993, national regulations on import and export of chemicals of 1991 and 1992, and the *Wet voorkoming gebruik chemicalieën* (Law on the Prevention of the Abuse of Chemicals) enacted in 1995 that made production and trade of precursor chemicals illegal, all gave the law enforcement agencies new tools to combat the supply of chemicals to the illegal drug industry, but did not succeed in ending it.[140] By the mid-1990s the materials needed for synthetic drug production were not produced in the Netherlands itself, with the exception of acetone and sulphuric acid. For instance PMK, lysergic acid, or ephedrine (a basic material for amphetamine production) came from abroad. It was, however, not much of a problem for criminal entrepreneurs to get their hands upon supplies. One could smuggle them in from Eastern Europe. One smuggler explained that he could telephone a Russian factory with the information that he could pay in American dollars, and then pick up what he needed and bring it in a road tanker to the Netherlands.

Another smuggler transported in 1995 and 1996 14,000 kilograms of precursors to the Netherlands. By that time the chemicals were also advertised on the emerging Internet.[141]

Smuggling

The XTC business was simply too profitable, especially when production was destined for smuggling to other countries. This smuggling started early on: 'In October 1989, [three Dutch newspapers] all printed articles about the French police's successful roll-up of an ecstasy drug line between the Netherlands and France.'[142] XTC manufacturers followed in the tradition of the Brabant and Limburg smuggling and amphetamine cultures, establishing collaborations over the border with Belgium. The police began to speak of an 'international professional drugs mafia'.[143]

In August 1992 the Belgian police raided an XTC lab in the village of Kessenich-Kinrooi, just across the border from Limburg, and arrested three Dutchmen: two chemists and one man wanted by the Dutch police. The lab produced XTC for distribution in Belgium and the Netherlands and for export to the UK, smuggled in the petrol tanks of the trucks of a Belgian transport company.[144] One combination of two smugglers started operations in 1990. After making the right contacts and attracting start-up capital, over the following year they smuggled cargoes of XTC of around 4,000 tablets hidden in their car to a client in Italy fifteen times. Initially they were motivated by a thirst for adventure, enjoying the adrenalin rush of a successful operation. However, when they were ripped at gunpoint during deliveries and deprived of 75,000 guilders the fun went out of the project and they quit the business.[145] In 1991 the smuggling of 100,000 XTC tablets hidden in an industrial oven from the Netherlands to England was discovered. Another 100,000 tablets were found in the UK in the boot of a car and turned out to have been smuggled from the Netherlands on board a Dutch yacht.[146] EVA tablets appeared in Belgium, Germany, and Switzerland.[147]

The smuggling of XTC out of the Netherlands took place on all kinds of scales. Some smugglers operated as partners. One Dutchman smuggled 10,000 tablets to the UK on a monthly basis. As he explained to a criminologist, he had a group of around forty people working for him. Five were organizers, planners, and bookkeepers; these were 'people you could socialize with'. For the technical side there were the clandestine manufacturers and the maintenance caretakers. Technicians were not easily replaceable, but couriers were. They took the most chances and earned the least money and therefore 'were treated most nicely by everybody'.[148]

In one police investigation the IRT investigating one of the smuggler gangs actually facilitated transport in the hope of catching the 'big' criminals behind the operation. In 1992 Minke Kok and Jan Femer decided on the transport of a large consignment of XTC to the UK. They contacted 'Haagse Kees' C ('Kees from The Hague', aka King Boko), a stolen-car dealer who arranged for the chauffeur and the transport: a road tanker carrying egg pulp (purchased from a businessman from Limburg who was in on the operation). Half a million tablets were hidden in a secret compartment in the tanker and in early 1993 driven to the UK. Four million pounds sterling in cash were taken back by the chauffeur, who delivered four more consignments before he was caught by the British police. It then turned out that Haagse Kees was a police informer and had arranged for the transport, together with his runners from the police.[149]

Apart from this kind of large-scale smuggler, the international XTC trade was sufficiently profitable to be interesting to small-scale smugglers. A criminological investigation of Dutch couriers held in German prisons in 2002 showed that small-time smugglers with experience in the field (gained in cocaine or cigarette smuggling) bought supplies of tablets from dealers they knew and smuggled them by train or car over the border, making profits of 1,000 to 10,000 guilders each trip. Aachen in Germany was an important transit hub, as it had been in the interwar period.[150]

To smuggle tablets to the USA couriers were recruited who hid consignments of XTC pills on their body, in their clothes, or in their luggage. Sizes of the consignments varied between 5,000 and 25,000 pills. Although these couriers are often portrayed as victims, it turned out that they frequently had a penal record and that they worked for financial gain: one trip could earn them quick money of up to 1,000 guilders. However, couriers interviewed in American prisons in 2002 did not work for Dutch, but for Colombian smugglers: or at least, that was what they thought.[151]

In 1994 three-quarters of all XTC seized by law enforcement agencies in Europe – and three-quarters of all XTC seized in the UK – was produced in the Netherlands. In France 81 per cent of the 255,000 tablets seized came from the Netherlands (and 13 per cent from Belgium, which developed an XTC industry of its own). Most of the seizures were meant for transit to Spain, Italy, and the UK.[152] The Dutch drug industry took direct orders from clients from abroad. In 1994 an XTC lab, at the time the largest ever raided, was discovered by the police in Wormerveer, close to Amsterdam. It worked on a grander scale than earlier labs, being 500 square metres and having a production capacity of 500,000 tablets every day, and ordering its chemicals through a cover at Dutch companies. It was situated next to a channel into which the chemical waste was dumped. The operation worked for a group of Israeli criminal entrepreneurs who aimed to supply both European and North American markets.[153]

The idealistic XTC producers and smugglers of the first years were by now supplanted by entrepreneurs that were already involved in the trade in other illegal drugs. One Dutchman had started dealing cocaine to finance his own use and progressed in five years to multiple operations: the smuggling of cocaine from South America mostly to the UK; the smuggling of on average 50,000 kilograms of cannabis annually from Morocco and Lebanon; and participation in the setting up of two amphetamine labs. The step from the latter to XTC manufacture was quickly made. However, in 1991 this Dutchman quit the business and broke off his contacts with the criminal world for the sake of his family.[154]

While the world of XTC smuggling, as that of cannabis, cocaine, and heroin, was mainly a masculine world, women were active here as well. One Dutchwoman in the 1980s made a career in the organization of cocaine smuggling from South America (3 or 4 kilograms were sent out every two months), and of an incidental cargo of 100,000 or 200,000 kilograms of cannabis from Morocco. In 1988 she went into partnership with American XTC traders whom she had met on the party scene on Ibiza, leaving the, in her words, *opgefokte* ('messed-up') cocaine business. In the XTC trade much bigger profits promised to be made. In the Summer of Love of 1988 she sold 0.5 million XTC tablets throughout Europe. When the Americans went into retirement the Dutchwoman set up fifteen different XTC labs in different countries. She dismantled each of the labs immediately after producing a batch in order to avoid detection by the police. By 1991 she had made enough money to decide to retire.[155]

Since the Netherlands was a production centre, the retail price of an XTC tablet in the country dramatically decreased. By the beginning of the twenty-first century, when the euro had replaced the guilder, Dutch consumers could buy the drug for only 3 to 4.50 euros. The costs of production of one tablet were estimated by the police at just 0.22 euros. Smuggling over the border, to France for instance where an XTC tablet fetched a price of 12 euros, or across the ocean where in the United States users paid 34 euros for a pill, was even more profitable. In 1999 9.7 million pills produced in the Netherlands were seized in foreign countries; in 2002 this number had risen to 38 million. Of the 25.7 million Dutch pills seized by foreign law enforcement agencies in 2001, 6 million were seized in the UK, 4.3 million in Germany, and 4 million in the USA.[156] Dutch XTC production and trade had become a very successful export industry.

Organized crime syndicates?

Clandestine XTC production kept growing, despite the operations of special police units or IRTs. The synthetic drug market remained basically a free market, to which it was easy to gain access.[157] To combat the increase, in 1998 a special police taskforce, the *Unit Synthetische Drugs* (Synthetic Drugs Unit), was founded with its headquarters in Helmond in Brabant. While the officers of the unit thought that there were four major producers at the time, three of them in the south, one in the west, they mostly raided small labs, dismantling thirty or forty each year.[158] Successful investigations by the unit in the south meant only a displacement of production: Amsterdam became by 2000 the centre of the synthetic drug trade. According to a DEA report, from 2001 80 per cent of all XTC production in the world continued to take place in the Netherlands and in Belgium.[159]

While early XTC production was for an important part minimally commercially driven, criminal entrepreneurs had jumped on the bandwagon, attracted by the huge profits to be made. Ronnie Undink had a background in the Amsterdam building industry, laundered money for friends such as cannabis smuggler Steve Brown, and set up XTC smuggling to Sweden.[160] Stanley Hillis, who had reputedly worked with Yugoslav criminals and was even designated by two journalists as the '*capo di tutti capi*' of drug lords in the Netherlands (*if*, they added, such a man existed), became a prominent player in the cannabis and XTC trade in the 1990s, together with Mink 'Thinker' Kok and burglar Jan 'Moustache' Femer.[161] In the Amsterdam of the 1980s Hillis, Kok and Femer had been known as the *Denkers* (Thinkers), responsible for a series of successful bank robberies.

The operations of another group of criminal entrepreneurs became better known to the police because they had recruited the chemist Leclère as an informer. For ten months this group, consisting of labour broker Ton van Dalen, criminal entrepreneur and kamper Roland van Essen, and financial advisor Willem Endstra, was allowed by an IRT team to export XTC tablets manufactured in its clandestine labs to the UK, making 300 million guilders in revenue. In February 1992 the IRT team raided thirty-one locations in eleven different municipalities, including two labs with an estimated production capacity of 250,000 tablets per day. They seized 2.5 million tablets of MDA, together with 200,000 litres of chemicals and thirteen firearms; forty people were arrested. Van Dalen, seen as the chief organizer, would receive a sentence of ten years in prison. However, the police operation could not unravel the whole network connected to the smugglers' operations. Part of the XTC tablets seized on transport to England were not manufactured in the laboratories of the Van Dalen group, but in other clandestine labs in the south of the Netherlands. The 'big' laboratory that supposedly supplied the successors of Bruinsma's organization was never found (according to one source it had been moved a few days before the raid to a bunker in the polder near the city of Almere, to the east of Amsterdam).

Despite the success of the police operation, XTC supply in the Netherlands was not really affected. Rather than one organization with central leaders, investigations unravelled a continuous shifting network of opportunistic alliances.[162] The illegal Dutch XTC industry was based on a network in which everyone who was involved knew each other and made temporary deals with each other: financers, producers, smugglers, customers.[163] Sometimes suppliers of chemicals worked for different labs, but there was no central coordination in these kinds of networks.[164] The explosion in demand for XTC had created a new illegal market, and criminal entrepreneurs and their networks, with track records in the illegal cannabis, cocaine, and amphetamines trade, were ideally suited to organize supply for these markets on the lines of criminal anarchy. The XTC industry was flexible and able to recover quickly after any strike by law enforcement.¹⁶⁵

Outlaw motorcycle gangs

The Dutch synthetic drugs industry was socially and historically embedded in different parts of society. Most of them we have already encountered. The smuggling villages and cultures of Brabant and Limburg were one part. A second were the criminal subcultures of the larger cities that had entered the illegal cannabis trade as early as 1971. Drug subcultures with enthusiastic users of LSD, XTC, and other hallucinogenic and synthetic drugs were a third part of society. The kampers were a fourth, and the so-called 'outlaw motorcycle gangs' such as the Hell's Angels a fifth. We need to say a little more about them. In 2018 a Dutch court ruled that the Hell's Angels were not a criminal organization; at present, however, another Dutch court has reversed this decision and banned the Angel chapters in the Netherlands, as earlier court decisions have banned three more motorcycle clubs, the Bandidos, Satudarah, and No Surrender (although enforcement of these court decisions have legal and practical complications). The involvement of motorcycle clubs in the illegal drug trade is comparable to that of the Chinese secret societies. Rather than organizations with the express aim of conducting an illegal drug trade, they are social and cultural environments that facilitate members active in this trade.¹⁶⁶

Outlaw motorcycle gangs such as the Hell's Angels are organized in local chapters. Like the Chinese societies, they are not secret, but rather mutual aid societies unified by a common culture, of which individual members can be involved in illegal activities. A British Hell's Angel explained to a journalist: 'I'd say that almost no one is joining the Angels specifically to be a criminal or get involved in drug dealing. Some just end up that way.'¹⁶⁷ The structure of the group as a whole facilitates network building and embeds the illegal activities in the club houses, meetings, and so on, and offers some form of protection to members in conflicts with outsiders.

Central in police investigations was the Amsterdam chapter of the Hell's Angels. The founders of this chapter in the Kinkerbuurt neighbourhood of city, a working-class district, were acquaintances of future notorious criminal entrepreneurs from that district such as the Thinkers mentioned above. The origins of the Hell's Angels in Amsterdam are in the youth gangs of the neighbourhood. Later the Angels became an important actor in the red-light district of Amsterdam, owning cafés and buildings, offering protection, and active in the illegal drugs and arms trade. The step to involvement in smuggling to other countries was not so great. In 1993 the CRI for the first time proposed a closer investigation into the activities of the Angels. By then they also had chapters in other cities and an associated club in Heerlen; all in all, there were around ten local motorcycle gangs active in the Netherlands.[168]

One important asset for the Hell's Angels was their international contacts. Just as members of Chinese triads could ask for support among triad members living in other countries, the Angels could turn to chapters of their brethren over the borders. A story investigated by a British crime journalist gives some detail on how Angel cooperation worked. One Angel, nicknamed 'English Bill' because he had lived in England, operated as facilitator for cannabis transports from the Netherlands to the UK. One particular deal he made in 1992 was with a Liverpool crime family of four brothers who gave him a substantial down payment for the delivery of a supply of cannabis from Amsterdam. Unfortunately the shipment was seized by British customs officers in Manchester, leaving 140,000 pounds sterling still to be paid to Bill. The Angel took the position that the shipment was his responsibility until it entered British waters; after that, it was the responsibility of the Liverpool crime family. The latter refused to pay up, and so Bill involved the Wolverhampton and Windsor chapters of the Angels in an attempt to get his money. Warnings and threats finally led to a meeting of the Liverpudlians with the Angels in a car park; on this occasion the Angels were on the receiving end of violence when one of the other side pumped four bullets from a handgun into one of the bikers.[169]

Violence

While flexible cooperation and alliances were one of the characteristics of the criminal anarchy that drove the synthetic drug industry in the south of the Netherlands, violence performed essential roles too. Increased profitability and increased competition as well as the involvement of armed robbers might account for a hardening of the smuggling that by the end of the 1980s led to attempted killings. In 1988 and 1989 two failed murder attempts (a car bomb and a grenade attack on his house) were made on Peter van D. Ten years later an assassin fired four bullets at him in front of his house in Schinveld, but Peter survived; a few months earlier two of his business associates had been murdered. Van D himself was suspected of involvement in two assassinations in 2004 and 2005.[170] A Luxembourg physician involved in the cannabis, amphetamine, and XTC trade was shot dead on parole from prison.[171] Informers were especially at risk: in 1993, a year after his involvement had led to the end of the Van Dalen operation, chemist Leclère was killed.[172]

One smuggler was astonished when he first went to a lab in the south of the country to pick up a consignment of XTC.

> Almost every one of those people walked around with a sawn-off shotgun. One time I had to go to a guy I did not know to make a deal. The one who sent me to the guy gave me a gun. 'Just in case, you never know with these people.' Once in the car the guy actually drew a big gun from a kind of leg holster and put it on the dashboard: 'So, we do not need this one, do we?' I was too scared to say that I also had a gun and was quite nervous driving the journey. We went to a man who had a large container with something like 40,000 tablets. I was supposed to look to see if they were all right and then possibly buy 5,000. I tasted that it was shit and did not want them, but the man started to threaten me […] to get rid of him I finally bought 500 tablets.[173]

Increased involvement of South Americans from the cocaine trade into the XTC trade from 1990 onwards was given as an explanation by one Dutch smuggler for the increased violence and the spread of the habit of always carrying a gun.[174] However, as in the cannabis trade, in the synthetic drug trade many networks functioned without any internal violence. Furthermore, violence was not the only internal sanction available to criminal networks. One retail dealer on questioning by the police confessed that he had bought his merchandise from a man in a photograph shown to him by police interrogators and identified his wholesale dealer. When the latter became aware of this, he did not punish the retail dealer by violence, but took care that the man was unable to buy any products from any distributor in the Netherlands any more. The small size of the whole synthetic drug distribution network, where everyone knew each other, made ostracism another available sanction.[175]

Conclusion

The regulation of amphetamines, starting in 1968 and resulting in their prohibition under the revised Opium Act of 1976, had the unintended consequences that were the usual result of the drug regulatory regime. It did not stop the further development of an international illicit trade; rather, it fulfilled two essential conditions for this development: the prohibition of alternative legal sources of supply and the illegalization of demand. Prohibition also led to the development of an underground production that in the 1990s would partly shift to the production of XTC and supplied Europe with a large part of its illegal synthetic drugs.

The geographical position of the Netherlands, its logistical infrastructure and excellent transport routes by car or ferry into the rest of Europe all contributed to the rise of this export industry. So did the presence of a chemical industry that supplied the underground with the necessary raw materials and precursor chemicals. When this led to further regulation and control of the chemical industry by the state, underground manufacturers obtained their chemicals from Eastern Europe.

Different cultures came together in the constitution of underground chemistry and trade. Idealists convinced they would create a better world by a better chemistry set up an illegal LSD production and trade that was embedded in the counterculture of the 1960s and 1970s and remained somewhat apart from amphetamine and XTC production. Idealists were also involved in establishing the first production lines of MDMA and related compounds. To these idealists there was a mystical purpose to the production of mind-expanding drugs. Borderlines between idealists and criminals became blurred as regulation intervened and production and smuggling became more and more profitable. When regulation made markets illegal while demand soared at the same time, criminal entrepreneurs noticed and took their chances and came to dominate the supply side. Criminal entrepreneurs connected to the smuggling cultures of the south of the Netherlands, as well as from the cities in other parts of the country, and later outlaw motorcycle gangs moved in on the amphetamine and XTC production and trade, sometimes in alliance with idealists.

The Dutch illegal synthetic drug industry has been as capable of solving problems and puzzles to further its expansion as the legal pharmaceutical drug industry. The drug regulatory regime, the illegalization of the market, and increased pressure by law enforcement agencies were answered by revolutionary changes and tactics: illegal liquor distilleries were transformed in amphetamine labs; underground chemists learned to synthesize new drugs; idealist chemist-users collaborated with criminal entrepreneurs. The result was relatively simple production processes that could easily be dismantled and reassembled. Chemical expertise came partly from the idealists, and partly from the illegal liquor distillation that had developed in the southern smuggling cultures. Underground chemistry was low tech and low cost. Even where more expensive laboratory equipment was needed, it could easily be financed out of the profit margins of the illegal drug trade. Underground chemistry was also flexible and organized as 'guerrilla production', producing batches of the product in one place, then dismantling and moving to another location. The flexibility and fragmentation of production fitted perfectly into the pattern of criminal anarchy. The use of spaces invisible to law enforcement, such as buildings in the agricultural landscape, made detection difficult. Difficult but not impossible: the police could claim many successes in raiding labs and arresting producers. However, there were always others to take their place.

Underground chemistry together with demand and with the social and cultural embeddedness of production and smuggling in Dutch society created a fragmented and decentralized drug industry that reconstituted itself after every police operation. While there have been a few very influential players in the illegal drug market and social networks and relations, cultural affinities, and family connections have all been important, access to the drug market remained relatively easy. Actors made multiple appearances in different collaborations. The result was that, especially after the prohibition of MDMA, the floodgates of criminal anarchy have opened up in the Netherlands.

Notes

1 Centrum voor Criminaliteitspreventie en Veiligheid, 'Taskforce Brabant-Zeeland publiceert resultaten', 22 February 2017, https://hetccv.nl/nieuws/nieuws-detail/article/taskforce-brabant-zeeland-publiceert-resultaten (accessed 7 August 2020).
2 E.g., B. Beke, E. van der Torre and M. van Duin, *Stads- en regioscan in de grootste Brabantse gemeenten. De achtergronden van onveilige GVI*

scores (Apeldoorn: Politie & Wetenschap, 2012); P. Tops and J. Tromp, *De achterkant van Nederland. Hoe onder- en bovenwereld verstrengeld raken* (Amsterdam: Balans, 2017); P. Tops, J. van Valkenhoef et al., *Waar een klein land groot in kan zijn. Nederland en synthetische drugs in de afgelopen 50 jaar* (The Hague: Boom, 2018); A. van Wijk and A. Lenders, 'Betonrot. Een kwalitatief onderzoek naar het fenomeen ondermijnende criminaliteit in Brabant-Zeeland, de effecten van en richtingen voor de overheidsaanpak' (Bureau Beke, 2018), https://bureaubeke.nl/wp-content/uploads/2018/12/Betonrot_Bekereeks-2.pdf (accessed 7 August 2020).

3   H. Moors and T. Spapens, *Criminele families in Noord-Brabant. Een verkenning van generatie-effecten in de georganiseerde misdaad* (Apeldoorn: Politie & Wetenschap, 2017).

4   van Wijk and Lenders, 'Betonrot', p. 21.

5   F. Bovenkerk, *Misdaadprofielen* (Amsterdam: Meulenhoff, 2001), pp. 232–5.

6   N. Rasmussen, *On Speed: The Many Lives of Amphetamines* (New York: New York University Press, 2008).

7   E.g., Delpher digitized newspaper archive (ww.delpher.nl/nl/kranten, hereafter D): *Nieuws van den Dag voor Nederlandsch-Indië* 2 July 1937.

8   *Pharmaceutisch Weekblad*, at pw.nl/archief/historisch-archief (hereafter PW), 1939, p. 1260; N. V. Koninklijke Pharmaceutische Fabrieken v/h Brocades, Shteeman & Pharmacia, Municipal Archive of Delft, no. 188, no. 157, minutes of meeting of directors, 8 January 1940.

9   D: *Volksdagblad* 6 February 1940.

10 Advertisement in *Nederlandsch Tijdschrift voor Geneeskunde* 28 June 1941; S. Snelders and T. Pieters, 'Speed in the Third Reich: Metamphetamine (Pervitin) use and a drug history from delow', *Social History of Medicine* 24 (2011) 686–99.

11 Centraal Bureau voor de Statistiek, *Economische en sociale kroniek der oorlogsjaren 1940–1945* (Utrecht: W. De Haan, 1947); H. A. M. Klemann, *Nederland 1938–1948. Economie en samenleving in jaren van oorlog en bezetting* (Amsterdam: Boom, 2002), pp. 331–8.

12 W. Pieper (ed.), *Nazis on Speed: Drogen im 3. Reich*, 2 vols (Löhrbach: Werner Pieper & The Grüne Kraft, nd.); Rasmussen, *On Speed*; N. Ohler, *Der Totale Rausch. Drogen im Dritten Reich* (Cologne: Verlag Kiepenhauer & Witsch, 2015).

13 H. Pinkhof, 'Schadelijke werking van Pervitine', *Nederlands Tijdschrift voor Geneeskunde* 85 (1941) 2896; H. Pinkhof, 'Een bezwaar van naamverandering van sterk werkende geneesmiddelen', *Nederlands Tijdschrift voor Geneeskunde* 85 (1941) 3786.

14 PW, 15 November 1940; minutes of Pharmaceutical Inspectorate, 16 May 1941, archive of Pharmaceutical Inspectorate 1921–1961, National Archive, The Hague, inv. no. 2.15.39, 10.
15 Snelders and Pieters, 'Speed in the Third Reich'.
16 A. T. Knoppers, 'Over de wekamines (amphetamine, pervitine en dergelijke)', *Nederlands Tijdschrift voor Geneeskunde* 86 (1942) 3323–8.
17 B. H. Rypkema, 'Een onderzoek naar het geneesmiddelgebruik in Nederland' (PhD thesis, University of Amsterdam, 1954).
18 M. de Kort, *Tussen patiënt en delinquent. Geschiedenis van het Nederlandse drugsbeleid* (Hilversum: Verloren, 1995), p. 173.
19 'Rapport inzake het gebruik van wekaminen', Gezondheidsraad no. 29/69, 20 August 1971, archive of Pharmaceutical Inspectorate (Staatstoezicht op de Volksgezondheid: Hoofdinspectie Geneesmiddelen) 1962–1994, National Archive, The Hague, inv. no. 2.27.5033, 108.
20 D: *De Telegraaf* 19 August 1967.
21 de Kort, *Tussen patiënt en delinquent*, pp. 174–5.
22 'Rapport inzake het gebruik van wekaminen'.
23 'Het heroinegebruik in Amsterdam: een signalement', in Erik Fromberg Archive in International Institute of Social History, Amsterdam, no. ARCH 03137, no inventory (hereafter IISH-EF).
24 de Kort, *Tussen patiënt en delinquent*, p. 175.
25 Police report 1 June 1949, in archive of Municipal Police of Amsterdam (Gemeentepolitie Amsterdam) 1957–1993, City Archive Amsterdam, inv. no. 5225A (hereafter GPA), 3837.
26 D: *De Telegraaf* 30 August 1963.
27 International Narcotics Control Board, annual reports and documents, incb.org (hereafter INCB), annual report 1977, p. 18.
28 de Kort, *Tussen patiënt en delinquent*, pp. 172–3; S. A. M. Snelders, 'LSD en de psychiatrie in Nederland' (PhD thesis, VU-University Amsterdam, 1999), pp. 150–1.
29 Snelders, 'LSD en de psychiatrie', pp. 153–4.
30 Snelders, 'LSD en de psychiatrie', p, 161.
31 C. C. Bisbee, P. Bisbee et al. (eds), *Psychedelic Prophets: The Letters of Aldous Huxley and Humphry Osmond* (Montreal: Mc-ill-Queen's University Press, 2018), pp. 519–26.
32 H. Cohen, *Drugs, druggebruikers en drug-scene* (Alphen aan den Rijn: Samsom, 1975), p. 62.
33 Cohen, *Drugs*, p. 63; D. van Weerlee (ed.), *Allemaal rebellen: Amsterdam 1955–1965* (Amsterdam: Tabula, 1984), pp. 74–9; Snelders, 'LSD en de psychiatrie', p. 149; A. Roberts, *Albion Dreaming: A Popular History of LSD in Britain* (Singapore: Marshall Cavendish, 2012), p. 126.

34 See D: 'Recept ligt voor het grijpen. Grondstoffen LSD vrij verkrijgbaar', *Trouw* 25 October 1985.
35 Uncle Fester, *Practical LSD Manufacture*, 3rd edn (Green Bay: Festering Publications, 2006), p. 4.
36 'LSD Manufacture', Schaffer Library of Drug Policy, www.druglibrary.org/schaffer/dea/pubs/lsd/LSD-5.htm (accessed 7 August 2020).
37 Uncle Fester, *Practical LSD Manufacture*, p. 1.
38 Roberts, *Albion Dreaming*, pp. 172–3.
39 Uncle Fester, *Practical LSD Manufacture*, p. 2. See also 'LSD Manufacture'.
40 L. Fielding, *To Live Outside the Law: A Memoir* (London: Serpent's Tail, 201), p. 59.
41 Police reports on Operation Julie, 9 August and 21 September 1978, and P. J. Gomm and I. J. Humphreys, 'The role of the Home Office Central Research Establishment Drugs Intelligence Laboratory in Operation Julie', April 1978 in Home Office Archive, National Archives, Kew, HO 319/315; L. Ebenezer, *Operation Julie: The World's Greatest LSD Bust* (Talybont: Y Lolfa, 2010); Fielding, *To Live Outside the Law*; Roberts, *Albion Dreaming*, pp. 177–8.
42 Fielding, *To Live Outside the Law*, p. 59.
43 Fielding, *To Live Outside the Law*, pp. 226–67.
44 Snelders, 'LSD en de psychiatrie', p. 151.
45 Weijenburg, *Drugs en drugsbestrijding*, pp. 147–8; Snelders, 'LSD en de psychiatrie', pp. 151–2.
46 D: 'Politie rolt LSD-laboratorium op', *NRC Handelsblad* 8 Augustus 1985; 'Voor maken LSD achttien maanden', *Trouw* 8 November 1985; 'LSD-fabrikanten veroordeeld', *De Volkskrant* 9 November 1985.
47 Centrale Recherche Informatiedienst (CRI), annual report 1982; INCB: annual report 1984, p. 32; D: 'Nederland ziet zich niet als LSD-centrum van West-Europa', *De Telegraaf* 2 February 1985.
48 CRI, annual report 1989, p. 88, 96.
49 CRI, annual report 1987, pp. 25–6.
50 Weijenburg, *Drugs en drugsbestrijding*, p. 134.
51 Weijenburg, *Drugs en drugsbestrijding*, p. 149.
52 CRI, annual report 1993, p. 10.
53 CRI, annual report 1993, p. 10; D: 'Laboratorium voor pillen ontmanteld', *NRC Handelsblad* 19 August 1993; Weijenburg, *Drugs en drugsbestrijding*, p. 149.
54 de Kort, *Tussen patiënt en delinquent*, p. 175.
55 P. Spapens and A. van Oirschot, *Smokkelen in Brabant. Een grensgeschiedenis 1830–1970* (Hapert: De Kempenpers, 1988), p. 58.
56 D. J. H. N. den Beer Portugael, *De Marechaussee grijpt in* (Utrecht: A. W. Bruna, 1954), p. 170.

57 Spapens and van Oirschot, *Smokkelen in Brabant*, p. 122.
58 Spapens and van Oirschot, *Smokkelen in Brabant*, p. 122.
59 T. Pfeil, *Van tollenaar tot poortwachter. Geschiedenis van de douane, de oudste rijksdienst van Nederland* (Rotterdam: Trichis, 2012), p. 281.
60 P. Spapens and P. Horsten, *Tappen uit een geheim vaatje. De geschiedenis van illegale alcoholstokerijen in Nederland* (Hapert: De Kempenpers, 1990).
61 Pfeil, *Van tollenaar tot poortwachter*, pp. 258–67.
62 den Beer Portugael, *Marechaussee grijpt in*, p. 19; W. H. Nagel, *De criminaliteit van Oss* (The Hague: D. A. Daemen, 1949); A. B. J. A. Nijdam, *Goirle. Een sociografische studie over de criminaliteit en de moraliteit van een grensgemeente rond de Tweede Wereldoorlog* (Wageningen: H. Veenman, 1950); A. F. A. Schreurs, *Het kerkdorp St. Willebrord (Het Heike). Een sociaal-geografische en criminologische studie* (Utrecht: Dekker & Van de Vegt, 1947).
63 Nijdam, *Goirle*, p. 115.
64 Klemann, *Nederland 1938–1948*, p. 337.
65 Nijdam, *Goirle*, p. 185.
66 F. Egmond, 'Georganiseerde misdaad en de overheid in het verleden: Nederland tijdens de 17^e en 18^e eeuw', in C. J. C. F. Fijnaut (ed.), *Georganiseerde misdaad en strafrechtelijk politiebeleid* (Lochem: J.B. van den Brink, 1989), pp. 11–22; F. Egmond, *Underworlds: Organized Crime in the Netherlands 1650–1800* (Cambridge: Polity Press, 1993).
67 J. Visscher, 'Val van een Brabantse drugsbende', *Reformatorish Dagblad* 23 October 1999, at www.digibron.nl/search/detail/012dddece18106a1ve45d07d2/val-van-een-brabantse-drugsbende (accessed 7 August 2020).
68 Nagel, *Criminaliteit van Oss*.
69 See Moors and Spapens, *Criminele families*, p. 10.
70 D: 'Zes jaar opiumsmokkel langs Zeeuwse grens', *Het Vrije Volk* 3 August 1960.
71 D: R. Govaars and H. Korver, 'Einde van een smokkelkoning', *De Telegraaf* 2 October 1976.
72 On Mink and his gang: R. A. Gonsalves and G. J. Verhoog, *Mr. Gonsalves: Memoires* (Amsterdam: De Arbeiderspers, 1999), pp. 161–76; R. Couwenhoven, *De affaire Noortman. Kunsthandelaar, stichter van de Tefaf, ereburger van Maastricht en kunstcrimineel* (Meppel: Just Publishers, 2017), pp. 40–2, 50–65.
73 E. M. Brecher et al. 'The Consumers Union Report on Licit and Illicit Drugs', 1972, Schaffer Library of Drug Policy, www.druglibrary.org/schaffer/LIBRARY/studies/cu/CU39.html (accessed 7 August 2020).

74 On his sentence see D: *Het Vrije Volk* 1 April 1972.
75 On arrest in 1970, see D: 'Brandkastenkraker gepakt in Zweden', *Het Vrije Volk* 3 December 1970.
76 D: *Het Vrije Volk* 1 April 1972.
77 'D: Volgens de Avro Machtsstrijd in Limburgse onderwereld', *Limburgs Dagblad* 10 March 1971.
78 Spapens and Horsten, *Tappen*, p. 165; M. Husken and F. Vuijst, *XTC smokkel* (Amsterdam: Zwarte Beertjes, 2004), p. 234.
79 Husken and Vuijst, *XTC smokkel*, p. 15.
80 Interviews with amphetamine producers and traders in D. Korf and H. Verbraeck, 'Dealers en dienders. Dynamiek tussen drugsbestrijding en de midden- en hogere niveaus van de cannabis-, cocaine-, amfetamine- en ecstasyhandel in Amsterdam (University of Amsterdam, Bonger Institutoe of Criminology, 1993), pp. 15–53.
81 P. C. Duyne, *Het spook en de dreiging van de georganiseerde misdaad* (The Hague: Sdu, 1995), p. 89.
82 Husken and Vuijst, *XTC smokkel*, pp. 16–17.
83 Weijenburg, *Drugs en drugsbestrijding*, pp. 135–6.
84 Korf and Verbraeck, 'Dealers en dienders', p. 155.
85 P. Spapens, 'Sluikstoken en smokkelen, een grensoverschrijdende activiteit. Belgen en Nederlanders broederlijk in illegale praktijken', in E. Van Schoonenberghe, P. Spapens et al., *Tersluiks. Alcoholsmokkel en sluikstokerij in de Lage Landen* (Heule: Snoeck, 2012), pp. 32–49.
86 *Limburgsch Dagblad* 7 November 1987.
87 CRI, annual report 1989, p. 87.
88 A. Elissen, 'Synthetische drugs', *Recherche Informatie* 14:2 (1993), p. 12.
89 Korf and Verbraeck, 'Dealers en dienders', pp. 150–7.
90 C. Fijnaut, 'Georganiseerde criminaliteit in Nederland: de rol van autochtone criminele groepen', Parlementaire Enquêtecommissie Opsporingsmethoden, Tweede Kamer der Staten-Generaal, 1995–1996, 24 072 (hereafter PEO), 17, pp. 42–3.
91 Weijenburg, *Drugs en drugsbestrijding*, p. 131.
92 P. C. van Duyne, R. F. Kouwenberg, and G. Romeijn, *Misdaadondernemingen. Ondernemende misdadigers in Nederland* (Gouda: Quint, 1990), pp. 51–3.
93 van Duyne et al., *Misdaadondernemingen*, pp. 43–54; van Duyne, *Het spook en de dreiging*, pp. 89–94.
94 van Duyne et al., *Misdaadondernemingen*, pp. 51–4.
95 van Duyne et al., *Het spook en de dreiging*, pp. 91–4.
96 Korf and Verbraeck, 'Dealers en dienders', pp. 152-3.
97 Price in 1989: CRI, annual report 1989, p. 87.

98 Value of kronor from InflationTool, www.inflationtool.com/swedish-krona/1982-to-present-value (accessed 7 August 2020).
99 K. Sturesson, *Bland langare och profitörer. Ur en narkotikapolis dagbok* (Stockholm: Hjalmarson & Högberg, 2004).
100 Sturesson, *Bland langare och profitörer*.
101 van Duyne, *Het spook en de dreiging*, p. 87.
102 Weijenburg, *Drugs en drugsbestrijding*, p. 132.
103 Sturesson, *Bland langare och profitörer*; D: 'Politie ontdekt in Limburg amfetaminelaboratorium', *De Volkskrant* 21 September 1989; 'Zweden', *Limburgsch Dagblad* 21 September 1989.
104 Smuggling to Sweden: Sturesson, *Bland langare och profitörer*.
105 Husken and Vuijst, *XTC smokkel*, p. 24.
106 Sturesson, *Bland langare och profitörer*; D: 'Bij uitgebreide politieactie amfetaminehandel opgerold', *NRC Handelsblad* 21 August 1990.
107 Husken and Freke Vuijst, *XTC smokkel*, pp. 30–1.
108 D: 'Arno Mink vordert in beslag genomen twaalf mille terug', *Limburgsch Dagblad* 8 July 1970; 'Amfetamine-bende Heerlen opgerold', *De Telegraaf* 8 July 1993.
109 Sturesson, *Bland langare och profitörer*.
110 H. J. Korterink, 'Zondag 7 juni: "Foute man" in Zevenhoven & de brandkastbende van Arno Mink' 7 June 2009, www.misdaadjournalist.nl/2009/06/zondag-7-juni-m (accessed 7 August 2020); J. and M. van Kampen, 'De pretpil in Limburg: wat zit erachter?', *De Limburger*, 16 January 2016, www.limburger.nl/cnt/dmf20160115_00006446/wat-zit-achter-de-pretpil-in-limburg (accessed 7 August 2020). Interview with Hollemans in Hans Moll, 'Drugproducent wil fabriek bouwen in Tholen', *NRC Handelsblad* 13 August 1994.
111 Tops and Tromp, *Achterkant*, p. 101.
112 Elissen, 'Synthetische drugs', p. 13; Weijenburg, *Drugs en drugsbestrijding*, p. 133.
113 A. Shulgin and A. Shulgin, *PiKHAL: A Chemical Love Story* (Berkeley: Transform Press, 2015), pp. 66–74.
114 On the early history of XTC and house: E. Fromberg, *XTC. Harddrug of onschuldig genotmiddel?* (Amsterdam: Swets & Zeitlinger, 1991); A. Adelaars, *XTC. Alles over Ecstasy* (Amsterdam: In de Knipscheer, 1996), pp. 30–41; Korf and Verbraeck, *Dealers en dienders*, pp. 169–72; B. Eisner, *Ecstasy: The MDMA Story* (Berkeley: Ronin Books, 1994); N. Saunders, *Ecstasy and the Dance Culture* (London: N. Saunders, 1995); M. Collin, *Altered State: The Story of Ecstasy Culture and Acid House* (London: Serpent's Tail, 1997).
115 Fromberg, *XTC*, p. 50. On MDA: Shulgin and Shulgin, *PiKHAL*, pp. 714–19; Elissen, 'Synthetische drugs', p. 2.

116 Husken and Vuijst, *XTC smokkel*, pp. 17–18. The journalists suggest that Van L and Van D were the former associates who set up the underground laboratory in cooperation with Hollemans. See p. 15.
117 Husken and Vuijst, *XTC smokkel*, p. 55; Gruppo Abele, 'Synthetic drugs trafficking in three European cities: Major trends and the involvement of organised crime' (Turin: Gruppo Abele, 2003), pp. 45–6.
118 Korf and Verbraeck, 'Dealers en dienders', p. 171; Weijenburg, *Drugs en drugsbestrijding*, p. 139.
119 Fromberg, *XTC*, pp. 59–60.
120 C. de Koning, 'De ontwikkeling van de Nederlandse ecstasymarkt. De ontwikkeling van de Nederlandse ecstasymarkt sinds de strafbaarstelling van ecstasy in november 1988' (thesis, University of Amsterdam, Bonger Institute of Criminology, 1992), p. 38, in IISH-EF.
121 e.g., 'A complete MDMA synthesis for the first-time chemist', part of site archive at https://erowid.org/archive/rhodium/chemistry/brightstar.mdma.html (accessed 7 August 2020). On the production of MDMA see also Fromberg, *XTC*, pp. 55–60; . For a photograph of a seized underground laboratory see Elissen, 'Synthetische drugs', p. 6. For an example of the synthesis of MDMA: Shulgin and Shulgin, *PiKHAL*, pp. 733–6.
122 Elissen, 'Synthetische drugs', pp. 5–7.
123 'Fenomeenonderzoek Synthetische Drugs, Een eerste verkenning' (IRT Zuid-Nederland, June 1996), pp. 32–3, in IISH-EF.
124 Adelaars, *XTC*, pp. 54–9; Korf and Verbraeck, 'Dealers en dienders', pp. 175–7.
125 de Koning, 'Ontwikkeling', p. 26, in IISH-EF.
126 B. van der Molen, 'Othering, criminalization and accommodation of ecstasy use in Dutch newspapers between 1985 and 1990' (paper for the Alcohol and Drugs History Society conference, Shanghai University 12–15 June 2019).
127 Fijnaut, 'Georganiseerde criminaliteit', PEO, 17, p. 41.
128 Korf and Verbraeck, 'Dealers en dienders', pp. 170–82; CRI, annual report 1988, p. 52; Elissen, 'Synthetische drugs', p. 3; van der Molen, 'Othering, criminalization and accommodation'.
129 Elissen, 'Synthetische drugs', p. 2.
130 Weijenburg, *Drugs en drugsbestrijding*, p. 136.
131 Elissen, 'Synthetische drugs', pp. 2–3.
132 Shulgin and Shulgin, *PiKHAL*, p. 729.
133 H. Moll, 'Justitie al langer op de hoogte van druggebruik met MDEA; MDEA is nog niet toegevoegd aan lijst van verboden stoffen', *NRC Handelsblad* 3 December 1992; Elissen, 'Synthetische drugs', pp. 3–4; Husken and Vuijst, *XTC smokkel*, pp. 17–19.

134 C. van Zwol, "Legale house-pil' MDEA vanaf morgen verboden', *NRC Handelsblad* 27 July 1993; Elissen, 'Synthetische drugs', p. 4; Weijenburg, *Drugs en drugsbestrijding*, p. 146.
135 Elissen, 'Synthetische drugs', pp. 2–3.
136 Fijnaut, 'Georganiseerde criminaliteit', PEO, 17, p. 41. See for the problem of resources: Korf and Verbraeck, 'Dealers en dienders', pp. 175–7; Elissen, 'Synthetische drugs', pp. 9, 13; 'Fenomeenonderzoek Synthetische Drugs', p. 17, in IISH-EF.
137 Husken and Vuijst, *XTC smokkel*, p. 68; M. Husken, *Deals met justitie. De inside story van infiltranten en kroongetuigen* (Amsterdam: Meulenhoff, 2000), p. 61.
138 R. van de Roer, 'Grondstof gifgas in beslag genomen', *NRC Handelsblad* 13 November 1990.
139 Husken and Vuijst, *XTC smokkel*, pp. 68–9; Husken, *Deals met justitie*, pp. 62–9.
140 Elissen, 'Synthetische drugs', pp. 15–16.
141 'Fenomeenonderzoek Synthetische Drugs', pp. 17–26, in IISH-EF; Synthetic Drugs Unit, annual report 1998, in IISH-EF.
142 van der Molen, 'Othering, criminalization, and accommodation'.
143 G. Cortebeeck, *De XTC-mafia* (Antwerp: Hadewijch, 1994), p. 136.
144 Cortebeeck, *XTC-mafia*, pp. 136–7.
145 de Koning, 'Ontwikkeling', p. 35, in IISH-EF.
146 Weijenburg, *Drugs en drugsbestrijding*, p. 139.
147 Elissen, 'Synthetische drugs', p. 4.
148 Korf and Verbraeck, 'Dealers en dienders', p. 173.
149 Husken and Vuijst, *XTC smokkel*, pp. 62–3.
150 H. van de Bunt, D. Kunst and D. Siegel, *XTC over de grens. Een studie naar XTC-koeriers en kleine smokkelaars* (The Hague: Boom Juridische uitgevers, 2003), pp. 33–6.
151 van de Bunt et al., *XTC over de grens*, pp. 23–7.
152 Weijenburg, *Drugs en drugsbestrijding*, p. 133–4.
153 Weijenburg, *Drugs en drugsbestrijding*, p. 140–1.
154 de Koning, 'Ontwikkeling', p. 36, in IISH-EF.
155 de Koning, 'Ontwikkeling', pp. 37, 41, in IISH-EF.
156 van de Bunt et al., *XTC over de grens*, p. 1.
157 Gruppo Abele, 'Synthetic drugs trafficking', p. 49.
158 Husken and Vuijst, *XTC smokkel*, p. 35.
159 Gruppo Abele, 'Synthetic drugs trafficking', p. 40.
160 B. Middelburg and K. van Es, *Operatie Delta. Hoe de drugsmafia het IRT opblies*, 3rd rev. edn (Amsterdam: L. J. Veen, 1996), pp. 31–2, 71–3.
161 Husken and Vuijst, *XTC smokkel*, pp. 60–6; Bovenkerk, *Misdaadprofielen*, pp. 85–6; B. Middelburg and P. Vugts, *De oorlog in de Amsterdamse*

onderwereld (Amsterdam: Nieuw Amsterdam, 2006). '*Capo di tutti capi*': M. Husken and H. Lensink, *Handboek Holleeder. Wie is wie in het proces van de eeuw* (Amsterdam: Balans, 2007), p. 79.

162 Elissen, 'Synthetische drugs', pp. 10–11; Husken and Vuijst, *XTC smokkel*, pp. 56–9; Weijenburg, *Drugs en drugsbestrijding*, pp. 136–7.

163 Husken and Vuijst, *XTC smokkel*, pp. 67–9. See also B. van Hout, *De jacht op 'de erven Bruinsma' en de Delta-organisatie: hoe de CID-Haarlem het IRT opblies* (Amsterdam: PS, 2000).

164 Fijnaut, 'Georganiseerde criminaliteit', PEO, 17, p. 44.

165 Cf. also T. Spapens, *Interactie tussen criminaliteit en opsporing. De gevolgen van opsporingstechnieken voor de organisatie en afscherming van xtc-productie en –handel in Nederland* (Antwerp: Intersentra, 2006); T. Blickman, 'The ecstasy industry: Exploring the global market' (Transnational Institute Briefing Series 2004, no. 9).

166 See A. Blokland, M. Soudijn and E. Terg, '"We zijn geen padvinders". Een verkennend onderzoek naar de criminele carrières van één procent motorclubs', *Tijdschrift voor Criminologie* 56 (2014) 3–28; A. Blokland and J. David, 'Outlaw bikers voor de rechter. Een analyse van rechterlijke uitspraken in de periode 1999–2015', *Tijdschrift voor Criminologie* 58 (2016) 42–64.

167 T. Thompson, *Gangland Britain* (London: Hodder and Stoughton, 1996), p. 178.

168 Fijnaut, 'Georganiseerde criminaliteit', PEO, 17, pp. 46–7; C. Fijnaut and F. Bovenkerk, 'Georganiseerde criminaliteit in Nederland. Een analyse van de situatie in Amsterdam', PEO, 20, pp. 43, 60–2; H. Schutten, P. Vugts and B. Middelburg, *Hells Angels. Motorclub of misdaadbende?* (Utrecht: Monitor Books, 2005); W. Marsden and J. Sher, *Helse engelen* (Amsterdam: Luitingh, 2006), pp. 221–59; Gruppo Abele, 'Synthetic drugs trafficking', pp. 57–8.

169 Thompson, *Gangland Britain*, pp. 151–9.

170 Husken and Vuijst, *XTC smokkel*, p. 33; 'Peter van Dijk – XTC-koning van Nederland', DutchMultiMedia, 10 January 2019, www.dutchmultimedia.nl/peter-van-dijk-xtc-koning-van-nederland (accessed 7 August 2020).

171 van Duyne, *Het spook en de dreiging*, pp. 91–4.

172 Husken and Vuijst, *XTC smokkel*, pp. 59–62.

173 Korf and Verbraeck, 'Dealers en dienders', p. 187.

174 de Koning, 'Ontwikkeling', p. 54.

175 Korf and Verbraeck, 'Dealers en dienders', p. 163.

9

Conclusion

In 1994 a journalist reported on a court case against a group of Dutch cannabis smugglers. The members of this group were a criminal entrepreneur and his associates from the maritime upperworld: a director of a Rotterdam-based investment company, a shipowner, and a shipping agent. The police thought that the group was involved in the infamous 'Octopus' network that supposedly ruled Dutch drug smuggling. The journalist observed that a map of the world showing the routes of the group's cannabis transports hung in the court. The routes went from the Far East around the Cape of Good Hope to Canada. The journalist wrote: 'The shipping routes evoke remembrances of the heroic enterprises of merchant ships in the past. The fact that the Dutch with their merchandise once again navigate the oceans is one of the reasons why the Octopus network is later [in the process] repeatedly compared to the VOC. Only the vessels are adjusted to current needs.'[1]

The message of the public prosecutors in the trial was clear. A new multinational had come into existence, only this time it was an illegal one that in spreading its tentacles of trade over the world was undermining society and the rule of the state. There was also a strange undertone in the message: one of admiration and even pride. One police officer said: 'If this had been a legal organization we would have been proud of it.'[2] After all, adventuring on the world seas and global trading is something deeply connected to Dutch national identity. The comparison between the VOC and Dutch drug smuggling showed some shared cultural values and attitudes between underworld and upperworld. These shared values, together with motives of profit and greed, contribute to explain the relative ease in which these worlds have collaborated in operations of smuggling and illegal production.

A comparison between trade under the VOC and drug smuggling is enlightening from another perspective as well. The VOC claimed the monopoly on trade in the East Indies, but its regulatory regime to implement this monopoly was a failure. An illegal market led to illegal operations. Prohibiting trade created opportunities for smugglers and led to a spontaneous counter-order of illegal operations. Not only sailors, but also high-ranking servants of the company and even its investigating officers were involved.[3]

The attempts by the VOC to control the opium trade opened up opportunities for smugglers in a manifestation of criminal anarchy. Similarly, the attempts of the Dutch state to implement the international drug regulatory regime in the Netherlands after 1919 opened up opportunities for smugglers. The expansion of criminal anarchy that has been the result has contributed to major domestic problems in the country, and especially to fears about the subversion of authority and democracy by organized crime. Ironically the introduction of the drug regulatory regime created problems rather than solving them – ironically, since after all the policy was instituted because of changing international relations, at a time when in the Netherlands itself there was no drug problem. In the one part of the Dutch Empire where there was a significant drug problem, the Dutch East Indies, the Dutch chose a different regime. Instead of prohibiting non-medical production, distribution, and consumption, the colonial state itself produced and distributed (under certain regulations) opium in the East Indies.

It is a strange paradox that in the Netherlands significant increase in demand for drugs has generally occurred after their prohibition. Responses to the drug regulatory regime in the Netherlands have shown common characteristics since 1919. The characteristics can already be observed in the interwar period and would gain volume and force after the mid-1960s. State regulations did not do away with consumer demand for now illicit drugs. In 1919 a Chinese labour force existed in the Netherlands for whom opium use was part of everyday life. Native Dutch consumers in the interwar period wanted illegal cocaine and morphine. Cannabis use was only incidental in the Netherlands until the mid-1950s, but rose significantly after the scheduling of the drug in the Opium Act in 1953. Demand for cannabis started to soar in a youthful counterculture after 1965 and became more and more normalized after 1980. In the early 1970s new groups of heroin consumers threatened public order in Dutch cities and created significant problems of addiction. In 1988 MDMA was scheduled under the Opium Act; demand for the drug has since multiplied. Failure of the regime to control the drug markets led to a continual imperative for more regulation: to bring more drugs in the prohibitive framework, to increase sentences, to regulate industries that facilitate the drug trade. All these strategies of the state have certainly won battles in the war against drugs, but the war itself could never be won.

This book has investigated the specifics of why drug smuggling has been so successful in Dutch society. Domestic demand was an important impetus for the development of the supply side, but not the only one. The demand in the Netherlands was far from unique; all over the Western world consumer demand for illegal drugs developed in similar ways in the twentieth century. The geographical location of the Netherlands, a hub in the shipping and transport routes to Europe and around the world, facilitated the development of an illegal transit trade to other countries as well. In the interwar period opium followed the routes of the steamship companies and the drug went through the Netherlands to other parts of Europe and the Americas. Cars and river barges transported narcotics from pharmaceutical factories in Germany to the Netherlands and elsewhere. Amphetamine smuggling actually started because of a demand in another country, Sweden, rather than in the Netherlands itself. From around 1970 onwards smugglers used fishing boats, yachts, and freight containers on maritime routes, as well as trucks and cars on the motorway system connecting the Netherlands to the rest of Europe and to Asia, to transport illegal drugs. By the 1980s Dutch entrepreneurs used their experience and contacts in the maritime world to bypass the Netherlands altogether, directly transporting cannabis from Afghanistan and Pakistan to North America.

Geography and the availability of transport were two crucial factors in the successful development of narcotics smuggling. The ability to utilize them, though, was dependent on social and cultural factors. Despite its lack of formal organization, narcotics smuggling on a larger scale was not the sole activity of lone individuals, but needed to be embedded in social and cultural environments. Because of this embeddedness personal relationships could be built and utilized, resources mobilized, and demand and supply connected. Even smugglers operating as individuals had to be embedded or at least had to find connections to environments where they could trade their contraband. The 'traditional' sailor smugglers were embedded in a maritime culture where small-scale smuggling was almost commonplace. They connected to bars in port towns where criminal entrepreneurs took on the drug trade as a sideline to other activities. Individual hippie smugglers of the 1960s were embedded in their own cultural environment, trading their merchandise to their contacts in the counterculture. The Chinese opiate smugglers were embedded in mutual aid societies, ship's crews, and Chinatowns. Dutch criminal entrepreneurs turning to narcotics smuggling were embedded in the criminal cultures of the larger cities and in the smuggling cultures of the south of the country, while Turkish and Kurdish heroin smugglers were integrated in the migrant communities of the Netherlands.

For foreign smugglers who failed to have this kind of embeddedness a successful alternative was making alliances based on personal relationships with those who had. This was the path taken by the Greeks and the Colombians. Altogether this created by the end of the century networks of literally hundreds of smuggling groups of various ethnic, social, and cultural compositions. Some of them smuggled only one drug, others a variety. Some of them only smuggled drugs, a few were involved in a multiplicity of criminal activities. Some of them were connected to mutual aid societies such as the Chinese triads or the outlaw motorcycle gangs, but most of them were not attached to any formal organization whatsoever. There were some conflicts between these groups, but also many shifting alliances. They were fragmented and decentralized, based on personal relationships and the personal charisma of key figures connected to the specialized expertise of others. They did not turn into monopolistic formal organizations vulnerable to police strategies. As a consequence, drug markets in the Netherlands were never monopolized.

Social and cultural embeddedness produced the social and cultural capital (relationships, attitudes and values, and expertise and knowledge) that combined with factors of geography and transport to make successful smuggling possible. It proved relatively easy to make alliances in countries of production to ensure regular supply. Social and cultural embeddedness also ensured conditions for the successful setting up of production in the Netherlands itself. The production of LSD and MDMA and the cultivation of nederwiet originated in the counter-culture, while criminal entrepreneurs moved in at some point and further embedded production in their own cultures. Amphetamine production developed from the illegal liquor distillation in the south and later combined with MDMA production. Nederwiet found a social and cultural embeddedness among cultivators with a low socio-economic status in the cities and among kampers.

Social and cultural embeddedness was not limited to the smugglers themselves and their direct environment. For smuggling to be successful, contacts within the upperworld were also crucial: with transport companies; within the maritime and chemical industries; sometimes with police officials or customs personnel willing to turn a blind eye; and with citizens who at first sight seemed to be law-abiding but who provided places for stashes or underground laboratories. From the perspectives of both supply and demand the illegal drug market was not a parasitic outgrowth on 'regular' society, but very much interwoven in these societies, reconstituting itself after every setback. The practices of narcotics smugglers were part of everyday life in Dutch society, even if they remained in darkness to the outside observer.

This book has traced the rise of a spontaneous counter-order to the twentieth-century Netherlands drug regulatory regime. Historical research into the Dutch experience leads us to question myths that infuse today's drug debates and drug policies. The first of these myths is that of 'organized crime'. Sinister and powerful organizations or mafias are routinely presented as a – or even as the – major cause of the drug problem. Discussions are then centred on the kind of resources and powers law enforcement organizations need to combat these organizations. Historical research shows that these images of criminal organizations driving the drug trade go back at least to the 1930s. It also shows that these images are basically misrepresentations and misinterpretations. The Dutch example demonstrates that the success of the illegal drug trade is based on the very different organizational model of criminal anarchy. The ways of operation of smugglers and illegal drug producers were not decreed 'from above' but the result of initiatives by individuals and small groups 'from below', organized in fluid connecting networks.

A second myth that the historical analysis of the Dutch experience dismantles is that the drug trade actually drives illegal drug consumption. The markets show themselves instead as demand-driven. Criminality only moves in when this demand can no longer be supplied by legal means. Legislation fuels criminal activity. What made criminal anarchy ultimately so successful was that it connected to the demand for illegal goods and services of a 'legitimate' public that continued to exist after 1920, increased enormously after 1965, and was not created by the underworld of drug trafficking itself. As Al Capone reputedly said about running an illegal alcohol trade in the USA in the time of Prohibition: 'If people did not want beer and wouldn't drink it, a fellow would be crazy for going around trying to sell it.'[4]

Demand for illegal drugs, caused by the regulation of the market by the state, meant that criminal anarchy *could* flourish. The organization model of criminal anarchy and its embeddedness in society ensured that it *did*, and does, flourish. In a dialectical interaction with the drug regulatory regime, criminal anarchy reconstructed the political economy of the drug market, within an ongoing cycle of regulation leading to more criminal anarchy, leading to the imperative for more regulation, leading to more criminal anarchy, and so on to the present day.

Notes

1 H. Schutten, *De jacht op Octopus. Hoe Nederlandse drugscriminelen greep kregen op de bovenwereld* (Amsterdam: Meulenhoff, 1996), p. 88.
2 Schutten, *Jacht op Octopus*, p. 9.
3 F. S. Gaastra, *De geschiedenis van de VOC* (Zutpen: Walburg Pers, 2002), pp. 94–101.
4 M. H. Haller, *Illegal Enterprise* (Lanham: University Press of America, 2013), p. 62.

Appendix: Graphs of arrests and seizures

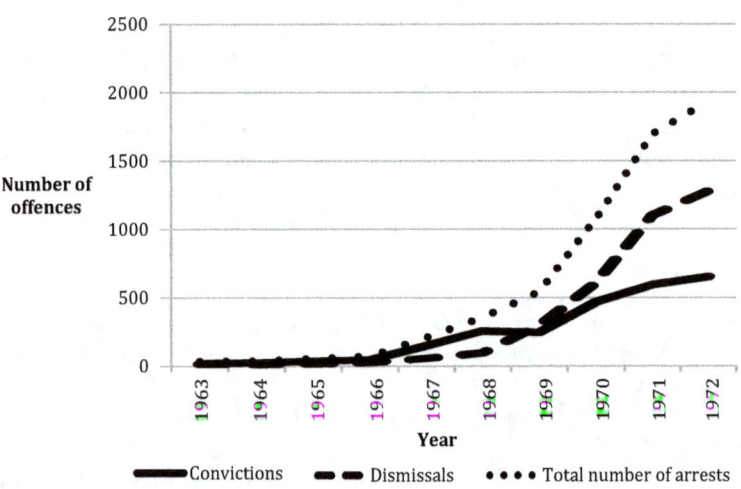

Figure 1 Offences against the Opium Act, 1963–1972

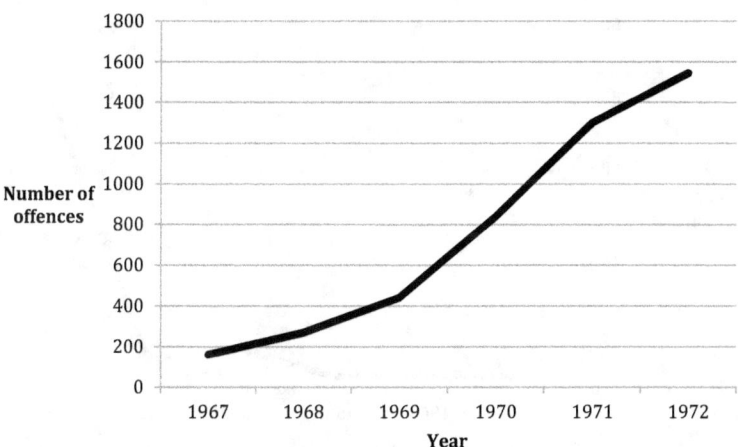

Figure 2 Offences against the Opium Act in relation to cannabis, 1967–1972

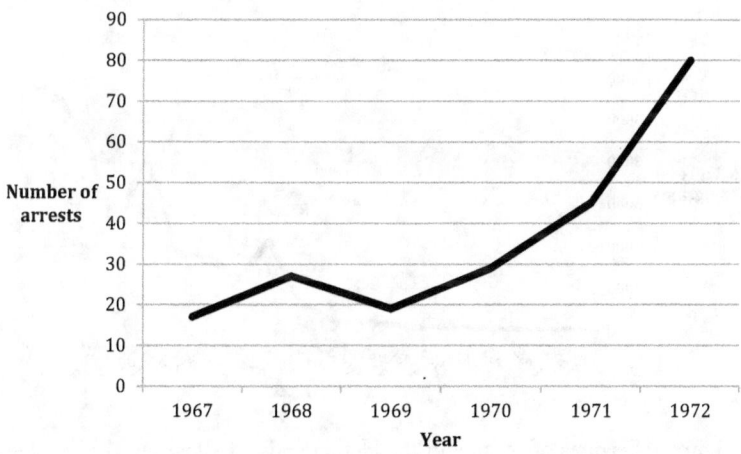

Figure 3 Arrests of importers of illegal drugs in the Netherlands, 1967–1972

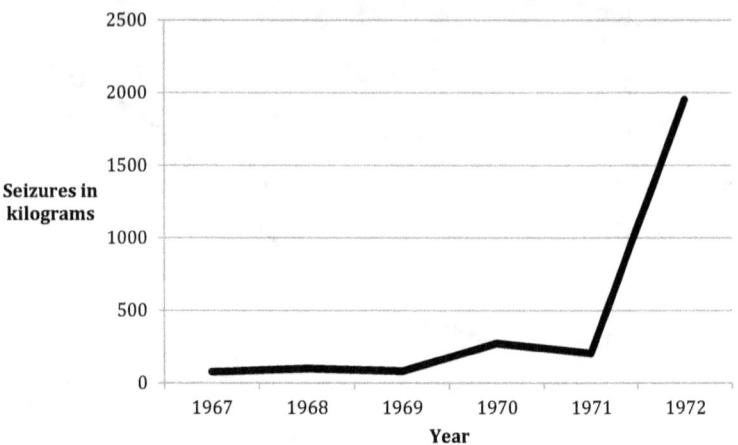

Figure 4 Seizures of marihuana and hashish in the Netherlands, in kilograms, 1967–1972

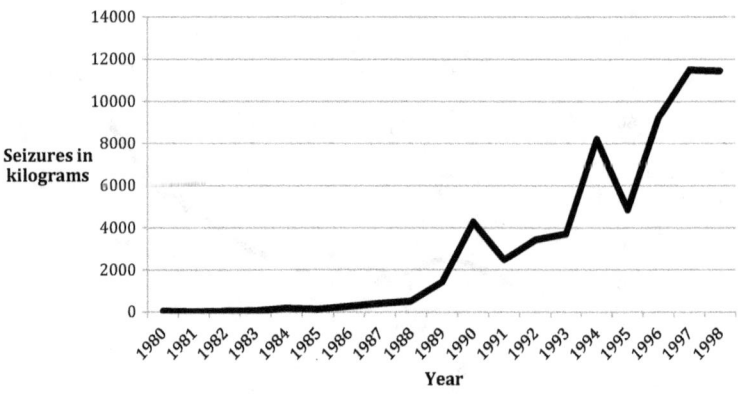

Figure 5 Seizures of cocaine in the Netherlands, in kilograms, 1980–1998

Bibliography

Primary sources, unpublished

GPA: Archive of Municipal police of Amsterdam (Gemeentepolitie Amsterdam) 1957–1993, City Archive Amsterdam, inv. no. 5225A.
Home Office, National Archives, Kew.
IISH-EF: Erik Fromberg Archive, International Institute of Social History, Amsterdam, inv. no. ARCH 03137.
League of Nations: United Nations Office at Geneva Archives.
NA/FA: Ministry of Foreign Affairs, A-files, National Archive, The Hague, inv. no. 2.05.03.
NA/FAII: Ministry of Foreign Affairs Code Archive 1945–1954, National Archive, The Hague, inv. no. 2.05.117.
NA/FAIII: Ministry of Foreign Affairs 1955–1964, National Archive, The Hague, inv. no. 2.05.118.
NA/FAIV: Ministry of Foreign Affairs 1965–1974, National Archive, The Hague, inv. no. 2.05.313.
N. V. Koninklijke Pharmaceutische Fabrieken v/h Brocades, Shteeman & Pharmacia N.V., Municipal Archive Delft, inv. no. 188.
Pharmaceutical Inspectorate (Farmaceutische Hoofdinspectie) 1921–1961, National Archive, The Hague, inv. no. 2.15.39.
Pharmaceutical Inspectorate (Staatstoezicht op de Volksgezondheid: Hoofdinspectie Geneesmiddelen) 1962–1994, National Archive, The Hague, inv. no. 2.27.5033.
Simon Vinkenoog, International Institute of Social History, Amsterdam, inv. no. ARCH01561.

Primary sources available online

D: Delpher digitized newspaper article archive: www.delpher.nl/nl/kranten.
INCB: International Narcotics Control Board, annual reports and documents: incb.org.

Proceedings of the Dutch parliament: Handelingen Staten-Generaal: https://zoek.officielebekendmakingen.nl/uitgebreidzoeken/historisch.
PW: *Pharmaceutisch Weekblad* 1864–1996: pw.nl/archief/historisch-archief.
WODC: Scientific Research and Documentation Centre Ministry of Justice and Security: www.wodc.nl/publicaties.

Primary sources, printed

CRI: Centrale Recherche Informatiedienst, annual reports 1987–1991.
GB: *Gouvernementsblad voor de Kolonie Suriname* (Paramaribo: Gouvernement Suriname, 1816–1950).
PEO: Parlementaire Enquêtecommissie Opsporingsmethoden, Tweede Kamer der Staten-Generaal, 1995–1996, 24 072.

Books, articles, and reports

Aa, J. van der, 'Opkomst en ondergang van een Brabantse misdaadbaas: Janus van W.', in K. Scharrenberg and J. van der Aa, *Georganiseerde misdaad in de Lage Landen* (n.p.: Just Publishers, 2011), pp. 77–97.
Adelaars, A., *XTC. Alles over Ecstasy* (Amsterdam: In de Knipscheer, 1996).
Afsahi, K., 'Cannabis cultivation practices in the Moroccan Rif', in T. Decorte, G. Potter and M. Bouchard (eds), *World Wide Weed: Global Trends in Cannabis Cultivation and its Control* (Farnham: Ashgate, 2011), pp. 39–54.
Aftab, S., 'Post 2014: The regional drug economy and its implications for Pakistan', report (CIDOB: Barcelona, 2014).
Akinbingöl, O. F., 'De Zwarte Driehoek. Politie, politici en de drugsmaffia in Turkije', *Justitiële Verkenningen* 26 (2000) 45–57.
Albert, L., 'Afghanistan: A perspective', in L. Dupree and L. Albert (eds), *Afghanistan in the 1970s* (New York: Praeger Press, 1974), pp. 249–59.
Alverson, C., 'Ketama: Morocco's hash capital', *Rolling Stone* 5 Augustus 1971.
Andrade, T., *Lost Colony: The Untold Story of China's First Great Victory over the West* (Princeton: Princeton University Press, 2011).
Antony, R. J., *Like Froth Floating on the Sea: The World of Pirates and Seafarers in Late Imperial South China* (Berkeley: Institute of East Asian Studies, University of California, 2003).
Aune, B. R., 'Maritime drug trafficking: An underrated problem' (Vienna: UNODC, 1990). www.unodc.org/unodc/en/data-and-analysis/bulletin/bulletin_1990-01-01_1_page008.html (accessed 7 August 2020).
Baud, J. C., ' Proeve van eene geschiedenis van den handel en het verbruik van opium in Nederlandsch Indië', *Bijdragen tot de taal-, land- en volkenkunde* 1 (1853): 79–220.

Becker, J., and M. Dewey (eds), *The Architecture of Illegal Markets: Towards an Economic Sociology of Illegality in the Economy* (Oxford: Oxford University Press, 2017).

Beer Portugael, D. J. H. N. den, *De Marechaussee grijpt in* (Utrecht: A. W. Bruna, 1954).

Beke, B., E. van der Torre, and M. van Duin, *Stads- en regioscan in de grootste Brabantse gemeenten. De achtergronden van onveilige GVI scores* (Apeldoorn: Politie & Wetenschap, 2012).

Benton, G., and H. Vermeulen (eds), *De Chinezen* (Muiderberg: Dick Coutinho, 1987).

Berridge, V., *Opium and the People: Opiate Use and Drug Control Policy in Nineteenth and Early Twentieth Century England*, rev. edn (London: Free Association Books, 1999).

Bewley-Taylor, D. R., *The United States and International Drug Control 1909–1997* (London: Continuum, 2001).

Bieleman, B., A. Diaz et al. (eds), *Lines Across Europe: Nature and Extent of Cocaine Use in Barcelona, Rotterdam and Turin* (Amsterdam: Swets and Zeitlinger, 1993).

Billingsley, P., *Bandits in Republican China* (Stanford: Stanford University Press, 1988).

Bisbee, C. C., P. Bisbee et al. (eds), *Psychedelic Prophets: The Letters of Aldous Huxley and Humphry Osmond* (Montreal: McGill-Queen's University Press, 2018).

Blaauw, J. A., 'De bestrijding van de georganiseerde misdaad in Nederland', *Algemeen Politieblad* 123 (1974) 227–36.

Blaauw, J. A., *Narcoticabrigade. De eindeloze strijd tegen drugshandelaren* (Baarn: De Fontein, 1997).

Blickman, T., 'The ecstasy industry: exploring the global market' (Transnational Institute Briefing Series 2004, no. 9).

Block, A., *East Side – West Side: Organizing Crime in New York 1930–1950* (Cardiff: University College Cardiff Press, 1980).

Block, A. A., 'European drug traffic and traffickers between the wars: The policy of suppression and its consequences', *Journal of Social History* 23 (1989) 315–37.

Block, A. A., and W. J. Chambliss, *Organizing Crime* (New York: Elsevier, 1981).

Blok, G., '"We the avant-garde": A history from below of Dutch heroin use in the 1970s', *BMGN – Low Countries Historical Review* 132 (2017) 104–25.

Blok, G., *Ziek of zwak. Geschiedenis van de verslavingszorg in Nederland* (Amsterdam: Uitgeverij Nieuwezijds, 2011).

Blokland, A., and J. David, 'Outlaw bikers voor de rechter. Een analyse van rechterlijke uitspraken in de periode 1999–2015', *Tijdschrift voor Criminologie* 58 (2016) 42–64.

Blokland, A., M. Soudijn, and E. Terg, '"We zijn geen padvinders". Een verkennend onderzoek naar de criminele carrières van één procent motorclubs', *Tijdschrift voor Criminologie* 56 (2014) 3–28.

Blom, T., *Opiumwetgeving en drugsbeleid* (Deventer: Wolters Kluwer, 2015).

Blythe, W., *The Impact of Chinese Secret Societies in Malaya: A Historical Study* (London: Oxford University Press, 1969).

Bock, C., *The Headhunters of Borneo* (Singapore: Marshall Cavendish, 2009).

Boekhoorn, P., A. G. van Dijk et al., 'Softdrugs in Nederland. Consumptie en handel' (Amsterdam: Van Dijk, Van Someren & Partners, 1995).

Boekhout van Solinge, T., *Drugs and Decision-Making in the European Union* (Amsterdam: Mets & Schilt, 2002).

Booth, M., *The Dragon Syndicates: The Global Phenomenon of the Triads* (London: Bantam, 2000).

Booth, M., *Cannabis: A History* (London: Bantam Books, 2004).

Bosman, H. H., 'The history of the Nederlandsche Cocaïne Fabriek and its successors as manufacturers of narcotic drugs, analysed from an international perspective', 2 vols (PhD thesis, Maastricht University, 2012).

Bovenkerk, F., 'Cocaïnesmokkelaar in Colombiaanse dienst', *Vrij Nederland* 15 April 1995.

Bovenkerk, F. (ed.), *De georganiseerde criminaliteit in Nederland. Het criminologisch onderzoek voor de parlementaire enquêtecommissie opsporingsmethoden in discussie* (Deventer: Gouda Quint, 1996).

Bovenkerk, F., *Misdaadprofielen* (Amsterdam: Meulenhoff, 2001).

Bovenkerk, F., *La Bella Bettien. Het levensverhaal van een Nederlandse go-between voor de Colombiaanse drugskartels* (n.p.: Pandora, 2008).

Bovenkerk, F., and Y. Yesilgöz, 'Antwoord aan Richard Staring', *Migrantenstudies* 14 (1998) 198–202.

Bovenkerk, F., and Y. Yesilgöz, *The Turkish Mafia: A History of the Heroin Godfathers* (Wrea Green: Milo Books, 2007).

Bradford, J., 'Linking East and West: How hash helped to globalize the Afghan drug trade' (unpublished paper for the conference Cannabis: Global Histories, Strathclyde University, Glasgow, 19–20 April 2018).

Bresler, F., *The Trail of the Triads: An Investigation into International Crime* (London: Weidenfeld & Nicolson, 1980).

Brook, T., *Vermeer's Hat: The Seventeenth Century and the Dawn of the Modern World* (New York: Bloomsbury Press, 2008).

Brook, T., and B. Tadashi Wakabayashi (eds), *Opium Regimes: China, Britain and Japan, 1839–1952* (Berkeley: University of California Press, 2000).

Brown, S., *Drugsbaron in spijkerbroek. De opzienbarende biografie van een rechtenstudent* (Rijswijk: Elmar, 2001).

Buddingh', H., *De geschiedenis van Suriname* (n.p.: Nieuw Amsterdam, 2012).

Buikhuisen, W., H. Timmerman, and J. De Jong, 'De ontwikkeling van het druggebruik onder middelbare scholieren tussen 1969 en 1973' (Criminologisch Instituut, University of Groningen, n.d.).

Bunt, H. van de, D. Kunst, and D. Siegel, *XTC over de grens. Een studie naar XTC-koeriers en kleine smokkelaars* (The Hague: Boom Juridische uitgevers, 2003).

Bunt, H. van de, D. Siegel, and D. Zaitch, 'The social embeddedness of organized crime', in L. Paoli (ed.), *The Oxford Handbook of Organized Crime* (New York: Oxford University Press, 2014), pp. 321–39.

Camacho-Guizado, A., and A. López-Restrepo, 'From smugglers to drug lords', in C. Welna and G. Gallón (eds), *Peace, Democracy, and Human Rights in Colombia* (Notre Dame: University of Notre Dame Press, 2007), pp. 60–89.

Carretero, N., *Snow on the Atlantic: How Cocaine Came to Europe* (London: Zed Books, 2018).

Castells, M., *End of Millennium*, rev. edn (Oxford: Blackwell, 2000).

Centraal Bureau voor de Statistiek, *Economische en sociale kroniek der oorlogsjaren 1940–1945* (Utrecht: W. De Haan, 1947).

Certeau, M. de, *The Practice of Everyday Life* (Berkeley: University of California Press, 1984).

Chandra, S., 'The role of government policy in increasing drug use: Java, 1875–1914', *Journal of Economic History* 62 (2002) 1116–21.

Charpentier, C. J., 'The use of haschish and opium in Afghanistan', *Anthropos* 68 (1973) 482–90.

Cherniak, L., *The Great Book of Hashish*, vol. 1, book 1 (Berkeley: And/Or Press, 1979).

Chong, Y., *De Chinezen van de Binnen Bantammerstraat* (Amsterdam: Het Spinhuis, 2005).

Chu, Y. K., *International Triad Movements: The Threat of Chinese Organised Crime* (London: Research Institute for the Study of Conflict and Terrorism, 1996).

Chu, Y. K., *The Triads as Business* (London: Routledge, 2000).

Clarke, R. C., *Hashish!* (Los Angeles: Red Eye Press, 1998).

Clawson, P. L., and Rensselaer W. Lee III, *The Andean Cocaine Industry* (Houndmills: Macmillan, 1996).

Cohen, H., 'Psychologie, sociale psychologie en sociologie van het deviante drug-gebruik. Een tussentijds rapport' (Instituut voor Sociale Geneeskunde, University of Amsterdam, 1969).

Cohen, H., *Drugs, druggebruikers en drug-scene* (Alphen aan den Rijn: Samsom, 1975).

Cohen, H., 'De hasjcultuur anno 1980: een overlijdensbericht', in C. J. M. Goos and H. J. van der Wal (eds), *Druggebruiken: verslaving en hulpverlening* (Alphen aan den Rijn: Samsom, 1981), pp. 13–24.

Cohen, P., 'Cocaine use in Amsterdam in non deviant subcultures' (University of Amsterdam, Department of Human Geography, 1989).

Cohen, P., and A. Sas, 'Ten years of cocaine: A follow-up study of 64 cocaine users in Amsterdam' (University of Amsterdam, Department of Human Geography, 1993).

Collin, M., *Altered State: The Story of Ecstasy Culture and Acid House* (London: Serpent's Tail, 1997).

Coomber, R., and L. Moyle, 'Beyond drug dealing: Developing and extending the concept of "social supply" of illicit drugs to "minimally commercial supply"', *Drugs Education, Policy and Prevention* 21:2 (2013) 157–64.

Corsino, L., *The Neighborhood Outfit: Organized Crime in Chicago Heights* (Urbana: University of Illinois Press, 2014).

Cortebeeck, G., *De XTC-mafia* (Antwerp: Hadewijch, 1994).

Cottaar, A., L. Lucassen, and W. Willems, 'Woonwagenbewoners en georganiseerde criminaliteit', *Contrast* 14 (25 April 1996) 4–5.

Cottaar, J. C. A. M., 'Kooplui, kermisklanten en andere woonwagenbewoners. Groepsvorming en beleid 1870–1945' (PhD thesis, VU-University Amsterdam, 1996).

Courtwright, D., *Dark Paradise: Opium Addiction in America before 1940* (Cambridge: Harvard University Press, 1982).

Couwenhoven, R., *De affaire Noortman. Kunsthandelaar, stichter van de Tefaf, ereburger van Maastricht en kunstcrimineel* (Meppel: Just Publishers, 2017).

Cressey, D. R., *Theft of the Nation: The Structure and Operations of Organized Crime in America* (New York: Harper & Row, 1969).

Davenport-Hines, R., *The Pursuit of Oblivion: A Social History of Drugs* (London: Weidenfeld & Nicolson, 2001).

Decorte T. (ed.), *Cannabisteelt in de Lage Landen. Perspectieven op de cannabismarkt in België en Nederland* (Leuven: Acco, 2008).

Dedem, W. K. Baron van, *Eene bijdrage tot de studie der opiumquaestie op Java. De officiëele literatuur* (Amsterdam: J. H. de Bussy, 1881).

Derks, H., *History of the Opium Problem: The Assault on the East, ca. 1600–1950* (Leiden: Brill, 2012).

Derksen, T., *Verknipt bewijs. De zaak-Baybasin* (Leusden: ISVW Uitgevers, 2014).

Dijk, L. C. D. van, 'Bijvoegsels tot de proeve eener geschiedenis van den handel en het verbruik van opium in Ned. Indië', *Bijdragen tot de taal-, land- en volkenkunde* 2 (1854) 189–211.

Dikötter, F., L. Laamann, and Z. Xun, *Narcotic Culture: A History of Drugs in China*, rev. edn (London: Hurst & Company, 2016).

Dorn, N., K. Murji, and N. South, *Traffickers: Drug Markets and Law Enforcement* (London: Routledge, 1992).

Downes, D. M., *Contrasts in Tolerance: Post-War Penal Policy in the Netherlands and England and Wales* (Oxford: Clarendon Press, 1988).
Driessen, H., 'Smuggling as a border way of life: A Mediterranean case', in M. Rösler and T. Wendl (eds), *Frontiers and Borderlands: Anthropological Perspectives* (Frankfurt am Main: Peter Lang, 1999), pp. 117–27.
Dudley, S., Bonello, D. et al., 'Mexico's role in the deadly rise of fentanyl' (Washington: Woodrow Wilson Center, Mexico Institute, 2019).
Duymaer van Twist, A. J., 'Het Hemel-Aarde-Verbond, Tien-Ti-Hoei, een geheim genootschap in China en onder de Chinezen in Indië', *Bijdragen tot de taal-, land- en volkenkunde* 1 (1853) 260–90.
Duyne, P. C. van, *Het spook en de dreiging van de georganiseerde misdaad* (The Hague: Sdu, 1995).
Duyne, P. C. van, R. F. Kouwenberg, and G. Romeijn, *Misdaadondernemingen. Ondernemende misdadigers in Nederland* (The Hague: Sdu, 1990).
Ebenezer, L., *Operation Julie: The World's Greatest LSD Bust* (Talybont: Y Lolfa, 2010).
Edens, B., and M. Bruil, 'Inclusion of non-observed economy in Dutch national accounts after the 2010 ESA revision' (The Hague: Centraal Bureau voor de Statistiek, 2014).
'Editorial', *Tijdschrift voor Alcohol, Drugs en Andere Psychotrope Stoffen* 1 (1975) 1.
Eerenbeemt, M. van den and M. Kruijt, 'Opmars der onderwereldeconomen', *De Volkskrant* 30 November 1996, www.volkskrant.nl/mensen/opmars-der-onderwereld-economen~b82e3539 (accessed 7 August 2020).
Egmond, F., 'Georganiseerde misdaad en de overheid in het verleden: Nederland tijdens de 17ᵉ en 18ᵉ eeuw', in C. J. C. F. Fijnaut (ed.), *Georganiseerde misdaad en strafrechtelijk politiebeleid* (Lochem: J.B. van den Brink, 1989), pp. 11–22.
Egmond, F., *Underworlds: Organized Crime in the Netherlands 1650–1800* (Cambridge: Polity Press, 1993).
Eisner, B., *Ecstasy: The MDMA Story* (Berkeley: Ronin Books, 1994).
Elissen, A., 'Synthetische drugs', *Recherche Informatie* 14:2 (1993).
European Monitoring Centre for Drugs and Drug Addiction and Europol, 'EU drug markets report: In-depth analysis' (EMCDDA–Europol joint publication, Luxembourg: Publications Office of the European Union, 2016).
European Monitoring Centre for Drugs and Drug Addiction, 'United Kingdom country drug report' (EMCDDA–Europol joint publication, Luxembourg: Publications Office of the European Union, 2018).
Farrell, G., K. Mansur, and M. Tulis, 'Cocaine and heroin in Europe 1983–93', *British Journal of Criminology* 36 (1996) 255–81.
Fielding, L., *To Live Outside the Law: A Memoir* (London: Serpent's Tail, 2012).
Fijnaut, C. J. C. F. (ed.), *Georganiseerde misdaad en strafrechtelijk politiebeleid* (Lochem: Van den Brink, 1989).

Foster, A. L., 'The Philippines, the United States, and the origins of global narcotics prohibition', *Social History of Alcohol and Drugs* 33 (2019) 13–36.
Freitag, Dr, 'Rauschgifte und ihre Opfer', *Kriminalistische Monatshefte* 8 (1934) 199–202.
Fromberg, E, *XTC. Harddrug of onschuldig genotmiddel?* (Amsterdam: Swets & Zeitlinger, 1991).
Gaastra, F. S., *De geschiedenis van de VOC* (Zutpen: Walburg Pers, 2002).
Gadourek, I., and J. L. Jessen, 'Prescription and acceptance of drug-taking habits in the Netherlands', *Mens en Maatschappij* 46 (1971) 376–410.
Galeotti, M., 'Turkish organized crime: Where state, crime and rebellion conspire', *Transnational Organized Crime* 4 (1998) 25–41.
Galeotti, M., 'Turkish organized crime: From tradition to business', in D. Siegel and H. van de Bunt (eds), *Traditional Organized Crime in the Modern World: Responses to Socioeconomic Change* (New York: Springer, 2012) 49–64.
Gerritsen, J.-W., *The Control of Fuddle and Flash: A Sociological History of the Regulation of Alcohol and Opiates* (Leiden: Brill, 2000).
Gingeras, R., *Heroin, Organized Crime, and the Making of Modern Turkey* (Oxford: Oxford University Press, 2014).
Gkotsinas, K., 'Attitudes towards heroin addicts and addiction in inter-war Greece', *Central Europe* 12 (2014) 174–94.
Gkotsinas, K., '"Genuine and natural": Opiates and nation-building in Greece, 1923–1940' (unpublished paper, Association for the Study of Nationalities conference, 2018).
Gonsalves, R. A., and G. J. Verhoog, *Mr. Gonsalves: Memoires* (Amsterdam: De Arbeiderspers, 1999).
Gootenberg, P., *Andean Cocaine: The Making of a Global Drug* (Chapel Hill: University of North Carolina Press, 2008).
Groot, J. J. M. de, *Het kongsiwezen van Borneo. Eene voorbereiding over den grondslag en den aard der Chineesche politieke vereenigingen in de koloniën, met eene Chineesche geschiedenis van de kongsi Lanfong* (The Hague: Martinus Nijhoff, 1885).
Gruppo Abele, 'Synthetic drugs trafficking in three European cities: Major trends and the involvement of organised crime' (Turin: Gruppo Abele, 2003).
Haenen, M., *Baas Bouterse. De krankzinnige jacht op het Surinaamse drugskartel* (Amsterdam: Sirene, 2000).
Haenen, M., and H. Buddingh', *De Danser. Hoe de drugshandel Nederland veroverde* (Amsterdam: De Arbeiderspers, 1994).
Haller, M. H., *Illegal Enterprise* (Lanham: University Press of America, 2013).
Harvey, S., *Smuggling: Seven Centuries of Contraband* (London: Reaktion Books, 2016).
Heek, F. van, *Chineesche immigranten in Nederland* (Amsterdam: J. Emmering, 1936).

Hemmes, G. D., 'Over het gebruik van morphine', *Nederlandsch Tijdschrift voor Geneeskunde* 91 (1947) 550–2.
Heuvel, J. van den, *De jacht op Desi Bouterse. Hoe het Suri-kartel de Nederlandse drugsmarkt veroverde* (The Hague: BZZTôH, 1999).
Hickman, T. A., 'Drugs and race in American culture: Orientalism in the turn-of-the-century discourse of narcotic addiction', *American Studies* 41 (2000) 71–92.
Hirschland, F., *Dossier Moengo '290' uur* (The Hague: Cast Publishing, 1993).
Hoefte, R., *In Place of Slavery: A Social History of British Indian and Javanese Laborers in Suriname* (Gainesville: University Press of Florida, 1998).
Hoogenboom, A. B., *Schaduwen over Van Traa* (The Hague: Koninklijke Vermande, 2000).
Houlbrook, M., *Prince of Tricksters: The Incredible True Story of Netley Lucas, Gentleman Crook* (Chicago: University of Chicago Press, 2016).
Hout, B. van, *De jacht op 'de erven Bruinsma' en de Delta-organisatie: hoe de CID-Haarlem het IRT opblies* (Amsterdam: PS, 2000).
[Hulsman, L. H. C.], *Ruimte in het drugbeleid. Rapport van een werkgroep van de Stichting Algemeen Centraal Bureau voor de Geestelijke Volksgezondheid* (Meppel: Boom, 1971).
Husken, M., *Deals met justitie. Van infiltrant 'Haagse Kees' tot kroongetuige Peter La S.* (Amsterdam: Meulenhoff, 2000).
Husken, M., and H. Lensink, *Handboek Holleeder. Wie is wie in het proces van de eeuw* (Amsterdam: Balans, 2007).
Husken, M. and F. Vuijst, *XTC smokkel* (Amsterdam: Zwarte Beertjes, 2004).
Jansen, A. C. M., *Cannabis in Amsterdam. Een geografie van hashish en marijuana* (Muiderberg: Dick Coutinho, 1989).
Jansen, A. C. M., 'De Nederlandse marihuanasector', *Economisch-Statistische Berichten* 78 (1993) 294–6.
Jansen, A. C. M., 'Prijsvorming in de Nederlandse marihuana-sector 1990–1995. Een beleidsperspectief', *Economisch-Statistische Berichten* 81 (1996) 257–9.
Jansen, A. C. M., 'Een halve eeuw productie en consumptie van cannabis in de westerse wereld', in T. Decorte (ed.), *Cannabisteelt in de Lage Landen. Perspectieven op de cannabismarkt in België en Nederland* (Leuven: Acco, 2008), pp. 17–28.
Janssen, O., and K. Swietstra, 'Heroïnegebruikers in Nederland. Een typologie van levensstijlen' (Kriminologisch Instituut Rijksuniversiteit Groningen, 1982).
Johnson, G., *The Cartel: The Inside Story of Britain's Biggest Drugs Gang* (Edinburgh: Mainstream Publishing, 2013).
Johnson, N., *Grass Roots: A History of Cannabis in the American West* (Corvallis: Oregon State University Press, 2017).

Karras, A., *Smuggling: Contraband and Corruption in World History* (Lanham: Rowman & Littlefield, 2009).

Kazemier, B., A. Bruil et al., 'The contribution of illegal activities to national income in the Netherlands', *Public Finance Review* 41:5 (2013) 544–77.

Kenney, M., 'The architecture of drug trafficking: Network forms of organisation in the Colombian cocaine trade', *Global Crime* 8 (2007) 233–59.

Kenney, M., 'The evolution of the international drugs trade: The case of Colombia, 1930–2000', in F. Allum and S. Gilmour (eds), *Routledge Handbook of Transnational Organized Crime* (London: Routledge, 2012), pp. 201–17.

Khonraad, S., *Woonwagenbewoners, burgers in de risicomaatschappij* (Utrecht: Jan van Arkel, 2000).

Kielstra, E. B., 'Bijdragen tot de geschiedenis van Borneo's Westerafdeling, X–XIII', *Indische Gids* 12 (1890) 450–77, 682–91, 857–78, 1085–9.

Kleemans, E. R., E. I. A. M. van den Berg, and H. G. van de Bunt, 'Georganiseerde criminaliteit in Nederland. Rapportage op basis van de WODC-monitor' (The Hague: WODC, 1998).

Klemann, H. A. M., *Nederland 1938–1948. Economie en samenleving in jaren van oorlog en bezetting* (Amsterdam: Boom, 2002).

Klerks, P. P. H. M., *Groot in de hasj. Theorie en praktijk van de georganiseerde criminaliteit* (Antwerp: Samsom, 2000).

Klooster, W., *Illicit Riches: Dutch Trade in the Caribbean, 1648–1795* (Leiden: KITLV Press, 1998).

Knepper, P., *International Crime in the 20th Century: The League of Nations Era, 1919–1939* (Houndmills: Palgrave Macmillan, 2011).

Knoppers, A. T., 'Over de wekamines (amphetamine, pervitine en dergelijke)', *Nederlands Tijdschrift voor Geneeskunde* 86 (1942) 3323–8.

Knotter, J., D. J. Korf, and H. Y. Lau, *Slangekoppen en tijgerjagers. Illegaliteit en criminaliteit onder Chinezen in Nederland* (The Hague: Boom, 2009).

Korf, D. J., and M. de Kort, 'Drugshandel en drugsbestrijding' (University of Amsterdam, Bonger Institute of Criminology, 1990).

Korf, D., and H. Verbraeck, 'Dealers en dienders. Dynamiek tussen drugsbestrijding en de midden- en hogere niveaus van de cannabis-, cocaine-, amfetamine- en ecstasyhandel in Amsterdam' (University of Amsterdam, Bonger Institute of Criminology, 1993).

Kort, M. de, *Tussen patiënt en delinquent. Geschiedenis van het Nederlandse drugsbeleid* (Hilversum: Verloren, 1995).

Kuzmarov, J., *The Myth of the Addicted Army: Vietnam and the Modern War on Drugs* (Amherst: University of Massachusetts Press, 2009).

Leuw, E., 'Het gebruik van cannabis onder leerlingen van voortgezet onderwijs: een poging tot interpretatie', *Nederlands Tijdschrift voor Criminologie* 14 (1972) 243–74.

Limbeek, J. van, M. C. A. Buster, and G. H. A. van Brussel, 'Epidemiologie van drugsverslaving in Nederland', *Nederlands Tijdschrift voor Geneeskunde* 139 (1995) 2614–18.

Lines, R., *Drug Control and Human Rights in International Law* (Cambridge: Cambridge University Press, 2017).

Lintner, B., *Blood Brothers: Crime, Business and Politics in Asia* (Chiang Mai: Silkworm Books, 2002).

Luger, J., *De kleine misdaad voor den politierechter* (Amsterdam: Blitz, c. 1935).

Luijk, E. V. V. van, and J. C. van Ours, 'The effect of government policy on drug use: Java, 1875–1904', *Journal of Economic History* 61 (2007) 1–18.

Maalsté, N., *Het kruid, de krant en de kroongetuigen. De geschiedenis van hennep van 1950 tot 1970* (Utrecht: Stichting WGU, 1993), pp. 29–48.

Maalsté, N., 'Nieuw licht op ontwikkelingen in de Nederlandse cannabissector', in: T. Decorte (ed.), *Cannabisteelt in de Lage Landen. Perspectieven op de cannabismarkt in België en Nederland* (Leuven: Acco, 2008).

McBride, R. B., 'Business as usual: Heroin distribution in the United States', *Journal of Drug Issues* 13:1 (1983) 147–66.

MacCoun, R. J., and P. Reuter, *Drug War Heresies: Learning from Other Vices, Times, and Places* (Cambridge: Cambridge University Press, 2001).

McCoy, A. W., *The Politics of Heroin: CIA Complicity in the Global Drug Trade*, rev. edn (Chicago: Lawrence Hill Books, 2003).

McDowall, D., *A Modern History of the Kurds* (London: Tauris, 1996).

Marks, H., *Mr Nice* (London: Vintage, 1998).

Marsden, W., and J. Sher, *Helse engelen* (Amsterdam: Luitingh, 2006).

Marshall, J. V., *The Lebanese Connection: Corruption, Civil War, and the International Drug Traffic* (Stanford: Stanford University Press, 2012).

Mazure, A., *Dick Bos. Alle avonturen*, vol. 1 (The Hague: Panda, 2005).

Meershoek, G., 'Terug naar de burgers. Wijkteams en buurtregie 1965–2004', in P. de Rooy (ed.), *Waakzaam in Amsterdam, Hoofdstad en politie vanaf 1275* (Amsterdam: Boom, 2011), pp. 517–55.

Meijring, K. H., *Recht en verdovende middelen* (The Hague: VUGA-Boekerij, 1974).

Meyer, K., and T. Parssinen, *Webs of Smoke: Smugglers, Warlords, Spies, and the History of the International Drug Trade* (Lanham: Rowman & Littlefield, 1998).

Middelburg, B., *De mafia in Amsterdam* (Amsterdam: De Arbeiderspers, 1988).

Middelburg, B., *De dominee. Opkomst en ondergang van mafiabaas Klaas Bruinsma* (Amsterdam: L. J. Veen, 1993).

Middelburg, B., *De Godmother. De criminele carrière van Thea Moear, medeoprichter van de Bruinsma-groep* (Amsterdam: Pandora, 2004).

Middelburg, B., and K. van Es, *Operatie Delta. Hoe de drugsmafia het IRT opblies*, 3rd rev. edn (Amsterdam: L. J. Veen, 1996).

Middelburg, B., and P. Vugts, *De oorlog in de Amsterdamse onderwereld* (Amsterdam: Nieuw Amsterdam, 2006).

Molen, B. van der, 'Othering, criminalization and accommodation of ecstasy use in Dutch newspapers between 1985 and 1990' (paper for the Alcohol and Drugs History Society conference, Shanghai University, 12–15 June 2019).

Moore, B. L., *Cultural Power, Resistance and Pluralism: Colonial Guyana 1838–1900* (Montreal: McGill-Queen's University Press, 1995).

Moors, H., and T. Spapens, *Criminele families in Noord-Brabant. Een verkenning van generatie-effecten in de georganiseerde misdaad* (Apeldoorn: Politie & Wetenschap, 2017).

Morgan, W. P., *Triad Societies in Hong Kong* (London: Routledge, 2002).

Nabben, T., and D. Korf, 'Cocaine and crack in Amsterdam: Diverging subcultures', *Journal of Drug Issues* 29 (1999) 627–52.

Nagel, W. H., *De criminaliteit van Oss* (The Hague: D. A. Daemen, 1949).

Nagtegaal, L., Riding the Dutch Tiger: The Dutch East Indies Company and the Northeast Coast of Java 1680–1743 (Leiden: KITLV Press, 1996).

Nieuwboer, D., 'De gewelddadige vrijheidsstrijd van de PKK', *Historisch Nieuwsblad* 27 (2007), www.historischnieuwsblad.nl/de-gewelddadige-vrijheidsstrijd-van-de-pkk/ (accessed 7 August 2020).

Nijdam, A. B. J. A., *Goirle. Een sociografische studie over de criminaliteit en de moraliteit van een grensgemeente rond de Tweede Wereldoorlog* (Wageningen: H. Veenman, 1950).

Nuijten, A., 'Regulating paradise: The rise and fall of the housedealer' (paper for the Cannabis: Global Histories conference, University of Strathclyde, Glasgow, 19–20 April 2018).

Offerhaus, C., and C. G. Baert, *Anaesthetica. Speciaal cocaine en novocaine, mede in verband met den smokkelhandel* (Amsterdam: D. B. Centen, 1936).

Ohler, N., *Der Totale Rausch. Drogen im Dritten Reich* (Cologne: Verlag Kiepenhauer & Witsch, 2015).

Orlando Melo, J., 'The drug trade, politics, and the economy: The Colombian experience', in E. Joyce and C. Malamud (eds), *Latin America and the Multinational Drug Trade* (Houndmills: Macmillan Press, 1998), pp. 63–96.

Ours, J. C. van, 'The price elasticity of hard drugs', *Journal of Political Economy* 103 (1995) 261–79.

Ownby, D., and M. S. Heidhues (eds), *'Secret Societies' Reconsidered: Perspectives on the Social History of Modern South China and Southeast Asia* (Armonk: M. E. Sharpe, 1993).

Paoli, L., *Mafia Brotherhoods: Organized Crime, Italian Style* (New York: Oxford University Press, 2003).

Paoli, L., V. A. Greenfield, and P. Reuter, *The World Heroin Market: Can Supply Be Cut?* (Oxford: Oxford University Press, 2009).

Pfeil, T., *Van tollenaar tot poortwachter. Geschiedenis van de douane, de oudste rijksdienst van Nederland* (Rotterdam: Trichis, 2012).

Pharmacopoea Amstelredamensis, of d' Amsterdammer apotheek, in welke allerlei medicamenten, tot Amsterdam in 't gebruik zynde, konstiglyk bereyd worden, 7th edn (Amsterdam: Jan ten Hoorn, 1714).

Pieper, W. (ed.), *Nazis on Speed: Drogen im 3. Reich*, 2 vols (Löhrbach: Werner Pieper & The Grüne Kraft, n.d.).

Pinkhof, H., 'Een bezwaar van naamverandering van sterk werkende geneesmiddelen', *Nederlands Tijdschrift voor Geneeskunde* 85 (1941) 3786.

Pinkhof, H., 'Schadelijke werking van Pervitine', *Nederlands Tijdschrift voor Geneeskunde* 85 (1941) 2896.

Poel, S. van der, 'De herovering van een no-go area', *Sociologisch Tijdschrift* 25 (1998) 128–30.

Poel, S. van der, 'De vulkanische relatie tussen overheid en woonwagenbewoners', *Tijdschrift voor Criminologie* 40 (1998) 235–56.

Poel, S. van der, 'Onder en boven de wet: woonwagenbewoners in Noord-Brabant', in M. Moerings, C. M. Pelser, and C. H. Brants (eds), *Morele kwesties in het strafrecht* (Deventer: Gouda Quint, 1999), pp. 75–99.

Port, M. van de, *Geliquideerd. Criminele afrekeningen in Nederland* (Amsterdam: Meulenhoff, 2001).

Prakash, O., *The Dutch East India Company and the Economy of Bengal, 1630–1720* (Princeton: Princeton University Press, 1985).

Pronk, B., *Verkenningen op het gebied van de criminaliteit in Suriname* (The Hague: Martinus Nijhoff, 1962).

Punch, M., *Policing the Inner City: A Study of Amsterdam's Warmoesstraat* (London: Macmillan, 1979).

Quadros Rigoni, R. de, '"Drugs paradise": Dutch stereotypes and substance regulation in European collaborations on drug policies in the 1970s', *Contemporary Drug Problems* 46 (2019) 219–40.

Ram, H., 'Hashishophobia and the Jewish ethnic question in Mandatory Palestine and the state of Israel', in J. Mills and L. Ritchert (eds), *Cannabis: Global Histories* (Cambridge, MIT Press: 2021).

Rasmussen, N., *On Speed: The Many Lives of Amphetamines* (New York: New York University Press, 2008).

Rees, W. A. van, *Montrado. Geschied- en krijgskundige bijdrage betreffende de onderwerping der Chinezen op Borneo* ('s-Hertogenbosch: Gebr. Muller, 1858).

Rensman, M., 'Illegale activiteiten in de nationale rekeningen', in *De Nederlandse economie in 2013* (The Hague: Centraal Bureau voor de Statistiek, 2014), pp. 178–93.

Reuter, P., *Disorganized Crime: The Economics of the Visible Hand* (Cambridge: MIT Press, 1984).

Rimner, S., *Opium's Long Shadow: From Asian Revolt to Global Drug Control* (Cambridge: Harvard University Press, 2018).

Roberts, A., *Albion Dreaming: A Popular History of LSD in Britain* (Singapore: Marshall Cavendish, 2012).

Robertson, F., *The Triangle of Death: Inside Story of the Triads* (London: Corgi, 1978).

Rossum, M. van, *Hand aan Hand (Blank en Bruin). Solidariteit en de werking van globalisering, etniciteit en klasse onder zeelieden op de Nederlandse koopvaardij, 1900–1945* (Amsterdam: Aksant, 2009).

Ruggiero, V., and N. South, *Eurodrugs: Drug Use, Markets and Trafficking in Europe* (London: UCL Press, 1995).

Ruggiero, V., and N. South, 'The late-modern city as a bazaar: Drug markets, illegal enterprise and the "barricades"', *British Journal of Sociology* 48 (1997) 54–70.

Rush, J. R., 'Opium farms in nineteenth century Java: Institutional continuity and change in a colonial society' (PhD thesis, Yale University, 1977).

Rypkema, B. H., 'Een onderzoek naar het geneesmiddelgebruik in Nederland' (PhD thesis, University of Amsterdam, 1954).

Saunders, N., *Ecstasy and the Dance Culture* (London: N. Saunders, 1995).

Sayer, J., and D. Botting, *Nazi Gold: The Story of the World's Greatest Robbery and its Aftermath* (London: Granada, 1984).

Schaank, S. H., 'De kongsi's van Montrado. Bijdrage tot de geschiedenis en de kennis van het wezen der Chineesche vereenigingen op de westkust van Borneo', *Tijdschrift voor Indische Taal-, Land- en Volkenkunde* 35 (1893) 498–612.

Schayegh, C., 'The many worlds of 'Abud Yasin; or, what narcotics trafficking in the interwar Middle East can tell us about territorialization', *American Historical Review* 116 (2011) 273–306.

Scholtens, J., 'Mededeelingen over het gebruik van Gânjâh (Cannabis Indica) in Suriname en over de krankzinnigheid, die er het gevolg van is (cannabinismus)', *Psychiatrische en Neurologische Bladen* 9 (1905) 244–53

Schou, N., *Orange Sunshine: The Brotherhood of Eternal Love and Its Quest to Spread Peace, Love, and Acid to the World* (New York: Thomas Dunne Books, 2010).

Schreurs, A. F. A., *Het kerkdorp St. Willebrord (Het Heike). Een sociaal-geografische en criminologische studie* (Utrecht: Dekker & Van de Vegt, 1947).

Schutten, H., *De jacht op Octopus. Hoe Nederlandse drugscriminelen greep kregen op de bovenwereld* (Amsterdam: Meulenhoff: 1996).

Schutten, H., P. Vugts, and B. Middelburg, *Hells Angels. Motorclub of misdaadbende?* (Utrecht: Monitor Books, 2005).

Seddon, D., *Moroccan Peasants: A Century of Change in the Eastern Rif 1870–1970* (Folkestone: Dawson, 1981).

Shaw, M., 'Organised crime in late apartheid and the transition to a new criminal order: The rise and fall of the Johannesburg "bouncer mafia"', *Journal of Southern African Studies* 42 (2016) 577–94.

Shulgin, A., and A. Shulgin, *PiKHAL: A Chemical Love Story* (Berkeley: Transform Press, 2015).

Sioe, K. T., and T. K. Hong, 'The mass treatment of drug addiction by the Medinos' phlycten method', in D. G. Baedyagun and L. S. Subhakich (eds), *Transactions of the Eight Congress of the Far Eastern Association of Tropical Medicine held in Siam December 1930* (Bangkok: Times Press, 1931), pp. 52–64.

Snelders, S., 'Het gebruik van psychedelische middelen in Nederland in de jaren zestig. Een hoofdstuk uit de sociale geschiedenis van druggebruik', *Tijdschrift voor Sociale Geschiedenis* 21 (1995) 37–60.

Snelders, S. A. M., 'LSD en de psychiatrie in Nederland' (PhD thesis, VU-University Amsterdam, 1999).

Snelders, S., 'The adventures of Tintin in the opium empire', Points blog, 9 July 2012, https://pointsadhsblog.wordpress.com/2012/07/09/the-adventures-of-tintin-in-the-opium-empire (accessed 7 August 2020).

Snelders, S., *The Devil's Anarchy: The Sea Robberies of the Most Famous Pirate Claes G. Compaen, and Very Remarkable Travels of Jan Erasmus Reyning*, 2nd edn (Brooklyn: Autonomedia, 2014).

Snelders, S., P. Huijnen et al., 'A digital humanities approach to the history of culture and science', in J. Odijk and A. van Hessen (eds), *CLARIN in the Low Countries* (London: Ubiquity Press, 2017), pp. 325–35.

Snelders, S., and T. Pieters, 'Speed in the Third Reich: Metamphetamine (Pervitin) use and a drug history from below', *Social History of Medicine* 24 (2011) 686–99.

Spapens, P., 'Sluikstoken en smokkelen, een grensoverschrijdende activiteit. Belgen en Nederlanders broederlijk in illegale praktijken', in E. Van Schoonenberghe, P. Spapens et al., *Tersluiks. Alcoholsmokkel en sluikstokerij in de Lage Landen* (Heule: Snoeck, 2012), pp. 32–49.

Spapens, P., and P. Horsten, *Tappen uit een geheim vaatje. De geschiedenis van illegale alcoholstokerijen in Nederland* (Hapert: De Kempenpers, 1990).

Spapens, P., and A. van Oirschot, *Smokkelen in Brabant. Een grensgeschiedenis 1830–1970* (Hapert: De Kempenpers, 1988).

Spapens, T., *Interactie tussen criminaliteit en opsporing. De gevolgen van opsporingstechnieken voor de organisatie en afscherming van xtc-productie en –handel in Nederland* (Antwerp: Intersentra, 2006).

Spapens, T., 'Dutch crime networks', in G. Bruinsma and D. Weisbund (eds), *Encyclopedia of Criminology and Criminal Justice* (New York: Springer, 2014), pp. 1211–19.

Spapens, T., T. Müller, and H. van de Bunt, 'The Dutch drug policy from a regulatory perspective'. *European Journal of Crime Policy Research* 21 (2015) 191–205.

Spence, J., 'Das Opiumrauchen im China der Ch'ing-Zeit (1644–1911)', *Saeculum* 23 (1972) 397–425.

Spence, J., 'Opium smoking in Ch'in China', in F. Wakeman, Jr. and C. Grant (eds), *Conflict and Control in Late Imperial China* (Berkeley: University of California Press, 1975), pp. 143–73.

Staring, R., 'Het criminologische tekort. Turkse migranten en georganiseerde drugscriminaliteit', *Migrantenstudies* 14 (1998) 191–7.

Staring, R., 'Nawoord', *Migrantenstudies* 14 (1998) 203–4.

Stel, J. C. van der, *Drinken, drank en dronkenschap. Vijf eeuwen drankbestrijding en alcoholhulpverlening in Nederland* (Hilversum: Verloren, 1995).

Straten, J. van, 'For export: Chinese triad societies', *International Crime Police Review* (February 1977) 49–53.

Sturesson, K., *Bland langare och profitörer. Ur en narkotikapolis dagbok* (Stockholm: Hjalmarson & Högberg, 2004).

Tagliacozzo, E., 'Kettle on a slow boil: Batavia's threat perceptions in the Indies' Outer Islands, 1870–1910', *Journal of Southeast Asian Studies* 31 (2000) 70–100.

Tagliacozzo, E., *Secret Traders, Porous Borders: Smuggling and States along a Southeast Asian Frontier, 1865–1915* (New Haven: Yale University Press, 2005).

Tendler, S., and D. May, *The Brotherhood of Eternal Love: From Flower Power to Hippie Mafia* (London: Cyan Books, 2007).

Thompson, T., *Gangland Britain* (London: Hodder and Stoughton, 1996).

Thompson, T., 'Heroin "emperor" brings terror to UK streets', *Observer* 17 November 2002.

Thoumi, F. E., *Political Economy and Illegal Drugs in Colombia* (Boulder: Lynne Rienner, 1995).

Thoumi, F. E., *Illegal Drugs, Economy, and Society in the Andes* (Washington: Woodrow Wilson Center Press, 2003).

Thoumi, F. E., 'The rise of the two drug tigers: The development of the illegal drugs industry and drug policy failure in Afghanistan and Colombia', in F. Bovenkerk and M. Levi (eds), *The Organized Crime Community* (n.p.: Springer, 2007), pp. 125–48.

Tops, P., and J. Tromp, *De achterkant van Nederland. Hoe onder- en bovenwereld verstrengeld raken* (Amsterdam: Balans, 2017).

Tops, P., J. van Valkenhoef et al., *Waar een klein land groot in kan zijn. Nederland en synthetische drugs in de afgelopen 50 jaar* (The Hague: Boom, 2018).

Trocki, C. A., 'The rise of Singapore's great opium syndicate, 1840–86', *Journal of Southeastern Studies* 18 (1987) 58–80.
Trocki, C. A., *Opium, Empire and the Global Political Economy: A Study of the Asian Opium Trade, 1750–1950* (London: Routledge, 1999).
Tullis, L., *Unintended Consequences: Illegal Drugs and Drug Policies in Nine Countries* (Boulder: Lynne Rienner, 1995).
'Turkse heroïnesmokkel over de weg', report IRT Noord- en Oost-Nederland Nijverdal, 1997.
Uncle Fester, *Practical LSD Manufacture*, 3rd edn (Green Bay: Festering Publications, 2006).
United States Senate Committee on the Judiciary, *Hashish Smuggling and Passport Fraud: 'The Brotherhood of Eternal Love'* (Washington: US Government Printing Office, 1973).
Valentine, D., *The Strength of the Wolf: The Secret History of America's War on Drugs* (London: Verso, 2006).
Vanvugt, E., *Wettig opium. 350 jaar Nederlandse opiumhandel in de Indische archipel* (Haarlem: In de Knipscheer, 1985).
Varese, F., *Mafias on the Move: How Organized Crime Conquers New Territories* (Princeton: Princeton University Press, 2011).
Verbeek, N., *Pablo Escobar. De zoektocht naar de man achter de mythe* (n.p.: Pandora, 2008).
Voordewind, H., *De commissaris vertelt verder* (The Hague: D. A. Daamen, 1950).
Vries, P. R. de, *Uit de dossiers van commissaris Toorenaar* (Baarn: Fontein, 1985).
Ward, C., *Anarchy in Action* (London: Freedom Press, 1982).
Warren, J. F., *Rickshaw Coolie: A People's History of Singapore (1880–1940)* (Singapore: Oxford University Press, 1986).
Weerlee, D. van (ed.), *Allemaal rebellen: Amsterdam 1955–1965* (Amsterdam: Tabula, 1984).
Weijenburg, M. A. M. H., 'De opsporing van softdrugs in Nederland', *Justitiële Verkenningen* 19 (1993) 60–76.
Weijenburg, R., *Drugs en drugsbestrijding in Nederland. Een beschrijving van de aanpak van het gebruik en misbruik van en de (illegal) handel in verdovende middelen* (The Hague: VUGA, 1996).
Wijk A., van, and A. Lenders, 'Betonrot. Een kwalitatief onderzoek naar het fenomeen ondermijnende criminaliteit in Brabant-Zeeland, de effecten van en richtingen voor de overheidsaanpak' (Arnhem: Bureau Beke, 2018), https://bureaubeke.nl/wp-content/uploads/2018/12/Betonrot_Bekereeks-2.pdf (accessed 7 August 2020).
Wijngaart, G. F. van de, 'Competing perspectives on drug use: The Dutch experience' (PhD thesis, Utrecht University, 1996).

Winterton, M. J., 'The collation of crime intelligence with regard to Chinese triads in Holland', *Police Journal* 54 (1981) 34–57.

Wubben, H. J. J., *'Chineezen en ander Aziatisch ongedierte'. Lotgevallen van Chinese immigranten in Nederland, 1911–1940* (Zutphen: De Walburg Pers, 1986).

Yangwen, Z., *The Social Life of Opium in China* (Cambridge: Cambridge University Press, 2005).

Yesilgöz, Y., A. Lempens, and F. Bovenkerk, 'Georganiseerde misdaad als buurtprobleem', *De Gids* 159 (1996) 644–54.

Zaitch, D., 'From Cali to Rotterdam: Perceptions of Colombian cocaine traffickers on the Dutch port', *Crime, Law & Social Change* 38 (2002) 239–66.

Zaitch, D., *Trafficking Cocaine: Colombian Drug Entrepreneurs in the Netherlands* (The Hague: Kluwers, 2002).

Zeven, B., 'Balancerend op de rand van Nederland. De Chinese minderheid in de jaren 1910–1940', in G. Benton and H. Vermeulen (eds), *De Chinezen* (Muiderberg: Dick Coutinho, 1987), pp. 40–64.

Index

14K 52, 121–8

Aachen 33–4, 248
addiction 35, 46, 76, 87, 115, 218–19
Adkins, Roy 166–7, 169, 178
Afghanistan 74, 85–90, 92, 129–31, 139, 156–7, 161, 165
Ah Kong 125–7
amphetamines 162, 215–20, 229–38, 244
  prices 234–5
  production 231–2
  regulation 6, 188, 218–19
  users 118, 217–19
Amsterdam 30, 41, 54–62, 64–5, 75–8, 90–1, 94–5, 97–100, 113, 116–27, 129, 141, 154–5, 161–8, 174–5, 188, 202, 205, 207–8, 220–5, 229, 232, 234, 239–40, 242–4, 250–4
anarchy as organization 13–14
Antwerp 10, 166, 196, 226, 229
Arnhem 138–9, 142
Aruba 198, 201

Baybasin, Hüseyin 138–9
Belgium 34–5, 96, 98–9, 102, 133, 166, 199, 204, 225, 227, 232, 234, 245, 247, 249–50
Blaauw, Jan 2–3, 101–2
Blonde Greet 94, 98, 100, 162–3
Bolivia 189–90, 194
Bo On 55, 59–62, 123
Bouterse, Desi 199–200
Bovenkerk, Frank 136, 138, 142–3, 204, 206
Brabant 134, 216, 227–8, 231–3, 237–8, 242, 250

Brotherhood of Eternal Love 86–7
Brown, Steve 175, 178, 250
Bruinsma, Klaas 94, 100, 160–70, 175, 178, 204–5
Brunswijk, Ronnie 200
butter smuggling 226–9, 231

Cali 'cartel' 193, 195–6, 204–6
Canada 166, 174–5
cannabis 74–105, 153–81, 194, 229, 234, 249, 251
  cultivation 78–83, 85–6, 88
  decriminalization 153, 159
  estimates of smuggled amounts 77, 156–7
  normalization 78, 106, 157
  prices 85–6, 156–8, 166, 177
  production of hashish 80, 82–4, 86–7, 165
  quality 83, 85, 87–8, 156, 165
  regulation 6, 74–6, 97
  users 77–8, 155–7
  value of market 154
  see also nederwiet
Capone, Al 14–15
Centrale, the *see* Nederlandsche Centrale tot bestrijding van de smokkelhandel in verdoovende middelen
Certeau, Michel de 12
Chemical Factory Naarden 28–9
chemical supply industry 131–2, 222, 224–5, 231, 234, 244–6
chemical waste 216, 249
China 4–5, 28–9, 43–4, 46, 48–9, 51, 56–7
  see also Fujian; Guangdong

INDEX

Chinatowns 41, 54, 57–8, 60, 119–20
Chinese
  first Chinese war 60–1
  in the Netherlands 53–4, 57–9, 112, 125, 127–8
  second Chinese war 125–7, 129
  smugglers 41, 64–6, 76, 111–13, 125, 176
  third Chinese war 128
  see also Chinese triads; Dutch East Indies; shipping masters
Chinese triads 41–2, 46–53, 56, 100, 119, 122, 125–6
  see also 14K; Ah Kong; Bo On; Dai Huen Jai; Three Fingers
Chung Mon 60, 123–6
clandestine chemical laboratories 256
  amphetamines 220, 231–4, 236–7, 241
  LSD 221–5
  XTC 231–2, 240–5, 249
cocaine 29, 33–5, 55, 75, 79, 168, 178, 188–209, 234, 244, 249
  prices 8, 32, 190–1
  production 27, 189–90, 194
  regulation 6
  users 188
  value of market 190, 201
codeine 27, 35, 64, 244
coffee shops 153, 155–6, 163–4, 178, 205
Cohen, Herman 78, 90–1, 95, 156
Colombia 160–1, 189–95, 205–8
Colombian cartels *see* Colombian export syndicates
Colombian export syndicates 193–4, 203–7
Colombians in the Netherlands 202
Colombian smugglers 160, 176, 189, 193–8, 202–6, 234, 248
co-management of crime 62, 116–17, 121, 124–5, 155
containers 101, 159, 165–6, 170, 174, 205
corporate non-compliance 28
corruption 35, 45–6, 79, 83, 86, 99, 124–5, 133, 140, 165, 169
counterculture 78, 117, 120, 220–1, 224
CRI (Centrale Recherche Informatiedienst) 3, 135, 159, 167, 195, 198, 201, 253
criminal anarchy 8, 11–14, 37, 67, 106, 128, 139–40, 143, 172–3, 175, 191, 205–6, 229, 237, 251, 256, 271

criminal underworld 96–102, 163, 206–7, 230
Curaçao 58, 196, 198, 201

Dai Huen Jai 128
Dalen, Ton van 251
Denis family 238
drug markets
  number of users 77–8
  prices 7–8
  structure 7–8
  value 1
drug regulatory regime 3, 8–9, 74
  Dutch 6–7
  see also Opium Act
  global 3–6, 76
Dutch East India Company *see* VOC
Dutch East Indies 57
  Chinese 26, 43–8, 50, 60
  opium regulation 4, 25–6, 45–6

Eliopoulos, Elie 10, 31
embeddedness, social and cultural 14, 34, 37, 41, 66, 91, 105, 112, 129, 139–44, 181, 191, 196, 205, 224, 227–8, 231, 252, 269–70
enterprise syndicate 14, 129, 167
Escobar, Pablo 193–5
Esser, Stanley Karel 170

Faas, Sjefke 229
Femer, Jan 248, 251
Fielding, Leaf 92–3, 224
Fijnaut, Cyrille 161, 173, 179–80, 233, 245
France 133, 159, 166, 199, 224–5, 247, 249–50
Frits van de Wereld 98–100, 162–4
Fujian 44, 55–6, 113

German army, drug supplies of 74–6
Germany 32–5, 75, 97, 166, 225, 235–8, 245, 248, 250
Grajales family 205–6, 208
Greece 62–5, 78, 236
Greek smugglers 41, 62–6
Guangdong 44, 55–6, 112, 114, 125

Hakkelaar, the 173–5, 178, 181
hallucinogens *see* LSD

INDEX

Hamburg 57, 64, 126–7, 196
hashish *see* cannabis
Heerlen 33–5, 230, 237, 243
Hell's Angels 234, 252–3
heroin 29, 36, 46, 64, 79, 100, 110–44, 176
  epidemic 114, 117–20
  prices 8, 115, 120, 127, 130
  production 27, 63–4, 115, 139
  regulation 6
  retail trade 119–20, 127, 141
  users 114, 117–19
Hillis, Stanley 250–1
hippie trail 81–2, 85, 90–3
Hollemans, Robert 232, 239, 243–4
Hong Kong 52, 55, 59, 113–14, 121–3, 125, 128
Hoornstra, Salomon 29–31

IJmuiden 197, 205–6
India 90, 114, 176
indoor cultivation *see* nederwiet
Iran 102, 130–1, 139

Jansen, C. H. 31
John H 228

kampers 171–3, 179
Kok, Minke 248, 251
Kurdish smugglers 127–33, 138–43

League of Nations 4–5, 28–30, 32
Leary, Timothy 86–7, 221
Lebanon 74, 78–80, 90–2, 96, 102, 139–40, 156, 161, 164–5, 169, 176
Leclère, Danny 240, 251, 254
Limburg 33–4, 97, 226, 228–32, 234–8, 242–3, 247–8, 254
LSD 86, 220–6, 238–9, 244
  regulation 6, 220
  users 220–1

Mahmut the Anarchist 139
marihuana *see* cannabis; nederwiet
maritime smuggling 90, 93–5, 97, 111, 267
  see also Chinese, in the Netherlands; transport, by sea
Marks, Howard 87, 170

Marseilles 57, 60, 63–5, 114
Martens, Bettien 204
MDA 239, 241, 243
MDEA 241, 243–4
MDMA 238–4
  see also XTC
Medellin 'cartel' 193–6, 201
Merck 33–4, 75, 238
methamphetamine 217–19, 220
minimally commercially driven traders 13, 17, 86, 91, 93, 243, 250
Mink, Anno 230, 237–8
Moear, Thea 94, 162–7
Moroccans 141, 175
Morocco 74, 77, 81–5, 90–3, 102, 157–8, 161, 164–5, 169–70, 175, 177
morphine 29, 35, 46, 75–6, 119, 218
  production 27
  regulation 6
Moustache, the 162–6

Nederlandsche Centrale tot bestrijding van de smokkelhandel in verdoovende middelen 31–2, 35, 75
Nederlandsche Cocaïne Fabriek 27, 34
nederwiet 154, 156, 158, 170–2, 234
  indoor cultivation 170–1
  value of market 1
Nepal 86, 90, 156–7, 165
Ng Young 59–62
Nieuwenhuis, F. M. 29–31, 34, 36
North Brabant *see* Brabant

opium 25, 27, 35, 42–7, 54–8, 64–6, 76, 111–13, 115–20, 129–31, 229
  cultivation 62–3, 88, 131
  prices 57, 88, 119, 131
  regulation 6
  use 57–8, 117
  see also Dutch East Indies
Opium Act 6–7, 23–5, 27, 75
  revision of 1976 153–4
outlaw motorcycle gangs 216, 252–3
  see also Hell's Angels

Pakistan 77, 87–90, 129–31, 137, 139, 156–7, 161, 164, 175
Pakistani smugglers 94–6, 127–30, 166, 174–6

parliamentary inquiry of 1994–1996 3, 142–3, 161, 168, 173, 179–80
Pauksch, Kalle 226, 237
Peru 189–90, 194–5
Peter van D 231, 237, 245–6, 254
Pharmaceutical-Chemical Products 27, 31
pharmaceutical industry 27–33, 36, 191, 217, 221, 240
Pharmaceutical Inspectorate 29–32, 35–6, 75
pharmacies 34, 219
power syndicate 14, 126, 167
precursor chemicals 132, 168, 191–2, 222–5, 231, 234, 240–1, 244–7

Robbie van L 229–31, 235, 237
Rotterdam 28, 32–3, 36, 41, 54–62, 64–5, 77–8, 92, 94, 97–101, 112, 116–20, 123, 127, 139, 159, 177, 198, 204–5, 229, 236

St Maarten 196
Schiphol airport 92, 95, 97, 175, 198, 201, 225
shipping companies 41, 53–4, 57–9, 64–5, 112
shipping masters 42, 58–61
Singapore 48, 50–2, 114, 121, 125–6
Sirks, A. H. 31–3, 57, 62
Spain 133, 170, 196–7, 235, 239, 249
subversion of the state 216
Suriname 126, 198–201
  regulation 26–7
Surinamese 118–19, 198–9
Surinamese smugglers 175, 198–202, 206–7
Sweden 158, 215, 226, 230, 235–7, 250
synthetic drugs 1
  see also amphetamines; LSD; MDMA; XTC

Tchai, Ai Kui 60
Terneuzen 96–7, 229, 232
Thinkers gang 251, 253
Three Fingers 59–61
Toorenaar, Gerard 122, 124, 127
transport
  by air 87, 92, 96–7, 121, 126–7, 129, 133, 193, 199–200, 225, 248
  see also Schiphol airport
  by ferry 235–6
  by river 33
  by road 34–5, 86–9, 103, 129, 132–4, 141, 160, 165, 170, 177, 235–6, 247–8
  by sea 55–6, 64–5, 82, 89, 96, 99–101, 159–61, 164–6, 174–7, 197–9, 205–8, 236, 247
  by train 65, 133, 248
transport companies 133–4, 175, 177, 198, 247
Turkey 57, 62–4, 66, 114, 130–2, 135–41
Turkish crime families 135–8
Turkish smugglers 127–43, 160, 175–6
Turks in the Netherlands 141–3

underworld–upperworld connections 34–5, 136, 138–43, 164–5, 167, 169, 176, 192–4, 196, 198–202, 205–6, 245–6
United Kingdom 133, 157–9, 166, 176–7, 207–8, 223, 235–6, 247–50, 253
United Nations 4–6, 76, 175, 205, 239
United States 4–5, 28, 30, 63, 79, 82, 87–8, 101, 114–16, 130, 170–1, 188–9, 193–5, 199–200, 228, 238–9, 248, 250
Urka, Etienne 167–9
US Army
  in Vietnam 113, 115–16
  in West Germany 75–6, 101, 113

violence, attitudes to 170, 178–80, 203–4, 206–7, 226, 234, 253–4
VOC (Dutch East India Company) 4, 25, 43, 93, 266–7
Vosseveld, Karel 169–70

WODC 11, 168

XTC 168, 175, 215–16, 228, 235, 237–52
  prices 242–3, 250
  production 239–42, 250
  regulation 6, 239, 243–4
  users 238–9
  see also MDA; MDEA; MDMA

Zeeland 216, 229, 232–3

EU authorised representative for GPSR:
Easy Access System Europe, Mustamäe tee 50,
10621 Tallinn, Estonia
gpsr.requests@easproject.com

www.ingramcontent.com/pod-product-compliance
Lightning Source LLC
Chambersburg PA
CBHW051602230426
43668CB00013B/1953